MW00782858

# Using
# Propensity Scores
## in Quasi-Experimental
# Designs

# Using
# **Propensity Scores**
# in **Quasi-Experimental**
# Designs

# William M. Holmes

Los Angeles | London | New Delhi
Singapore | Washington DC

Los Angeles | London | New Delhi
Singapore | Washington DC

FOR INFORMATION:

SAGE Publications, Inc.
2455 Teller Road
Thousand Oaks, California 91320
E-mail: order@sagepub.com

SAGE Publications Ltd.
1 Oliver's Yard
55 City Road
London EC1Y 1SP
United Kingdom

SAGE Publications India Pvt. Ltd.
B 1/I 1 Mohan Cooperative Industrial Area
Mathura Road, New Delhi 110 044
India

SAGE Publications Asia-Pacific Pte. Ltd.
3 Church Street
#10-04 Samsung Hub
Singapore 049483

Acquisitions Editor:  Vicki Knight
Editorial Assistant:  Jessica Miller
Digital Content Editor:  Kalie Koscielak
Permissions Editor:  Karen Ehrmann
Marketing Manager:  Nicole Elliott
Project Editor:  Veronica Stapleton Hooper
Copy Editor:  QuADS Prepress (P) Ltd.
Typesetter:  C&M Digitals (P) Ltd.
Proofreader:  Scott Oney
Indexer:  Sheila Bodell
Cover Designer:  Anupama Krishnan

Copyright © 2014 by SAGE Publications, Inc.

All rights reserved. No part of this book may be reproduced or utilized in any form or by any means, electronic or mechanical, including photocopying, recording, or by any information storage and retrieval system, without permission in writing from the publisher.

Printed in the United States of America

*Library of Congress Cataloging-in-Publication Data*

Holmes, William M.

Using propensity scores in quasi-experimental designs / William M. Holmes, University of Massachusetts at Boston.

pages cm
Includes bibliographical references and index.

ISBN 978-1-4522-0526-7 (pbk. : alk. paper)

1. Statistical decision. 2. Experimental design. I. Title.

QA279.4.H64 2013
001.4′34—dc23          2013005294

This book is printed on acid-free paper.

13 14 15 16 17 10 9 8 7 6 5 4 3 2 1

# BRIEF CONTENTS

# DETAILED CONTENTS

# PREFACE

This text reviews problems of working with data from quasi-experiments and making causal inferences. It compares problems of making inferences from quasi-experiments with those from experiments. It discusses and illustrates how data from experimental and quasi-experimental designs are analyzed and how propensity scores are used to address their problems and improve inferences with such data.

There are two basic problems with quasi-experiments. Groups being compared are usually not the same when an intervention, treatment, or other supposed causal factor occurs; and, even if they do start off the same, factors other than the one of interest can also have an influence. These other factors confound making an inference because of the difficulty in knowing whether observed changes in the groups are a result of the intervention or of the other confounding factors.

With experiments, the groups usually (but not always) start off the same. Controls of the experiment are designed to prevent confounding factors from having different effects between the groups. However, problems arise in the implementation of the procedures for the experiment. This allows confounding factors to have differential effects between the groups and undermines valid inferences from the data. Propensity scores may be used to compensate for the effect of confounding variables.

With quasi-experiments, the groups usually start off different. Characteristics of the intervention group do not start off the same as that of a comparison group. Constraints on the research prevent a design that might control these factors. Propensity scores may be used to compensate for their effects.

## APPROACH OF THE BOOK

This text describes how propensity scores can be used in a variety of quasi-experimental designs to improve the validity of estimates of the relationship between variables. It assumes that the reader is familiar with basic statistics and is acquainted with regression analysis. It is helpful, but not necessary, if the reader also has knowledge of logistic regression or discriminant function analysis. Explaining how quasi-experiments may benefit from propensity scores depends on noting how they differ from well-designed experiments and how they may undermine the validity of the analytical results.

The following chapters will discuss how to analyze data from broken experiments and quasi-experiments that take into consideration the role of confounding influences. For each type of design, the likely confounding influences will be discussed, as well as strategies for reducing their influence, of which using propensity scores is an important element. The book will also address common sources of broken experiments and how one may attempt to repair them so they still produce usable inferences.

In discussing whether evidence provides reasonable support for inferences, criteria will be offered that reflect standards that other statisticians have chosen and professional journals have specified for article submission and the author's extensive experience in statistical analysis. While these recommendations provide reasonable grounds for making inferences, no recommendations will work all the time. The reader is urged to use his or her own professional judgment when applying them to specific situations.

*Target Audience.* The text is intended for students who have basic statistical knowledge. Experience with multiple regression analysis is assumed. Experience with logistic regression is helpful but not required. Depending on a program, it might be used at the advanced undergraduate or master's level. It may also be used as a reference by those engaged in experimental, quasi-experimental, or evaluation research who currently know some of these techniques but want information on how propensity scores are used with them. The references cited provide more advanced treatment of issues the user may wish to pursue.

## EXAMPLE DATA

In subsequent chapters, examples of using propensity scores and means for analyzing quasi-experimental data will be given from published literature and from available public data. Two public data sets will be used so that the reader may access them, replicate the examples, and try the procedures. Replicating the examples will verify that the reader is correctly using the procedures and provide a common data experience. Users will be able to compare their results and learn from the experience of others. Some published examples for these data will also be provided to illustrate the procedures using these data and provide the user an opportunity to build on the work of others. In addition, users will be able to apply the procedures they learned to publications using the data and determine whether using propensity scores or other procedures produces different results.

The two data sets are the General Social Survey (GSS) 2008 panel survey (Davis, Smith, & Marsden, 2010) and the national Health and Retirement Study (HRS; 2011; National Institute on Aging, 2008). They were chosen because they represent a wide range of issues. Both data sources provide a variety of measures relevant to economics, health, sociology, education, policy science, gerontology, criminal justice, social work, and psychology. Both data sets have been used in policy analysis, testing theories, and examining applied issues. These data have resulted in extensive analyses and publications. Both data sets have websites that list many of the publications resulting from their use. These are noted below. Users may find it interesting and useful to build on some of the published results by applying the techniques and guidelines provided.

Users may select measures relevant to their discipline when generating their own examples. The examples given in the text are based on unweighted data, unless otherwise noted. This is intended to facilitate replication of the results by the user. If users wish to replicate or extend published research, sample weighted data should be used.

## *The General Social Survey Panel*

The GSS 2008 panel is part of the GSS (Davis et al., 2010), administered biannually. It is a nationally representative sample of U.S. households. The 2008 panel is a two-wave panel replicating questions for the same respondents in 2006 and 2008, with some questions asked only in 2006 and others only in 2008. It is coordinated with the International Social Survey Program, which is a consortium of affiliated social survey programs in 45 nations. Some questions from the U.S. GSS are replicated in the surveys conducted by the other member programs, which allows the possibility of cross-national analysis for those who work with data from the member countries.

The GSS 2008 panel has data on 2,000 respondents, of which 1,536 have two wave data. These data may be downloaded from http://www.norc.org/GSS+Website/Download/. Documentation is available from http://www.norc.org/GSS+Website/. Copies of the data may be obtained from authorized users at institutions that are members of the Inter-University Consortium for Political and Social Research. Most colleges, universities, and research organizations are eligible for membership. The faculty may also provide students copies of the data. Lists of publications may be found at http://www.norc.org/GSS+Website/Publications/Bibliography/ or by doing electronic searches through an institution's library website.

## *The Health and Retirement Study*

The HRS is a nationally representative sample of households with adults of age 50 years and above. The study interviews 22,000 Americans 50 years and above every 2 years on subjects like health care, housing, income, assets, pensions, employment, health, and disability (HRS, 2011). Many of its questions have been replicated in similar studies in Europe, Mexico, India, Korea, Japan, and China. For example purposes, only data from the 2006 and 2008 surveys will be used. There are 20,000 respondents who participated in either survey, of which 17,000 participated in both surveys.

To download HRS data, one must first register with the HRS project. The web address for registration and data is http://hrsonline.isr.umich.edu/index .php?p=reg. For documentation, the URL is http://hrsonline.isr.umich.edu/index.php?p=docs. Lists of publications using the data may be obtained from http://hrsonline.isr.umich.edu/index.php?p=pubs. Searching electronic databases or Google Scholar will also identify publications using these data. Copies may be available from other users if they also register with HRS. Students who obtain copies of a prepared HRS data set from faculty in a course must also register with the website.

## IMPROVING KNOWLEDGE

While care has been taken to ensure accuracy, there is always the possibility of typos, omissions, and errors. If users replicate any of the analyses reported below and find what they think are errors, they are encouraged to report this to propensity01@google.com. Please attach a file containing the program code and the results. If the error is verified, the correction with the user's name will be posted on the emendation page of the propensity website. The URL for the book website is http://www.sagepub.com/holmes. The URL for the author's website is http://faculty.umb.edu/william_holmes/propensity.htm.

# ACKNOWLEDGMENTS

The author is grateful for the support of his wife, Lenore Olsen, whose encouragement and assistance made this work possible. The incisive and helpful comments of an originally anonymous panel of reviewers immeasurably helped make this a better work, including M. H. Clark, University of Central Florida; Peggy S. Keller, University of Kentucky; David LaHuis, Wright State University; Douglas Luke, Washington University in St. Louis; Michael A. Milburn, University of Massachusetts, Boston; Robert G. Morris, The University of Texas at Dallas; Dmitriy Poznyak, University of Cincinnati; and Tina Savla, Virginia Tech. Support for the research leading to this work was provided by Children's Friend and Service, Providence, Rhode Island, and by the United States Children's Bureau. The author owes much to the inspiration of the work of Peter Austin, Onur Baser, Rajeev Dehejia, James Heckman, Guido Imbens, Paul Rosenbaum, David Rubin, Jasjeet Sekhon, William Shadish, Elizabeth Stuart, and too many others to mention. He owes deep gratitude to his editor, Vicki Knight, who helped bring this work to fruition.

# About the Author

William M. Holmes is a faculty member at the University of Massachusetts at Boston in the College of Public and Community Services. He has evaluated criminal justice and community programs serving families, children, the abused, and those with substance abuse problems. He coauthored *Portrait of Divorce*, with Kay Kitson, which won the William Goode Award from the Family Section of the American Sociological Association. He coauthored *Family Abuse: Consequences, Theories, and Responses*, with Calvin Larsen and Sylvia Mignon.

# CHAPTER 1

# QUASI-EXPERIMENTS AND NONEQUIVALENT GROUPS

A propensity score is the probability that a person will be in a treatment group, given his or her specific characteristics. This text describes how propensity scores can be used in a variety of experimental and quasi-experimental designs to improve the validity and reduce the bias of estimates of the effect of treatments, interventions, and other causal influences.

Explaining how experiments and quasi-experiments benefit from propensity score use depends on noting how actual research differs from the ideal of well-designed experiments. This chapter will summarize the ways in which such designs affect the ability to make reliable causal inferences from the results.

## EXPERIMENTS AND INFERENCE

Experiments are regarded by many as the gold standard by which the quality of research is judged. This is largely because experiments, if done properly, most closely approximate the conditions under which one may make valid causal inferences following the "Counterfactual" model of causal inference. Under the counterfactual model, one may infer that one thing has a causal influence on another when one demonstrates that an outcome is present when the cause is present and absent when the cause is absent—and no other confounding factor influences the outcome (Rubin, 1974). The difficulty with counterfactual inference is in observing what happens when the cause is present and when it is absent for the same subject. This is not usually possible. Instead, one observes average effects of what happens when the cause is present and average effects of when it is not. This difference is taken as the model for the

1

average causal effect (sometimes called the average treatment effect, **ATE**). This logic goes back to John Stuart Mill (1848) and his principle of concomitant variation.

All models of causal inference in science have three components: (1) a scientific theory, (2) a specific mathematical or statistical model that represents the theoretical relationships, and (3) empirical data that allow estimating and testing the models (Blalock, 1971; Heckman, 2005). A scientific theory implies a hypothetical statement (or hypothesis) and its opposite (a counterfactual statement or a null hypothesis). The causal effects are estimated with data and compared with what is hypothesized by the theory. Each hypothesis must be represented as a specific mathematical or statistical equation. Data allow estimating the parameters of the equation and comparing those estimates with what would be predicted by the theory.

The divergence of the estimated model from the hypothesized model is used to test the model and the hypotheses on which it is based. The various quasi-experimental designs have different statistical models. One of the purposes of this text is to clarify which statistical model is most appropriate for testing particular types of hypotheses. This allows a researcher to know whether the assumptions of the hypothesized model correspond to those of the statistical model. It indicates whether the hypotheses one wishes to test can be adequately tested with a particular model. When a hypothesized model cannot be adequately tested with a given statistical model, additional evidence or modifications to the model are needed.

A well-done experiment has many strengths that allow for making reasonable causal inferences. Quasi-experiments do not meet all the strict requirements of an experiment. Additional evidence must be offered to provide a basis for valid inference. Broken experiments are those where implementation of the experiment deviates from that required by strict experimental protocol. The ability to infer a causal effect from it is impaired. With broken experiments, additional evidence must also be offered so that the deviations from protocol do not undermine the ability to make reasonable inferences from the data.

*Rubin Causal Inference.* The requirements for an experiment have been summarized by Donald Rubin as stable unit treatment value assumption (**SUTVA**; Rubin, 2010). They are based on the work of Donald Campbell on threats to validity (Cook & Campbell, 1979) and the statistical work done by Cochran (Cochran & Cox, 1957) and Neyman (1935) on randomization. SUTVA requires that groups being compared be all essentially similar, that the treatment be the same for all experimental subjects, and that the outcome not be dependent on the assignment procedure.

Treatments may refer to any type of intervention or event that is under control of the experimenter. They may be drugs, income experiments, punishments used, or actions taken (or withheld) concerning a subject. Experiments have stable treatments by standardizing the treatment and nontreatment and by randomizing the assignment of subjects to the experimental and control group(s). Successful randomization is seen as essential to making the experimental and control groups the same on all characteristics at the beginning of the experiment. If some subjects are not randomly assigned, the two groups may differ on characteristics other than receiving the treatment, a problem referred to as sample selectivity. These other factors confound one's ability to infer a treatment effect if they represent variables that are correlated both with the group to which a subject is assigned and with the outcome being studied. If the confounding variable precedes the treatment, it creates spurious correlation between the treatment and the outcome. The spurious correlation either increases (reinforces) or decreases (suppresses) the effect of the treatment. This approach to causal inference rests on a basic principle that alternative influences on the outcome that also correlate with the intervention must be controlled, either by design or by statistical manipulation.

If the randomization is successful, the other factors can be ignored because both groups are likely to have the same distribution of the factors. This produces what is sometimes called internal validity for the study, the ability to correctly determine if there is a relationship between two variables—in this case, between the treatment and the outcome. The absence of a difference between the experimental group and the control group implies that there are no factors confounding one's assessment of a relationship between the treatment and the outcome. This is also referred to as the strong ignorability assumption. Sometimes there are compromises to randomization that do not jeopardize one's ability to make inferences from the data. The groups might differ on some characteristic, but the difference is not significantly associated with the outcome variable. If this is the case, it would be referred to as weak ignorability or weak confoundedness. This approach to making causal inferences from experiments has come to be known as the Rubin Causal Model (RCM; Shadish, 2010).

The RCM approach would be to design an experiment in which counseling was randomly assigned to one group and not to another group. Without randomization, the two groups would be adjusted, matched, stratified, or weighted so that differences between the two groups on the other factors would be minimized or eliminated. When data are normally distributed, it can be represented as the difference in the group means (or difference in proportions if the outcomes are discrete).

$$\hat{\tau}_{ys} = \overline{Y}_1 - \overline{Y}_0, \tag{1.1}$$

where $\hat{\tau}_{ys}$ is the effect of treatment $S$ on outcome $Y$, $\overline{Y}_1$ is the treatment group mean of $Y$, and $\overline{Y}_0$ is the control group mean of $Y$. This is easily estimated and tested using a $t$ test or a one-way analysis of variance (ANOVA). When the data are not normally distributed, other measures of central tendency must be used, and the equation is expressed as a difference in expected values, rather than as a difference of means.

$$\hat{\tau}_{ys} = E(Y|S = 1) - E(Y|S = 0), \tag{1.2}$$

where $E$ indicates mathematical expectations; $Y|S = 1$ indicates the value of $Y$ for the condition where $S$ equals 1; and $Y|S = 0$ indicates the value of $Y$ for the condition where $S$ equals 0. $S$ is coded 1 for treatment cases and 0 for comparison or control cases.

*Structural Equation Modeling Causal Inference.* The approach of Balke and Pearl (1997), Blalock (1971), Goldberger and Duncan (1973), Pearl (1995), and Wright (1921) to obtaining evidence for causal inference contrasts with that of Rubin (1974) and Holland (1986). Their approach has been referred to as **structural equation modeling (SEM)**. This approach uses diagrams of causal models combined with sets of equations that correspond to the diagrams. As such, it attempts to model all the influences on an outcome. The RCM approach controls possible alternative influences by research design or statistical adjustments to the data. It does not attempt to model all the influences on an outcome but, rather, to model the relationship between a particular influence and the outcome with everything else held constant.

For example, the structural equation approach might examine influences on depression as an outcome by measuring counseling, parental depression, and substance abuse. The relationships among these factors might be diagramed and represented as a series of equations that would be estimated and evaluated to infer which of these factors had direct or indirect causal effects on depression (see Figure 1.1).

In the diagram, $Y$ is respondent depression; $W$ is parental depression; $X$ is substance abuse; and $S$ is counseling (where $S$ is a dichotomous variable coded

**Figure 1.1**  Example Structural Diagram

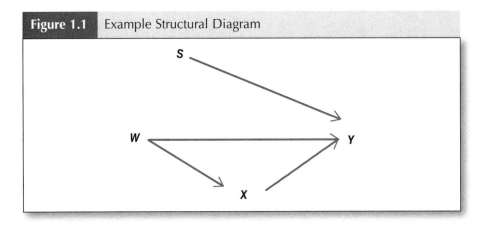

0 for no counseling and 1 for counseling). In this model, $W$, $S$, and $X$ all have a causal effect on $Y$. In addition, $W$ has an indirect effect through $X$. So its total effect is greater than the direct effect alone. Some of the correlation between substance abuse and respondent depression is a spurious effect caused by their joint influence by $W$ (parental depression). This illustrative model assumes that there are no confounding variables that affect $S$, $W$, or $X$ that also affect $Y$. The equations that correspond to this model are as follows:

$$X = \alpha_x + \beta_{xw}W, \tag{1.3}$$

$$Y = \alpha_y + \beta_{yw \cdot xs}W + \beta_{yx \cdot ws}X + \beta_{ys \cdot xw}S. \tag{1.4}$$

The treatment effect of counseling in this model is $\beta_{ys \cdot xw}$, the effect of $S$ on $Y$ controlling for $X$ and $W$. *Note:* If parental depression does not influence the likelihood of one having counseling (a supposition of this model), then one could estimate the treatment effect by also regressing depression solely on counseling, since parental depression and substance abuse are not confounding variables of the effect of counseling on depression. In the simple case where two equal groups are randomly assigned to counseling and noncounseling, estimating the effect using the RCM approach and two-way ANOVA produces the same result as using the SEM approach and regression analysis of dummy variables.

This leads us to the first condition under which we may reasonably make a causal inference:

*Condition 1:* randomization, with double blind conditions, and evidence of no social effects confounding the results.

When Condition 1 is met, the assumption of strong ignorability is met—as are the requirements for SUTVA. The randomization removes average differences in confounding influences. The double blind removes some social influences. Social effects might confound the result if the experimenters treat the subjects in each group differently or if the subjects determine which group they are in and modify their behavior in response to that. The reason for requiring evidence of no social effects is to base one's inference on evidence rather than on the unsupported belief that the experiment wasn't compromised.

Evidence of no social effects requires collecting information after the intervention about the subject's experiences during the period of the study. Carefully worded "debriefing" questions can indicate whether there were any actions by the subjects or the research staff that might skew the results. If the results of debriefing indicate that they did not try to skew the results, this is evidence of no social effects. Not debriefing the subjects and not asking about their behavior or that of the experimenters during the experiment is not evidence of no social effects. It is the absence of evidence concerning social effects. If debriefing information is not available and a study finds differences between the two groups, the estimated effect may be real. However, it is not certain that the estimated causal effect is real. The most that can be said is that the causal effect is plausible, not that it is certain.

If no causal effects are found in this situation, one doesn't even know if it is a false negative, a result of social influences confounding the result. This is why it is always desirable to have debriefing information from the subjects in an experimental study. Condition 1 is not met if there is no debriefing information regarding possible social effects. This approach to causal inference is based on offering evidence that potential risks of a given approach are not realized. Causal inference is supported when evidence demonstrates that the known risks do not bias the findings. No causal inference is supported when evidence is not offered that known risks are absent. The type of supporting evidence needed is specified for each condition of causal inference discussed. This position is similar to both the RCM and SEM. It brings together the importance of design and the known problems inherent in the RCM with the empirical, evidence-based approach of SEM.

## The Classic Experiment

When confounding variables can be ignored and one uses a posttest-only design, the estimation of treatment effects is simple. As noted above, it can be represented as the difference in the group means (or difference in proportions if the outcomes are discrete):

$$\hat{\tau}_{ys} = \overline{Y}_1 - \overline{Y}_0, \tag{1.5}$$

where $\hat{\tau}_{ys}$ is the effect of treatment $S$ on outcome $Y$, $\overline{Y}_1$ is the treatment group mean of $Y$, and $\overline{Y}_0$ is the control group mean of $Y$. This is easily estimated and tested using a $t$ test or a one-way ANOVA.

When one has a pre–post experiment, there are two common options available for estimating the treatment effect. The first option is to use the difference-of-differences approach:

$$\hat{\tau}_{ysld} = \left(\overline{Y}_{12} - \overline{Y}_{11}\right) - \left(\overline{Y}_{02} - \overline{Y}_{01}\right), \tag{1.6}$$

where $\hat{\tau}_{ysld}$ is the effect of treatment $S$ on $Y$, estimated by the difference-of-differences method; $\overline{Y}_{12}$ is the treatment mean at Time 2; $\overline{Y}_{11}$ is the treatment mean at Time 1; $\overline{Y}_{02}$ is the control mean at Time 2; and $\overline{Y}_{01}$ is the control mean at Time 1. This difference-of-differences approach is most appropriate when regression to the mean is an issue in the treatment group but not in the control group (Holland, 1986). It is also appropriate when there is an interaction effect with the treatment. It can be estimated and tested using the change scores between Time 1 and Time 2 for the outcome measures if there are no interaction effects. If one uses change scores, a $t$ test or a one-way ANOVA estimates the treatment effect. When regression effects are the same in both groups, testing the difference of change scores produces the same result as the second approach, regression with lagged variables. The estimate of the treatment effect is

$$\hat{\tau}_{ysll} = \alpha + \beta_s \overline{Y}_s - \beta_p \overline{Y}_p, \tag{1.7}$$

where $\hat{\tau}_{ysll}$ is the value of the treatment result of $S$ on $Y$ estimated using the lagged approach with a two-way ANOVA; $\alpha$ is the intercept of the prediction equation; $Y_s$ is a dummy variable coded 0 for comparison group and 1 for treatment group, and $Y_p$ is another dummy variable coded 0 for pretest and 1 for posttest; $\beta$ is the effect of each dummy variable; and the treatment effect is $\beta^s$. This estimation procedure assumes that each observation on a subject is treated as a separate record of data. In this case, each subject would have two records, one for pretest and the other for posttest. Alternatively, if the pre- and postdata are stored on the same record (one record per subject), then the causal effect is estimated as

$$\hat{\tau}_{ys} = \alpha + \beta_{y\delta s}\bar{\delta}_s, \tag{1.8}$$

where $\hat{\tau}_{ys}$ is the treatment effect of $S$ on $Y$, $\beta_{y\delta s}$ is the effect of the change in $S$ on $Y$, and $\bar{\delta}_s$ is the mean change in $S$. This is estimated with a $t$ test or one-way ANOVA using the change score in the outcome as the dependent variable. These two procedures give the same result if there are no interaction effects. When there are interaction effects, the two procedures may give different results, depending on the nature of the interaction. The difference-of-differences approach is used more often in this case, unless a researcher adds an interaction term to the estimation using a change score. If Condition 1 is met, then estimating Equations 1.5, 1.6, 1.7, and 1.8 produces reliable estimates of the causal effects of a treatment or intervention. If Condition 1 is not met, the data should be analyzed as if they came from a quasi-experiment, which has procedures for dealing with the problems arising from not meeting Condition 1.

Figure 1.2 illustrates a simple example of group differences. It shows that those in the 2008 General Social Survey who did not have babies in their household had a higher household income than those who did have babies. The chart displays the confidence interval and the range of income for the two groups.

Table 1.1 provides a quantitative summary of the example one-way ANOVA for estimating effects. In this case, it examines the effect of having babies in a household on the income of the household, under the supposition that time allocated to baby care takes away from time allocated to producing income (without assuming how much time each parent allocates to baby care). Presence or absence of babies is treated as a factor in the analysis. Household income is treated as a continuous outcome. For this example, we assume no confounding factors and normal distribution of income. Subsequent examples will examine these assumptions and demonstrate how propensity scores may result in more credible estimates. The data are from the General Social Survey 2008 panel study (Davis, Smith, & Marsden, 2010).

These findings suggest that having babies in the household reduces income by about $11,800. The effect of babies is weak, however. Eta equals .08.

One may argue that the assumption of no confounding factors is not credible. This may be examined by looking at the correlations of having babies

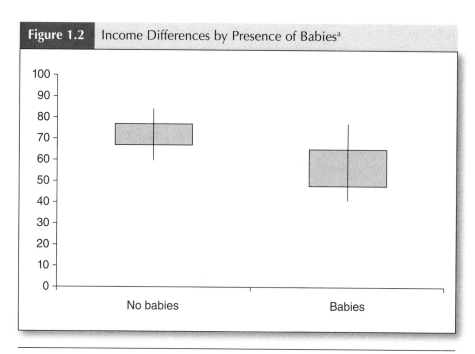

| Figure 1.2 | Income Differences by Presence of Babies[a] |

a. Income in thousands. Data are from General Social Survey. N = 1,341.

| Table 1.1 | Income and Having Babies[a] |

| Groups | t Test | | | | ANOVA | | | |
|---|---|---|---|---|---|---|---|---|
| | Means | t | df | p | Means | f | df | p |
| No babies 2006 | $69,423 | 2.98 | 1,390 | .003 | $69,423 | 8.93 | 1,390 | .003 |
| Babies 2006 | $57,647 | | | | $57,647 | | | |

*Note.* ANOVA, analysis of variance; *df*, degrees of freedom.

a. Income in 2008 by baby in household in 2006, unweighted data. $\eta = .08$; $t^2$ does not equal *F* due to rounding error.

and income with other variables. If the potential confounding factors are categorical variables, then the confounding factors could be examined using cross-tabulation or ANOVA (depending on the level of measurement of the factors). Table 1.2 provides the correlations of the factors in the model (babies and income) with other variables in the data set.

Table 1.2 shows that education and marital status are both correlated with having babies and income. Those with more years of education in 2006 were less likely to have babies in their household. Those who were not married in 2006 were also not likely to have babies in their household. Both of these variables confound the assessment of the effect of having babies on income. Subsequent examples will show how some of this confounding may be removed.

## QUASI-EXPERIMENTS AND INFERENCE

All the quasi-experimental designs discussed contain threats to the ignorability assumption. They violate SUTVA. They fail one or more of the requirements for causal inference because of potential threats of confoundedness in their design. Those threats are not always realized. When they are realized, actions need to be taken to reduce or eliminate the confoundedness. The following chapters discuss these designs: how their data are analyzed and what evidence may be offered that potential confoundedness may be ignored and that reasonable inferences may be made from those designs. Some of the more common designs are discussed within this chapter to introduce concepts important to understanding how problems of statistical and causal inference are interrelated. Addressing the problems for one has implications for the other.

If an experiment is not designed well or there is a problem in implementation, this is likely to fail SUTVA and the requirements for causal inference. Other variables may confound one's inference about the effect of the intervention. Quasi-experiments, as a consequence of their design, always have a

| Table 1.2 | Correlates of Babies and Income ($N = 1,390$) | | | | | |
|---|---|---|---|---|---|---|
| | Babies | Income | Work Status | Education | Race | Marital Status |
| Babies | 1.0 | −0.148** | 0.040 | −0.187** | −0.017 | −0.059** |
| Income | −0.148** | 1.0 | −0.080** | 0.353** | −0.087 | −0.195** |

**Significant at $p < .01$.

potential confounding influence. These confounding influences need to be reduced or controlled. It is preferable to control them by design. If they cannot be controlled by design, they need to be controlled statistically or a compelling argument must be given why the failure to control them does not confound the inference made. Controlling them statistically is discussed more in the next chapter.

Offering a compelling argument to ignore a potential threat needs strong justification. Giving just any kind of reason to not control for a confounding variable is inadequate. The reason must be compelling. There must be no logical reason for rejecting the argument. For example, if clients who also have problems of substance abuse are accepted into a parent education program, the substance abuse may make it more difficult to get positive effects from the parent education program. If analysis shows that parent education helps parenting skills despite the influence of substance abuse, then one could still infer that the intervention helped, other things being equal. If the findings are opposite that of the confounding effect, one can cautiously conclude that an effect is there and possibly stronger than the amount estimated, although one may still question how much stronger the effect might be.

## Threats to Valid Inference

The threats to valid inference come from three sources: (1) confoundedness of variables, (2) making incorrect causal assumptions, and (3) difficulties in implementing the design. Addressing confoundedness and testing one's assumptions about the statistics produced improves statistical conclusion validity. Testing one's assumptions about the causal relationships enhances internal validity. Implementation difficulties are a problem mainly because they affect statistical conclusion validity and internal validity. They produce confoundedness, challenge one's assumptions about the causal relationships, and may bias the estimation process. Addressing implementation difficulties improves statistical conclusion validity, internal validity, and decisions about the estimation process. These threats will be discussed for each quasi-experimental design. Strategies for dealing with those threats will be described. Criteria for assessing the seriousness of the threats will also be presented.

The threats to internal validity are well-known and discussed extensively in texts such as Shadish, Cook, and Campbell (2002). These include the following: ambiguous temporal precedence, sample selectivity, history, maturation, regression, attrition, testing, instrumentation, and interactive effects among the threats. In addition, there are social factors that may confound an experiment: subjects' awareness of their research group, diffusion of treatment between groups, compensatory rivalry, resentful demoralization, and compensatory equalization.

It may be difficult to implement an experiment or quasi-experiment because of legal, ethical, or practical constraints on the study. For example, the subjects in the intervention group may all be assigned by a court that is unwilling to randomly withhold punishment or treatment. The researchers may treat subjects unequally and compromise the research protocol. As such, these are threats to quasi-experimental designs. Substantive knowledge of the issue being studied is usually necessary to anticipate what some of these factors or problems might be. As noted by Heckman (1989), good causal inference needs contextual knowledge about the issue as well as good statistical procedures.

## *Propensity Scores*

Propensity scores are one way of attempting to deal with confoundedness when the threat is realized. The subsequent sections describe the ways in which each design may have threats to valid inference and identify what issues need to be addressed concerning each design. The final section discusses the ways in which broken experiments may violate strong and weak ignorability and the issues involved in repairing them.

A propensity score is the conditional probability that a subject will be in the treatment group, given his or her characteristics. If a research subject in an experimental group has a propensity score of .80, this means that, given information about prior variables in the study, the case is estimated as having an 80% chance of falling in the experimental group. Such scores, or probabilities, are estimated using knowledge of the characteristics of the prior variables for the groups being compared. They allow controlling for much, if not all, of the pregroup differences (Rubin, 1974). They improve the internal validity of between-group comparisons so that an estimate of the effect of the variable represented by the groups will be as close as possible to the true effect of the variable. In optimal circumstances, they may even allow an unbiased estimate of this effect.

Propensity scores can be used in a variety of ways with quasi-experimental data. They may be used to create matched samples, uniform subgroups, and weights for balancing characteristics between groups and used as variables for controlling or adjusting data. Each quasi-experimental design has ways in which the risk of confounding is higher. However propensity scores are used, the focus is always on reducing the risks that are most prominent with a particular design.

There are four ways that propensity scores are commonly estimated: (1) using logistic regression, (2) discriminant function analysis, (3) regression with a dummy dependent variable, and (4) probit regression. Because dummy variable regression and probit estimates are very similar, they will be treated here as the same. The propensity is the probability of being classified in a given group. It is sometimes defined as the conditional probability of classification given specified characteristics. It is most commonly estimated using logistic regression, mainly because it is easy to use when the dependent variable is dichotomous. Discriminant analysis is mainly used when there are multiple intervention groups. Regression analysis is mainly used to get a simple estimate of the propensity. Probit regression is mainly used if probit analysis is also used as one's analytical technique for estimating intervention effects.

Currently, there are no criteria for choosing one procedure over another. They all produce probabilities that have a monotone relationship with each other. They all rank the cases the same with their probabilities. The discriminant estimated probabilities may even be a linear function of the probit or regression estimated probabilities. However, the probabilities for classifying estimated by the three strategies are not identical. The propensity scores estimated by logistic regression come out less similar to those of regression or discriminant analysis. As noted in Chapter 4, the relationship may even be curvilinear (though monotone). The trade-offs between using each of these three procedures for estimating propensity scores are discussed in Chapter 4.

Since there are no criteria for preferring one procedure over another, the following is recommended. One should use the same or similar procedure to estimate a propensity score that one will use to estimate effect coefficients of one's model. If logistic regression is the statistical procedure that will be used in estimating the effect coefficients, then the propensity should be estimated using logistic regression. If the effect coefficients of one's model will be estimated using some version of regression analysis, then the propensities should be estimated using either discriminant function or regression analysis. The choice between discriminant function and regression analysis is essentially arbitrary, since the values estimated will be a linear function of the other (the difference due to scaling factors). This is because in the case of only one discriminant function, the procedure is equivalent to regression analysis with a dummy dependent variable. With normally distributed data, it produces the same result as a probit analysis. The rationale for this recommendation is that if a different procedure is used to estimate the propensities than is used to estimate the effect coefficients, the propensity estimates may be inconsistent estimates of the true propensity. The full ability of propensity scores to remove confounding influences will not be realized, even though the amount of bias may be small.

In all cases of estimating propensities, the basic strategy is to estimate the probability of membership in the treatment group(s), have the program save the classification probabilities, and use the classification probabilities as propensity variables. More about estimation of propensity scores will be discussed in Chapter 3. Computer code for simple procedures for estimating propensity scores is given on the website for the book. The URL for the website is http://www.faculty.umb.edu/william_holmes/propensity.htm.

Table 1.2 showed that the relationship between having babies and household income was confounded by education and marital status. This confounding can be reduced by using propensity scores. To do so, we need to estimate propensity scores for the probability of classification in the two groups of having babies or not. Table 1.3 provides an example of simple propensity score estimation. Using data from the General Social Survey (Davis et al., 2010), propensity scores are estimated for classification of families as either having babies in the household or not having babies in the household (scored 0 for no babies and 1 for babies in household). The variables used to estimate the propensity scores were the following: education, race, geographic mobility since the age of 16, work status, and marital status.

This estimation is done to look at the effects of having young children in the household. Estimates were generated using logistic regression, least squares regression, and discriminant function analysis. The estimated dependent variable (the classification probability) for each procedure was stored as a separate variable. A more elaborate discussion of estimating propensity scores is given in Chapter 4. Table 1.3 shows slight differences between the estimates of logistic regression and least squares regression. The probabilities estimated by

| Table 1.3 | Propensities Estimated by Alternative Procedures | | |
|---|---|---|---|
| | *Logistic Regression Estimate* | *Least Squares Regression Estimate* | *Discriminant Analysis Estimate* |
| Mean | 0.12787 | 0.12788 | 0.48909 |
| *SD* | 0.0379 | 0.0375 | 0.0824 |
| Range | 0.065–0.312 | 0.048–0.266 | 0.316–0.771 |
| *N* | 1,984 | 1,984 | 1,984 |

discriminant analysis, however, are larger and have a broader range. This greater dispersion of scores produces the same order of cases ranked by propensity. Indeed, these propensities are nearly a linear function of the least squares estimate. It may mean, however, that a larger criterion (called a caliper) might be needed when matching cases (see Chapter 3).

## QUASI-EXPERIMENTS AND OBSERVATIONAL STUDIES

The variables that can confound a particular quasi-experiment depend on the design of the experiment, the variables' measures, and the implementation of the study. Every quasi-experiment has some design weakness. Some important variables may go unmeasured. Unexpected difficulties may arise in implementing the research protocol. Any of these may lead to confounded results. Every quasi-experiment may be confounded by sample selectivity, maturation, history, testing, instrumentation, mortality, or an interaction among them. The biggest problem is often selectivity, because if groups differ at the beginning, they may experience maturation, history, testing, instrumentation, or dropout differently. For example, those not in a job training program may be more depressed in their job search efforts than those in a job training program. The depression may impede job searching, making the comparison group even less successful than the training group.

### Cross-Sectional Designs

A cross-sectional design can utilize propensity scores, because the groups compared almost always differ in some characteristics. This design is a classic example of having nonequivalent groups. When there is an intervention group compared with a nonintervention group, Shadish et al. (2002) refer to this as a posttest-only with nonequivalent groups. Such designs have a high risk that many factors will influence in which group the subjects will fall, which is a problem of sample selectivity or selection bias. When a factor in which the groups differ is known to have occurred prior to the treatment, that factor is referred to as an antecedent variable. It happens before the treatment. If antecedent variables also correlate with the outcome variables, confounding results. A common strategy with such a design is to identify as many antecedent variables as possible and use them as statistical controls to remove pregroup differences. When a factor in which the groups differ has an effect known to have occurred after the intervention begins, it is called an intervening effect; and the factor is an intervening variable. It happens after the treatment and before the outcome. Measures of intervening variables may be included in studies to examine the process by which a treatment produces its effect. If an intervening variable correlates with the outcome, using it as a control helps identify this process.

Controlling intervening variables helps clarify the process by which an effect occurs. However, the effect of the treatment is a result of the **direct effect** of the intervention (the effect of the intervention controlling for all other factors) and the indirect effect through specified intervening variables. This is referred to as the **total effect** or the **net effect** of the intervention. This total effect is the sum of the direct effect and the indirect effects. Indirect effects are calculated by multiplying the effects of the treatment on the intervening variables by the effect of the intervening variables on the outcome. That is,

$$\tau_n = \tau_{sy} + \beta_{sx}\, \beta_{xy}, \tag{1.9}$$

where $\tau_n$ is the net effect, $\tau_{sy}$ is the direct effect of $Y$ on $S$, $\beta_{xy}$ is the direct effect of $Y$ on $X$, and $\beta_{sx}$ is the direct effect of $X$ on $S$.

It is difficult to know what pregroup differences there are and whether all their confounding effects have been removed by using the measured antecedent variables as control variables or to adjust estimated effects. A thorough literature review can identify some of the antecedent confounding factors. Ideally, one measures all the confounding factors that cannot be controlled by design; and then they are controlled statistically. It is rare that all identified factors can be measured. It is hoped that the unmeasured factors correlate with the measured factors. If they do, controlling for the measured factors will, in part, control the unmeasured factors. With posttest-only nonequivalent groups, it is important to use as many control variables as possible, because the risk of unmeasured confounders may be high. Even with many control variables, there may still be sources of confounding independent of the control variables. One must closely examine the published literature on the outcome studied to identify whether there are any important correlates that remain unmeasured and to consider what the effect of not controlling for those factors might be on estimates of the outcome.

One group of factors should not be controlled even if they correlate with the intervention and with the outcome. These are the **consequent variables**, those that are known to occur after the outcome. It makes no temporal sense to control for things that happen after the outcome, even if one thinks that "anticipation of the outcome" might be a confounding factor. If the anticipation of an event is not measured directly, one cannot assume it was anticipated just because the event occurs.

All known threats to validity apply to posttest-only nonequivalent group designs. The only threat that might not apply is when the temporal ordering of the intervention and the outcome is clear. One should attempt to measure as many of the sources of validity threats as possible, since they aren't controlled in this type of design.

## Pre–Post Comparison Groups

While pre–post comparison groups have a similarity to the pre–post experiment, units of analysis are not randomly assigned to the groups. Like cross-sectional studies, antecedent variables in the study may correlate with the groups compared and with outcome variables, confounding the results. A pre–post comparison allows controlling for more pregroup differences than a cross-sectional design. However, it does not usually measure all the potential factors by which the groups may differ. In the words of Shadish et al. (2002), "The absence of pretest differences in a quasi-experiment is never proof that selection bias is absent" (p. 138). However, the absence of pretest differences in variables known to correlate with the outcome strengthens one's argument that pretest differences are weak or absent. It strengthens the claim of strong or weak ignorability, even though it does not prove it.

In principle, history and maturation are both controlled because both groups are exposed to the same history and period of maturation. However, the nonequivalency of the pretest groups means that there could be interaction between selectivity and history or maturation. For example, if a control group of students in an educational program have less supportive parents than an intervention group, then economic stress on the parents may cause the less supportive parents to be even less helpful to their children than the parents of students in the treatment group. This would inflate the estimate of the intervention.

## Dose–Response Designs

A dose–response design is used when there are multiple interventions of different types or magnitudes. It allows comparing between intentions and with a nonintervention comparison group (Shadish et al., 2002). With this design, the intervention is typically administered in increasing amounts, such as different amounts of a drug or hours of participation in a program. The levels of treatment may be randomly assigned to the subjects, be assigned according to specific criteria, or naturally result from variable participation in a program. Except in the case of strict random assignment, the different levels of the intervention may be related to other characteristics of the subjects. These other characteristics may also be correlated with the outcome. For example, individuals with a more severe mental health problem may receive more hours of counseling or a greater amount of a drug than those with a less severe mental health problem. The factors that produced a more severe problem to begin with may also be associated with the severity of the outcome, which would confound any analysis of the effect of different amounts of the intervention.

Some researchers do not regard dose–response designs as having a comparison or control group. This is partly because some dose–response designs do not have a group with no treatment at all. They only have varying amounts of treatment. Some dose–response designs have groups that receive no intervention, which makes them indistinguishable from a comparison group for which there was nonrandom assignment (i.e., subject to sample selectivity). Designs that have a no treatment group are often a result of nonrandom assignment (e.g., dropouts from the study who may have incomplete outcome information). As a result, analysts using dose–response data often focus on estimating a dose–response effect (the effect of different levels of intervention), rather than the counterfactual effect (the effect of no intervention). In any case, comparisons are being made between different levels of treatment. If the dose levels correspond to an underlying continuous measure, it may even be possible to estimate what the effect of no treatment might be. Whether one chooses to describe a dose–response design as one having a comparison group or not, it still makes comparisons between groups and raises the question as to how many pretest differences there are in the groups at the start of the study. It is for these pretest differences that propensity scores may be used in trying to make the groups equivalent.

## Panel Studies

Quasi-experimental panel studies, like pre–post comparison group designs, do not have random assignment of subjects to groups at the start of the study. They are less likely to have results with low internal validity because the groups are followed across time. This allows some control over trends, such as history and maturation. It is especially important to consider trends when one is studying a variable subject to a developmental process—such as alcoholism, career trajectory, or aging. Unfortunately, panel studies only allow examining short-term trends. To consider longer-term trends, one may need a longitudinal design. As with a pre–post nonequivalent comparison group design, there may also be interaction between selectivity and history or maturation. So measures of selectivity factors as well as history and maturation factors are needed. Procedures appropriate for panel studies are discussed in Chapter 10.

## *Longitudinal Studies*

Longitudinal studies are most powerful when they involve comparison groups. The longer-term trends in the intervention and comparison groups can be more accurately estimated and controlled. Multiple measures are taken before and after the intervention. If there is no separate comparison group for which data are collected, then the preintervention trend is taken as the comparison group and the postintervention as the treatment group.

Longitudinal quasi-experiments, however, do not have random assignment to groups. As with pre–post designs, the groups may start out different and be subject to separate maturation processes or history effects, which can confound the results. It is important for longitudinal studies that measures of possible maturation or relevant history factors be collected along with other data. This will help document pretest differences, as well as differential changes in confounding factors. It will also allow using them either in the estimation of propensity scores or as instrumental variables to obtain more consistent estimates. The treatment effect may be spuriously inflated (a **reinforcer effect**) or spuriously reduced (a **suppression effect**). Reducing the pregroup differences will reduce the confounding. The procedures appropriate for longitudinal designs are discussed in Chapter 10.

## *Broken Experiments*

Sometimes, a study begins as an experiment; but the research protocol breaks down. The subjects who drop out of one group may differ from those in the other group. There may be communication between people in each group, leading them to know or believe which group they are in and what the expected result might be. For example, there was an experiment in which the researcher was studying the effect of vitamin C on the common cold. Subjects were randomly given little white capsules in which one half of the subjects got vitamin C and the other half got powdered sugar. The subjects were medical personnel, who proceeded to open the capsules and taste the substance. They could easily tell the difference between ascorbic acid and powdered sugar. The experiment was seriously compromised (Miller et al., 1977). Similarly, randomly assigning classes in schools to a treatment and a control group may break down if the children communicate over lunch period about what is happening in their classes.

The breakdown is often a result of social actions that occur during the experiment or of failure to anticipate factors that will interrupt the experiment. Subjects may become aware of their research group and deliberately conform with or violate what they think the experimenter predicts. Communication may occur between subjects in different groups, confounding the results. The groups may compete with each other to achieve better results. A group may become angry and sabotage the experiment. The experimenter may have failed to anticipate effects of the treatment that interact with the outcome. These kinds of factors need to be considered in the design of any experimental and quasi-experimental study. It means that the researcher may need to collect information during the intervention or debrief the subjects afterward to examine their beliefs, feelings, and actions during the intervention. When one is doing secondary analysis of existing data where such information was not collected, one can do little more than examine comments by others about the quality of the research study to see if there is any evidence of protocol breakdown. Talking with the original researchers may also provide information not available in print.

## ADEQUACY AND SUFFICIENCY OF CAUSAL INFERENCE

A causal inference is reliable when it is based on a statistical model that is both adequate and sufficient. These terms are here used in a technical sense that the model estimated from the data meets specific criteria. If the criteria are not met, the estimated model is not statistically adequate or sufficient. Causal inferences should not be based on models that are not adequate or sufficient. A causal model is **statistically adequate** when assumptions of the model correspond to assumptions of the statistics used to estimate the model. The level of measurement of the constructs and the level appropriate to the statistical procedures used should correspond. The model should not be misspecified. If the statistical procedure is appropriate for estimating the model and if the model is correctly specified, then the resulting estimates of the model parameters are statistically adequate. If the causal model is not correctly specified and if the measurement level of the indicators and procedures do not correspond, then statistical estimates based on it are likely to be biased. They fail the test of statistical adequacy.

Rubin's assumption of strong ignorability addresses statistical adequacy of effects. If it is correct that there are no unobserved confounding variables, then his model for estimating causal influences is not misspecified—so long as the causal effects are estimated using procedures that are appropriate to the level of measurement of the indicators. As Heckman (1986) notes, if the assumption of strong ignorability does not hold, the estimated effects are biased. No biased estimate meets the standard of statistical adequacy.

The assumption of weak ignorability does not produce statistically adequate estimates. The presence of unobserved weakly confounding variables means that there is some bias in the estimate, however small. As the weak confoundedness approaches zero, so does the bias. The estimate approaches adequacy. The bias may be so small that an estimate based on weak confoundedness is indistinguishable from an adequate estimate.

The structural equation approach to causal inference also addresses statistical adequacy. An essential element of all structural equation models is an assessment of whether there is evidence of misspecification of the model. Tests are used to examine whether the model is correctly identified. If there is no misspecification and if the assumptions of the estimation procedures correspond to those of the causal model, adequate estimates of causal effects are provided.

A causal model is substantively adequate when evidence fails to support a conclusion that the model is misspecified. The researcher must undertake tests of misspecification, and the results must be negative. Inferences based on a model that fails to provide evidence of valid specification are not substantively adequate. Both the RCM and the SEM approach use tests of their models to see if they are properly identified. For the various causal models discussed in subsequent chapters, tests of misspecification will be offered. Failure to test for misspecification means the model is not substantively adequate. A causal inference is adequate when the inference is based on a causal model that is both statistically and substantively adequate.

A causal model is statistically sufficient when no additional information would change that estimate of the statistic. For example, the sample mean is an unbiased estimate of the population mean with normal distributions. No other measure of central tendency provides additional information about the population mean of a normal distribution. This is why with such a distribution, the mean equals the median, which in turn equals the mode. Many maximum likelihood estimates are sufficient statistics when assumptions for maximum likelihood estimation are met.

Statistics used to estimate a causal effect, such as a mean difference or a regression coefficient, are sufficient estimates when no alternative estimator provides additional information about the causal effect. When this condition is met, well-done replication studies will produce similar estimates of the causal effects. When replication studies produce dissimilar results, one or more of the estimates cannot be statistically sufficient. Studies that produce such results are likely to fail adequacy criteria as well. They may be misspecified, or assumptions for use of the statistics are not met.

Estimates of a causal effect may be adequate without being sufficient. There may be alternative statistical procedures whose assumptions are consistent with a causal model, but whose statistics provide additional information about the effect. However, a failure of adequacy implies that the estimator will also fail sufficiency. Inferences based on these statistics will be neither adequate nor sufficient.

In examining adequacy and sufficiency of causal inferences, three questions are important to address: (1) Do the assumptions of a statistical procedure correspond to those of the causal model from which inferences will be made? (2) Have all identifiable confounding variables been controlled by the design or estimation procedure? (3) Are the statistics used to estimate the model sufficient? If the answer to all the three questions is yes, this gives us the second condition under which causal inference is reliable:

*Condition 2:* comparison groups in which all pretest differences either are controlled or for which there is a compelling argument that the difference will not confound the causal inference and the estimated model is adequate and sufficient.

Pretest differences refer to all factors that prior research, theory, or design specifications require to occur prior to the treatment or the intervention. If a research study ignores or excludes previously identified factors, then Condition 2 is not met. There may be valid reasons why a given factor is ignored or excluded (e.g., if including a measure would require engaging in an illegal or unethical act). Nevertheless, such a study can only offer plausible evidence of a causal effect. It cannot be said to offer conclusive evidence. On the other hand, if all identifiable factors are either controlled or excludable by compelling argument, then Condition 2 is met, and a reliable causal conclusion can be made. The assumption of strong ignorability when applied to quasi-experiments meets Condition 2, as does the assumption of weak con-foundedness (provided the weakness of the confounding influence is smaller than can be statistically detected). Structural equation models can also meet Condition 2 when all the variables in the model correspond to the identifiable factors. In both the cases of the RCM and SEM, the estimated model must also be adequate and sufficient.

# CHAPTER 2

# CAUSAL INFERENCE USING CONTROL VARIABLES

This chapter reviews how control variables are used to reduce problems of causal inference. It examines trade-offs between different strategies in using control variables. Issues unresolved by control variables are identified and discussed. The various ways in which propensity scores are used to control confounding variables are addressed. Their use with alternative designs will be discussed in Chapter 4.

While it is preferable to control confounding factors with appropriate design characteristics, reasons have already been given why this is not always legal, moral, or feasible. Things that confound inference about causal effects that cannot be controlled by research design need to be controlled statistically. Five approaches are used to statistically control confounding factors: (1) matching, (2) stratifying, (3) weighting, (4) adjusting, and (5) using multivariate structural models. Each approach has its own strengths and weaknesses. No approach works all the time. Indeed, any approach can make things worse under certain circumstances. On the other hand, some approaches can produce unbiased estimates of treatment effects if the right conditions are met. This is why it is necessary to assess the adequacy and sufficiency of the causal model being used. Selecting an approach whose assumptions closely match those of one's causal model generally produces better results. This and subsequent chapters will discuss which assumptions are most relevant for deciding whether a particular approach seems likely to produce acceptable results. Using a misspecified causal model to control confounding factors can produce less accurate results than not controlling those factors at all. Assessing the degree of misspecification provides evidence on whether the results are improved or worsened by using control procedures.

This chapter addresses approaches that adjust data to remove the biasing effects of confounding variables or control them in simple multivariate models. The adjustment approach attempts to measure the confounding factors and remove their effects statistically. The control approach uses the confounding variables in a causal model as alternative causal influences on the outcome. The effect of the intervention is estimated after controlling for the alternative causal influences.

The existence of confounding influences represents violation of the ignorability assumption. The chapter addresses some of the strategies for identifying confounding factors and controlling their influence. The chapter includes a treatment of instrumental variables (IV) and two-stage least squares (2SLS) regression because adjusting estimates of program effects using IV is mathematically equivalent to using instruments in the same way as control variables. Most issues that apply to control variables also apply to IV. Issues that are unique to IV derive from assumptions about IV that often don't apply to other control variables but do apply to control variables in specialized circumstances. As will be explained later in the chapter, 2SLS can even be directly estimated where the IV are included as exogenous variables in a structural equation model.

This chapter does not include extensive treatment of structural equation modeling (SEM) because most such models are more complex than that implied by IV or 2SLS use, especially if they include measurement models for unobserved variables. The greater complexity raises additional issues beyond those covered in this chapter. The general use of SEM and the issues arising therefrom will be discussed in Chapter 9.

## CONTROLLING CONFOUNDEDNESS

The relationship between marital status and education is an example of a confounding variable. If one gets married at an early age, he or she may drop out of secondary school or never attend college. This relationship is illustrated in Figure 2.1

This figure is a mirror histogram. It shows that the highest level of education for the married is more likely to be high school graduation or less, whereas the highest level of education for the singles is more likely to be high school graduation or more. The singles are more likely to graduate from college. The married are more likely to drop out of school before graduation.

A mirror histogram like this can be graphed using a population pyramid histogram found in every major statistical package. The outcome variable is used instead of population. The "treatment variable" (in this case, marital status) is used instead of gender.

Five procedures are commonly used for controlling the influence of confounding variables: (1) matching, (2) stratifying, (3) weighting, (4) adjusting,

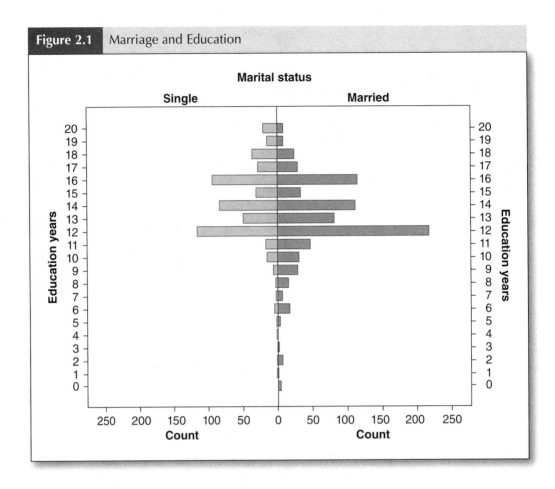

Figure 2.1    Marriage and Education

and (5) multivariate modeling. Although matching is a popular way of using propensity scores to control confoundedness, these scores can be used with any of the procedures noted above. The procedures may also be combined and used either simultaneously or sequentially. Matching and adjusting combined was one of the techniques that Rubin evaluated (and recommended) in his 1974 article on estimating causal effects.

Each of these procedures attempts to achieve a similar result by using different means. The result desired is that the groups being compared be as identical as possible. Matching does this by finding subjects in each group that have very similar characteristics. Stratifying creates separate groups of individuals having similar characteristics and averages the results across the groups. Weighting makes the groups similar by replicating cases in each group so that a similar number of cases have the same characteristics. Adjusting uses a statistical approach to remove characteristics that are associated with confounding factors. Multivariate modeling uses measures of confounding factors as control variables in a multivariate model. Often the model is ordinary least squares (OLS) regression, analysis of covariance (ANCOVA), logistic regression (LR), or a general linear model (GLM). The procedures discussed here primarily use OLS or a modification thereof. ANCOVA, LR, and GLM will be discussed in Chapter 9.

## *Matching as Controlling*

Matching is one way of removing preintervention differences. If two or more groups are formed where each member of a group is matched in one or more characteristics with a member of the other group(s), then the groups start out having the same characteristics. There are no pregroup differences—provided that there are no characteristics unmatched related to the outcome measures and the choice of groups in which cases are placed (i.e., no unmatched confounding factors; Rubin, 1974). For matching, the principal issue is selecting the right variables to use for matching. As demonstrated by Heckman and Navarro-Lozano (2004), if you leave out important confounding factors, the matching procedure will be biased and inefficient. Rosenbaum and Rubin (1983), however, have argued that matching is preferable because regression adjustment with control variables requires a linear relationship between the confounding variables and the outcome, which is not always the case. One can use nonlinear transformations of variables to address curvilinearity; but this is seen as a more problematic strategy. In principle, if a regression model with control variables is correctly specified, it can do matching as well. Rubin's simulations, however, generally show that matching does a better job of estimating true causal effects than regression adjustment, although the improvement is usually modest (Rubin, 1974).

Strict 1–1 matching does a good job of controlling confounding factors because it ensures that each case in one group has a corresponding member in another group that has the same characteristics. This ensures that there are no pretest differences in any of the characteristics that were used to estimate the propensity scores. It doesn't ensure balance in the pretest characteristics for those variables that were not included in estimating the propensity scores. Unmeasured variables are among those not included in the estimation. Matching can only be done for those variables that are measured.

### Stratifying as Controlling

When one divides a sample into several groups according to characteristics of a potentially confounding variable, this produces a control over its influence. Each group allows examining the conditional effect of the treatment on the outcome. Averaging the estimates across the conditional groups produces an estimate of the treatment effect controlling for the confounding variable. Cochran (1968) has estimated that using even five subgroups of cases grouped by propensity scores can control as much as 90% of pretest differences, though this depends on the groups having a similar number of cases.

Grouping cases according to quintiles of propensity scores gives results very similar to those from using propensity scores as control variables in regression. The reason is that the effect estimated by regression controls is equivalent to creating subgroups for each unique value of the control variable, calculating the mean outcome of each group, and then computing a weighted average of those means across all the groups (the weights depend on the number of cases in each group and the variance of the mean). With subclassification, only five groups are used instead of all the values of the propensity scores. Calculating the mean for each value of the propensity score is usually not feasible. There are rarely enough cases for each propensity value. The regression approach doesn't create subgroups but, rather, is able to get the same result from the variance–covariance matrix of the independent variables and the outcome.

### Weighting as Controlling

Weighting the cases in a sample can remove preintervention differences. Weighting can increase cases that are too few in one group compared with another or decrease cases that occur too often in another group. As a simple example, suppose the experimental group has 50 men and 50 women and the comparison group has 60 men and 40 women. The comparison group can be made to resemble the experimental group by giving the women in the comparison group a weight of 1.5. This will increase the number of women in the weighted comparison sample to be the same as that for men, although it will produce a weighted sample size for this group of 120 subjects. To avoid inflating the calculated degrees of freedom (*df*), one might weight the men in the comparison group by 0.833 and the women by 1.25, which produces a weighted sample size of 100 subjects, which will have 50 men and 50 women in it. Since the result produces an equal number of men and women in each group, the potential influence of gender is statistically controlled.

Weighting is a procedure that improves one's statistical estimates of causal effects. It improves internal validity. In so doing, it produces a weighted sample whose profile does not match the unweighted sample. The estimate of the causal effect applies to the weighted sample. It does not apply to the unweighted sample. This means that in the real world where other factors are not controlled, different results might apply. This can be said for randomized experiments as well. The results do not always generalize to the broader population, an issue referred to as the problem of external validity. The causal effects may be valid for the sample studied (internal validity); but different results may be produced in a nonexperimental broader environment (external invalidity).

## *Adjusting as Controlling*

Adjusting for the influence of a confounding factor has come to mean two different things in statistical analysis. One use of adjusting involves examining the effect of an intervention under each of the conditions of a confounding factor. For example, looking at the effect of a drug treatment for groups that have high blood pressure and low blood pressure adjusts for the potential confounding effect of blood pressure. The effect within each group is the marginal or conditional effect of the treatment, given a group's characteristic. In the language of correlation analysis, this would be referred to as a **part association**.

In contrast, if one averages the effect across all groups, this represents the partial association between the intervention and the outcome. Some researchers use "conditional effects" to mean both marginal and partial effects. To avoid confusion, in this text conditional effects will only refer to marginal effects—that is, for a subgroup characteristic of a third variable. Effects averaged across characteristics of a third variable or with the third variable controlled will only be referred to as partial effects. Adjusting data using propensity scores will be discussed in more detail in the next chapter.

## *Multivariate Models for Controlling*

Multivariate modeling controls the effects of confounding factors by estimating the intervention effects as a partial measure of association with the outcome while controlling for the other variables in the model. A simple example of this would be where the intervention is treated as a dichotomous variable in a regression equation along with all of the measured confounding variables. The regression coefficient for the intervention would represent the treatment effect with the confounding effects removed (assuming all confounding factors have been measured and included in the regression equation). Alternatively, the treatment may be used in ANCOVA, LR, GLM, or SEM, which are discussed in a later chapter.

Table 2.1 presents the results of an ANCOVA for the relationship between having babies and household income, controlling for a third variable. The presence of babies in the home is treated as an intervention in this case because it is potentially subject to the control of household members. Education, a previously identified confounding factor, is used as a control variable. After education is controlled, the effect of babies in the household disappears. When control variables make the intervention coefficient become nonsignificant, the intervention effect is inferred to be zero. The only exception to this is if there is counterevidence that the analysis was underpowered and the results represent a "false negative" or the control variable is shown to be a variable intervening after the treatment factor. How to examine the power adequacy of the sample will be discussed in a later chapter. The role of intervening variables will be discussed more in the section on 2SLS.

This approach to multivariate modeling is not without limitations. The models must use valid measures, be identifiable, and be properly specified. Tests for misspecification are particularly important for multivariate modeling. In addition, error terms of endogenous variables must not be correlated with any antecedent variable in the model. The latter part of the chapter discusses strategies for situations in which these requirements are not met.

| Table 2.1 | Babies and Income, Controlling for Education | | |
|---|---|---|---|
| | Tests of Model Effects | | |
| Source | Wald $\chi^2$ | df | Significance |
| Intercept | 8.029 | 1 | .005 |
| Babies in home | 2.723 | 1 | .099 |
| Years of education | 190.145 | 1 | .000 |

Note. Overall $\chi^2 = 187.1$; $df = 2$; $p < .001$; $N = 1,461$.

## SELECTING CONTROL VARIABLES

Whichever approach for controlling confounding influences is used, there is still the problem of how to identify which factors need controlling. Four strategies for identifying confounding factors are commonly used: (1) theorizing, (2) using prior research, (3) ad hoc selection, and (4) using pretest measures.

### *Theory-Selected Controls*

Theory is used to identify potential confounding factors because it can specify supposed causal linkages and which variables are antecedent to others. Any factor that theory says affects the outcome (directly or indirectly) and which is also related to sample selection is a candidate for confounding. One difficulty with using such factors, however, is that it is not known if there is a difference between the groups until after the data are collected. The data analyst has to measure and see if there is a difference between the groups to find out if the potential confounder is an actual confounder. This may require testing a number of variables to see if they are related to sample selection when there are multiple theories about the outcome and the intervention.

Typically, one chooses the most plausible theories or the ones supported by prior research to make this more manageable. Not covering all the credible theories, however, leaves one open to the charge that confounding factors were uncontrolled and the results are biased. The only defense against this charge is to empirically test such factors or have a strong theoretical argument as to why the alternative theory doesn't apply. Unfortunately, reasonable people can disagree as to whether a particular theory applies. One can appeal to prior research that fails to show such factors related to the outcome. If research contradicts theory about an outcome and there are no credible studies that show a relationship with the outcome, one has a defense against the charge of an uncontrolled theoretical confounder.

### *Research-Selected Controls*

Reviewing prior research has always been a way to identify confounding factors. Published research will usually state a rationale for why variables are included in the analysis. This may include theoretical arguments, other research, or substantive grounds for the temporal ordering of one's variables. Reviewing the research will not only identify empirical correlates but also identify reasons why variables should be regarded as confounding factors. The research should be examined closely to be sure that these variables do not intervene between the intervention and the outcome. If such correlates are antecedent or contemporaneous with the start of the intervention, they may be treated as confounding factors.

Research may disagree as to whether certain factors are confounding. While it may seem reasonable to include all variables that any study has ever found confounding, this can be unwieldy. It can divert one's attention from the most important confounders. It is also likely to include variables that were statistically significant because of chance variation (a false positive). Such variables may well drop out of significance due to regression to the mean, but their inclusion does consume time and resources. If a variable was found to be a significant correlate in only one study and there are no substantive or theoretical grounds for thinking it should have an effect, a researcher may make a judgment as to whether it should be included. If excluded, however, it should be explicitly noted in describing the design of the study.

## Ad Hoc Controls

The selection of control variables is not just a matter of reviewing research and theory. It requires substantive knowledge of the phenomenon under study and intelligent reasoning. Substantive knowledge may suggest potential confounding factors that prior research or theory has overlooked. Even if a researcher doesn't have much substantive experience with the subject under study, someone who does have such experience can be interviewed or be an adviser to the study. This will help ensure that confounding factors are not excluded because of ignorance.

Sometimes a researcher has a hunch or an idea that a particular factor might confound the results. There may be no prior research or theory that supports this. It may not even be based on substantive familiarity with the subject of the study. Yet it may be possible to fashion a reasonable argument as to why there might be a connection. Such arguments have a danger that they may stem from bias, ignorance, or stupidity; but they might also reflect a brilliant insight or a creative line of thought. The ad hoc inclusion of potential confounders should not be rejected out of hand; but they should receive careful thought before they are included.

## Pretest Controls

Pretest measures of the outcome are always good candidates as confounders. They are invariably correlated with the outcome. Nonrandomization at pretest makes unequal distribution among the groups for pretests of the outcome very likely. Errors of measurement in the outcome are also likely to be present in measurement of the pretest. Variables that influence the outcome may well also be an influence on the pretest.

It is a common practice that if pretest measures of the outcome are available, they are used as separate control variables. They may not be used as predictors of propensity scores. If the pretest variable is an important causal influence that one wishes to study, then it is usually treated as a separate variable. Studies of feedback or developmental processes are especially likely to use the pretest as a separate variable. In addition, if the error terms of the pre- and postmeasures are correlated, then including the pretest as an estimator of the propensity score will bias the estimated causal effect. Error in the estimated propensity will be correlated with error in the outcome. The estimated effect could be exaggerated (reinforced) or minimized (suppressed), depending on whether the correlation between the error terms is positive or negative.

If the pretest is not hypothesized as a causal influence, the outcome does not involve a developmental or feedback process, and tests of the error terms indicate that they are not correlated, then one can use a pretest measure for predicting the propensity score. Note that the pretest measure should not be used simultaneously to predict the propensity score and as a control variable. Doing this will introduce collinearity between the propensity score and the pretest. At the least, it will increase random error variance and decrease statistical power of the analysis. At the worst, it may rob the treatment of true covariance with the outcome and result in a false-negative conclusion of the treatment effects.

## Misspecification in Causal Models

Misspecification means that the causal relationships in one's model do not correspond to those that exist in the data. When there are causal influences that are neither included in the causal model nor controlled by the research design, it produces misspecification. They are unobserved and omitted. Misspecification also occurs when one includes a variable in one's causal model using invalid assumptions about the relationships between that variable and others in the model. For example, including a variable that is caused by the outcome and correlated with the treatment variable would bias the estimates of the treatment effects and also constitute misspecification. The one-way analysis of variance in Table 1.1 is an example of a misspecified model. When education was taken into consideration, the results changed. The original results were a biased estimate of the influence of babies in the household.

Several procedures are commonly used for providing evidence as to whether a specific causal model is misspecified or not. Some of these procedures are generally applicable. Others are only used with specific approaches to causal estimation. Tests of misspecification are discussed below.

## Consistency in Using Controls

Consistency is both a terminological and a statistical issue. Researchers in various disciplines use some terms differently. For example, some use the term *mediating variable* to refer to an intervening causal influence. Others use it to describe an interactive effect between two or more influences on a causal effect. In this text, it will be used only to describe an intervening effect. When interactive effects are discussed, the variables producing the effects will be described as interacting with, specifying, or having a marginal influence on the treatment effect. Some researchers will also say that the intervention effect is conditional on the value of the interacting variable.

When identifying potential control variables, the researcher must be careful that the sources on which he or she draws are consistent in how the causal relationships are described. When there may be ambiguity as to the directionality of a causal influence, some studies may say a variable is antecedent to another and other studies may say it is consequent. Whatever causal model is used in one's analysis should carefully evaluate the different descriptions of variables. When the research literature doesn't agree on the directionality or nature of a causal influence, the data analyst may need to posit alternative causal models, evaluate them, and base inferences on the results of the multiple models—rather than choosing what the presumed correct model is and just evaluating that.

**Statistical consistency** refers to whether a sample statistic approaches the population value as the sample size gets larger. Some sample statistics accurately describe the sample and the population from which the sample was drawn. The sample mean is an unbiased estimate of a population mean for samples that are unimodal and symmetrical. It is a consistent estimate of the population mean. For nonsymmetrical samples (skewed samples), the sample mean is not an unbiased estimate of the population mean.

An inconsistent estimate generally gets closer to the population value as the sample size increases, but it may converge on some value other than the population value. Some inconsistent estimates may, in fact, be close approximations of the population value; but they are generally not as good an approximation as a consistent estimate. If statisticians can prove mathematically that a sample statistic becomes indistinguishable from the population value as the sample approaches infinity, such a statistic is said to be **strongly consistent**. If simulations show the sample statistic approaches the population value though it is not demonstrated in a mathematical proof, the statistic is said to be **weakly consistent**. Estimates of causal effects that are consistent are always preferable to inconsistent estimates.

Interventions and treatments may be either exogenous or endogenous in one's causal model, depending on whether influences on the treatment status are included in the model. If no influences on the intervention are posited by the model, the treatment is exogenous. The estimate of the influence of a treatment on an outcome is a consistent estimate of the effect when the treatment is an exogenous variable in the model (other assumptions also being met). The estimate of the effect of an endogenous intervention is not a consistent estimate. It needs to be modified to become a consistent estimate.

## GETTING CONSISTENT ESTIMATES

Simple causal models that have neither intervening factors nor treatments that are conditioned by other specified factors produce consistent estimates of causal effects. The treatment or intervention is exogenous. When there are other exogenous variables that influence treatment assignment, but have no direct effect on the outcome, the treatment is endogenous. In this case, standard estimation procedures do not produce consistent estimates. The same is true if there are endogenous variables in the model other than the treatment.

One way of obtaining consistent estimates of causal effects is through the use of IVs. An **instrumental variable** is an exogenous variable that is correlated with a supposed causal influence in the model (either the treatment or an intervening variable between the treatment and outcome) and not correlated with the outcome or with confounding factors in the model. It can be used to improve the consistency of the estimated causal effect of the treatment and those of intervening variables.

IVs are used to obtain consistent estimates of intervention effects when the treatment is endogenous in a causal model. Programs that have entrance criteria or qualifying restrictions are endogenous because selection into the treatment group is a result of a subject's prior characteristics being applied to the entrance criteria. Obtaining consistent population estimates in this case is difficult because some subjects never participate in the program. They are excluded by the qualifying criteria. Other subjects are only exposed to part of a program and have not received "stable treatment" as defined by the Rubin Causal Model. One can deal with this by assuming that the never-takers will respond the same as the program participants or assuming that partial-takers (the dropouts or the noncompliants) will experience an effect proportional to their participation. Sometimes these assumptions are credible but not always so. When the assumptions are credible, then exogenous variables correlated with selectivity can be used to adjust the data using the procedures described below.

One limitation of this IV approach is that the assumptions necessary to estimate the treatment effect for a population that includes noncompliers and never-takers may not be credible assumptions. The never-takers may be so different from the program participants that it does not make any sense to assume that they will respond the same as the rest of the population. For example, a group of religious ascetics will probably not respond the same to a cash incentive program as a group from the general population. On the other hand, their immune systems will probably respond the same to inoculation against a disease as that of the general population. The assumptions of IV estimation need to be made explicit so that their credibility may be judged on a case-by-case basis. If, in a particular case, the assumptions are not credible, then standard IV estimation cannot (or should not) be done.

Angrist, Imbens, and Rubin (1996) have developed a restricted formulation of IV estimates that is estimable and also provides consistent estimates. They refer to these restricted estimates as local average treatment effects (**LATE**). The principal restriction of LATE estimates is that they are based on only those subjects that complete the program or comply with the treatment protocol. Such estimates are also called average treatment effects for the treated (**ATT**). Dropouts are excluded from the subjects on whom the estimates are based. The results are then only said to represent those who comply with the program. If the estimates cannot apply to a larger population, the analysis and results are limited to the population for which consistent estimates can be obtained. While this might seem to be unduly limiting, their assertion is that it is better to have a consistent estimate for a known subpopulation than to produce an inconsistent (and incredible) estimate for an unknown broader population.

Wald (1940) developed an estimator for LATE when there are dropouts or incomplete participation. He begins by calculating an intent-to-treat effect, which is the average effect for those who complete the program and those who refuse to participate (where the refusals are coded as having zero effect). The intent-to-treat effect is then divided by the percentage of the sample who were selected for treatment (including those who were selected for the intervention but refused to participate). The formula for Wald's estimate is as follows:

$$\hat{\tau}_w = \bar{Y}_c / (N_e / N_T), \qquad (2.1)$$

where $\hat{\tau}_w$ is the Wald estimated treatment effect, $\bar{Y}_c$ is the mean treatment effect for those who complete the program, $N_e$ is the number sampled for the experimental or treatment group (including refusals), and $N_T$ is the total number in the sample (including refusals).

Another limitation of IVs is that weak instruments may only remove part of the confounding influences. This may overstate the treatment effects in some subgroups. It is important to assess whether the instruments are sufficiently associated with the target endogenous variable (especially treatment assignment) so reliable results can be produced. One approach to assessing the strength of the IVs is to look at the relationship with the endogenous variable while controlling for other causal effects on that variable. If a simple causal model is being used in which there are no specified causal influences on treatment assignment, then one can examine the multiple correlation of the instruments with the treatment variable (i.e., the multiple $R$ of the instruments with the intervention variable). In this simple case, one can judge the strength using a standard criterion for the multiple $R$, the significance of its $F$ test or selection of a cutoff value for the $R$ (e.g., .30, .40, etc.) or for the $F$ (e.g., 10.0). Whatever criterion is chosen, it does not guarantee that the instruments are strong enough. It does, however, increase the likelihood that they are. In the more complicated case where there are multiple causal influences on the intervention, assessment of the weakness of the instruments requires removing correlation associated with those other influences. This is commonly done by looking at the strength of association of the instruments with the intervention while controlling for the other causal influences on the intervention. One needs to assess the partial (or conditional) strength of the instruments after controlling for other confounding factors. One approach to doing this is to look at the $R^2$ increment associated with the instruments after controlling for the causal variables. One can apply a criterion to $R^2$ increments the same as partial $r$'s (taking into consideration differences in degrees of freedom). The $F$ test for the $R^2$ increment is as follows:

$$F_i = (R_F^2 - R_R^2) / ((1 - R_F^2) / df_F), \qquad (2.2)$$

where $F_i$ is the $F$ value, $R_F^2$ is the $R^2$ for the multiple correlation of the confounders including the IV, $R_R^2$ is the $R^2$ for the multiple correlation of the confounders without the IV (a restricted $R^2$), and $df_F$ is the degrees of freedom for the unrestricted $R^2$. The degrees of freedom for this $F$ test is $(1, df)$, assuming only one IV is being tested at a time.

## Instrumental Variable Controls

When the intervention is an endogenous variable in the model or there is an intervening variable in the model, then using IVs can produce more consistent estimates of causal effects. If the IVs account for all the exogenous influences on an endogenous variable, it can result in consistent estimates. If the IVs account for some, but not all, of the exogenous influences, it will produce an estimate that is more consistent. The sample estimate of the population causal effect will be closer to the population value than if the IVs are not used. Angrist et al. (1996) have shown that IVs can be included in the RCM approach to produce consistent estimates. As they note, SEM approaches to causal inference, as well as Bayesian approaches, can include IVs. Inconsistent estimates can result from any of these approaches if their assumptions are violated. Using IVs to get more consistent estimates is appropriate for all of these approaches to causal inference when the assumptions are credible or the restrictive conditions are met.

One can identify IVs by looking for specific findings in the published literature and empirical evidence in one's data. If published research indicates that variables are correlated with receiving an intervention but not correlated with the outcome, these are possible IVs. Similarly, if research indicates there are correlates with an intervening variable that are not also direct causes of the outcome, these, too, may work as IVs. Empirically, one can correlate all variables in the data set (especially those antecedent to the intervention) and inspect the correlation matrix for factors correlated with endogenous variables that are not correlated with the outcome. This procedure will provide candidates for IVs using almost any measure of association (correlation coefficients, Cramer's $V$, odds ratios, Kendall's tau, etc.). Keep in mind, however, that correlating a lot of measures may produce false positives. The IVs should not necessarily be interpreted as having causal influences—unless they are already included in the causal model as causal factors or a credible, theoretically based argument can be provided to justify such an interpretation. They should, however, have at least a plausible causal influence on the intervention.

## *Estimating With Instrumental Variables*

Wald (1940) developed a procedure that Durbin (1954) uses to estimate treatment effects with IVs. The IVs in this approach are used to calculate the covariance between them and the treatment measure. This is equivalent to the covariance between the treatment measure estimated by the IVs and the observed treatment measure. The IV measures are also used to calculate the covariance between the estimated outcome measures and the observed outcome measures. The covariance between the instrumental outcome and the observed outcome is divided by the covariance between the instrumental intervention and the observed intervention. This is the IV estimated treatment effect. It is commonly referred to as a Wald estimate. The formula for the Wald estimate is as follows:

$$\hat{\beta}_{IV} = \widehat{COV}_{ZY} / \widehat{COV}_{ZS}, \tag{2.3}$$

where $\hat{\beta}_{IV}$ is the IV estimated treatment effect, $\widehat{COV}_{ZY}$ is the estimated covariance between the instruments and the outcome, and $\widehat{COV}_{ZS}$ is the estimated covariance between the instruments and the intervention (where the intervention measure is a dummy variable coded 0 and 1). This approach is applicable when one is estimating causal effects with SEM as well or when measures of entrance criteria are clearly specified and measured and dropping out or noncompliance is assumed to be random. If dropping out or noncompliance is not random, then procedures appropriate to handling missing data and imputing values may be used, which is discussed in the chapter on handling missing data.

An example of this Wald estimate is provided by the baby and income example from Table 1.1. Usable instruments were identified by correlating possible instruments with both the babies and the income variables and calculating their covariances (see Table 2.2).

Of the five variables considered, age of the respondent was the only one correlated with babies in the household and not correlated with family income (the requirements for an IV). We will assume that there is a causal relationship between age and presence of babies in the household. The covariance of age with income is –12,951 and with babies is –2.064.

The ratio of these (see Equation 2.2) is 6,274—more than a 50% reduction in the estimated effect of babies in the household on income. The instrument has removed some of the inflated effect due to error correlation. Whether this is the best estimate of this effect is discussed below.

| Table 2.2 | | Correlates of Babies and Income | | | | |
|---|---|---|---|---|---|---|
| | | Marital Status | Adults in Household | Age of Respondent | Ever Divorced | Gender of Respondent |
| Babies in household | Cor | −.079 | .074 | .346 | .111 | −.021 |
| | Sig | .000 | .001 | .000 | .162 | .352 |
| | Cov | −.043 | .021 | −2.064 | .018 | −.004 |
| | N | 1,390 | 1,406 | 1,403 | 796 | 1,406 |
| Income | Cor | −.195 | .107 | −.015 | .050 | −.133 |
| | Sig | .000 | .000 | .582 | .162 | .000 |
| | Cov | −16,093 | 4,463 | −12,951 | 1,149 | −3,475 |
| | N | 1,960 | 1,982 | 1,975 | 1,090 | 1,982 |

*Note.* Cor, correlation; Sig, significance; Cov, covariance.

The LATE approach is to limit the estimation to the sample of completers. This involves fewer assumptions because additional assumptions are not needed to generalize to a broader population. The causal estimates are only applied to those who complete the treatment or intervention. While this does allow making causal inferences about a subgroup of the population of interest, it doesn't allow inferences about program effects for those who drop out of an intervention prior to completion of the program. A LATE estimate of the effect of babies on income is not possible because some of those without babies in 2006 might have had them in the household earlier. We don't know who the "never had babies" households are. The original supposition says nothing about the effects of having babies who have grown out of babyhood, who died as infants, or who are removed from the home for other reasons prior to the study period. It is not reasonable to suppose that such events had no effects on income whatsoever.

A LATE estimate of the effects of college education on health is available in the Health and Retirement Study data. There were 140 individuals who provided educational information along with the health data. Of this, 50% had attended college; but only 28.9% completed college. That meant 111 either never attended or completed (see Table 2.3).

The average score of the completers on the overall health measure was 2.15 on a scale from 1 to 5, where 1 = *good* and 5 = *poor*. The never attendees had an average health score of 2.99, indicating worse average health (see Figure 2.2).

Restricting the comparison with just the completers versus the never attended, the average effect was 0.84, with a *t* of 2.76 and 109 *df*. From this LATE analysis that doesn't consider confounding factors, one would conclude that college education improves one's health. A subsequent example will examine whether the finding continues to hold when confounding factors are considered.

The number of IVs used is important. There needs to be at least as many IVs as there are treatments or interventions. The more, the better; provided one does not use up too many degrees of freedom. For modest size samples, this is an issue. While there is no agreement as to how small a sample poses a risk of

| Table 2.3 | College Education and Health | | |
|---|---|---|---|
| *Group* | *Mean* | *Standard Deviation* | *N* |
| Never attended | 2.99 | 1.014 | 70 |
| Completers | 2.15 | 0.937 | 41 |

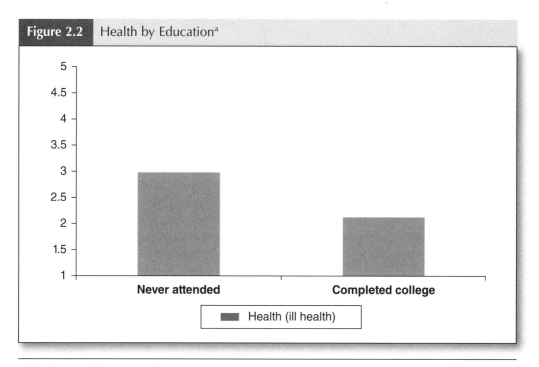

**Figure 2.2**    Health by Education[a]

a. Health is rated from 1 (*good*) to 5 (*poor*). N = 111.

unreliable results, samples smaller than 100 cases may quickly produce unreliable results when using up degrees of freedom. This doesn't mean that smaller samples are unusable. It does mean that as the sample size decreases, the researcher needs to pay closer attention to evidence of unstable statistical results.

## Two-Stage Least Squares

2SLS is the most common way in which IVs are used to obtain consistent estimates when there are intervening variables in a causal model. The two-stage approach has several advantages. The 2SLS approach does not make distributional assumptions for the independent variables (sometimes referred to as right-hand sided, RHS, because they appear on the right-hand side of structural equations representing the causal model). Since IV works with each equation separately, it isolates specification errors to individual equations. While it is more complicated than OLS regression, the OLS approach produces inconsistent estimates in situations where IVs can be used. IV estimates are less complicated than maximum likelihood solutions (MLS) that might be used instead of the IV approach, and evidence suggests that the results are more stable with small samples than MLS (Bollen, 1996).

The two stages are (1) estimate all endogenous variables, except the outcome, using IVs, then replace those observed endogenous variables with their estimated counterparts and (2) estimate the outcome variable using exogenous variables and estimated endogenous variables (the estimated intervening variables). The second step is the same as the normal estimation of an outcome variable, except some or all of the endogenous variables are replaced with their estimated values.

The problem of error correlation for babies and income addressed above by a Wald estimate can also be addressed by 2SLS. Table 2.4 contains the results of a 2SLS between babies in the household and income with age of the respondent as an instrument.

The Wald estimate of $6,274 is not the same as the 2SLS estimate of $5,187. There are two reasons for this. First, the Wald estimate is based on a variance–covariance matrix that uses pairwise deletion of missing cases. The 2SLS is based on listwise deletion of cases. If one wishes to produce a Wald estimate as similar as possible to the 2SLS estimate, one must use listwise deletion of cases. When one calculates the Wald estimate using listwise deletion for just the three variables from the 2SLS, the results are the same as 2SLS when the results are rounded to whole numbers.

| Table 2.4 | Two-Stage Least Squares for Babies and Income | | | |
|---|---|---|---|---|
| Variables | Coefficient | Standard Error | t | Significance |
| Constant | 67,050 | 2,165 | 30.967 | .000 |
| Babies in household | 5,187 | 9,627 | 0.539 | .590 |

The second reason the two estimates differ is that the 2SLS program uses a procedure that estimates the final solution in a single computational step. The rounding process is slightly different. This means the estimates may differ slightly due to rounding error. The 2SLS estimate is also more efficient. It has smaller standard errors than those produced by a Wald estimate. Thus, it is generally to be preferred. However, if one has access to a variance–covariance matrix and no access to the data producing it, a Wald estimate is a perfectly reasonable estimate. Both of these approaches are statistically adequate. Whether they are statistically sufficient is considered below.

What if there are endogenous variables for which no instruments can be found? If there are no instruments and no causes of the intervening variable other than what is in the model, then the inconsistency in the estimate of the intervening variable effect will be low or nonexistent. When there are no exogenous causes, there are no variables with which the error term of the intervening variable may be correlated. If there are other causes of an intervening variable that are not included in the model, then the model is misspecified. The results of estimating such a model will be inadequate and insufficient. It should not be estimated, except perhaps as a heuristic exercise in which the results are recognized as invalid. Such results should not be used to estimate causal effects or to make policy decisions about treatments or interventions.

What this means for assessing causal effects depends on whether or not the intervention is an endogenous variable in the model lacking instruments. If the treatment is a randomized experiment that hasn't broken down, then the treatment is an exogenous variable. A successfully carried out experiment doesn't have this problem. However, quasi-experiments and broken experiments do have this problem. If there are any selection effects, they act as causes of receiving the treatment. The intervention is then endogenous. This means the confounding effects must be removed—either by identifying IVs or by measuring the confounding variables. In the former case, one proceeds with 2SLS. In the latter case, one may proceed to propensity score estimation and use or to SEM to deal with the problem. One may do both. If the intervention is endogenous and confounders are measured, propensity scores may be used to create matched pairs for the intervention/nonintervention groups, as control variables in the regression (assuming the control variables have some interpretability), as weights by using weighted regression in the second stage, or to create homogeneous subgroups in which 2SLS is run within each subgroup and the results are averaged across groups.

2SLS does have some limitations. One must check that the residuals from the second stage of the regression are now uncorrelated with the independent variables. If correlation remains, then more instruments must be found and the equations are reestimated. If there are additional instruments available, it is wise to replicate the analysis using the alternative instruments. Sometimes the results vary between the choice of instruments. If similar results are produced with alternative instruments, the analyst can have more confidence in the stability of the estimates. If the model is **nonrecursive** (if there is mutual causation between variables), one or more of the mutually influencing variables may need to be lagged and used as instruments (assuming panel or longitudinal data). While the 2SLS approach can provide adequate estimates, it does not always provide sufficient estimates. The MLS uses more information than 2SLS. With large samples, MLS provides more efficient estimates. The use of more information by MLS may mean that it provides sufficient estimates when 2SLS does not. Nevertheless, the MLS approach (discussed more fully in Chapter 9) also tends to make more demanding assumptions about specification of relationships and the distributions of variables and their error terms. The analysis must assess the credibility of the assumptions that each approach makes. If there is insufficient information to build a credible structural model, it may be more appropriate to first estimate causal effects using 2SLS, recognizing that future research may eventually lead to those results being replaced by more efficient, even sufficient, estimates if and when they become available. Reliable adequate estimates are preferable to incredible sufficient estimates.

## *Detecting Selection Bias*

Sample selection bias may be detected with 2SLS using propensity scores. As noted by Heinrich (1998), possible selectivity factors may be used to estimate propensity scores of a bivariate treatment variable. Any selectivity factors significantly associated in the regression with the treatment variable indicate differences between the groups. When there are significant selectivity factors identified, the groups are said to be imbalanced. They don't have the same average characteristic of some variable in both groups. In the second stage of 2SLS, the propensity scores are used as an independent variable in predicting the outcome, along with all other variables specified as causes of the outcome in one's causal model. If the propensity score is statistically significantly associated with the outcome (using standard $t$ tests or $F$ tests), then there was selection bias in the intervention variable. If the regression coefficient of the propensity score is not significant, one may conclude that there is no significant selection bias—provided that no major selection factors were omitted from the original calculation of the propensity scores. If the hypothesis of selectivity is rejected, the coefficients of other variables predicting the outcome should be nearly the same if the regression is rerun without the propensity score. In the unlikely event they are different between inclusion and exclusion of the propensity score, further investigation of possible inclusion selectivity or collinearity should be done.

This procedure of using propensity scores to test for sample selectivity has some limitations. It assumes that all major selectivity factors are measured and included in the regression predicting the propensity score. It does not test for curvilinearity or interaction among the predictors unless it is explicitly included in the model. Also, if the propensity score and the intervention variable are highly collinear, the significance tests of their coefficients may be biased or unreliable—leading to erroneous conclusions as to whether there are selectivity and/or treatment effects. The first problem can be dealt with by inspecting the research literature about the intervention (if any) for factors that have been previously identified, a process similar to that for identifying confounding factors. One should also have a person knowledgeable about the intervention identify factors he or she has found related to the treatment. For the second problem, one can also inspect prior literature and do regression runs exploring possible curvilinear relationships and interaction effects. For the third issue, one can do an analysis of variance between the intervention variable and the propensity score. The eta coefficient, if significant, will indicate how strong the collinearity is. Alternatively, one could compute a Pearson correlation between a dummy variable for the intervention and the propensity score and judge how large that correlation is.

## Removing Selection Bias

Propensity scores may be used to remove selection bias in 2SLS in four ways. They may be used to match cases in the treatment and comparison group. This is matching cases on a composite score of the measured selectivity factors. Propensity scores may be used as control variables in multiple regression or in the second stage of 2SLS. Indeed, the same regression that detects selection bias by including propensity scores will also provide an estimate of the causal effect of the intervention with the selectivity removed. The propensity scores can be used for creating subgroups of cases that are homogeneous on the selectivity factors. Averaging the results for each subgroup will produce an estimate of the causal effect with the selectivity removed. The propensity scores can also be used with weighted regression (a modification of OLS) or in the second stage of 2SLS. In addition, if the propensity score can be substantively or theoretically interpreted, it may also be used as a measured variable in SEM.

All of these procedures attempt to remove the effects of sample selectivity with the intervention and the comparison group. The control variable approach does this by measuring sources of selectivity and calculating partial or conditional effects. IV and 2SLS do this by removing correlation between errors in the outcome measure and confounding variables. The adequacy of these procedures depends on specifying factors that confound the relationship between the intervention and the outcome. If the list of confounding factors is misspecified, the procedures will not be adequate. Whether one of these procedures is statistically sufficient depends on obtaining consistent estimates of the treatment effect. If all the confounding factors are measured and controlled (if strong ignorability is met) and assumptions for use of a statistic are met, the results will usually be consistent and sufficient. If all of the correlation between the measurement errors in the outcome with the confounding variables is removed, then biased and inconsistent estimates become consistent. Either one must have a positive argument that there are no credible confounding factors that were unobserved or the evidence from IV or 2SLS use must demonstrate that correlation with the error term has been removed. If a researcher can identify credible unobserved confounding factors, evidence must be offered that their effects have been removed to make causal inferences that are adequate and sufficient. This generally means demonstrating that correlations with error terms are absent or have been removed.

This leads us to two more conditions under which causal inference may be reliably made:

*Condition 3:* use of all known confounding factors as control variables with evidence the causal model in which they are used is not misspecified and

*Condition 4:* presence of unobserved confounders with evidence that the resulting error correlations have been removed.

The essential element of these conditions is that evidence must be offered that the known problems for causal inference in these situations have been removed. This means that the models must have tests of misspecification performed and presented. It also means that one must test for the presence of correlation between errors in the outcome and confounding factors. If evidence of proper specification and zero error correlation is not provided, there is no way of knowing if the estimates are adequate or sufficient. Causal inferences made without providing this evidence can only be said to be based on suggestive evidence, and further research would be needed to establish how reliable the inferences are.

Having a clearly identified process for selecting people into the treatment or comparison group is an important element of Conditions 3 and 4. One cannot know the likely confounders if one does not know how cases were selected into the groups. As noted by Cochran and Cox (1957) in their comparison of experiments and quasi-experiments, studies that had a clearly identified selection process were more likely to produce quasi-experimental causal estimates close to the experimental estimates than studies that did not have a clearly defined selection process. When the selection process is nonrandom, a clearly defined process is more likely to allow identifying, measuring, and controlling confounding factors. In addition, it makes it easier to identify variables that are potential instruments with moderate correlation with treatment assignment.

To meet the requirements for Condition 3, the measured confounders must be statistically controlled. This can be done in a variety of ways, including multiple correlation or regression, logit analysis, or other multivariate procedures. The analysis must present the results of the procedure used that indicates this has been done. A test for misspecification must also be done for one to know that Condition 3 has been met. Presenting these two results will generally establish the statistical adequacy of the results. To establish the sufficiency of the results, one must also argue or present evidence that using additional information or alternative procedures will not produce a better estimate. OLS multiple regression is statistically sufficient in all circumstances where OLS produces the same result as MLS. An MLS is sufficient in all circumstances except when curvilinearity between variables in the model causes the program to estimate a local maximum, rather than the overall maximum, or with nonnormally distributed data. This is discussed more in Chapter 9. 2SLS is usually neither statistically sufficient nor statistically efficient. The reasons why it may not be efficient have been discussed previously. It is unlikely to be statistically sufficient because it doesn't usually use as much information in estimating the causal effect as would be done by MLS. However, when there is curvilinearity or use of dummy variables that creates nonnormal distribution of the errors in estimating the outcomes, 2SLS may produce more stable and reliable results.

To meet the requirements for Condition 4, one has to demonstrate that the error terms of the endogenous variables are not correlated with antecedent variables or with each other. The latter can be easily checked by computing the correlations among the residuals for the endogenous variables. If none are statistically significant, one can argue that the errors are not correlated among themselves. One can also compute correlations between error terms and antecedent variables. This is suggestive that that there is no correlation between the error terms and the antecedents. Given the possible curvilinearity or disjunctions in distributions, it is wise to also look at scattergrams between the error terms and the antecedents to have greater confidence that correlation is absent.

## Checking for Misspecification

This section discusses three approaches to checking for misspecification of a causal model: (1) distribution checks, (2) plot checks, and (3) predictive checks. These are the more applicable procedures. Other ways of checking for misspecification are discussed in subsequent chapters where the checks are appropriate to specific estimation procedures. Distribution checks look at the distribution of errors in predicting endogenous variables. Plot checks examine scattergrams between errors and antecedent variables. Predictive checks use replicated (simulated) data to compare the observed results with what the results would be if the model were completely correct.

*Distribution Checks.* If a model is misspecified, then the residuals from prediction (the errors in prediction) may be distributed contrary to assumptions of the model. For models using OLS, the residuals are expected to be normally distributed with a mean of zero. For MLS, IV, and 2SLS estimation procedures, the errors in prediction may only need to be monomodal and symmetrical. If one is using OLS regression, the distribution of the residuals should be graphed to see if they look normal with a mean of zero. One may also do a chi-square test of the normality of the distribution. The chi-square test is done by dividing the residuals into a small number of groups (five to seven), estimating how many cases would be expected in each group if the distribution were normal, and calculating a chi-square between the observed and expected number of cases for the groups. The degrees of freedom for this test is the number of groups minus 1. One may also do this test using the cumulative distribution function. The chi-square test works better for moderate to large samples (>200 cases). Alternatively, one may use the Kolmogorov–Smirnov one-sample test or the Anderson–Darling test. They work fine for smaller samples. For MLS, IV, and 2SLS, one may inspect the distribution of residuals to see if they appear monomodal and symmetrical. Asymmetry of the distribution may also be tested by comparing its skewness statistic (Fisher's $g_1$ statistic) with the standard error for $g_1$. This produces a $t$ test with the degrees of freedom equal to the sample size minus 3.

Inequality between the errors in different groups can also indicate misspecification. This is known as heteroscedasticity. Errors in different groups should have the same dispersion (homoscedasticity) if there is no misspecification. One can perform an $F$ test in the variances of the errors in predicting the outcome comparing the intervention and comparison group. Several other tests of heteroscedasticity are available (see MacKinnon & White, 1985), but the work of Long and Ervin (1998) offers evidence that such tests should not be applied routinely as they do not catch some forms of heteroscedasticity. When the tests are significant, errors are not homoscedastic. When the tests are not significant, heteroscedasticity may still be present. It doesn't hurt to look at the distribution of errors between the groups to also do a visual check. Long and Ervin (1998) recommended always using a correction factor for heteroscedasticity, but it is not generally available in statistical analysis programs. The most feasible approach when confronted with heteroscedasticity at present is to use a nonparametric approach to estimating causal effects, which doesn't depend on homoscedasticity.

*Plot Checks.* Misspecification is sometimes indicated by examining the scattergram between the residuals and antecedent variables. If the causal model is misspecified, one may observe a distinct pattern between the errors in prediction and the values of the antecedents. This is a warning that the model may be misspecified. It is not proof that the model is misspecified. If a pattern is observed, one must also perform a predictive test to verify that the pattern would not be expected even if the model were correct. Patterns between errors and predictors can occur as a random artifact in the data, but they are a significant warning sign that further investigation is needed.

Plots between the predicted and observed values also provide information on misspecification. The plots can be produced separately for each group in the study. The slope of the relationship between predicted and observed values should be the same in all groups. If the slopes are different, this indicates that interactive effects may be present that were not included in the prediction equation. This would constitute misspecification. The analyst can perform a $t$ test of the difference between the slopes using the values of the slopes and their standard errors.

There is no standard procedure for detecting a pattern by this method. It depends on the visual acuity and insight of the researcher. Plot inspection may produce ambiguous results. If other researchers observe the plot and perceive the same pattern, this adds strength to the argument that the model might be misspecified. The uncertainty and judgmental nature of this procedure is why a predictive test for verification is desirable. Nonetheless, a researcher's capacity for perceiving patterns in data should not be dismissed. If disputed, it should be verified with additional evidence.

*Predictive Checks.* A predictive check for misspecification begins by creating a replicated (simulated) copy of the data. Variables are calculated having the means and standard deviations of those in the sample. Relationships between the variables are imposed that correspond to those estimated by the model. The causal effects are then estimated using the replicated data. The results of checking for misspecification with the replicated data are compared with those for the observed data. If they are similar, this implies that any patterns observed are a result of random factors—not misspecification.

Some researchers also perform a chi-square test of the difference between observed and replicated data. If the test is not significant, this supports the argument that the model is not misspecified. If the test is significant, then the specification of the model needs reassessment. This chi-square test, however, is not absolute proof that the model is correctly specified. One must exercise professional judgment in deciding whether the model is correctly specified.

## SUMMARY

Using control variables breaks down into three steps: (1) identifying control variables, (2) matching their assumptions with a statistical procedure, and (3) evaluating the results of those choices. Theory, prior research, and substantive experience help identify confounders. Propensity scores promote a match between statistical procedure and results by helping identify confounding variables and increasing control over them.

# CHAPTER 3

# CAUSAL INFERENCE USING COUNTERFACTUAL DESIGNS

This chapter reviews how counterfactual designs are used to reduce problems of causal inference. It identifies challenges in developing counterfactual designs. It addresses the role of counterfactual evidence and randomization in inference. It discusses trade-offs between different designs and issues unresolved by counterfactual design. It also introduces propensity matching and propensity weighting and their roles in causal inference.

## CONTROLLED EXPERIMENTS

As discussed in Chapter 1, controlled experiments provide a model for causal inference. They start out with the cases in each group having the same average characteristics. This is a result of random assignment of cases to each group. Any differences after the intervention are attributed to the intervention, provided the two groups continue to have the same experiences during the experiment. The threats to validity, mentioned in Chapter 1, either threaten random assignment or provide differing experiences to the groups. Varieties of experimental design mean that there are many ways in which the randomization may be violated or control over the experimental conditions may break down. Counterfactual inference breaks down in the absence of randomization and control conditions. Propensity scores attempt to remove the effects of nonrandomization and differential experience by replacing the processes of nonrandomization and protocol violation, having unknown probabilities for confounding the data, with a process having known probabilities. The better the estimates of the propensity scores, the more the unknown probabilities of distorted data are replaced with known probabilities of the groups starting out the same.

## Random Assignment

At the heart of the classic experiment is random assignment. Cases are assigned by a random process to the groups. It could be a coin toss, selection of a random number, or a card pulled from a well-shuffled deck. The randomness breaks down because some subjects refuse to be included in a particular group. The researcher may choose to put subjects in a particular group. The instructions for the assignment process may not be understood. There may be ethical, legal, or practical barriers to assigning some subjects to a particular group.

When random assignment breaks down, counterfactual inference is undermined. Counterfactual inference depends on one group being exposed to the intervention and another not being exposed to the intervention when both groups start out the same. Since the experimenter cannot observe subjects that are both exposed and not exposed, the inference is based on the average differences between the groups after the intervention. The average differences on outcome indicate the effect of the intervention only if the groups start out the same. As noted in Chapter 1, the difference-of-differences approach attempts to adjust for prior differences. It doesn't work when experimental controls break down, because the two groups may have different experiences beyond the intervention—unless one can measure and statistically control for these differences.

Propensity scores, being the probability of inclusion in a group prior to intervention, are estimates of the distortion in assignment to the groups. If cases have unequal probabilities of being classified in the treatment and control groups, the process is not random. If cases are selected so that they have equal probabilities of being in each group, the average result is the same as if they had been randomly assigned.

Differing probabilities of assignment don't always mean that there is no randomness in the assignment. For example, if one wished to have unequal group sizes, a die could be used, and subjects could be selected for one group if the "1" face came up and for the other groups if the "2" through "6" faces came up. The subjects would be assigned according to different probabilities (in this example, .1666 and .8333). The probabilities would differ even though the process was still random. As long as the different probabilities are known, one can make statistical adjustments to calculate what the result would be if there had been equal probabilities for inclusion.

## Criteria Assignment

Sometimes, some or all the cases are assigned according to specific criteria or subject characteristics. When the prevalence of the characteristics is known for the population, this is equivalent to having a known probability of assignment. When the prevalence in the population is not known, this undermines random assignment. The results cannot be directly adjusted to be equivalent to equal assignment. One might assume that the prevalence in the sample is the same as the population; but if this is not a probability sample from a known population, that assumption is dubious. The alternative is to estimate the probability of assignment using propensity scores. They can be used as weights to produce an equal distribution of characteristics, as matching criteria to only select cases for analysis that have pairs in each group with the same probability of inclusion, as covariates to adjust the outcome means for differential probabilities, or as criteria for creating strata where all the cases in each stratum have similar probabilities.

Rubin (1977) has shown that when a criterion is used to assign cases to intervention and comparison groups, there is a risk that the distributions of the outcome measures and the propensity scores may not overlap between the two groups or may have only a small amount of overlap. The groups may be too dissimilar to contain enough similar cases that the differences can be removed. When this happens, propensity scores and other adjustment procedures will be unable to make the two groups equivalent (Dehejia & Wahba, 2002; Rubin, 1977). An example of propensity scores with little overlap between groups is given in Figure 3.1. Rubin also notes that because the groups will be different is some respects (due to using different criteria for membership in each group), it is also important to test that the regression slopes in each group are the same. If the slopes are not the same, then one must consider adding interactive effects to the selectivity model or the causal model. A simple additive model will produce biased results when slopes in the two groups differ. A standard $t$ test for the equality of regression slopes or for the equality of logistic regression coefficients can be used to test whether this is the case. If the slopes are the same, then average treatment effects can still be computed without revising the selectivity or causal model.

## *Dropping Out*

When the cases that drop out of one experimental group are different from those that drop out of another group, it is referred to as differential sample mortality. This undermines the original random assignment of cases. If the cases that drop out had an equal chance of being in the experimental or control group, random assignment would be preserved. When the drop-out rate is different, it raises the possibility that cases in each group don't have the same probability of remaining in the study. It is possible for cases to drop out of each

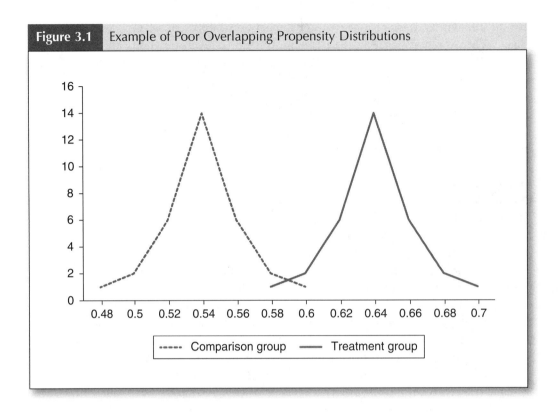

**Figure 3.1**    Example of Poor Overlapping Propensity Distributions

group for reasons unrelated to the study and resemble a random process. If the researcher doesn't know all the reasons for dropping out, however, it is unknown whether the mortality process (the process of cases dropping out of a study) is a random process.

There are standard procedures for examining drop-out rates. Most commonly, a dummy variable is created indicating whether a case dropped out or not, and this is correlated with pretest characteristics of the sample. This association may be examined using correlation analysis, analysis of variance (ANOVA), cross-tabulation, logit analysis, or some other procedure. If dropping out is not associated with pretest characteristics, it is inferred that differential sample mortality is not a problem. This procedure, however, only works if the baseline or Time 1 variables are believed to be related to the outcome measures. If dropping out is associated with Time 1 characteristics that are also correlated with the outcome, differential sample mortality is a problem. If dropping out correlates with sample inclusion (or retention) and correlates with variables associated with the outcome, dropping out has the same effect as a confounding variable. It produces biased estimates of the causal effect. It produces unequal distribution of characteristics at outcome that were equal at pretest. It alters the probability for cases being in a given group at outcome.

Propensity scores may be used to reduce the effect of differential sample mortality. Variables correlated with dropping out may be used to predict the propensity for inclusion in a given group. Propensity scores can then be used to match cases, weight the sample to adjust the distribution of characteristics, and stratify the sample to achieve equal probability groups or be used as control variables in the analysis. Since those variables correlate with dropping out, removing their differences with propensity scores also reduces differential sample mortality. Imputation or estimation of data missing from dropouts may also be done, issues that are discussed in Chapter 11.

In Table 2.3, examining the effect of babies on income in 2008, there were 589 cases with missing data for the recoded income variable. A dummy variable was created indicating whether a case was missing income data. This was correlated with confounding factors used to estimate the propensity scores for sample inclusion. The correlations are presented in Table 3.1.

All of the confounding factors used for propensity estimation were also associated with patterns of missing data. If there had been significant confounders not included in the propensity estimation, then the missing data would have created error in estimating the effects of the causal variable. Using propensity scores in this case also reduced problems with missing data. Whether there are remaining problems with missing data and what more can be done about it are discussed in Chapters 5 and 11.

| Table 3.1 | Correlates of Missing Data ($N$ = 1,968; Listwise Deletion) | | | |
|---|---|---|---|---|
| Variables | Marital Status | Education | Race | Mobility Since Age 16 |
| Missing income data | .056* | −.117** | .067** | .047* |

*$p$ < .05. **$p$ < .01.

## CHALLENGES TO COUNTERFACTUAL DESIGNS

Counterfactual experiments are difficult to design because there is not always a clear conception of who should make up the comparison group and what is meant by "absence of the intervention." Theoretically, the best comparison is self-comparison, where the presence and absence of the treatment is compared for the same individuals. This allows comparing an observed outcome of the intervention with the potential outcome without the intervention. However, it is not possible to do this at the same time. Consequently, it is either done for the same individuals at different times or different individuals are used. The "absence" treatment is also an issue. With drug trials, it might seem like "giving a placebo" or "not giving the drug" would be the clear counterfactual condition. However, even with placebos and nontreatments, events arise in the course of the trial. For example, those getting the placebo might get worse. The doctors running the study cannot ethically allow the subjects to just get worse without doing something (even though, in the past, that is precisely what some doctors did). The control condition might be an alternative drug currently used, but this only shows how much better or worse the experimental treatment is compared with the alternative treatment, not what the treatment is compared with the counterfactual condition. Even if the control group has the intervention withheld and if there are no other differences between the groups to begin with, circumstances in the course of the study may force a change in the protocol. For example, when an experimental trial was done using multiple drugs to treat AIDS, it became apparent that the experimental group was doing much better than the control group. Even though the trial was scheduled to run 18 months, it was terminated early so that the control group subjects could also get the drug combination. Trade-offs have to be made between adhering to the original research protocol and meeting ethical demands and legal constraints of research on human subjects. This can lead to sample selectivity. When there is selectivity, the average treatment effect cannot be estimated without bias. The various strategies discussed in the book are attempts to minimize that bias. As Rosenbaum and Rubin (1983) note, the bias in estimating the intervention effect can be removed if it is a result of observed measures in the study. Matching and other methods of removing bias depend on measuring the confounding factors and specifying an appropriate causal model for which their influence can be controlled.

These issues lead to several ongoing challenges to counterfactual inference and use of propensity scores:

1. When modifications to the research protocol are made during the study, it may alter selectivity factors in the samples. Researchers should attempt to collect information at the time of the change. This will provide

evidence whether selectivity continues, remaining the same after the changes, or whether new selectivity factors are introduced. Analysis of the data should include examining such measures as intervening or confounding factors.

2. When more than one intervention takes place, different selectivity processes may occur. Each intervention needs separate estimation of propensity scores. If the separately estimated propensities turn out the same, then only one may be needed; but they don't always turn out the same. Separate propensity adjustments may be needed for each intervention.

3. Omitted confounding variables may leave bias in the estimate of the intervention effect. When important omitted variables are known to exist (as is often the case with secondary analysis of preexisting data), propensity analysis should be combined with additional procedures (e.g., use of instrumental variables or two-stage least squares). These methods are not mutually exclusive. As Dehejia (2005) notes, there are times when multiple methods need to be used together to reduce bias and improve estimated effects.

4. Propensity scores may be sensitive to the choice of the variables used to estimate them. It is generally better to use as many confounding variables as possible for which one has measures. The only confounding variables that might be reasonable to be omitted are those whose relationship with the outcome disappears when controlling for other measured confounding factors. In addition, the sensitivity of the results of propensity use should be examined to have greater confidence in those results. Methods for sensitivity analysis are discussed in Chapter 11.

## Natural Experiments

Natural experiments differ from controlled experiments in that the process of assignment to the groups is not determined by the researcher. It is a result of decision processes that people make in their normal life. The decision might be that of a doctor in choosing a treatment. It might be that of a program having more applicants than treatment slots in deciding who receives an intervention. It might be that of a parent in deciding whether to have his or her child immunized for measles. The essential element of a natural experiment is that one or more treatment and comparison groups are created by a person in everyday life, who makes the decision without controlling the threats to valid inference. It is sometimes described as a haphazard assignment process, because not all the factors that go into the assignment to groups are known. Haphazard decisions can be random, but often they are not. A significant problem with natural experiments is that the haphazard assignment creates uncertainty in the treatment assignment process.

A drug manufacturer may provide free samples of a new drug to doctors who prescribe it for patients instead of a competitor drug. The doctor may then provide feedback to the manufacturer on how the patients who got the drug responded compared with those who received the usual drug. Unless the doctor had clinical criteria for assigning the new drug, its distribution would be haphazard—and the meaning of the comparison would be uncertain.

Since natural experiments are not known to have random assignment and do not occur with a research design controlling the threats of valid inference, they are subject to potential confounding factors. It is unlikely that those who receive the treatment are the same as those who do not. The probabilities of assignment into the intervention or comparison group, however, are not entirely known. What is usually known are some of the characteristics of the subjects prior to the decision being made. Differences between the groups may be examined based on their pretest characteristics. With natural experiments, it is common to test for pregroup differences to assess how similar or dissimilar the groups are prior to the intervention.

Some of the variables that show group differences may also be related to the outcome being studied. Those variables are confounding factors. They can be used to estimate propensity scores for subjects in the groups resulting from the decision process. The propensity scores can then be used to address preintervention differences between the groups. They may be used to match cases, weight the sample, or stratify the sample, or they may be used as control variables in the analysis. The variables that show group differences that are not related to the outcome can be considered for use as instrumental variables to remove any additional bias from correlated error terms.

## MATCHING SAMPLES

Matched samples are used in quasi-experimental designs because they reduce pretreatment differences for the intervention and comparison groups. Theoretically, if cases are matched preintervention on all confounding factors and if both groups experience the same intervention, then any differences at the end of the intervention are due to the intervention. It can, in theory, provide an unbiased estimate of the effect of the intervention. The problem lies with the difficulty in matching the characteristics of all confounding factors. To do this for individual subjects when you are matching even half a dozen characteristics is extraordinarily difficult. In the situation where there are identified key variables, matching on them can reduce the imbalance between groups. Key variables are discussed subsequently in this chapter. Matching on key variables improves similarity of the two groups. It is unlikely to eliminate all differences. However, there are maximum likelihood procedures available for accomplishing this when one has a large sample of data (Conniffe, Gash, & O'Connell, 2000), and evidence suggests that they may produce more efficient estimates than matching on propensity scores alone. Unfortunately, it can only be applied with large samples, and there is uncertainty as to whether it drops more or fewer unmatched cases from the sample than propensity matching.

## *Propensity Matching*

Propensity scores reduce difficulty of matching. The probabilities estimated represent a linear sum of the influences on selectivity. If randomization is successful, all cases have the same probability of inclusion in either group. Differences in propensity between groups are a consequence of sample selectivity. Matching cases on propensity scores is the same as matching on the characteristics of all the confounding factors that are used to estimate the propensity scores. If you do exact matching of propensity scores for cases in each group, you remove all confoundedness associated with those factors and any bias in estimating treatment effects that result (Rubin, 1974).

There are three difficulties in matching propensity scores. First, exact matching requires that propensity scores in all groups matched be the same up to the limits of measurement precision (which might be four, six, or eight digits to the right of the decimal point). There may be no cases matching with that precision. Second, not all the confounding factors may be measured. This produces errors in estimating the propensity scores and reduces precision in how many significant digits of the estimated probability can be relied on as accurate. This is especially a problem when different researchers use different variables to estimate the propensity scores. Finally, there are different approaches to matching propensity scores when exact matching is not done. Knowing which approach to matching is most appropriate in a given situation is uncertain. Even though there are approaches to matching that represent statistically optimal matches, some bias may remain if important confounding factors were not measured and included in estimating the propensity scores. This is why so much emphasis was given in earlier chapters on identifying and measuring all important confounding factors. If this is not done, the program effects estimated using matched samples may still be biased. The degree of bias depends on how important are the confounding factors unmeasured. If the unmeasured confounders are weak, the degree of bias may be small. It may even fall below what can be detected by the statistical power of the data.

*Criteria for Matching.* If exact matching is not generally feasible, the question is how close a match must there be to say it is good enough? This question is called the question of caliper. A caliper is a tool that is used in measurement. For propensity scores, it is a standard of how close the propensity scores must be to say they are a match. Values of .05, .02, or one quarter of the standard deviation of the propensity scores is commonly used. A standard of .01 would select cases that are better matches, but it also excludes more cases from the sample as unmatched. A standard of .10 provides a poorer match but includes more cases. Generally, using the one-quarter rule excludes more matches than using the .05 standard, but it results in closer matches. In the example given, the standard deviation of the propensity scores is .03; one quarter of that would be .0075—a very tight match. This tight match would delete most of the cases. If too many cases are dropped, one may try a looser criterion and check to see if the imbalance is still removed. Alternatively, one can start with a looser match, check to see if the imbalance is removed, and tighten the criterion if it is not.

There is no inherent reason why either standard is used, nor any agreed criterion for how many dropped cases are too many. The trade-off is between power and bias. The more power you give up, the less bias you have in your matched samples. If more than 20% of the cases have been dropped, however, it is a good idea to check the sensitivity of the results to using different criteria. Even though these criteria are not hard-and-fast rules, they have proven useful. Much of the time, they allow matching many of the cases in one's sample without excluding large numbers.

One doesn't know which caliper to use in advance of matching. Only after matching can one check to see if there still are pretest differences between the groups and whether there are enough cases retained that the analysis has sufficient statistical power to detect the effects of the intervention. This implies two things. (1) After matching, a researcher must go back and check to see if the differences between the groups have been reduced enough to be nonsignificant. (2) A researcher must also check to see if so many cases were dropped that it is likely to have made the analysis too weak to detect the expected effects. These two procedures are discussed later in this chapter.

*Procedures for Matching.* A researcher may match each case in one group with a case in another group. This procedure is referred to as 1–1 matching.

This type of matching has the advantage that it ensures an equal number of subjects in each of the groups. Adjustments do not have to be made for unequal group size. It adds confidence that the two groups are equal. A researcher may also match each case in one group with multiple cases in another group. This is 1–many matching. This allows having more cases in the analysis and increases the statistical power of the study. However, 1–many matching still uses a caliper. The multiple cases that are matched with the one case do not all have the same exact propensity score. Indeed, some of the cases may have propensity scores that differ from their matched partners in the same group by more than the caliper if the matching software does not impose this as an additional criterion. This may add error variance to the estimates of the effects, even though the larger sample size is reducing random error variance. To examine this possibility, one needs to know whether the computer program used for matching imposes a constraint on the 1–many matches to prevent this. The currently available programs for matching do not generally address this issue in documentation. For most of the examples given, 1–1 matching is used to more easily illustrate the matching process. When 1–many matching is done, this will be noted. The trade-offs between different propensity matching procedures will be discussed in more detail in Chapter 4.

*Quota Matching.* Quota matching is used to ensure that an adequate number of subjects will be included in the sample having specific characteristics. Usually, these are individuals whom one wishes to analyze as a group in comparison with other groups. With random assignment of cases, such individuals are likely to appear in treatment and control groups. With quasi-experimental and natural experiment designs, however, such individuals may be over- or underrepresented in the treatment or comparison group. There may not be enough cases in the subgroups to make comparisons. If a researcher has a high degree of control over the selection process, he or she can do stratified sampling to ensure an adequate number of cases. If the researcher does not have a high degree of control over the selection process, however, quota sampling may still be possible. Stratified sampling is preferable to quota sampling because the subjects have a known probability of selection. Quota sampling may be done when one does not know the population distribution of a given characteristic. For example, the religious affiliation of those involved in the black market economy is unknown. If one wanted to look at the effect of religious affiliation on such activity, one would have to use quota matching. Quota matching occurs when quotas for sample selection are set for both the intervention and the comparison groups. For each member of a population having a specified characteristic selected into the treatment group, a corresponding person is selected into the comparison group. This form of matching has been used very widely in a variety of research areas (Moser, 1952; Walter, 1988)—even though it has been criticized as undermining probability sampling.

When one uses quota matching, the distribution of characteristics in each group are usually compared to ensure that an equal number have been selected. Equality of the distributions doesn't always occur because there may be difficulties in obtaining subjects having the right characteristics. Those with the desired characteristics may refuse to participate in one or another of the groups. Propensity scores may be used to improve the match between the two samples. The scores may be computed using variables where the two groups differ, especially quota characteristics where they differ. The subjects in each group may then be matched a second time based on the similarity of their propensity score. The two groups will be more similar on the quota characteristics after this process than before.

*Matching With Replacement.* Sampling without replacement has generally been preferred over sampling with replacement. This is because the replacement cases do not always have the same characteristics as those who refused to participate or who were unavailable. A similar process applies with matching cases. The replacements who are matched with known characteristics do not always have the same characteristics as the nonparticipants for those variables that were not used in the matching process. Those other characteristics may even influence whether a person is available for matching or not, as well as influence the outcome (i.e., they may be confounding factors). On the other hand, if one matches without replacement, those same confounding factors may still bias the estimate of treatment effect, a form of differential sample mortality. The risk may be lower with nonreplacement, but the problem is still there. Matching propensity scores in a sample with replacement, however, has the opposite effect (Dehejia & Wahba, 2002). The replacements have propensity scores closer to the case for which a match is sought. This increases the similarity of the intervention and comparison groups. It reduces bias.

Doing propensity score matching in addition to matching with (or without) replacement reduces the risk of a biased estimate. Variables that were not used in the original matching process can be used to estimate propensity scores for the intervention and comparison groups, provided they are confounding variables. The propensity scores can then be used to improve the match and reduce preintervention differences on those characteristics that were not used for the matching.

*Greedy Matching.* Greedy is usually a type of 1–1 matching (though it can be used in 1–many matching). It is regarded as simple to understand. It is so simple that for a modest number of cases, it can even be done by hand. The programs that do greedy matching are also seen as easy to use. Examples of them are posted on the book's website (http://www.sagepub.com/holmes). This procedure is called greedy matching because programs that do this matching will match a case in the first group with the first case it finds in the second group whose propensity meets the criteria for matching. The matched case is withheld from matching with any other cases. With simple greedy matching, this is even if there is another case in the second group whose propensity is closer to that of the case in the first group. An alternative greedy matching criterion is to select the case in the comparison group whose propensity is closest to that of the case in the treatment group, a form of greedy matching called nearest-neighbor matching, sometimes abbreviated N-N. The discussion here will focus on simple greedy matching as it easily illustrates the matching process. The nearest-neighbor matching will be examined in Chapter 5. Greedy matching does not result in the best possible matches being found for all cases that are matched, but it does tend to minimize the number of cases that are dropped as not having matches. If too many cases are excluded by an alternative propensity matching process, greedy matching can be tried to see if it finds enough matches. As is the case for any form of propensity score matching, one must check the results of the greedy matching to be sure that it sufficiently reduces preintervention differences before analyzing the greedy matched sample.

To do this form of matching, a data file may need the propensity scores and case IDs for members of each group to be treated as separate variables in the file. This is sometimes organized in a format called horizontal file organization. Table 3.2 displays an example of this type of file.

| Table 3.2 | Horizontal File | | | | |
|---|---|---|---|---|---|
| ID Group 1 | Propensity Group 1 | Flag for Group 1 | ID Group 2 | Propensity Group 2 | Flag for Group 2 |
| 101 | .6501 | 0 | 104 | .5897 | 1 |
| 105 | .5925 | 1 | 106 | .5824 | 1 |
| 107 | .5801 | 1 | 103 | .4567 | 0 |
| 102 | .4001 | 1 | 109 | .4022 | 1 |
| 108 | .3310 | 1 | 110 | .3321 | 1 |

There are several notable things about this file. First, data are not stored with each case having its own unique record. Instead, the data for each case are stored in several columns in the file. In this case, the data in the first three columns are cases in the first group that have been stored in the rank order of the propensity score for Group 1 (some programs store highest to lowest; others, lowest to highest). When two cases have the same propensity score, the ordering of these cases is generally randomized among the tied cases. The data in the fourth to sixth columns are cases in the second group that have been stored in the rank order for the propensity score for Group 2. It has two variables, one for each group, that will flag whether that case is part of a match or not (usually coded 0 or 1). The computer matching program first compares the propensity for Group 1 with the propensity for Group 2 in the same record. If they are within the caliper criteria, then the flag variables for each group are set to 1, indicating that each case is part of a match. If the propensity of the case in the second group is more than the propensity for Group 1 and falls outside the caliper, then the flag for this case is set to 0, indicating it is not part of a matched pair. This unmatched case in the second group is then deleted, since there can be no other case in the first group that will match this case. The data in the columns for Group 2 are shifted upward. The program repeats this process until it finds a match for the case in Group 1 and flags it as a match or until the propensity in Group 2 is less than the caliper. If the propensity is less than the caliper and the case in Group 1 does not have a match, then the flag in Group 1 is set to 0. If a match is found, the program goes to the next case in Group 1 and repeats the process. If a match for the Group 1 case is not found, then the Group 1 case is deleted. The columns for Group 1 are shifted up, and the process repeats itself. For the data in Table 3.2, if we assume a caliper of .05, we see that the propensity for the first case in Group 1 (ID 101) is not within the caliper when applied to the case in Group 2 (ID 104). Since the propensity for the Group 2 case is less than the caliper, then the flag for the Group 1 case is set to 0. That case will be deleted from Columns 1 through 3 and the cases below shifted upward. A similar process happens for Case ID 103. No match is found for this Group 2 case within Group 1. The Group 2 flag for Case 103 is set to 0, and the case will be deleted from the file. At the end of this process, the only cases remaining in the file are those that have matches. Some computer programs that do matching do not use horizontal file organization. They retain one case per record format. They use a series of program loops that scan all comparison cases and select the one that matches (or is closest to) the treatment case being considered. The result is the same as using horizontal files. Computer programs that do greedy matching are listed in the appendixes and are posted in the book's website. Other procedures for propensity score matching are discussed in subsequent chapters.

Table 3.3 illustrates the kind of difference propensity matching can make in group differences. In this example, the intervention group is "parents smoking" and the nonintervention group is "parents not smoking" when the respondent was a child. These groups are different for all five measures in the table when one looks at the unmatched sample of cases. This is compared with a matched subsample of cases in which the groups are not statistically significantly different on any of these variables. A subsample was used for illustrative purposes.

## KEY VARIABLE MATCHING

Key variable matching is done when one wishes to use a relatively small number of variables for matching and wants to maximize the similarity of the groups. This entails identifying variables that are important to the study and using them for matching. If such key variables are important to the outcomes of the study, then matching on them will tend to make the groups homogeneous at the point of the intervention. There may, however, be disagreements as to which factors are important to the outcome or which should be used for matching.

| Table 3.3 | Group Differences Between Unmatched and Matched Samples[a] | | | |
|---|---|---|---|---|
| | All Cases | | Matched Cases | |
| | Parents Smoked | | Parents Smoked | |
| Variables | Yes (%) | No (%) | Yes (%) | No (%) |
| Respiratory disorder at age <16 | 10.8 | 8.8 | 2.9 | 2.0 |
| Allergy at age <16 | 8.0 | 5.6 | 2.4 | 1.3 |
| Heart trouble at age <16 | 2.3 | 1.5 | 0.9 | 0.6 |
| Drug/alcohol problem at age <16 | 0.7 | 0.1 | 1.5 | 0.0 |
| Depression at age <16 | 2.7 | 1.9 | 1.1 | 0.4 |
| n | 7,772 | 4,450 | 557 | 555 |

a. Percentage difference for all cases are all significant at $p < .01$. No percentage difference for matched cases is significant at $p < .05$. Matching was by greedy matching with caliper <.01. The greedy matching for this example was done using a macro program within SPSS distributed by John Painter (2010).

Indeed, there may also be key factors thought to be important for which no observational data are available. The common strategy in this case is to match on those key variables for which one has data and issue qualifying remarks about those key variables for which one has no data. If the unobserved key variables are very important, it can raise serious questions about the worth of the results altogether. Propensity scores allow improving on this situation in a manner discussed below.

### Identifying Key Variables

The crux of key variable matching is finding those variables important to the outcomes being studied. Prior research may have identified some variables. Theories may suggest important variables. Public debate, stereotypes, or cultural beliefs may suggest other variables (initially ignoring whether such variables are actually related to the outcomes). This process is, in fact, the same process by which one identifies confounding variables. There are only three reasons why variables are regarded as keys. They have an association with the outcome. They are important to the values of the public, or people misunderstand the outcomes. Take, for example, infant death. It used to be thought that the poor had higher rates of infant mortality due to the immoral lifestyle of the mother. Research showed that it had more to do with the availability of adequate nutrition, low birth weight, and prematurity (Cramer, 1987; Dollfus, Patetta, Siegel, & Cross, 1990). Now, nutrition and health care are regarded as key variables regarding infant survival. The morality of the mother is thought to be less important. Identifying key variables can be done in the same manner as identifying confounding variables. The only exception is when public beliefs hold that some factor is important, even though there are no data to support that belief. If one wishes to have a study regarded as producing credible results, the researcher may need to include variables for which there is weak or nonexistent evidence as being related to the outcome. The purpose of including such a variable would be to demonstrate that it is not a key variable and that other factors are. In the absence of such evidence, critics will claim that the failure to include the other factor undermines the results of the study.

### Using Key Variables and Propensity Scores

When one uses key variable matching, two problems in particular may arise. (1) The groups may not be sufficiently equivalent pretreatment and (2) unobserved factors may create correlated errors between the outcome measures and treatment selection. Propensity scores may be used to address these issues. After matching by key variables, propensity scores can be computed using the measured confounding factors. The propensity scores can then be used to enhance the matching process, provide control variables to reduce confounding bias, provide weights to adjust the distribution of case characteristics, or provide criteria for creating homogeneous strata for subgroup comparisons. In addition, if the residuals for the outcome measures are correlated with group differences, instrumental variable or two-stage least squares procedures discussed in the preceding chapter can be used to address this problem.

## Distance Matching

Cases can be matched either by comparing simple differences between propensity scores (Euclidean distance matching) or by comparing distance measures based on all the confounding variables used to estimate the propensity scores (Mahalanobis distance matching). The former strategy maximizes the probability of including similar cases. The latter strategy minimizes the dissimilarity of the cases. Usually, the two strategies produce very similar matches of cases, although the Mahalanobis distance criteria produce slightly better matches of cases having more extreme values (Baser, 2006).

*Euclidean Distance.* Matching cases based on the similarity of their propensity score is matching based on the Euclidean distance between the two scores. It is what is usually meant when one says he or she matched propensity scores. It is a very common strategy. It can produce matches even with moderate-sized samples. It avoids having to decide whether some variables should be given more weight in matching than other variables (since they are automatically weighted based on their association with the treatment and comparison groups). It is less cumbersome to use as one works with only two, or a few, propensity scores. In the bivariate case, the Euclidean distance is the simple difference between the values of the variables. That is,

$$D_E = (X_i - X_j). \tag{3.1}$$

Greedy matching is the simplest form of Euclidean distance matching. An example of this form of Euclidean matching has been given above. Simple greedy matching is far from being the only Euclidean approach to matching. It has already been mentioned that nearest-neighbor matching is a form of greedy matching. So it is a form of Euclidean distance matching. An example of this will be given in Chapter 5. Beyond this, there are a variety of approaches to this type of matching.

*Mahalanobis Distance.* When combinations of the confounding factors are compared for cases in different groups, this is what is usually meant by Mahalanobis distance matching. This generally gives more weight in calculating similarity of cases to the more extreme values. This is apparent from the formula for calculating the Mahalanobis distance. Diamond and Sekhon (2006) provide the matrix form of the formula:

$$D_M = \{(X_i - X_j)'S^{-1}(X_i - X_j)\}^{1/2}, \tag{3.2}$$

where $S$ is the covariance matrix of $X_i$ and $X_j$. This can be simplified to

$$D_M = \{(X_i - X_j)\ \mathrm{COV}_{xij}(X_i - X_j)\}^{1/2}, \tag{3.3}$$

which is the square root of the difference between the values times the covariance times the difference. The Euclidean distance $(X_i - X_j)$ is adjusted for the covariance between $X_i$ and $X_j$. It is the square root of three products, which tends to inflate the importance of more extreme values.

The matches produced tend to reduce preintervention differences slightly better than Euclidean matching. Mahalanobis matching is more likely to find matches for a broader range of cases. Rubin (1979) has shown that the results of Mahalanobis matching can be improved further by combining it with covariate regression adjustment. This implies that propensity score use and Mahalanobis distance matching need not be alternative strategies. One can get better results using Mahalanobis matching combined with propensity score covariate adjustment than with Mahalanobis matching alone.

## ASSESSING MATCHING RESULTS

All forms of matching require testing and assessing how good the match is. It should be noted that the test of how good the match is depends on its ability to reduce pregroup differences, not purely on minimizing the average difference of propensity scores. It is always necessary after matching to examine how much of the differences between the groups has been removed. This involves using statistical tests of differences between groups, as well as using substantive criteria for judging whether the differences have been reduced enough to allow meaningful estimation of program effects.

*Testing for Nonequivalent Groups.* Statistical tests to determine group differences after the matching include those that were used to detect nonequivalency (imbalance) prior to intervention. Cross-tabulations, ANOVA, *t* tests, and other statistics that were run before matching need to be repeated after matching to verify that there has been a reduction. The associated statistical tests (chi-square tests, *F* tests, *t* tests, etc.) may be used. However, it should be remembered that the matched sample may have somewhat fewer cases than the original sample. For very large data sets, this is not an issue. For moderate- or modest-sized samples, this can be an issue. One way of dealing with it is to examine the original tests and recalculate their significance based on the assumption of using the smaller, matched sample. If the original differences remain significant and the matched differences are not significant, then matching has reduced preintervention differences.

*Assessing Nonequivalence of Groups.* The nonequivalency of the groups after matching needs to be assessed using the same procedures that were used to assess imbalance prior to the matching. If *t* tests or ANOVA *F* tests were used to test intervention and comparison groups for imbalance in characteristics of the confounding factors, they should be rerun. If cross-tabulation or logit analysis were used to look for differences in qualitative characteristics, they should be repeated.

In assessing nonequivalence of groups, two things need to be considered: (1) statistical significance and (2) substantive difference. The inferential tests allow assessing how likely the groups are to be the same. If the differences are not statistically significant (and the sample size has not fallen too greatly), one may infer that the groups compared are now essentially the same. The substantive information on the differences between the groups (difference of means, percentages, odds ratios, etc.) allows judging how much of a difference in the outcome the prior difference between the groups is likely to make (assuming this difference is statistically significant). This can be judged by multiplying the residual difference (the difference between the groups after matching) by the coefficient of regressing the outcome on the variable being compared. When working with categorical variables, a similar process can be used for estimating changes in percentages or odds attributed to the remaining prior difference. These estimated remaining effects can be compared with clinical standards, policy criteria, or professional judgment to assess whether the difference is big enough to require further action.

*Assessing Sample Size Power.* The loss of cases due to nonmatching is not necessarily a problem. It depends on whether so many cases have been dropped that the samples no longer have enough statistical power to tell whether the

estimated effects are a result of random sampling variation. When one is working with large samples, losing a number of cases may still result in adequate
statistical power. However, it can raise a question as to whether the estimated
effects are local average treatment effects applicable only to a subpopulation
and not average treatment effects applicable to a broader population. With
more moderate-sized samples, the power reduction may be sufficient that the
true treatment effects do not approach statistical significance, resulting in a
"false-negative" conclusion.

One way to assess the effect of power reduction is to compare results
between alternative matching procedures that have a different number of cases.
Different matching procedures can reduce imbalance while retaining a different
number of cases. If a matching procedure that retains more cases produces
similar results to a more stringent matching procedure having fewer cases, it is
evidence that the latter procedure did not give up too much power. One might
ask, Why do the more stringent procedure if the less stringent procedure
produces the same result? One doesn't know whether the less stringent procedure produces the same result unless it is compared with a more stringent
procedure. Similarly, a "false-positive" effect might be estimated by the less
stringent procedure. If the effect remains under a more stringent procedure, it
is evidence that the result is reliable. Judging sample size adequacy is helped if
one has substantive knowledge of the phenomenon being studied. If one has an
idea of how large an estimated effect one would like to result from an intervention, then one can tell how large the matched sample needs to be to be able to
detect that magnitude of a result.

*Revising Propensity Score Matches.* The matches that result from using
propensity scores may or may not remove significant prior differences. They
do remove differences associated with the confounding factors included in
their estimation, but that may not be all the differences there are. As noted
above, one must assess how much of the differences are removed by a matching procedure. If one concludes that there are still significant pregroup differences remaining, one must either revise the estimates of the propensity scores
or change the matching procedure.

The estimates of the propensity scores are revised either by adding more
confounding variables to the estimation equation or by changing the estimation procedure. Admittedly, if one has done a thorough job of searching for
confounding variables, there may not be any more to be found. Yet sometimes
researchers will reject possible confounders as unlikely or as far-fetched.
When looking for additional confounders, one needs to consider those suggested by theories that are less likely. One can also discuss the issue with

professionals knowledgeable about the subject being studied. Sometimes, their experience can suggest options that one might overlook. It should be kept in mind, however, that there may be no other confounders. The prior differences between the groups may be so big or nonoverlapping that nothing can be done to improve the results. It should be noted that in rare circumstances, dropping a confounding variable can improve the matching of the propensity scores. If inclusion of a measure adds systematic error variance into the propensity estimate, it can introduce bias in the results. This may manifest itself in correlated errors, which should be part of the normal checking procedures of any causal modeling.

Switching estimation procedures for the propensity scores to get a better matching result is not commonly done or even recognized much as a possibility. There are two reasons why it might make a difference, even though the odds are not very high. The propensity scores estimated by logit and probit can differ, though not by much. This slight difference can reduce the overlap of multiple matches, making a false selection of a local maximum match less likely. Also, it may spread out the probabilities more uniformly, which also results in a more efficient and less error-prone matching procedure. It was also recommended above that one use an estimation procedure for propensity scores that corresponds with the analytical procedure for estimating the causal effects. Even though a mismatch of estimation procedure does not often seem to create problems, in theory it can. Thus, one might try switching from logistic to probit estimates or vice versa to see if that produces better results.

The matching procedure can be changed by choosing a procedure that alters the closeness of the match and/or the number of cases that are dropped by the procedure. Switching from nearest-neighbor to optimized or the reverse will alter the number of cases that are matched and the reduction in differences between the groups. If significant differences remain after doing all that is possible with the propensity scores, one may need to try optimized matching (or its equivalent, genetic matching), discussed in Chapter 6, keeping in mind that one may still not have enough power, given the size of the matched sample. If a matched sample is underpowered, one can try switching to a procedure that drops fewer cases (e.g., increasing the caliper); but this does have a risk of not removing enough of the group differences. Sometimes, one has to try several strategies to find an approach that removes significant differences and retains enough cases that there is adequate statistical power. Other times, nothing works because the groups are too different or the matched samples are too small.

## Sample Weighting

Samples can be weighted to ensure a particular distribution of sample characteristics. It is commonly done so that a sample is representative of a population. The statistics of the weighted sample are unbiased estimates of the population parameters. Weighting for this purpose is parametric weighting. Samples can also be weighted to remove disparities in the distribution of the sample characteristics. Propensity scores can be used in this way to remove differences in the distribution of characteristics for confounding variables. Weighting for this purpose is propensity weighting.

*Parametric Weighting.* Weighting a sample to resemble a population is done to enhance generalizability (external validity) of the findings. For example, if a sample is collected using disproportionate sampling to ensure an adequate number of cases of people having various characteristics, the inverse of the disproportionate weights may be used so that the weighted sample has the same distribution of characteristics as the population from which it was taken. Both the General Social Survey and the Health and Retirement Study have weights provided so that if one wishes to generalize to the U.S. national population, one can use the weights to obtain a weighted sample representative of that population. The weights are used so that the sample characteristics match the population characteristics. It is matching aggregate characteristics rather than individual case matching. Parametric weighting also allows simulating what the effects of the intervention would be when the confounding effects of uncontrolled, real-world situations are present.

*Propensity Weighting.* Weighting a sample with propensity scores is done to remove differences in characteristics of the intervention and comparison groups. When samples are weighted using propensity scores, the aggregate characteristics of the samples should be nearly identical on those variables that were used to estimate the propensity scores and nearly every other variable that is correlated with those variables. It removes pretest differences.

The sample weights used to balance between group differences are based on the inverse of the propensity scores. As noted in Guo and Fraser (2010), the weights for estimating average treatment effects (the ATE) is as follows:

$$W_{P(ATE,1)} = 1/P \qquad (3.4)$$

and

$$W_{P(ATE,0)} = 1/(1 - P), \qquad (3.5)$$

where $W_{P(ATE,1)}$ is the weight for the treatment group, $W_{P(ATE,0)}$ is the weight for the comparison group, and $P$ is the propensity score. Different weights are needed if one is estimating the average treatment effect for the treated (the ATT):

$$W_{P(ATT,1)} = 1 \qquad\qquad (3.6)$$

and

$$W_{P(ATT,0)} = P/(1 - P), \qquad\qquad (3.7)$$

where $W_{P(ATT,1)}$ is the weight for the treatment group, $W_{P(ATT,0)}$ is the weight for the comparison group, and $P$ is the propensity score. For either ATE or ATT estimation, a variable is calculated having the appropriate weights for the treatment of comparison groups. This variable is used as a weighting variable.

As with propensity scores used for other purposes, propensity weighting is sensitive to the specification of the selectivity model. If there is misspecification in estimating the propensity scores, there will be errors in propensity weights. This can result in biased weights and completely wrong weighted samples. If propensities are used for weights, then the original propensity estimation process needs to offer evidence that the selectivity model is not misspecified. When the model is properly specified, then using propensity scores as weights is appropriate.

To examine whether propensity weighting removes prior differences, a process similar to that for matching is used, except that it must allow weighting. The two most common procedures are to use weighted regression for continuous confounding variables and logistic weighted regression for categorical confounding variables. In this case, the confounding variables are used as dependent variables and the intervention or comparison variable is used as an independent variable. With weighted regression, the intervention or comparison variable is used as a dummy independent. If there are multiple treatment or comparison groups, multiple dummy variables may be needed. With logistic regression, the intervention and comparison groups can be used as a factor. The appropriate weighted variable is used as the weight for either procedure. If the coefficient between the confounding variable with the treatment or comparison variable is not significant, then weighting has removed the differences in this confounder between the groups. If the coefficient is significant, one needs to go back to the estimation process for the propensity scores and follow the procedures for revising estimates of propensities. Remember, if the propensities don't overlap between the groups, there may be no propensity weighting that will remove differences between the groups.

## ADEQUACY AND SUFFICIENCY OF MATCHING

Statistical adequacy of a matching procedure depends on selecting a procedure whose assumptions correspond with the causal model being tested and for which there is evidence of proper specification of the matching evidence. There must be a discussion of the model of sample selectivity and the variables that contribute to that model. There must be measures of those variables. There must also be evidence the variables used to estimate the propensity scores or the distance measures include the variables in the selectivity model. Other authors have previously called for researchers to specify their model of sample selectivity. Here, it is noted that if that model is not discussed with evidence provided that the model is correct, the analysis does not meet criteria for statistical adequacy.

If the criteria for statistical adequacy are met, it is likely that the matching procedure will also be regarded as substantively adequate. That is, the matching procedure will produce a matched sample that has comparable groups. If the selectivity model is adequate, then all important confounding factors will be included in the estimation of the propensity scores or the distance measures. This corresponds to the conditions demonstrated by Rosenbaum and Rubin (1983) that the estimated propensity is an unbiased estimate of the true propensity.

Statistical sufficiency of a matching procedure is demonstrated when the addition of no other information improves on the matched sample. Optimized matching (discussed in Chapter 6) meets this criterion. Greedy matching does not. The reason is that the greedy procedure selects the first matches that meet the caliper. Given that multiple members in both groups may fall within a caliper range, the solution that is chosen by the greedy criteria may not be the solution that minimizes overall differences between the groups. Nevertheless, if the propensity scores are relatively uniformly distributed across the range of probabilities for those scores, a greedy match may turn out to be the best possible match. Even if greedy matching is not statistically sufficient, if it is based on a statistically adequate selectivity model, it can still produce matches that reduce or remove significant prior differences between the groups. Whether it does is an empirical question; the researcher will have to rely on inspecting the results of the matching to discover whether the matches are substantively adequate. The statistical sufficiency of matching will be discussed further when we address other matching procedures.

### Causal Inference With Matching

Although propensity scores and distance measures are used for stratifying, weighting, and controlling, this section only discusses causal inference with matching. Inference with the other uses will be addressed in subsequent chapters where those procedures are discussed in more detail. The conditions for causal inference with matching are the following:

*Condition 5:* estimation of propensity scores or distance measures from all significant confounding factors, based on a specified model of selectivity, with evidence that no significant differences remain and that the sample has adequate power. This has four requirements. A specific model of sample selectivity needs to be presented. The propensity scores or the distance measures need to be based on all the variables specified in the model of sample selectivity. Evidence also needs to be provided that significant group differences have been removed and that the sample has adequate power to detect expected differences. To present a specific model of sample selectivity, the factors affecting selectivity should be identified and discussed. The list of factors affecting selectivity should also appear complete (i.e., all significant confounding factors should be identified). These two things would meet the first requirement. *Note:* Under randomization and control over the intervention, the selectivity model reduces to the absence of confounding factors with no need to match the samples. To meet the second requirement, the confounding factors specified in the selectivity model must be measured and included in the process of estimating the propensity scores or the distance measures. *Note:* If the relationship between a confounding factor and the outcomes disappears when the influence of the other confounding factors is controlled, that particular factor can be dropped from estimating the scores or distance measures. All others need to be included. To meet the third requirement, the reduction in prior group differences must be documented. This can be something as simple as doing *t* tests, ANOVAs, or cross-tabulations to show the differences before and after matching. Whatever procedure demonstrated group differences to begin with should also be used to show that those differences no longer remain. *Note:* If there are statistically significant differences that are substantively small, one may make an argument that inferences based on the findings approximate (but may not equal) the true treatment effect. A researcher should not expect everyone to accept the argument, however. Such inferences should not be claimed to rest on strong evidence. The most that can be said is that the evidence is adequate. Only if there are no significant differences using evidence based on statistically sufficient estimates can one say that the evidence is strong. The reason is that an estimate that is not statistically sufficient can be improved by additional information. Inferences using the additional evidence might differ from the original inferences. It should be noted, however, if the original estimates are unbiased estimates, the inferences are unlikely to change dramatically. They can usually be used for public discussion and policy planning. Finally, evidence of adequate statistical power needs to be provided.

The most convincing evidence is a demonstration that the sample has sufficient cases to detect a specified effect. For example, if changes of 10 units on a scale would move the average subject from being in the clinical range to a position of not needing intervention and if the sample was big enough to get statistically significant results with a 10-unit change, then that would be sufficient evidence of adequate statistical power. In the absence of an agreed-on standard, it may be necessary to propose an ad hoc standard (prior to conducting the study) and provide an argument why that standard should be accepted. This is a less defensible position. Inferences based on such evidence cannot be regarded as strongly based, but they can be regarded as adequate.

# CHAPTER 4

## PROPENSITY APPROACHES FOR QUASI-EXPERIMENTS

This chapter discusses the basics of propensity score estimation and use. It presents tests for the effectiveness of propensity scores for reducing imbalance or bias in the groups compared. It discusses how to improve propensity score estimates and how to judge whether the imbalance reduction is adequate for analysis. In addition, it reviews alternative propensity uses and how they may be combined and discusses trade-offs between the uses.

## ESTIMATING PROPENSITY SCORES

The probability that a given case will fall in a specified group is affected by the process of selecting cases into the groups. When randomization is used for the selection process, all cases have an equal chance of being in the intervention or control groups. The treatment effect is easily estimated as a difference in means, proportions, or rates. When different probabilities are used between the groups to assign the cases, the probabilities are known and the results can be adjusted to estimate the treatment effect. With quasi-experimental data, however, the selection process is not fully defined. The probabilities of selection into the treatment or comparison group are not totally known. To the extent that factors can be identified that appear to affect the selection, however, it may be possible to estimate those probabilities.

Estimating propensities depends on three things: (1) the variables, (2) the procedures, and (3) the criteria used for choosing an estimation result. The variables should be related both to group selection and to the outcome. The estimation procedures need to be appropriate for the data. The criteria should reflect trade-offs chosen for specific purposes.

The best variables for estimating propensity scores are those that are different between the groups and are related to the outcome factors. These are the typical confounding factors in estimating treatment effects. One should not include variables correlated with selection and the outcome when they are thought to intervene between the intervention and the outcome. Intervening variables cannot affect the selection process. They are affected by the selection process. One can search for other confounding variables in the process discussed in Chapter 2. One needs to be careful, however, that the variables identified by empirical association do not causally follow the selection. They need to represent the characteristics or experiences the subject had prior to the intervention. If it is unknown whether they precede or follow the intervention, their inclusion needs to be done with caution. It is important to include all possible confounding factors for which one has data and exclude correlates that could not affect the selection process. Omitting a confounder lowers the bias reduction. It leaves bias in the estimation of the treatment effect. Severity of that problem can be explored with sensitivity analysis, discussed in Chapter 11. Including a noncausal correlate can also bias the estimate.

One should not include variables uncorrelated with the outcome. Austin, Grootendorst, and Anderson (2007) have shown that including variables correlated with selection, but not with outcomes, adds little to the precision of estimating treatment effects and is likely to result in cases being dropped from the sample when doing matching. In addition, some variables will jointly correlate because they are the result of the intended outcome itself (which makes them a distal, or long-term, outcome). Just as omitting a confounding variable results in bias, so does including a variable that is consequent to the intervention. Including these as estimators of propensity scores will rob the treatment measures of estimated causal effects. It can result in falsely concluding that there is no intervention effect.

Excluding predictors of propensity scores is no trivial matter. Whenever a variable is considered for inclusion as a predictor, an assessment needs to be made as to whether it precedes, is contemporaneous with, or follows the intervention. With contemporaneous variables, there is greater uncertainty as to whether they should be included. Unless there are clear theoretical indications, the causal ordering is less certain. The two factors may even be mutually influencing (**simultaneous** or **nonrecursive** causal variables). Informed professional judgment may be the only grounds for including or excluding them. In either case, that decision should be explicitly noted.

Which estimation procedure to use? Should it be logistic regression, probit regression, discriminant analysis, or some other procedure? The procedure used to estimate the propensity scores should match the measurement levels of the indicators and the analytical procedure to be used in estimating causal effects. Using dummy dependent variables in a regression (as a probit-like analysis) is possible, but it depends on having a reasonable split between the two groups and a check to see that estimated values do not fall outside a 0 to 1 range. If there are more cases in one group than the other, it biases the estimates of the standard errors of the regression coefficients and makes valid inference more difficult. If the split is too extreme, something like logistic or probit regression should be considered. Researchers differ on their criteria for an extreme split, but an 80/20 split is usually regarded as extreme. Less than a 60/40 split is not usually regarded so.

The choice of estimation procedure depends on measurement properties of the variables, the statistical procedures to be used in analyzing the data, the significance tests likely to be used, and theoretical considerations. When continuous variables are not symmetrical, outliers can have different effects on propensity estimates when used in different procedures. When propensities are estimated using procedures that differ from those to be used in the analysis, they may not be adequate tools for removing group differences. Similarly, significance tests differ on their robustness and sensitivity. If one is going to use an analytical procedure whose significance tests are more robust or more sensitive than those used in estimating the propensity scores, then the propensity estimates may leave out confounding variables relevant to the analytical model. This leads to bias in estimating causal effects. If the procedures differ only slightly in their robustness and sensitivity, the bias may be small. It may be weakly ignorable.

Suppose two researchers are studying the effect of a health voucher program on frequency of medical visits. One estimates the propensities with logistic regression and the other with probit analysis. They both then use analysis of covariance (ANCOVA) to estimate the effect of the program and examine alternative influences on frequency of visits. Suppose further that the subclassification procedure of logit estimation results in variables dropping out due to large error variances because some categories have few cases. If estimated by probit analysis, the variables might remain in the prediction equation (depending on the criteria for inclusion and exclusion). The propensities estimated can then differ, and the ANCOVA that ultimately uses them will produce different results for the two researchers. A careful assessment of variables removed from the estimation process can help avoid this, but consistency in use of significance tests can help as well.

A causal theory provides the basis for which one expects a link between an intervention and an outcome. If the theory requires estimating statistics that use procedures different from those used in estimating the propensities, the

assumptions of the theory differ from the assumptions of the estimation procedure. These differences might not affect the results, but sometimes they can. If
possible, one should use techniques for estimating propensities whose assumptions are consistent with the causal theory of the treatment effect.

## Regression Estimation of Propensities

Regression analysis is the simplest way of estimating propensity scores. If a
dichotomous variable is coded 0 for control group and 1 for treatment group,
potential confounding variables can be used as regressors to predict the value
of the dichotomous variable. The predicted value will be the estimated probability that a given case is in the treatment group—the propensity score conditional on the confounding characteristics.

The formula for a regression estimate of the propensity is as follows:

$$P_S = \alpha_S + \beta_{SX}X, \qquad (4.1)$$

where $P_S$ is the probability of receiving treatment, $\alpha$ is a constant, and $\beta_{SX}$ is the
regression coefficient of the effect of $X$ on $S$ (a dichotomous treatment variable
coded 0 for no treatment and 1 for treatment), restricted within a 0 to 1 range.
This is the probit estimate of a propensity score.

Probit regression (regression with a dummy dependent variable) is most
appropriate when the cases are split evenly between the categories, and one will
focus on interpretation of the effect coefficients. It is recommended when the
outcomes are cast in terms of percentages or rates at which a characteristic or
event occurs. It also tends to perform better than logistic regression if there are
many continuous variables that will be used as control variables or whose
alternative influence will be examined.

The split of the cases between two groups is an important issue. An uneven
split is equivalent to a skewed distribution of a dependent variable in regression analysis. This can lead to a biased estimate of the variance estimated by
the regression program, which can throw off standard errors of the coefficients
for the treatment effect and covariates in the estimation equation. As noted
above, when the split is within 60/40, the bias is typically small. When it is
greater than 80/20, the bias is enough that using an alternative to regression
with a dummy dependent is recommended. In between these two splits, it's
mainly a matter of professional judgment as to whether the results are likely
to have significant bias. However, it doesn't hurt to replicate the analysis with
an alternative program to see if similar results are produced. Alternatives that

can be considered are discriminant function analysis and logistic regression. With both these procedures, however, the parameter coefficients produced need to be converted to percentages or rates to get a finding comparable with probit analysis.

When estimating propensity scores with a regression, the problems of collinearity of the predictors are present. A forward stepwise regression is not advisable, as variables that have a true relationship with the selection process may be excluded. Backward stepwise regression is more likely to result in a valid model of selection.

With regression estimation of propensities, there is also the risk that predicted probabilities will fall outside a 0 to 1 range. When predicted probabilities fall outside this range, a condition similar to complete or quasi-complete separation may be present. This can be a result of highly skewed distributions or collinearity of the predictors. Transforming the skewed predictors may help. If the skewed predictor is a dichotomy, however, it may be necessary to delete this variable from the prediction equation. In some cases, the problem can be resolved by dropping cases whose estimated propensity is 1.0 or 0.0. They generally would not have paired cases for matching in any case.

All the major statistical programs contain checks for complete separation. Most of the time, the programs issue a warning that the probability is 1.0 or 0.0 and try to continue, terminating if that is not possible. If a warning occurs and the program continues, the user should inspect the standard errors for the statistics provided to see if they are very large. If they are, the results are not meaningful.

The problem that predicted values fall outside a 0 to 1 range can be dealt with by recoding such values as falling just inside the range. However, the values chosen as the recoded value are typically ad hoc and may not have theoretical justification. The cases having such values, however, are likely to be dropped from matched samples as it is very difficult to find both treatment and comparison cases that have similar extreme values. Other problems posed by extreme propensity scores are discussed subsequently.

The results of a probit estimation of propensities are compared with logistic estimation in Figure 4.1. It shows that the predicted probabilities between the two procedures are close but are not identical. The straight line in the figure indicates the pattern if it were a perfect linear relationship.

It is commonly thought that it doesn't make a difference whether one uses regression estimation to estimate propensity scores or logistic regression. According to Rubin (1974), there is a monotonic relationship among the alternative estimates. These procedures result in estimates that maintain the same rank order of cases. There is, however, a circumstance in which they do not.

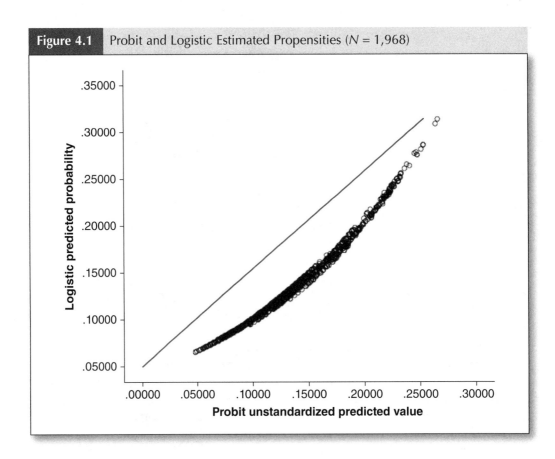

**Figure 4.1**   Probit and Logistic Estimated Propensities ($N = 1,968$)

When predictors are skewed and not symmetrical, the propensities estimated by the two procedures may differ, even when using the same variables. Logit and regression estimates give different weight to outliers in distributions. Cases that have outliers in some variables and not in others may have a higher or lower estimated propensity. If there is an adjacent case that has similar characteristics except for those that are more extreme, regression may estimate it as having a slightly higher propensity—which can change the distance between the propensities of similar cases. Extreme cases may have a different distance between adjacent propensity scores.

Since extreme propensities often do not overlap between groups when they are at the opposite end of the distribution of the propensities, they are often dropped by a matching process. The rank ordering of the overlapping propensity cases is not affected by the outliers. From a practical viewpoint, it doesn't make much of a difference when matching. However, if one wishes to use all the cases in weighted regression, covariate adjustment, or multivariate modeling, the outliers are not usually dropped. It can make a difference. Consequently, results can differ between methods of propensity estimation when outliers are present.

## Logistic Estimation of Propensities

The formulas for estimating the propensities differ between logit and regression. The formula for a logit estimate of the propensity given by Guo and Fraser (2010, p. 136) is as follows:

$$P_{SX} = 1/(1 + e^{-x\beta}),\qquad(4.2)$$

where $P_{SX}$ is the probability of receiving treatment given $X$, $X$ is one or more confounding variables, and $\beta$ is a logistic regression parameter. This equation has a nonlinear relation to the true propensity. It can be converted to a linear relation using the logarithm of the odds calculated from the propensity. The odds are

$$\Omega_S = P_S/(1 - P_S),\qquad(4.3)$$

where $\Omega_S$ is the odds of receiving treatment and $P_S$ is the probability of receiving treatment. The linear estimate of the propensity is as follows:

$$P_{Sl} = \log_e (\Omega_S),\qquad(4.4)$$

where $P_{Sl}$ is the linearized propensity and $\Omega$ is the odds of receiving treatment.

As noted above, there is a monotonic relationship between these equations—except when extreme outliers are present. The two equations, however, do not usually produce the same identical estimated propensities. The propensity distributions may differ by a scaling factor (a linear transformation) or they may be skewed differently (a nonlinear transformation). This difference is illustrated in Figure 4.2, a scatterplot of propensities estimated by logistic and discriminant analysis used in Table 1.3.

Figure 4.2 shows a curvilinear relationship between the logit and the discriminant estimates. A similar curvilinearity is present between the logit and probit estimate (Figure 4.1). The curvilinearity results because the propensity distribution for the logit estimates is somewhat more skewed than that for the discriminant estimates (see Table 4.1). The distribution of probabilities estimated

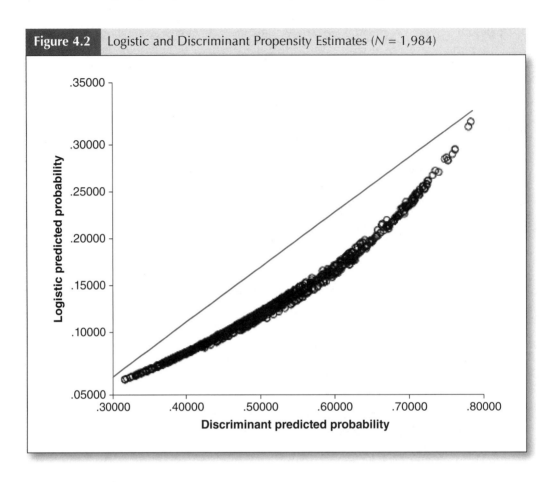

**Figure 4.2**    Logistic and Discriminant Propensity Estimates ($N = 1,984$)

by logistic regression is slightly less normal than that estimated by discriminant analysis (and by probit analysis). All of the tests of nonnormality are statistically significant. This is not too surprising given the number of cases for which propensities were estimated ($N = 1,984$).

All three of these approaches to testing normality are fairly sensitive. Small departures from normality may be statistically significant with large samples. Figure 4.3 is a bar diagram where the propensities have been divided into six groups, with an equal range of propensity in each group. These groups were created to perform the chi-square test of normality of the distribution. The figure clearly shows how skewed the distribution is.

The chi-square test of normality requires larger samples than the other tests because the expected number of cases in the smallest cell should be at least 5. With a normal distribution and six categories, at least 200 cases are needed to

| Table 4.1 | Normality Tests for Propensity Estimates | | | | | |
|---|---|---|---|---|---|---|
| *Estimation Method* | *Fisher's $g_1$* | *$p(g_1)$* | *Kolmogorov–Smirnov $p(K–S)$* | *$\chi^2$* | *df* | *$p(\chi^2)$* |
| Logistic | 1.404 | <.001 | <.001 | 9364.0 | 5 | <.001 |
| Discriminant/ probit | 0.737 | <.001 | <.001 | 1381.0 | 5 | <.001 |

| Figure 4.3 | Logistic Estimated Propensity ($N$ = 1,984) |
|---|---|

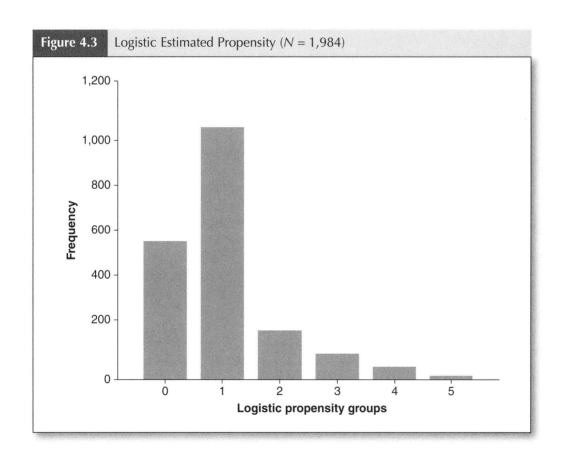

obtain 5 in the smallest cells. Fisher's $g_1$ and the Kolmogorov–Smirnov test can produce results with fewer cases. Fisher's $g_1$ statistic, moreover, also provides substantive information about skewness. Since it is the ratio of the average cubed deviations from the mean to the cube of the standard deviation, it can be interpreted as an imbalance ratio. The log-normal distribution, for example, has a skewness value of 3.0. This means that the average cubed deviations that are out of balance is three times the cubed standard deviation of the sample. If variables have a skewness value less than 3, then taking the log of that variable may overcompensate for the degree of skewness. Some researchers regard a skewness value less than 1.0 as not likely to be substantively important, even though it can be statistically significant (as is the case here). Sometimes a statistically significantly skewed variable can still provide estimates of covariances and mean differences that are very similar to known population values when skewness is within a ±1.0 range. This is not true for small samples.

To transform a distribution of propensities to a normal distribution, one should look at the variables used to estimate those propensities. If some of those variables are nonnormal, it may be possible to first transform them to normality before using them in the estimation or to use powers of the variables to add to the estimation. Variable transformation and adding powers of variables will be discussed further in the section on improving propensity estimates. Transformation to normality of a predictor will tend to produce a more normal distribution of estimated propensities.

One cannot always transform to normality. If dummy variables are used in the estimation, as is often the case, these cannot be transformed to normality. Adding other dummy variables imbalanced in the other direction can reduce the skewness of the predicted propensities; but they are not always available. It is better to make the distribution of propensities as close to symmetrical as possible, however. With matching, the problem is not quite as severe. The distortion may be negligible in the center of nearly symmetrical distributions. Using Rubin's terminology, it is ignorable. With procedures other than matching, the distortion may be greater. One may need to consider distribution-free analysis to estimate program effects. If so, one needs to reevaluate the propensity estimation procedure to ensure consistency with the nonparametric procedure employed.

## Discriminant Analysis Estimation

Discriminant analysis is most appropriate when one's focus is on the ability to predict the outcomes in discrete categories. It is especially desirable when the principal covariates are continuous variables, normally distributed, and there are multiple categories of interventions. In the special case that all the predictors are normally distributed, the discriminant estimate of the propensity is equivalent to a maximum likelihood estimate of the population propensity. In this case, the estimate will be statistically adequate and sufficient. If categorical variables are included in the estimation, the results are unbiased if the categorical variables are evenly split. In cases of significant nonnormality, a logistic regression approach may be preferable.

When there are more than two categories of treatment groups and categorical predictors, discriminant function analysis will sometimes be preferable to logistic regression to estimate propensities. With multiple treatment or comparison groups and categorical predictors, the probability of having empty cells for some combination of predictors and treatment increases geometrically with the number of categories. If there are empty cells, the maximum likelihood procedure of logistic regression fails to achieve a stable solution. In such a case, discriminant function estimation is preferable. However, complete separation can produce collinearity among predictors. There are times when the only way to achieve an estimated probability is to drop a predictor that creates both separation with logistic regression and collinearity with probit and discriminant function analysis. This rare situation truly represents ill-conditioned data.

## Linking Estimation and Analysis

This author recommends that the procedure used to estimate the propensities be similar to the procedure for estimating the causal effects. This is more likely to produce propensities whose distribution is consistent with one's analytical procedure than if estimated using an alternative procedure. This is especially true when one's measures have outliers. If the distribution of the propensities is inconsistent with the analytical procedure assumptions, this will reduce the ability to remove between-group differences. If the distribution doesn't match the assumptions, either the measure or the estimation procedure needs to be changed.

There is also a practical reason for preferring an estimation procedure that matches one's analytical procedure: It simplifies the computer programming one has to do. Estimating propensities often requires prior programming to have the measures in a form that the software can use to do the estimation. This is also true for analysis needed for estimating treatment effects. When the same or similar procedures are used, some of the thinking, planning, and programming done for the propensity estimation process may also be useful for the analytical process. It may improve the efficiency in carrying out the analysis.

Logistic regression is most appropriate when there are discrete outcomes, and theory does not favor analyzing the outcomes with survival analysis, hazard analysis, or event history analysis. It is also better to use this procedure if the cases are split unevenly between the categories and one's focus is on the likelihood of outcomes as opposed to the rate of a given outcome.

The procedures for doing logistic regression vary between computer programs. Certain issues, however, are common between the programs. The dependent variable needs to be dichotomous. Even though logistic programs can estimate equations with multiple categories, the application of probabilities to propensity classification in this case is less clear. The probability for group membership is in relation to the other groups, excluding one group as a reference group. Results vary by the choice of the reference group. If one can be confident as to what the reference group should be (e.g., if there is one placebo group and all others are treatment groups), one may proceed with the estimation.

The maximum likelihood process used in logistic regression, however, may not converge on a stable solution. This process revises the estimates through a series of iterations, using the results of the prior iteration to achieve a better estimate with a subsequent iteration. All logistic regression programs set a maximum number of iterations to avoid having the program run indefinitely. The iterations stop when a specified criterion is met. Usually, this is when the difference between the iterations of the estimate of a fit parameter (e.g., the maximum change in the parameters of the equation) is some small number, such as .0001. Some data do not converge very quickly and require much more than the default number of iterations. Other data do not converge at all (Allison, 2008). If estimation does not converge after a number of iterations, the results should be inspected to see how close the estimates are between iterations. If they are very close, though greater than the criterion, they may be regarded as possible solutions. However, such estimates are neither statistically adequate nor sufficient. They may be, however, the best approximations available. If the results between iterations do not seem very close, then convergence may not be possible, and maximum likelihood estimation should not be done. An alternative procedure should be used, such as using discriminant function analysis to estimate the propensities.

Another problem arises because different computer programs do not use the same algorithm for estimating logit maximum likelihood solutions. The Newton–Ralphson algorithm and Fisher's scoring method are used by different statistical programs. The estimates of the parameters are the same, but the standard errors of the estimates differ. Hence, opposing conclusions may be reached by using different programs, but only for interventions having borderline effects. SAS and R use Fisher's scoring method. Stata and SPSS use the more common Newton–Ralphson algorithm.

The sequence in which variables are entered into the logistic regression also affects the model parameters and which variables appear in the model (Schumacker, 2009). Forward stepwise logistic regression is not recommended for estimating propensity scores because different results can be obtained with slight variations in the criteria for entering or deleting variables. The variables entered at an earlier step can keep out variables that, if present, would not be dropped from the estimation. This is because the criteria for entering a variable are typically more stringent than for dropping a variable. For example, as a default, a variable might need to meet a .05 criterion for entering and a .10 criterion for dropping. These criteria can be changed by the user.

If one wishes to use logistic regression, a backward stepwise solution is preferable. It is less likely to exclude variables that have a true relation to the selectivity process. If the number of variables considered is large, one might start with a forward stepwise logistic regression but follow it with a backward stepwise that includes some of the variables excluded earlier—especially those that seem to be correlated with variables in the final solution.

To use a stepwise process, one needs a criterion for entering or deleting variables in the predictive equation. With a backward stepwise solution, all specified variables are entered in the initial prediction equation. The coefficients of the equation are estimated by a maximum likelihood process and evaluated for statistical significance; for example, whether their significance probability is greater than .05. This may be done using the Wald chi-square or the likelihood ratio chi-square. One may also consider whether the change in parameters between iterations is sufficiently small using either a default criterion or a user-specified criterion. Some value less than .001 is commonly used. The least significant predictor is dropped from the equation, and the predictive equation is reestimated with the remaining variables. This process is repeated until all remaining variables are statistically significant. A backward stepwise approach is unlikely to leave out variables that should be in the predictive equation—provided that they are included in the list of possible predictors in the first place. A forward stepwise process may result in fewer variables being included in the predictive equation, but it may also leave out variables that have an influence on the selection process.

With both stepwise procedures, if at any point empty cells result from including a variable, the maximum likelihood process may not find a stable solution. This is a situation called complete separation. With complete separation, there is no maximum likelihood solution. If a cell has only a few cases, this may produce quasi-complete separation—which can also prevent a maximum likelihood solution. Some programs do logistic regression tests for complete separation. If predicted probabilities equal 1.0 or the parameter variances approach infinity, complete separation is present. Quasi-complete separation is indicated by predicted probabilities near 1.0 (>.95) or parameter estimates that have large variances compared with other parameters. If separation is present, it may be necessary to delete the predictor variable to obtain a maximum likelihood solution. A backward stepwise procedure may abort if separation is detected. In such a case, one can run a forward stepwise procedure and use the results prior to it aborting. In this case, the likelihood ratio chi-square is more accurate, rather than the Wald chi-square, in judging significance of the parameters. On the other hand, if a maximum likelihood solution is found, it is usually a statistically sufficient solution.

## *Estimation Complications*

The estimation process is complicated by the use of categorical variables, the presence of tied values for the propensities, the risk of misspecified variables with which to do the estimation, and the presence of nonlinear relationships among the variables. Misspecification has been discussed earlier. Nonlinear relations are discussed in the section on improving imbalance reduction. Categorical variables pose issues because they limit the range of possible estimated propensities. The number of categories poses issues for a similar reason. Empty categories can make maximum likelihood estimation impossible. Ties in propensity scores mean arbitrary rules may need to be adopted to resolve the ties. Misspecification complicates estimation because variables may be included that shouldn't be included, and other variables may be omitted that should be included. Either can create biased estimates of propensities, in some cases underestimating and in other cases overestimating. Nonlinear relations can also create bias. Several strategies are available to deal with nonlinearity. Choosing among the strategies does not always have a clear rationale.

Categorical variables pose a problem because they often do not have even splits between the categories. This tends to result in nonnormal distributions of the propensities. The nonnormality may contribute to multiple modes in the distribution of the propensity scores, since multiple cases will fall in each category of the nominal variable. It will tend to skew the distribution if there are more cases in one category than in another. Increasing the number of categorical variables will tend to reduce this problem. It will increase the number of combinations of values predicted by the model, smoothing the distribution of probabilities. On the other hand, increasing the number of nominal variables will increase the chances of empty cells—which may discourage using logistic regression as a propensity estimator. It will not necessarily exclude it. It's an empirical question as to whether empty cells result.

Multimodality in the propensity distribution is also a problem because it creates ties in propensity scores. Many computer programs for matching randomize the sequence of cases that have tied propensity scores. This is done to prevent any bias in which a tied case is selected for a match. If there are more ties in the treatment group than in the comparison group, some treatment group members may be excluded as not having a sufficiently close match. This does not create bias, but it does result in a smaller sample of matched cases and reduce the power of the analysis. If there is skewness in the distribution of propensities, this may also result in different matched pairs.

## CHECKING IMBALANCE REDUCTION

Determining whether the imbalance has been reduced requires comparing differences before and after using propensity scores. For some statistics, testing a difference-of-differences is very straightforward. For others, the process is a little more complicated. Imbalance reduction may be examined using significance tests, standardized deviations, percent reduction, and clinical or substantive criteria. These approaches provide different information about the nature and severity of the imbalance. All of them may be used to gain a broader understanding of the nature and severity of the imbalance.

*Significance Tests.* The significance tests to determine imbalance depend on the measurement level of the variables. If the potential confounders are continuous variables with unimodal, symmetrical distributions, then $t$ or $F$ tests are most commonly employed. Austin (2008) has argued against using significance tests because assumptions for their use may not be met. There are, however, different views on the subject (Hansen, 2008; Stuart, 2008). One may use the significance probability of these tests with a significance-level criterion to judge whether differences remain. Some researchers use the $F$ value or $t$ value directly. The $F$ and the $t$ can be interpreted as relative ratios: the ratio of a squared difference to a standard squared difference ($F$) or the ratio of a difference to a standard deviation ($t$). Values less than 1.0 for either statistic cannot be statistically significant. If the distributions are highly skewed or multimodal, the Mann–Whitney $U$ test may be employed. If the potential confounders are categorical (nominal level) variables, then Pearson's chi-square (cross-tabulation) or the likelihood ratio (logit) may be used.

Performing a number of these tests creates a risk of false positives. One correction for this is to divide the alpha level for significance by the number of tests to be performed and use that as the corrected alpha level. For example, if one is using an alpha level of .05 and performing 5 imbalance tests, the .05

is divided by 5 to achieve a corrected alpha level of .01. This should be used instead of the original alpha level. Alternatively, grouped significance tests may be used (e.g., $T^2$ instead of $t$ tests).

## Standard Deviation Criteria

An effect coefficient based on the standard deviation within the treatment group is also used in judging imbalance. When means or percentages are compared, their difference is divided by the pooled standard deviation of the statistic for the treatment and comparison groups (Hedges, 1981). The statistic is called the standardized mean difference or the normalized difference. Some refer to the statistic as Hedges' $g$. This statistic "normalizes" the difference and allows comparisons between different measures. It allows comparisons of imbalance between different measures to determine where the greatest imbalance is. This statistic is also used as a standardized effect coefficient for comparing causal effects between different measures or different studies. One can also do this by comparing $\eta$ or $\eta^2$ statistics from an analysis of variance (ANOVA) or $\varphi$ or V from a cross-tabulation. Hedges' $g$ is not a true $z$ statistic, but it is similar to it. It is common to say that imbalance is present if the difference is more than one fifth of a standard deviation, that is, if the normalized difference is greater than 0.20 (although some use a difference of 0.25). The formula for the standardized difference is as follows:

$$g_w = 100\left((\bar{W}_1 - \bar{W}_0)/\sqrt{(s_1^2 + s_0^2)}\right), \tag{4.5}$$

where $g_w$ is the standardized difference for grouping variable $W$, $\bar{W}_1$ is the mean or a percentage for a confounding variable $W$ for the treatment group, $\bar{W}_0$ is the mean or percentage of the same confounding variable for the comparison group, $s_1^2$ is the variance of the mean or percentage for the treatment group, and $s_0^2$ is the variance of the mean or percentage for the comparison group. In other words, it is the difference of the means or percentages divided by their pooled standard deviation for the groups.

## Percent Reduction

Another way of judging imbalance is to compare the group difference before and after adjustment or matching with propensity scores. This judgment can use the percent reduction statistics. The equation for the percent reduction is as follows:

$$P_r = 100\left((\bar{W}_u - \bar{W}_m)/\bar{W}_m\right), \tag{4.6}$$

where $P_r$ is the percent reduction, $\bar{W}_u$ is the difference in means or percentages for the unmatched sample, and $\bar{W}_m$ is the difference in means or percentages for the matched sample.

It is the change in difference after using propensity scores divided by the difference after using them. If the percent reduction in difference is large, then imbalance is said to have been reduced. While this approach provides interesting information, there are no agreed-on criteria for judging how much a reduction is needed to say the imbalance has been effectively removed (60%? 80%? 90%?). It is more useful for comparing alternative propensity adjustments to determine which seem more effective.

## Clinical/Substantive Criteria

When there are clinical standards for a measure, they can be used in judging imbalance reduction. One can compare the percentage in each group that meets a clinical standard. If, after adjustment, the two groups have a similar percentage that meets the clinical standard, then imbalance may be said to have been eliminated.

## Graphical Criteria

Graphing frequency distributions and Q–Q plotting are two common procedures used to judge imbalance. If the propensity scores for the treatment group and the comparison group have frequency distributions with a similar shape, central tendency, dispersion, and skewness, they may be judged to have similar balance. The Q–Q plot performs a scattergram of the observed propensity scores with those of a normal distribution having the same mean and variance with the cases rank ordered. An example of Q–Q plotting is given in Figure 4.4.

When propensity scores are normally distributed, the scatterplot has the scores close to a straight line. When they seem to take an "S" shape or some other curvilinear shape, it indicates that the propensity scores are not normally distributed. If treatment and control groups both have a similar shape on their Q–Q plots, then they have similar balance—although a difference in central tendency may still be present. Figure 4.4 shows a "wiggly" relationship between the observed propensity scores and the line of normality with some curvilinearity. If treatment propensity scores and comparison propensity scores had similar such patterns, they might be balanced, but they would not be normally distributed.

## Improving Imbalance Reduction

Two strategies are used most often to improve the reduction in imbalance: (1) adding more variables to the prediction equation and (2) correcting for nonlinearity in relationships. The former strategy means trying to identify other factors that affect the selection process that are in one's data set and

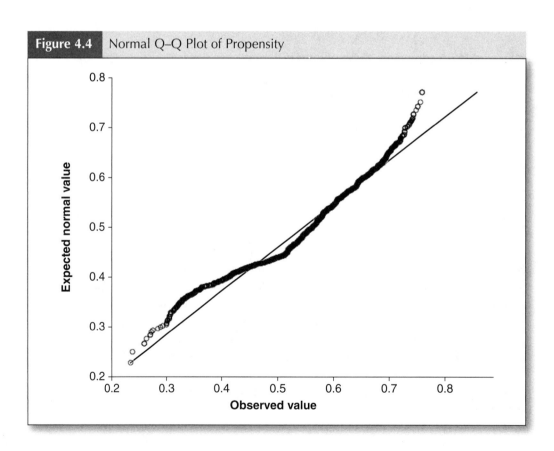

**Figure 4.4    Normal Q–Q Plot of Propensity**

adding them to the propensity estimation. The second strategy means adding variables already in the equation that are transformed by a quadratic or some other function.

In the initial selection of variables to estimate propensities, variables may have been excluded because there was no clear theoretical grounds for expecting them to affect selection—even though they were correlated with selection. Existing theory or suppositions may have indicated that some of these variables were simultaneous or intervening. These issues may be revisited. A wider search of the literature may discover grounds for including these omitted variables. One's own theorizing may also identify new reasons. This is not the same thing as speculating. The reasons have to be tied to a specific theory. One can also use empirical procedures similar to those for identifying confounding variables. Once additional correlates are identified, however, theoretical assessment of them still needs to be done to ensure that consequent variables are not added to the prediction equation.

Adding transformed variables to the equation can sometimes increase the predictive power of the equation. Common transforms include squaring, cubing, exponentiating, or taking the logarithm. Adding such transformed variables is also likely to increase the collinearity of the predictors. This means that even though the predictive power is better, as well as the corresponding reduction in imbalance of the propensities, the coefficients associated with each predictor are less reliable. This process can be used to get propensities that better reduce imbalance. The coefficients of the prediction equation should not be interpreted individually, due to the added collinearity. Both probit and discriminant procedures print warnings about collinearity when it becomes too severe.

## PROPENSITY SCORE USES

This section discusses how propensity scores are used. It compares the alternative procedures, discusses their strengths and weaknesses, and comments on how these procedures may be used together to improve the analysis of quasi-experimental data.

### Matching

Matching, if done well, can remove all prior group differences for the measured variables (Rosenbaum & Rubin, 1983; Rubin, 1979). It even removes some differences of unmeasured variables if they are correlated with the observed variables. Matching propensities is called multivariate matching because the propensity score reflects all the influences on selectivity of the multiple variables that went into the propensity estimation. This section will discuss three basic strategies to matching: (1) exact matching, (2) nearest-neighbor matching, and (3) caliper matching. More advanced matching procedures are discussed in later chapters. Computer programs for doing these procedures are presented in the appendixes and the book's website.

*Exact Matches.* Exact matching is the easiest procedure for matching, and the one likely to drop the most cases from analysis. All statistical packages can be used to do exact matching. If one creates a horizontal file in the manner discussed in Chapter 3, then cases can be selected when the treatment propensity matches the comparison group propensity. If the comparison group propensity does not match exactly, a flag can be set for deletion, the flag merged to the comparison group data file, and the case deleted. The comparison data can then be remerged with the treatment data, and the process continued. Programs that do nearest-neighbor matching can also be modified to do exact matching by setting the requirement for a match to be "equals" rather than "minimum difference."

Exact matching does an excellent job of removing group differences for the observed variables. Its weakness is in how many cases this process deletes. If it deletes too many cases, the remaining sample size may not have sufficient statistical power to detect true effects that may be present. If the estimated causal effects are statically significant, however, they are typically highly reliable.

*Nearest Matches.* Nearest-neighbor matching chooses cases where the propensities may not be the same, but they are very close. It selects as a match those cases whose propensity is closest to that of the treatment propensity (Dehejia & Wahba, 2002). If there is only one case whose propensity is at the minimal difference from the treatment propensity, then only one comparison group case will be selected. If there are ties in the nearest neighbor, some programs will randomly select one match. Other programs will select all matches, depending on whether one is doing 1–1 or 1–many matching.

Nearest-neighbor matching is popular both because there are computer programs easily available for doing it and because it has intuitive appeal. The accessibility and ease of use of programs for matching is a factor to consider. If using an easier procedure doesn't produce results, one can always try another program (assuming a matching solution is possible). In addition, the nearest-neighbor criterion has appeal as representing "the best individual match available." While optimal matching (discussed in a later chapter) can produce better overall matches, if individual matching produces adequate results, for many research purposes this may be acceptable.

*Caliper Matches.* Caliper matching is sometimes used as an adjunct of nearest-neighbor matching. It may specify a maximum difference one is willing to accept as a nearest neighbor. It can, however, be used without requiring the matched case to be the nearest neighbor. One can match all cases within the distance of the caliper. This is especially useful with 1–many matching. While it reduces the precision of the matches, it increases the power of the sample by retaining more cases. With caliper matching, it is especially important to check imbalance reduction because the reduced precision of matching may not adequately remove group differences.

There are no agreed-on standards for which value of the caliper to use. Most researchers either pick some value of a propensity difference they consider "small" or select a value related to the standard deviation of the propensity scores. For example, researchers will sometimes choose a value of $\pm.05$ for the value of acceptable difference in propensities. Other researchers may choose a value of one quarter of the standard deviation of the propensity distribution. If using one standard selects too few cases or fails to remove group differences, one may try another standard—always evaluating the result to see if group differences are removed and the resulting sample is not too small. Procedures for checking the sensitivity of the results to sample size are discussed in Chapter 11.

## Stratifying

Stratifying is the process of breaking a sample into subgroups, each of which is homogeneous on one or more characteristics. It is sometimes called subclassification. Cochran (1968) has shown that if one creates five subgroups, each of which is homogeneous on their propensity scores, this effectively controls more than 90% of the differences between treatment and comparison groups. It may control more than 95% of these differences (Rosenbaum & Rubin, 1984). If a researcher creates more than five groups, this will control even more of the differences. However, the size of the sample needed for creating more groups can get quite large. Enough cases are needed in each group to replicate the causal analysis in every group. The results are then combined with a weighted average.

It is technically possible to perform the calculations for something like a one-way ANOVA with only 20 cases in each group, but the standard errors of the parameters can be large. The sample may be underpowered to get significant results for a true difference. One hundred cases in each group is a modest amount, given degrees of freedom lost to the number of variables used and constraints of various statistical procedures. This means at least 500 cases are desirable for most stratifying uses. With more than 10 variables being used (including variables used in estimating propensity scores), considerably more than 500 cases may be needed.

Five groups are formed by dividing the range of propensity scores into five quintiles. Each quintile is treated as a separate group. If the range in propensity scores is small, each quintile will be relatively homogeneous; that is, the differences related to propensity scores will be controlled. If the range in propensity scores is moderate or large, there will remain some variation within each group. It is an empirical question as to whether sufficient variation has been controlled to remove differences between the treatment and comparison groups. One needs to examine these differences within each subgroup to determine whether the differences are no longer significant. If differences remain, it is necessary either to revise the propensity estimates and create new groups or to try an alternative use of the propensity scores.

The estimated effects (differences of means, proportions, rates, or odds) are combined with an average weighted by the number of cases in each group or the variances of the effect coefficients. When there are an equal number of cases in each subclassification, one may simply average the estimated effects (Rosenbaum & Rubin, 1984). If the results are statistically significant in every subgroup, the averaged effects will also be significant—unless the results are significant in one direction in some groups and in the opposite direction in other groups. This latter situation implies an interactive effect between one or more of the variables used to estimate propensity scores and the selection process—in which case, one needs to revisit the selectivity model used to estimate the propensity scores and take interactive effects into consideration.

## *Regressing*

Regression may be used in several ways with propensity scores to remove biasing effects of confounding factors. It may be used to adjust the estimated effect of treatment for confounding factors in sample selection. It may use propensity scores to weight the sample so it is balanced on confounding factors in the treatment and comparison groups. A propensity score measure may also be used as a control variable in a multivariate model.

*Adjustment.* Data may be adjusted to remove bias from confounding variables by using the propensity scores as a covariate in a regression. The simplest way of adjusting with propensity scores is to use ANCOVA, where the propensity is treated as a covariate and an intervention/comparison variable is treated as a factor. The covariate is entered prior to the factor. The effect of the factor controlling for the covariate is the estimated average treatment effect (ATE) with bias from the measured confounding factors removed. When one is working only with program completers, the estimated effect would be a limited average treatment effect (LATE) estimate.

*Weighting.* Propensity scores may be used as weights to balance characteristics of the intervention and comparison groups. This may be done either with least squares or maximum likelihood weighted regression or with logit weighted regression. If one needs to use an alternative analytic procedure, such as Cox regression or hazard analysis, the sample can be weighted separately before doing the analysis.

In principle, weighting with propensity scores can be as effective as (and in some cases superior to) matching in removing bias (Abadie & Imbens, 2006; Busso, DiNardo, & McCrary, 2009). Weighting uses all the information about variance associated with the confounding factors. Matching, because it is a classification process, uses only enough information to identify a match (if there is one). In practice, however, propensity weighting has not proven better than matching. Initially, this was because the optimal weighting function had not been identified. Originally, one used the inverse of the propensity as the weight. This was then rescaled so the propensity mean was 1.0 (Glynn & Quinn, 2009; Imbens, 2004). This maintains the weighted sample size as equal to the unweighted sample size. However, as Guo and Fraser (2010) note, to achieve the full benefit of weighting, different weights are needed for the intervention and comparison groups, depending on whether one is estimating ATE or LATE. These weights were given in Chapter 3 in the discussion of propensity weighting.

The analysis by Busso et al. (2009) clearly shows that weighting is more efficient and has smaller mean squared errors in its estimates than matching, provided the proper weights with unit rescaling are utilized. Unfortunately, regression with propensity weights (also called inverse propensity weighted estimation or IPW) tends to have large standard errors with small samples. There is a question as to how reliable it is with small samples. Empirical inspection of the results when one has a small sample, however, can provide information on this issue. There are special circumstances when an augmented inverse probability weight (or AIPW) may outperform IPW, principally when there is high collinearity between the confounding variables and the selection process and when there may be misspecification in propensity or effect estimation. The reader is referred to Glynn and Quinn (2009) if IPW does not perform well in those circumstances. Weighting is discussed in more detail in Chapter 7.

*Controlling.* Since propensity scores are a linear function of the covariance between the confounding variables and the selection process, a propensity score variable can be used as a control variable to remove the effects of the confounding variables. This is not a common practice, but one can go back to the work of Cochran (1968), in which he showed that propensity scores remove as much difference as the multiple variables used to estimate them. This was the justification for using propensity scores. If, however, the individual predictors can be used as covariates in a regression analysis or ANCOVA, then so can the propensity score variable.

The principal obstacle to using propensity scores as control variables is their interpretation. Individual variables can each be given an interpretation. How does one interpret the propensity score that is a linear function of multiple variables? Research on latent variables suggests that multiple measures may have a common, underlying component (Goldberger & Duncan, 1973). If a propensity score is a composite index representing the selection process, then propensities do have an interpretation as a measure of the probability of treatment assignment. A propensity score variable may be used as a variable in one's analysis. It may be used as a control variable to remove group differences. In fact, when 2SLS regression is estimated as a single process (see Chapter 2), propensity scores are used in precisely that fashion.

Propensity score variables have not been used as much as control variables in estimating causal effects compared with matching, stratifying, or weighting. This has mainly been a result of greater interest in modeling the causal effects of treatments than in modeling sampling selectivity per se. If, however, researchers wish to build multivariate models that account for causal effects and describe the role of selectivity, as might be done with structural equation modeling, then using propensity scores as measures of selectivity factors would be appropriate. They have also not been used much with small samples because their desirable properties are more prominent with large samples. However, results reported by Holmes and Olsen (2011) show that sometimes their use with small samples can be justified.

## ADEQUACY AND SUFFICIENCY OF PROPENSITY ESTIMATES

Propensity estimates are statistically adequate when the variables modeling the selectivity process are not misspecified and the estimation procedure is appropriate. For the model to be correctly specified, one needs to use the strategies discussed in Chapter 2 to identify confounding factors that are related to treatment selection and to the outcomes. If there are variables omitted that are related to selection and outcomes and those variables precede the intervention, they should be considered for inclusion. If variables follow the intervention, they should not be included as confounding factors or used to estimate propensity scores.

The appropriateness of the estimation procedure depends on the level of measurement of the outcome variables, assumptions one makes about the relationship between the intervention and outcome, and whether there is evidence of errors in estimation. Matching measurement level with estimation procedure is usually not problematic. However, sometimes it is unclear as to whether a rank order variable is continuous or not. Discrete outcomes usually need different estimation procedures than continuous ones, for example, logit, rather than regression or ANOVA. Assumptions about the relationship between the intervention and outcome identify whether the effects will be linear or curvilinear across time, which also affects the estimation process. Previous chapters have discussed what evidence is used to identify possible errors in estimating propensities and effects on outcomes. This evidence must be inspected to have confidence that the effects were estimated without error and that the estimates are statistically adequate.

Propensity estimates are statistically sufficient when the procedure used to estimate the propensities is adequate, efficient, and unbiased. To be unbiased requires that there be no confounding variables omitted from estimation of the propensity (Rosenbaum & Rubin, 1983). This implies that there is no additional information that can be added to the estimate that will improve the estimate (Nelson & Noorbaloochi, 2010). Since inefficient estimators can have their error variances improved on, they are not sufficient estimates. Using an inefficient estimate of propensities may be a good approximation, but how good is not usually known. Only efficient estimates are sufficient estimates. This directly implies that to make strong causal inferences using propensity scores, one must use efficient estimators. If one uses an inefficient estimator, the most that can be said is that the evidence is suggestive of a particular causal influence—not that it demonstrates that particular influence.

As noted previously, an adequate propensity estimate is one whose selection model correctly represents the selection process (strong ignorability) or which only omits variables uncorrelated with the other confounders (when it meets weak ignorability). The assumptions of the procedure used to estimate the propensity scores must also correspond to the selection model.

When propensity scores are both statistically adequate and sufficient, one has grounds for making causal inferences from the intervention or treatment, for whose selectivity process the propensity scores have been estimated. This specifies a condition under which one may make causal inferences using propensity scores.

*Condition 6*: completeness of selectivity factors, arguments regarding temporal ordering of selectivity factors and appropriateness of estimation procedures for measurement levels, efficiency of estimation procedures, and use of model checking procedures that provide evidence that the estimates are not biased. When these requirements are met, one can reliably make inferences about the causal effects of quasi-experimental data. If any of these elements are lacking, the most that can be said is that the evidence is suggestive.

# CHAPTER 5

## PROPENSITY MATCHING

This chapter focuses on 1–1 and 1–many matching. It compares matching by propensities and by distance measures. It explains greedy matching and the use of calipers. It discusses problems of dropped cases, unequal cases in the groups, and assessing adequacy and sufficiency of these forms of matching.

Propensity matching is a highly efficient way of matching. It solves the dimensionality problem when multiple variables are used to match cases. It reduces the number of dimensions from the number of matching variables to that of a single dimension (Rosenbaum & Rubin, 1983). It is a balancing measure in the sense that it can be used to balance the distribution of characteristics between two groups so that they are the same (Austin, Grootendorst, & Anderson, 2007; Rosenbaum & Rubin, 1985). It also provides a standardized, consistent, and uniform process for matching cases. The result is a process that equally reduces bias across cases, referred to as equal percent bias reducing (EPBR; Rosenbaum & Rubin, 1985; Rubin, 1976b, 1976c). If a matching procedure is not EPBR, there may be situations in which the matching process will increase sample bias rather than decrease it. The equal bias reduction means that the bias is reduced proportionately across cases. If the bias between two groups is represented as

$$\hat{\beta}_s = \bar{W}_1 - \bar{W}_0 \,, \tag{5.1}$$

where $\hat{\beta}_s$ is the bias between the treatment and comparison groups, indicated by variable $S$, and $\bar{W}_1$ and $\bar{W}_0$ are the mean or percentage of a characteristic $W$ for the treatment and comparison groups, respectively. It is the difference of the mean or percentage in each group. In contrast, after EPBR matching, the bias is

$$\hat{\beta}_{sm} = P\left(\bar{W}_1 - \bar{W}_0\right), \tag{5.2}$$

where $\hat{\beta}_{sm}$ is the reduced bias in $S$, $P$ is the percentage reduction, and $\bar{W}_1$ and $\bar{W}_0$ are the mean or percentage of a characteristic $W$ for the treatment and comparison groups, respectively. The ideal for all matching procedures is to minimize $\hat{\beta}_{sm}$ equally in all subgroups of the sample. If the reduction is not the same in each group, the propensities are not EPBR, and the model of selectivity used to estimate the propensities needs revision, usually by adding interactive terms to the prediction equation.

Table 5.1 illustrates the violation of EPBR. It provides the results of a cross-tabulation from the Health and Retirement Study data in which respiratory difficulty before age 16 is related to the respondent's parents smoking. Using all cases, there is a relationship between parents smoking and respiratory disease before age 16 in the children. Adults whose parents smoked were 20% more likely to have respiratory disease than adults whose parents did not smoke. The results are statistically significant. Cases were matched by propensity scores with a nearest-neighbor procedure for a subset of 1,061 cases (to reduce the computational time). When the groups are matched, this relationship disappears.

However, when we compare subgroups of those who are satisfied with their life and those who are not, the results differ. The relationship remains absent among those who are satisfied with their life. It reemerges for those who are dissatisfied with their life. In fact, there is greater imbalance in the subgroup of adults dissatisfied with their life. The percentage difference is greater than that in the unmatched sample, and the Phi coefficient is stronger. The negative percent reduction in this group implies that the difference is even greater in this sub-sample. The pattern of the odds ratio is similar. In this case, one can debate whether satisfaction is a cause or a consequence of respiratory disease. Anxiety or anger from dissatisfaction can produce physiological symptoms and vice versa. What is critical here is that the bias reduction is not the same in both the groups. The nonsignificance for the satisfied group is not an artifact of fewer cases because the dissatisfied group has even fewer cases and does have a significant relationship. The relationship in the satisfied group is also in the opposite direction as that of the dissatisfied group. Clearly, there has not been equal percentage reduction of bias by this match. In such a circumstance, one would have to revise the selectivity model used to estimate the propensity scores and redo the analysis.

The failure of the nearest-neighbor matching in this instance is not a result of a deficiency of the nearest-neighbor procedure. It requires normally distributed propensities to produce the best matches. The propensities in this case have been shown above to be not normally distributed. The failure of the matching to be

| Table 5.1 | Unequal Percent Bias Reduction for Respiratory Difficulty | | | | | |
| --- | --- | --- | --- | --- | --- | --- |
| Groups | Percent | N | Phi | Percent Difference | Odds ratio | Percent Bias Reduction |
| Unmatched sample** | | | −.032 | 2.0 | 0.7993 | |
| Parents smoke | 10.8 | 7,756 | | | | |
| Parents don't smoke | 8.8 | 4,417 | | | | |
| Matched sample | | | −.029 | 0.9 | 0.684 | 55.0 |
| Parents smoke | 2.9 | 557 | | | | |
| Parents don't smoke | 2.0 | 504 | | | | |
| Matched, health satisfied | | | .033 | −1.0 | 1.584 | 50.0 |
| Parents smoke | 1.6 | 365 | | | | |
| Parents don't smoke | 2.6 | 349 | | | | |
| Matched, health dissatisfied* | | | −.129 | 4.6 | 0.118 | −180.0 |
| Parents smoke | 5.2 | 155 | | | | |
| Parents don't smoke | 0.6 | 192 | | | | |

*Difference between groups is significant at $p < .05$. **Difference is significant at $p < .01$.

EPBR is partially a result of the nonnormality of the data. With normally distributed data, nearest-neighbor matching will be EPBR (Rubin, 2006, p. 120). The failure of EPBR also illustrates that the percent reduction for the confounders is not similar. Figure 5.1 illustrates what a line chart of change in percentage difference might look like before and after matching for confounder variables. The lines are nearly parallel, indicating equal percent reduction. The lines are negatively sloped, which indicates that there is a reduction in the differences between the unmatched and the matched groups. Ideally, these differences are significant in the unmatched sample and not significant in the matched sample. Figure 5.2 illustrates what a similar line chart looks like without EPBR for parent-smoking confounders. The lines for allergies, respiratory disorder, and heart trouble are nearly parallel. The differences for these variables are significant in the unmatched sample and not significant in the matched sample. The uniform negative slopes indicate a reduction in bias. The lines for measles and childhood smoking, however, are not parallel to the others. They even cross, which indicates that in the matched sample, the differences in having measles are worse than in the unmatched sample. These differences for measles and for childhood smoking in the matched sample are statistically significant, further indication in a breakdown in EPBR.

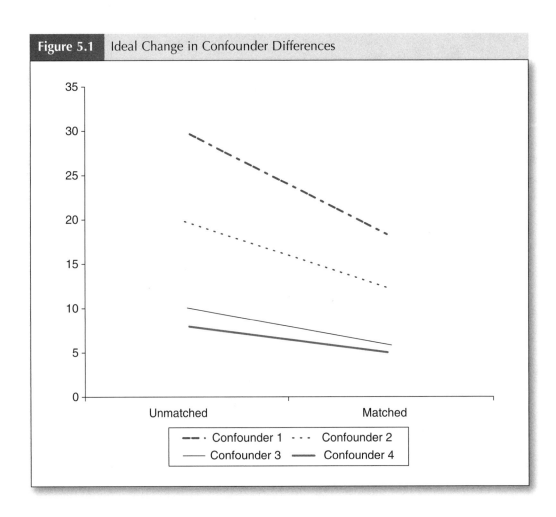

**Figure 5.1**     Ideal Change in Confounder Differences

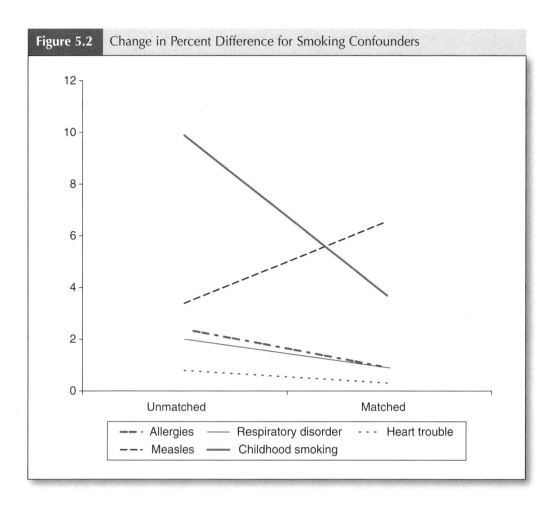

**Figure 5.2**    Change in Percent Difference for Smoking Confounders

## ONE-TO-ONE MATCHING

In the earlier discussion of 1–1 matching (also called one-to-one, pairwise, or paired matching), it was noted that each case in the treatment or intervention group was matched with one similar case in the comparison group. The principal advantage of this is that it forces the same number of cases to be in each group. Many statistical procedures are simpler when there are the same number of cases in each group. It is conceptually simpler to think of each person in one group associated with a single person in another group. It is also easier to write a statistical program that does 1–1 matching than to write a similar program that does 1–many matching.

One-to-one matching is generally preferred when the sample size of the treatment group is similar to the sample size of the comparison group. It allows using most of the cases and provides good matches. One-to-one matching is particularly preferred to 1–many matching when the closeness of the match is critical. One-to-many matching increases the number of cases in the matched sample. It increases statistical power and reduces error variances, but it is at the expense of how close the matches are. One-to-one always chooses the closest match between individual cases for those cases that are matched. One-to-many chooses a dissimilar match for the second and subsequent matches, provided there are no ties and there are other possible matches within the specified caliper. If one tries a 1–many match and differences remain between the treatment and comparison groups, then trying a 1–1 match may remove the differences—provided that too many cases don't drop out of the sample.

The principal disadvantage of 1–1 matching is that it results in many cases being dropped from analysis. It is frequent that at the end of a study there are different numbers of subjects in the intervention group and the comparison group. With this procedure, there can be no more matches than the number of cases in the smaller group. When the comparison group has been selected from available data, it may be much larger (e.g., everyone in a county receiving service other than the intervention). If the comparison group was created as part of the research design (where they start out with some common characteristics, even though they differ on others), there may be fewer subjects in the comparison group at the end of the study than in the intervention group. Since they are not necessarily receiving services for the issue that brought them to the study's attention and may be sitting on a waiting list, they may become discouraged or bored with the study and drop out. Even if they receive a placebo or conventional services for the issue, the benefits may not be large (otherwise, there would be little need for a new intervention). This may also lead to depression, anger, or envy if the comparison subjects prefer the new intervention. The author has evaluated treatment programs where comparison group members, referring to the intervention group, complained, "Why can't we have what they are getting?" The result in this circumstance is that there may be fewer members in the comparison group than in the intervention group at the end of the study. If one starts out with a large number of cases, this may not be much of a problem, although one still has to consider issues of differential sample mortality (discussed in Chapter 11).

Ties in the propensity scores create problems for 1–1 matching. If there are tied propensity scores in the comparison group, which subject does the intervention group member match with? The common solution is to randomize the order of cases tied on a propensity score. If the treatment group case randomly selects one of the ties, no bias will result. A problem is also created if there are ties in the intervention group. A similar solution is usually adopted: Randomize the order of cases among those having the same propensity score.

This approach to ties prevents bias when estimating causal effects. However, it adds random variance into the matches. It increases the standard errors of the coefficients. One is not using any information to get the best match among ties. Some matches with tied propensity scores may have different characteristics among confounding variables if two or more variables have different values, and increases to the propensity score contributed by one are offset by decreases of others. Using information about the cases can, in principle, result in matches having smaller error variances. For example, with tied cases, one can restrict the choice so that specified variables are matched exactly—such as on gender, race, symptomatology, or other characteristics.

Nearest-neighbor matching is a particularly popular form of 1–1 matching. It is conceptually easy to understand. Programs to do it are available for most major statistical packages. It also has desirable statistical properties. It performs well with normally or symmetrically distributed data. It tends to produce a similar amount of bias reduction across groups (a condition called equal percent bias reduction, discussed below). It can be done using propensities or distance measures in various combinations.

The principal disadvantage of nearest-neighbor matching derives from its use as a greedy matching procedure. It has high credibility as a matching procedure because it uses the best individual, paired matches possible. It provides very good, but not necessarily optimal, results, but it tends to have more unmatched cases than some alternative procedures. Various ways of doing nearest-neighbor matching are discussed below.

## *Matching Similar Propensities*

Matching propensity scores is a trivial activity when the scores are the same. This allows exact matching. One-to-one exact matching is a statistically optimal procedure because there are no differences in propensities between the matches. The total difference between the groups is zero. The effect of exact matching is illustrated in Figure 5.3, which simulates the difference between unmatched and matched groups.

Unfortunately, propensities to be matched often differ by some small amount. When they differ, there is a question as to how similar propensities should be to represent an acceptable match. When discussing calipers earlier, it was noted that a value within .20 of a standard deviation of the propensities is

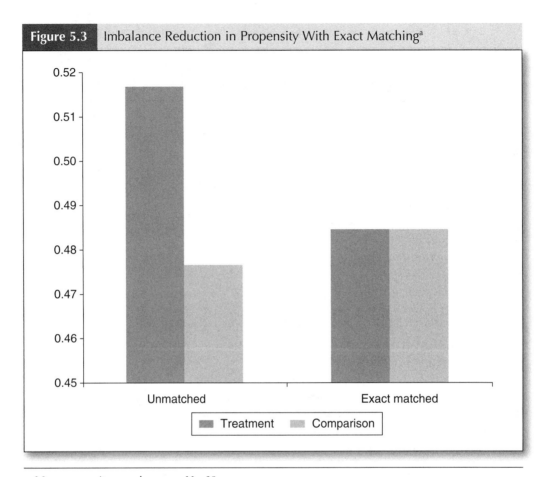

**Figure 5.3**     Imbalance Reduction in Propensity With Exact Matching[a]

a. Mean propensity score by group. $N = 30$.

sometimes used as a criterion. In the example in Table 2.1, the standard deviation of the propensity score was .060. Twenty percent of that is .012. If this were used as a criterion, many possible matches would be rejected. However, the remaining matches would be fairly close.

Austin (2010) has provided simulation evidence that using a .20 criterion produces results superior to other percentages of standard deviation. Accumulated practice has found it useful. However, there is no justification within statistical theory for the .20 criterion. The useful practice should not be disregarded, however, without justification. It is desirable to also have a criterion that derives from statistical theory. If the criterion has no basis in theory, the decisions made may be inconsistent with those decisions based on statistical theory. If it is kept in mind that propensities are probabilities or proportions, one can derive a confidence interval for each propensity and select only matches within the confidence interval. The formula for such a confidence interval is given in Equation 5.3:

$$\theta = \hat{p} \pm z\sqrt{\hat{p}(1-\hat{p})/n} \,, \tag{5.3}$$

where $\theta$ is the confidence interval, $\hat{p}$ is the estimated propensity, $z$ is the critical $z$ value for the confidence interval one wishes to use, and $n$ is the sample size. For a 95% confidence interval, $z$ is 1.96. In an example where the conventional criterion would be .012, the 95% confidence interval for a propensity of .50 would be .022, nearly twice the size of the informal criterion. This would provide more matches, but the result would have to be examined to see how much the imbalance is reduced. It should be noted that the confidence interval around a propensity decreases the closer one gets to either end of the range (0 or 1).

Using confidence intervals or significance tests provides stronger theoretical grounds for the match than accumulated practice. It is likely to remove group differences because this is equivalent to the covariates not differing statistically between the groups. While a formal proof has not been published, it is presented as a conjecture that if the difference in propensities between two groups is not statistically significant, then the overall difference in the covariates is not statistically significant.

With large samples, the confidence interval around the propensities is quite small. This criterion is likely to result in fewer matches with large samples; but the matches should be quite good. This again raises the trade-off between power and bias. A very narrow criterion will reduce or eliminate group differences and bias resulting therefrom, but it may also reduce the sample size to such a small number that a reasonable treatment effect cannot be detected. If the sample size reduction and loss of statistical power does not seem unreasonable, then one may use this criterion knowing that it follows in the traditions of significance testing, rather than solely following common practice, keeping in mind that there are different views on using significance tests.

Matching by propensity similarity may use other criteria. For example, one may define exact matching as occurring within a certain number of significant digits and saying that subsequent digits in a propensity score are not meaningful. This is also called **coarsened exact** matching. It is equivalent to using a tight caliper, since the same matches will result if one uses a caliper with one more significant digit. Nonetheless, it has high credibility and is generally effective in removing group differences. One may combine exact matching with calipers. Rosenbaum and Rubin (1985) matched one sample requiring that gender be matched exactly and that the propensity of possible matches be within a given range. They also combined propensity matching and distance matching. First, they selected a sample of comparison cases that met gender and caliper criteria. Then, they selected a single comparison case that was the closest Mahalanobis distance from the treatment case. This process is very similar to nearest-neighbor matching, except that the nearness is defined by minimizing the Mahalanobis distance rather than the propensity. Rosenbaum and Rubin have observed that the same matched pairs are often the result of such procedures. It seems likely to only make a substantive difference in modest-sized samples or if the covariate matrix of the confounders is nonellipsoidal (Rosenbaum & Rubin, 1983). When the covariate matrix is nonellipsoidal, propensity scores tend to produce a better result.

## Using Calipers

With respect to propensity scores, a caliper is a criterion by which to judge similarity of the propensity score in a comparison group with that in a treatment group. As noted above, it is common to use some ad hoc value of the raw propensity difference, such as .05, or of the normalized difference, such as .20. The range of values above and below the propensity that meets the criterion is the radius of the caliper. Matching procedures typically choose matches within the radius of the caliper. Nearest-neighbor matches choose the closest match within the radius. One-to-many matches choose all or some of the cases whose propensity score is within the radius. As noted above, the choice of the caliper is generally an ad hoc decision. It could correspond to some confidence interval around the average propensity of a group; but, at present, this is not generally considered.

While the radius of a caliper is conceptually used in defining the possible matches, some of the computer programs for matching use the radius in a manner that needlessly discards cases. For example, a nearest-neighbor, 1–1, greedy matching program may select a match that is also the nearest neighbor for another case. This second case, often a treatment case, is barred from matching with its neighbor because once a case is matched, it is deleted from the list of possible matches for subsequent cases. The second treatment case is then discarded if another nearest neighbor is not found. If there is more than one subject in the radius of the caliper for the first case, then it could be matched with its second nearest neighbor, and the original match can be linked with the next treatment case.

This principle is often used in optimized matching programs to increase the number of matches. It may trade off a slight reduction in degree of match for an increase in statistical power by having more cases. When optimizing procedures are used, the total error is generally reduced. For modest samples, the gain in statistical power may be more useful than a possible slight reduction in balance. The reduction in match can be compensated for by selecting a subsequent match whose difference has an opposite sign from that of the case whose match was changed, a procedure that is also used in some optimal programs. Nevertheless, even when a program doesn't make such adjustments to increase the number of cases, if a small caliper is chosen, bias will be reduced. The user may need to try several of the strategies mentioned above for adjusting propensities, selecting different matching procedures, or using a different caliper before finding one that removes group differences while retaining enough power to detect intervention effects that are there, always checking, however, whether the sample is too small to detect expected causal effects and whether there are no effects there to be detected. Checks on sample size will be discussed in Chapter 11.

## *Using Distance Criteria*

An exact match of two cases requires that they be the same in specified characteristics. They are dissimilar to the extent that their characteristics differ. If those characteristics are measured either with continuous indicators or using dichotomous variables indicating presence or absence, then the difference between the scores on those measures tells us about that difference. If we square those differences and add them up (because some are positive and others are negative), the result is total distance between the two cases. If those characteristics are all independent of each other, this is the Euclidean distance between the two cases. It can be used as a measure of the extent to which two cases do not match each other. The equation given by Mahalanobis (1936) for the Euclidean distance can be written as Equation 5.4:

$$d(\vec{x},\vec{y})_{\mathrm{E}} = \sqrt{\sum_{i=1}^{N} \frac{\left(x_i - y_i\right)^2}{\sigma_i^2}}, \tag{5.4}$$

where $d(\vec{x},\vec{y})_{\mathrm{E}}$ is the Euclidean distance between all the cases for $x$ and $y$, $N$ is the sample size, $x_i$ and $y_i$ are a set of characteristics for groups $x$ and $y$ having

$i$ number of characteristics, and $\sigma_i^2$ is the variance of each characteristic. In essence, this formula normalizes each squared difference by dividing it by the variance of the measure for that characteristic and then adding it up. The square root of this is taken to remove the exaggeration resulting from squaring the differences. Since it is common that confounding factors in selectivity are correlated among themselves, using the Euclidean distance measure is not usually appropriate for matching intervention and comparison group cases. A more generalized distance measure is needed.

Mahalanobis (1936) has generalized this principle to take into consideration the case where the characteristics are correlated with each other. See Equation 5.5:

$$d(\vec{x},\vec{y})_M = \sqrt{\sum_{i=1}^{N} \frac{\left(x_i - y_i\right)^2 \alpha^{ij}}{\sigma_i^2}}, \tag{5.5}$$

where $d(\vec{x},\vec{y})_M$ is the Mahalanobis distance between $x$ and $y$, $N$ is the sample size, $x_i$ and $y_i$ are a set of characteristics for groups $x$ and $y$ having $i$ number of characteristics, $\sigma_i^2$ is the variance of each characteristic, and $\alpha^{ij}$ is the inverse of covariance between $x_i$ and $y_i$ (the $x_i y_j$ element of the inverse covariance matrix).

If the confounding factors used to estimate propensities are not intercorrelated, then the Mahalanobis distance reduces to the Euclidean distance. Cases that have the minimum Mahalanobis distance between them are the best individual matches (Rubin, 1979).

As noted above, one may combine the use of propensity scores with Mahalanobis distance measures. While Rubin's earlier work (1979) suggested that Mahalanobis distance provided slightly better individual matches than using propensities, the combined use that he and Rosenbaum did in 1985 has not been compared with each individual use to document whether better overall matches result from the joint use. In principle, it should result in better matches because it uses information both from the propensities and from the Mahalanobis distances. That is undoubtedly why they used the combination in 1985.

## Dealing With Dropped Cases

Cases dropped by the matching process can bias the results only if subjects with a given characteristic are more likely to be dropped from one of the groups than the other. Cases dropped equally from both groups do not bias the estimates of causal effects. They do, however, reduce the statistical power of the sample. This can lead to a false-negative finding and bias the conclusions.

Four factors increase the loss of cases when matching: (1) presence of outliers in propensity distributions, (2) nonnormality of propensity distribution, (3) low degree of overlap between propensity distributions, and (4) a limited number of measured confounding variables. All these factors tend to produce different propensities estimated for subjects in different groups. Cases that have propensity estimates near 1.0 or 0.0 are unlikely to have matches. They may lead to complete or quasi-complete separation and inability to achieve a maximum likelihood solution for one's estimates. Outlier propensities also tend to have more separation between the values, which decreases the likelihood that propensities in one group will fall within the radius of the caliper of a propensity of a different group.

Nonnormality is related to the problem of outliers. Any skewed distribution of propensity scores is nonnormal and has outliers. If the particular matching procedure requires normally distributed propensities, then matching nonnormal distributions will not be statistically efficient or statistically adequate. The assumptions for the technique will not correspond to the data. Despite this, it may still be possible to obtain enough matches that the causal effect of an intervention can be estimated. It will not be the best estimate possible, but it may provide useful information so that better estimates can be made subsequently. Such results can be said to be suggestive of or consistent with a causal effect. If the results are not significant, the findings are still only suggestive of no causal effects because the sample may be underpowered. Sometimes the results are not very useful.

The problem of low overlap was introduced in Chapter 3. Figure 3.1 showed a small overlap between the comparison group and the treatment group, approximately 9% of the cases. If matching were done in this situation, more than 90% of the cases in the sample would be dropped. How much more than 90% would depend on the number of matches made within the overlapping 9%. If a researcher started with 1,000 cases to begin with (500 in the intervention group and 500 in the comparison group), then that would leave fewer than 45 matched pairs in the matched sample—not a satisfactory result. Increasing the caliper does not solve this problem. At most, one might pick up a few cases at the extreme end of the propensity distribution for each group. This is more likely to skew the distribution of matched propensities than to significantly increase the sample's statistical power.

Identifying characteristics for confounding variables that both groups are likely to have in common is one way of increasing the overlap. To the extent that common characteristics are identified and included in predicting propensities, this will tend to push the two distributions toward each other. Even so, it poses a dilemma. The characteristics have to occur in both groups to create overlap, but there still have to be some differences in the distribution of the characteristics between the groups, otherwise the measure will not represent a confounding factor. If a characteristic is the same in both groups, the measure of it will not correlate with the measure of the intervention group. It will not correlate with selectivity and not contribute to the estimate of the propensity. If a researcher has done a thorough job of reviewing all possible confounding factors present in a data set, there may be no other confounding factors to add. One may, however, try powers and transforms of variables already in the prediction equation—especially if the distribution of propensities is not completely normal to begin with. Sometimes, however, there are no other measures that can be added. In that case, the results of looking at the relationship between the intervention and the outcome can only be regarded as, at best, a correlation analysis that documents covariation and calls for further research having more extensive measures. It should not be described as documenting an effect. In such a situation, a researcher may try developing a more extensive theory of selectivity for the intervention so that subsequent research projects may benefit from his or her experience.

This leads to the fourth factor in sample attrition from matching, a limited number of measured confounding variables. The fewer the measured confounding variables, the fewer the possible predicted values for the propensity scores. This tends to leave the adjacent scores farther apart than if there are more predictors and more predicted values. Propensities fall in a bounded range. The more propensities you put in that range, the closer will be the average distance between adjacent propensity scores and the more likely that a comparison group propensity will fall within the caliper of an intervention group propensity. This is the reason, for example, that even adding more dichotomous predictors increases the number of possible predicted values and reduces the number of ties for propensities having ties. Other things being equal, adding more measures of confounders increases the number of matches.

Limited measured confounders also pose a problem theoretically. The variables used to predict propensity scores represent a model for the selectivity process. If there are few variables, it is the same as saying that there are only a few things that affect selection into or out of the intervention. While there may be instances where sample selection is affected by only a few things, there are good reasons to expect that many selectivity processes are affected by a number of things—especially for quasi-experimental designs where some factors are known to be not controlled.

This problem of limited measured confounders can only be addressed in the design stage of a study. When one is designing a quasi-experimental study (or even a randomized controlled trial, for that matter), a researcher needs to anticipate what else might be going on that can affect participation in the study. Experimenters need to know this to introduce appropriate control conditions. Quasi-experimenters need to know this to anticipate factors that affect sample selectivity and that pose a risk of confounding the results. The more factors are anticipated as possible confounders, the more they can be measured and controlled either by design or by statistical analysis. The consequence is that there will be more cases having propensity scores that meet the criteria for matching and less sample attrition.

## Computer Programs for One-to-One Matching

Programs for 1–1 matching are available using SPSS, SAS, Stata, and the R statistical language. The appendixes to the text and the book's website provide URLs for programs to do 1–1 matching, particularly nearest-neighbor matching. There are several principles for their use that they share in common. Before running a matching program, the user needs to have resolved any issues of nonnormality of the propensity distribution, insufficient overlapping of the distributions, and selected matching criteria. Most programs require data to be organized vertically, rather than horizontally. This means that there must be a variable that identifies the categories of intervention and comparison groups. Most of these programs are designed for one treatment group and one comparison group. The comparison group usually needs to be coded 0, and the treatment group needs to be coded 1. Cases in the treatment group whose propensity score exceeds the maximum propensity in the comparison group by the chosen criterion or caliper should be deleted from the file to be matched. None of those cases will find a match. Cases in the comparison group that are smaller than the minimum propensity in the intervention group by more than the criterion should also be deleted from this file. They will not find any matches either. Deleting these cases before beginning the matching process will speed up the matching programs with no reduction in resulting matches.

Choosing a program depends on three things: (1) the statistical programs with which one is familiar, (2) the statistic used for matching, and (3) the criteria used for matching. One-to-one matching programs are available in virtually all major statistical programs: SAS, SPSS, Stata, and R, as well as some stand-alone programs. One can choose the program with which one is most familiar to do 1–1 matching. However, not all statistical software has all the same features.

Some programs may have features that others do not. If one's chosen program does not have the desired feature, the user may need to either write a macro to augment the program (a sometimes demanding task) or choose to learn a new program. If all else fails, the R program alternatives are more extensive than the others, and a program can be written in R to meet user needs.

A program has recently been developed to do large-scale nearest-neighbor matching—the hd-PS program (Rassen & Schneeweiss, 2012). It combines elements of SAS, R, and Java. It is intended to screen and include a large number of predictor variables (up to 500). It has been tested and found satisfactory with relatively small samples (Rassen, Glynn, Brookhart, & Schneeweiss, 2011). It automates the process of selecting predictor variables by requiring that all the variables considered for inclusion must clearly precede the intervention. It has mainly been applied to medical and biological measures. Given that such measures may have correlated error terms across time, there is a need to check for correlation between the predictors and any intervening or contemporaneous variables (covariates). Such correlation could bias the results. Intervening variables may be included to examine the pathways by which an intervention has an effect. If such correlations are present, the variables identified by hd-PS might have to be used in a two-stage least squares regression to check the effect of that correlation.

Which statistic to use for matching is mainly a choice between propensity scores or distance measures. Propensity scores are preferred when a standardized measure produces adequate balance reduction. Distance measures, especially Mahalanobis distance, are preferred when propensity scores do not produce acceptably balanced matches. The preference for propensity scores has more to do with the ease of explaining how cases have equal probabilities of being in a group. Distance measures are harder to explain as summed, squared, and multivariate differences of means—although users familiar with analysis of variance should be able to explain it as minimizing the mean sum of squared differences between the matched cases.

One-to-one matching mainly uses four criteria for judging the degree of similarity: (1) exact matching, (2) coarsened exact matching, (3) radius (caliper) matching, and (4) augmented radius matching. Exact matching requires that the propensity or distance measure be the same within the statistical precision of the software. This produces the best matches. It is a special case of optimal paired matching, but it drops the most cases. If sufficient cases result, exact matching is preferred as a statistically optimal procedure. Coarsened exact matching is used to loosen the degree of match, perhaps requiring an exact match to two significant digits, when exact matching drops too many cases. As soon as the exactness is coarsened, the procedure is no longer an optimal match. Radius or caliper matching is used to increase the number of matches further. A small caliper can produce results similar to coarsened exact matching. Too generous a caliper, however, can leave the matched groups imbalanced after matching. If the groups remain imbalanced, the caliper can be reduced to produce a smaller radius and better matches—provided that it doesn't drop too many cases. Augmented radius matching extends the radius matching procedure to require that some characteristics be exact matches. Usually, these are qualitative characteristics (e.g., gender, race, marital status, or presenting symptoms) that might correlate with other confounding factors. Augmented radius matching generally produces better matches than radius matching alone, but not all software programs for 1–1 matching allow constraining the matches to require some characteristics be exact matches. This problem can be overcome by 1–1 matching subsamples of cases that have exact matches for the relevant criteria and then by combining the subsamples. These criteria for choosing a 1–1 procedure are summarized in Table 5.2.

## ONE-TO-MANY MATCHING

One-to-many matching may be greedy or nongreedy. All subjects meeting the criterion for a particular case may be matched with that case and then removed from the list. Alternatively, subjects that are matched with one case can have their match changed if a closer match subsequently appears. The latter strategy is used most often with optimal matching strategies, which may themselves be either 1–1 or 1–many. This section first discusses greedy 1–many strategies and then the nongreedy 1–many strategies.

| Table 5.2 | Selecting 1–1 Matching | |
|---|---|---|
| *Issue* | *Choices* | *Considerations* |
| Statistical program | SAS, SPSS, Stata, R, and S | Familiarity with program, need to use special features |
| Statistic used for matching | Propensity, Euclidean distance, and Mahalanobis distance | Ease of explanation, balance resulting from use |
| Criteria for matching | Exact, coarsened exact, radius/caliper, and augmented radius | Closeness of matches and balance, number of matches, desire for exact matches on special variables |

## Greedy Matching

One-to-many greedy matching is truly greedy. A treatment or intervention case is matched with as many comparison cases as possible, within limits specified. All of them are removed as possible matches for other cases. Subsequent intervention cases can only be matched with what's left. This increases the precision of the estimate of effect in the comparison group because it reduces the standard error of the coefficient (mean, percentage, ratio, or rate). On the other hand, it can increase the error variance of the coefficient in the intervention group. If treatment cases are dropped because their match was taken by an earlier treatment case, this reduces the number of matched treatment cases. One-to-many matching programs need to check if there is a subsequent treatment case that could be matched with one of those in a group already matched. It causes no loss in precision to match it with a treatment case otherwise dropped, especially if that case has a tied propensity score with the case already matched.

The big advantage of 1–many over 1–1 matching is the increase in sample size. This is especially advantageous if one has a moderate or modest number of intervention cases. It is one way of compensating for having a smaller number of treatment cases. It does, however, create issues related to unequal sample size in the groups. Those issues are discussed below. This section focuses on explaining the different types of 1–many matching, when they are used, and the trade-offs among the procedures.

Greedy 1–many matching has several advantages in addition to increasing the sample size. It is a faster procedure than optimal matching (which will be discussed in the next chapter). It is more likely to meet asymptotic (large sample) requirements of some of the analytical procedures for estimating treatment effects. It avoids some of the more complicated programming requirements of nongreedy procedures. It allows weighting cases on how similar they are to their matches.

Greedy 1–many matching has several disadvantages. It is, generally, less effective in reducing imbalance between the intervention and comparison groups. The additional cases matched are not as good matches, unless one is dealing with tied propensity scores. It is also a time-consuming procedure. The calculations can take hours to complete the matches with a moderate-sized sample and use of a personal computer. With smaller samples, it may even be faster to print out separate lists of propensity scores and IDs for the intervention and comparison groups and do the matching by hand—assuming one is consistently applying a standard criterion.

There are several varieties of 1–many matching. Like 1–1 matching, the most common are nearest neighbors, radius, and coarsened exact. The difference is that the matching procedures select some or all of the cases in the comparison group that meet the matching criteria of the treatment group. Nearest-neighbors matching follows the same procedures for nearest-neighbor 1–1 matching except that, instead of selecting only the one nearest neighbor, the program selects $k$ nearest neighbors. This procedure may be combined with radius matching to limit how different the nearest neighbors are allowed to be. One–$k$ radius matching defines a caliper and selects all matches (or a specified number of matches) within the radius.

Common 1–many procedures include "1–$k$" matching and kernel matching. The 1–$k$ matching involves selecting a specified number of matches that meet a criterion. For example, 1–2 matching could select the two closest neighbors, the two cases closest within a caliper radius, or the two closest within the coarsened exact radius. The number $k$ should be fewer than the number of variables used to estimate the propensity score. Gu and Rosenbaum (1993) have shown that the efficacy of the matches decreases as the number of matches approaches the number of predictive variables. They have shown that increasing $k$ beyond seven matches does not greatly improve the results. Austin (2008) has also shown, using simulated data, that using more than six matches does not significantly improve the results. In addition, it greatly increases the computational time to achieve the matches.

Kernel matching is a procedure that matches cases having a similar propensity and averages the effect estimate for those cases. The kernel is a mathematical function that defines how many and in what ways the effects are averaged. It is used most often when 1–$k$ matching does not produce satisfactory results. The effect is estimated for subgroups of cases. This is a generalization of calculating effects for samples stratified by propensity score and averaging them. There is more than one way of grouping cases and averaging the effects within a group. It is similar to calculating a smoothed regression line within a scatterplot when one has curvilinear relationships, which is why it is also referred to as nonparametric regression or local linear regression. In the special case where the effect is averaged for all the cases, the result is the same as the difference-of-differences method. An example is given in Figure 5.4. In this example, the kernel is the average of six adjacent data points. This results in four local linear lines that approximate the true curve.

There is more than one possible kernel. This is mainly because the number of cases to be averaged depends on how curvilinear one thinks the relationship is. The choice of the number of cases depends on one's professional judgment.

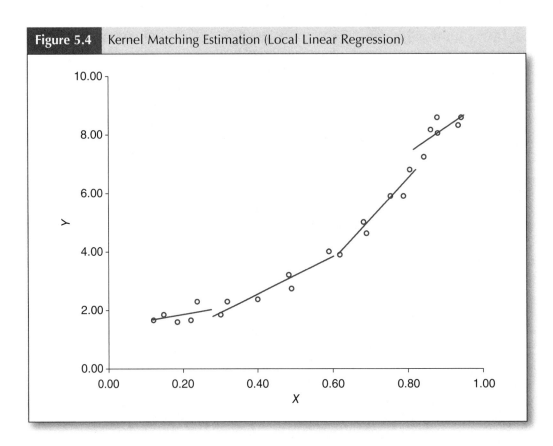

**Figure 5.4**   Kernel Matching Estimation (Local Linear Regression)

Arithmetic averaging is most commonly used. Kernel matching is a greedy procedure when cases to be averaged are not used in multiple averaging. The groups to be averaged do not overlap. This results in a coarser "smoothed" line than if the groups overlap. When they do, the result is similar to using a moving average.

### Nongreedy Matching

The two most common nongreedy, 1–many procedures are full matching and kernel matching where the cases averaged may overlap between groups. **Full matching** might be characterized as many–many matching, since each intervention or comparison case is matched with as many matches (within a specified criterion) as possible. It isn't a simultaneous many–many matching procedure. It uses a sequential process to select multiple interventions for each comparison case and multiple comparisons for each treatment case if there are multiple cases that meet the matching criterion.

Full matching can produce more matches than other 1–many procedures (Hansen & Klopfer, 2005). Full matching produces optimized matches for the criterion specified, but it can be constrained in ways that make it nonoptimizing. Full matching allows specifying constraints (e.g., women not matched with men, college graduates not matched with high school dropouts, or those with substance abuse not matched with those without). If one changes the constraints, different results can be obtained. The results are always optimized for whatever the constraints are, but constraining on a confounding variable may produce estimates that are different from when confounders are not constrained. When the constraints imposed are the same as those used for another optimized procedure, the results should be virtually the same. Any differences would be a result of reordering of cases when randomizing ties. Full matching will be discussed in more detail in Chapter 6.

A particular advantage of 1–many matching is that it increases the precision of an estimate of treatment effects. This is demonstrated by comparing the standard errors for estimated treatment effects for the treated (ETT) in a greedy analysis with the standard errors of ETT's estimated using 1–many procedures. This comparison uses the **relative risk ratio**, which is the ratio of the standard error under one procedure divided by the standard error under another procedure (see Equation 5.6, provided by Hansen, 2004).

$$R(S, \bar{S}_{w}) = S / \bar{S}_{w}, \tag{5.6}$$

where $S$ is the standard error using one procedure, and $\bar{S}_{w}$ is the standard error under weighted full matching. The standard error for the 1–many matching estimate is smaller than paired greedy matching.

## Using Calipers

Calipers facilitate 1–many matching. It is usually possible to find a caliper that will include multiple matches within its radius. The disadvantage is that it lowers the ability of the matches to reduce the group differences. Researchers who do radius 1–many matching may have to try more than one caliper to find a value that acceptably reduces differences and retains enough cases. Sometimes there is no caliper that will accomplish this task. Moreover, if using a caliper fails to find an acceptable result, coarsened exact matching will also fail. In such a situation, nearest-neighbor matching within a radius may find an acceptable balance and number of cases; but this is not a certainty. Sometimes, no matching procedure can accomplish both tasks.

### Using Distance Criteria

Mahalanobis distance measures have a few advantages over propensity scores for 1–many matching. Since they are not constrained in their range of values like propensities, they have greater variation in the values. Work by Rosenbaum and Rubin (1983) suggests that using Mahalanobis distances may slightly improve the matches. However, Rubin (1979) notes that because matching is a classification procedure using a range of values, most of the matches produced are the same between the two methods. In the above example regarding babies in the household, the matches were identical for all the 1–1 procedures—propensity as well as Mahalanobis.

In the above example for babies in the household where 1–3 matching was done, the matching was repeated using Mahalanobis distance measures. Of the potential 1,000 matched pairs, there were only 2 pairs where the matches differed. The imbalance reduction was the same. The estimated effect was virtually identical.

## MANAGING UNEQUAL CASES IN GROUPS

When multiple matches are made with a single intervention case, this can create heteroscedasticity in the variances of the outcome measures. One way of dealing with this is to weight the cases based on how similar they are to their match. This is similar to the same weighting procedure as that used in weighted regression, only the weights are applied to the differences between the groups.

Weighting also allows compensating for unequal cases in each group. When there is a large disparity of cases between groups, it is useful to weight the cases so that the results are not dominated solely by one group. Two different weighting procedures are used. Some weight according to how many cases are in each group. Others weight according to what the variance of the measure is in each group. Weighting according to the number of cases is a simpler procedure and often produces good results. If one weights according to the inverse of the proportions, rescaled so that the inverse proportions sum to one, this will treat the two groups as having the same number of cases. One can weight using variances in two ways. If one wishes to make the variances of the two groups equal, one weights by the inverse of the variances. If one wishes the total variance of the measures to be utilized, one weights according to the variance in each group.

The choice of weighting procedure depends on what the objectives are. If one wishes to get results as if the number of cases were equal, then weighting by numbers is appropriate. If one wishes to remove heteroscedasticity and treat the groups as having equal variances, then weighting by rescaled inverse variances is appropriate. If one regards the unequal variances as reflecting true differences between the groups and wishes to take that into consideration, then weighting by the variances is appropriate.

## ASSESSING ADEQUACY AND SUFFICIENCY OF MATCHING

Earlier in this chapter, it was mentioned that exact 1–1 matching was a special case of optimal paired matching. If the distribution of the propensity scores is unimodal and symmetrical, then exact 1–1 matching is statistically adequate and sufficient. Adding more information will not produce better matches. Note, however, that if the propensity distribution is not unimodal and symmetrical, then the matched sample resulting will not be statistically sufficient. Adding more information may produce a symmetrical distribution. Matching on that may become statistically sufficient. With nonsymmetrical distributions of the propensities, the most that can be said of causal effect estimates is that they suggest or are consistent with a given causal effect. They do not demonstrate or show a causal effect unless a sufficient procedure is used.

Coarsened exact matching can be adequate and sufficient. If the coarseness of the exact matching is close enough to exact matching that all the matches produced by exact matching are included in the coarsened exact matched sample, then the coarsened exact matched sample will be statistically adequate and sufficient. If there is a slightly less coarse sample that includes all the exact matches and additional matches, it would be statistically sufficient—rather than the coarser exact matched sample. Typically, however, even if a coarsened exact matched sample is not statistically sufficient, it is very close to the result of a sufficient procedure. Estimates of a sufficient coarsened exact sample may differ by only a small amount from a nonsufficient, but slightly coarsened, exact matched sample.

Nearest-neighbor matching is adequate and sufficient in some circumstances. If, for each case, there is only one nearest neighbor and that neighbor is not also nearest to some other treatment propensity (i.e., if no comparison group members share being nearest neighbor with more than one treatment member), then nearest-neighbor matching is statistically sufficient. The match cannot be improved on. In this restricted circumstance, the match is optimal. In all other circumstances, nearest-neighbor matching can be improved by using additional information. It is, however, still adequate.

Caliper (radius) matching is statistically sufficient when the caliper is close enough to exact matching that no less coarsened matching would improve the balance between the groups. One can normally know this only by trying less coarsened matches to discover if the match improves while maintaining enough cases to have the sensitivity of the statistical tests be maintained.

Full matching is a statistically adequate and sufficient procedure. It uses all the available information to make the matches. As such, there is no additional information to improve the match. Full matching always has an optimal solution. When the optimum is achieved, no better solution can be found for the available information. If there are unobserved confounders, however, the results may be improved on, and the solution may not be statistically sufficient. It depends on making a credible case that there are no remaining unobserved confounders.

Kernel matching is also statistically adequate. As a nonparametric procedure, it does not produce the most efficient estimates. If there is a more efficient estimator available in a given situation, then kernel matching is not statistically sufficient. However, sometimes it is sufficient. There may be no parametric procedure that meets the requirements for statistical adequacy when the data are nonnormal and curvilinear and the statistic to be estimated does not have well-defined parameters.

## SUMMARY

The choice of matching procedure depends on several considerations.

1. Among the 1–1 matching procedures, exact matching is preferable because it is optimal, statistically adequate, and sufficient. However, it may not produce enough pairs.

2. If exact matching does not produce enough matched pairs, coarsened exact matching can be tried. It still may not produce enough matched pairs, and it is not statistically optimal.

3. Nearest-neighbor or caliper matching can be tried if coarsened exact matching does not produce enough matched pairs. If the neighbors are

too far apart or the caliper too large, insufficient balance reduction may occur or there may still be too few matched pairs.

4. If none of the above procedures produce enough matched pairs, a 1–many approach can be tried. Using more than three or four "many" matches has diminishing returns in precision of estimating treatment effects.

5. If none of these procedures produce enough matches or a stable estimate of treatment effects, an optimized matching procedure will be needed. For that, see the next chapter.

# CHAPTER 6

# PROPENSITY SCORE OPTIMIZED MATCHING

This chapter focuses on optimized matching. It presents optimizing criteria, explains procedures for achieving optimized matches, and assesses the adequacy and sufficiency of the optimized match. It clarifies differences in the procedures for maximizing the number of cases with those for minimizing the distances between groups. It compares optimized matching with the more general approach of genetic matching and discusses the trade-offs between them.

Researchers have referred to matching procedures that minimize the total distance or dissimilarity between matched cases as optimal matching as well as optimized matching (Rosenbaum, 1989; Rubin, 1979). An optimized matching solution reduces average pregroup imbalance to a minimum, though it may leave some individual confounders slightly imbalanced. If total baseline imbalance cannot be reduced to zero using optimized procedures, there is no other procedure that can produce a better result, given the selection of confounding variables chosen to estimate the propensity score. An optimized solution with paired matching, however, may produce balance at the expense of using up so many cases that there are not adequate degrees of freedom to judge statistical significance of the findings. This is not likely when doing 1–many or full optimized matching. The full matching and genetic matching procedures discussed in this chapter allow 1–many optimization.

Optimized solutions that use 1–many matching drop fewer cases than paired matching. Such matching increases the total number of cases in the group having the many matches, although there still needs to be enough cases in the "1" group (usually treatment) to have a reliable estimate of the treatment effect.

For pairwise optimization, if sensitivity analysis indicates that too many cases have been dropped to get a reliable result, then a less-than-optimal matching procedure may be needed to retain sufficient cases. Alternatively, pairwise matching may have to be abandoned for 1–many matching. There is a trade-off between having enough cases and reducing enough imbalance. It is an empirical question whether the less optimal procedure will reduce the imbalance enough to say the groups are not significantly different. If the imbalance is not fully removed, the results may be biased; but the results may be approximately correct. This is analogous to using ridge regression when it reduces the mean square error of the estimate by being willing to accept a small amount of bias. On the other hand, using a 1–many optimization procedure will also retain cases; but some users regard the results as less credible if paired matching is not used.

However, if an adequate number of cases are retained by a greedy matching procedure when not all the imbalance is removed, then an optimized approach can be tried. This will provide the best chance for an unbiased estimate of the intervention effects. Like other matching procedures, however, one has to examine the imbalance after achieving an optimized result. Even an optimized solution can still have imbalance. Important confounders might have been unmeasured or not included when estimating the propensity scores. Derivatives of the propensity distribution may not exist or they may not be consistently estimated by standard estimation procedures. One must also examine the sensitivity of the results to judge the extent to which they are reliable.

Since greedy matching procedures can sometimes produce solutions that are also optimal solutions, the two approaches can produce the same result. Most of the time, the results are similar. The data typically need to be well behaved before greedy and optimal solutions converge. With poorly behaved data, the results can diverge. An optimized solution minimizes the total distance between all the matched pairs. Since minimizing the total difference also minimizes the average difference, an optimized solution is conceptually equivalent to minimizing average pregroup differences.

An optimized solution can be obtained using more than one strategy. If the propensity scores are symmetrically distributed, have a single mode, and overlap between the intervention and comparison groups (a circumstance that might be called well-behaved data), one can use standard matrix inversion procedures to obtain an optimized match. With well-behaved data, solutions that minimize differences are easily estimated using derivatives of the distribution. When derivatives of the distribution of propensity scores are not identified, finding solutions that minimize differences is often a multistage process of revising the selection model and using iterative optimized matching. An optimized solution may also be derived from network control theory (Rosenbaum, 1989; Sekhon, 2011) or from graph theory (Sekhon, 2011).

This issue is similar to the problem of finding the shortest route of a delivery truck. A greedy approach does this sequentially by choosing the shortest distance between adjacent stops. If the streets have a grid layout with no one-way streets, the solution is simple. If streets have odd angles and some are one-way, the solution can be far from simple. An optimized approach finds a solution by minimizing the total distance traveled. Minimizing the total distance also minimizes the average distance. Hence, there are no matched pair greedy solutions that are better than optimized solutions. This means optimized results are also statistically sufficient. On the other hand, because greedy solutions usually provide adequate matches and occasionally produce optimal matches, the improvement of an optimized solution over a greedy solution may sometimes be relatively small or nonexistent.

Greedy solutions are more likely to produce suboptimal results when large calipers are used in matching (Rosenbaum, 1989). Given that calipers are commonly used with propensity matching, the adequate solution of a greedy match is an approximation of the optimal match. Experience suggests that very poor results for greedy matching is uncommon, except when certain conditions are violated—mainly if important confounders are omitted from estimating the propensity scores or the distribution of the propensity scores is not well behaved.

This notion of well-behaved data is important in understanding when greedy matching is nearly as good as optimized matching. The parameters of well-behaved data can be easily and rapidly estimated. A continuous, symmetrical distribution with a single mode characterizes well-behaved data. Such distributions usually can have their parameters estimated using a simple process. The most well-behaved data distribution is the normal distribution. Its parameters are estimated using the sample mean and variance. The parameters of a well-behaved data distribution can also be estimated using the derivatives of the distribution. The inversion of a matrix of well-behaved data is easily achieved using a standard algorithm, such as the Newton–Ralphson algorithm. The conditions under which greedy matching doesn't work well do not apply to well-behaved data.

An example of data that are not well behaved is provided in Figure 6.1. In this figure, the variance around the regression line between the two variables var001 and var002 is not oval shaped. It is dumbbell shaped because the distributions of both variables are bimodal with few cases in the middle. In addition, it appears that the lower half of the data might have a different slope than the upper half. Standard optimized matching should not be used when the confounding variables have such relationships.

| Figure 6.1 | Scatterplot of Poorly Behaved Data |
|---|---|

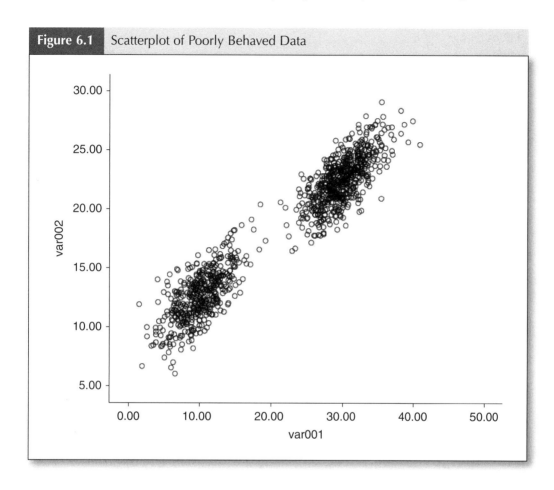

When data are not well behaved, estimation of the parameters of a distribution and inversion of a data matrix are far more complicated. They may even be impossible. Optimization algorithms for matching make use of these more complicated procedures. They are more computationally intensive, but they are more robust against violations of a supposition that the data are well behaved. If the data are approximately well behaved, the results of greedy procedures and optimized procedures will be similar. If the distribution of propensity scores is not well behaved, the results will diverge.

Figure 6.2 compares greedy matching with optimized matching when both use pairwise matches. It shows how a greedy, nearest-neighbor match would sequentially select each of the four possible pairs using a caliper of .05. In contrast, the optimized matching examines more than one possible match to a case and considers the total distance between the cases in the group. For the

| Figure 6.2 | Greedy Versus Optimized Matching | | | |
|---|---|---|---|---|
| | Greedy Matching | | Optimized Matching | |
| Cases | Treatment Group Propensities | Comparison Group Propensities | Treatment Group Propensities | Comparison Group Propensities |
| | .06 ⟶ *0.60* | ▶ .06 *0.60* | .06 *0.60* | .06 *0.60* |
| | .45 ⟶ | ▶ .55 | .45 | .55 |
| | .44 ⟶ | ▶ .45 | .44 | .45 |
| Sum of differences | | 0.11 | | 0.05 |
| Number of matches | | 3 | | 2 |
| Mean difference | | 0.037 | | 0.025 |

optimized solution, the first case is matched with the second case because that results in a smaller average distance between the propensity scores for all the matched pairs. It results in a smaller total imbalance and a smaller average imbalance. The trade-off is that one case of the treatment group and of the comparison group is dropped from analysis. It results in fewer cases and fewer degrees of freedom for analysis. For large samples, this may not be a significant problem. For moderate to small samples, however, pairwise optimization definitely requires checking the results for sensitivity to sample size to be sure that one retains enough cases to produce reliable results.

There may be more than one solution that results from a specific optimization procedure. There may be more than one combination of matched pairs that produces the same minimized total distance between the groups. This is likely when cases have tied propensity score estimates. Since the order of tied cases is randomized in most matching algorithms, multiple runs of the same data may select different cases tied on propensity scores for a given match. This is true for optimized pair matching and for optimized full matching. In the latter case, however, it is only an issue if the number of tied pairs exceeds the maximum number of matches permitted for individual cases. These differences in the estimates of treatment effects are typically small. This is one reason why it is useful to report the confidence interval for estimated effects. The slightly different estimates may all fall within the same confidence interval. If the number of tied pairs is less than or equal to the number of matches permitted in a full matching estimate, only one solution is possible.

The theory of full matching assumes that all the cases are used, that there are no limits on the number of cases that may be matched with a reference case (Stuart & Green, 2008). Theoretically, there is only one solution. However, the computational time increases geometrically with the number of matches. It may take so long that the user decides to limit the computation to obtain a result within a reasonable amount of time. Thus, users may impose a limit on the maximum number of matches when doing full matching.

A similar problem exists for genetic matching. The matches are improved iteratively. As long as an improvement can be detected using specified criteria, it will continue to try improving the matches. This, too, can take a long time. In some circumstances, it may not ever end. It may find itself in a loop of changing matches back and forth repeatedly. Consequently, practical considerations dictate that limits be placed on the number of iterations or on the criteria that are met for accepting a solution. The program developed by Sekhon and Mebane (1998) allows also using parallel processors to reduce the computational time of genetic estimation.

The estimated effects are unlikely to be much different for multiple optimized solutions. The multiple samples will differ only on the small number of tied cases that exceed the maximum number permitted in the estimate, but they may have a slight difference. Cases tied on their propensity scores are likely to have the same characteristics on the confounding variables, but this is not a certainty. The estimated effect may be slightly different because the confounding variables can be different when their effects counterbalance each other to produce the same propensity score. Factors other than observed confounding variables might also be in play.

## FULL MATCHING

Full matching is an optimized 1–many matching procedure. It has several advantages. As a 1–many procedure, it is more likely to preserve sufficient cases for meaningful analysis. As an optimizing procedure, no greedy solution can produce a more balanced result than full matching. Programs for doing full matching also have more flexibility in combining propensity matching with Mahalanobis distance matching and in imposing constraints on the solutions.

Full matching is accomplished by creating subgroups based on each unique value of the treatment group. As many of the comparison group cases are matched with the subgroup treatment case as possible. This allows computing the mean value of the comparison group for that value of the treatment group and provides an estimate of the treatment effect for that value of the treatment group. In a similar fashion, the procedure can be reversed and subgroups of the comparison group created, treatment cases matched for values of the comparison group, and estimates of the treatment effect for values of the comparison group provided.

If one creates a subgroup for each value of the propensity scores for the treatment group, there may be only one or a few cases in each group. This increases the standard errors for estimating the treatment effects. Consequently, it is common practice to reduce the number of groups so that an adequate number of cases are there in each group. Given that covariance adjustment is sometimes also used within groups (Stuart, 2010), it may be necessary to combine groups to have enough degrees of freedom within each group. The goal is to have as many groups as possible while preserving enough degrees of freedom within groups to proceed with the analysis. If too many groups are combined, there may be only a few left. An extreme case of this is if one creates five strata, similar to the stratification approach of propensity matching. The difference, however, is that matches are selected for the strata based on optimal criteria, rather than greedy criteria. With well-behaved data, the results will differ by very little. With less well-behaved data, even with five groups the results may differ.

If the values of the treatment group have a linear relationship with those of the comparison group, the estimated treatment effect of the treated, or ETT, can be calculated by averaging the estimates. The linearity of this relationship is usually easy to see using a Q–Q plot of the effect values for the two groups. If the relationship is not linear and the distribution of the effect coefficients is symmetrical and monomodal, the treatment effect can still be computed by averaging the estimated treatment effects. If the relationship is nonlinear and the distribution of effect coefficients is skewed or discontinuous, it is better to use a genetic matching estimate of the treatment effect.

Full matching is available using the **optmatch** program available from Hansen (2004). He provides an example of full matching (see Figure 6.3). In his examination of the effects of coaching on SAT (Scholastic Aptitude Test) score performance, he compared standardized bias measures for the unmatched sample with that of the full matching sample. For every pretest measure, the imbalance in the full matching sample (the black dots) is smaller than for the unmatched sample (the white dots).

A particular advantage of full matching is that it increases the **precision** of an estimate of treatment effects. A more precise estimate has a smaller error

---

**Figure 6.3    Balance of Unmatched and Full Matching**

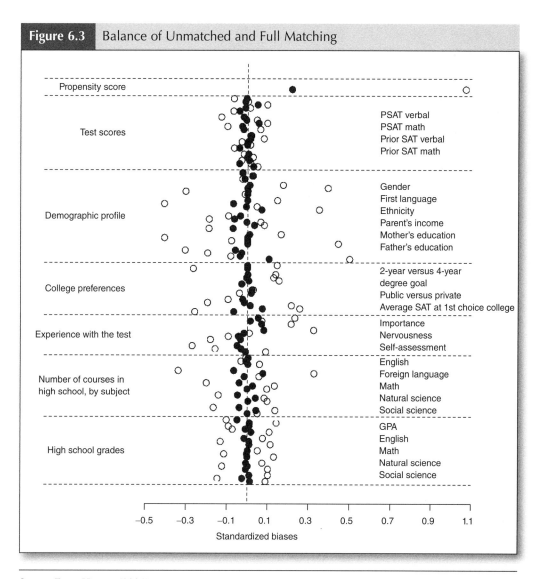

*Source.* From Hansen (2004).

*Note.* PSAT, Preliminary Scholastic Aptitude Test; GPA, grade point average. White dots represent unmatched imbalance in mean propensity score. Black dots represent full matching imbalance. Values closer to zero have the least imbalance.

variance. Hansen (2004) demonstrates this by comparing the standard errors for ETTs in his analysis of the effect on SAT scores of coaching students. He compares the standard errors using the **relative risk ratio**. The formula for the relative risk ratio is given in Equation 6.1:

$$R(S, \tilde{S}) = S / \tilde{S}, \tag{6.1}$$

where $R(S, \tilde{S})$ is the relative risk ratio, $S$ is the standard error for the unmatched sample, and $\tilde{S}$ is the standard error for the full matched sample. In Hansen's study, the standard error for the full matching estimate was about 25% smaller than that for 1–1 greedy matching.

While full matching may occasionally have greater imbalance for individual confounders, it is usually the other way. Most confounders will be more balanced. Stuart (2010) provides an example where she compares the standardized differences between intervention and comparison groups with and without full matching (see Figure 6.4). In this figure, all of the standardized differences for the unmatched data (labeled "all data") are larger than those for the full matched data.

Full matching may be done with propensity scores alone, with distance measures (e.g., Mahalanobis distance), or with both propensities and distance measures. When both are used, the difference measure that is minimized is a combination of the propensity scores and the distance measure for the confounding variables. Sometimes variables other than those used to estimate the propensity score are included among the distance measures. They may be added if they have particular substantive, policy, or theoretical significance. One may also impose constraints on the matches. For example, the matches can be restricted to only match cases of the same gender, symptomatology, economic, social, or psychological classification.

## OPTIMIZING CRITERIA

There are common principles that optimized matching programs follow. All optimal solutions maximize total similarity and minimize total distance for the cases selected. They all may impose constraints on matching for specified variables. Such variables may be required to match between the pairs. Optimization is always done by minimizing the total distance or the total dissimilarity between the two (or more) groups for propensity score or for the predictors of the propensity scores (when using Mahalanobis distance)—within the constraints that are imposed. Alternative measures of distance or dissimilarity can

| Figure 6.4 | Absolute Standardized Difference in Means |
|---|---|

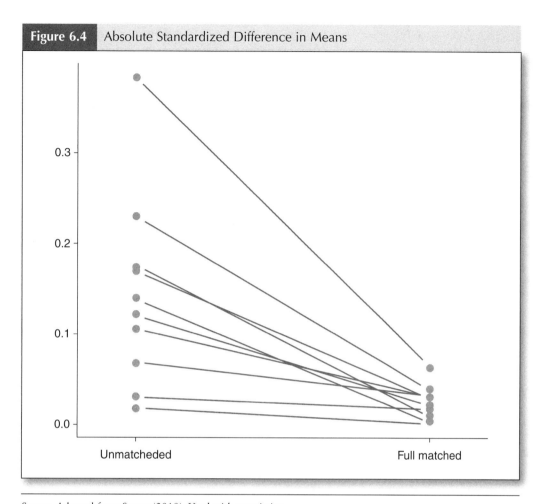

*Source.* Adapted from Stuart (2010). Used with permission.

be used. Mahalanobis distance and propensity score difference are the two most commonly used (Sekhon, 2007). The measures chosen may be used singly or in combination. Most optimizing programs allow the user to minimize group differences for whichever measures are used.

However, different researchers may use diverse criteria to achieve the optimized matches. There are trade-offs in the choice of criteria. Optimizing on the propensity score minimizes overall differences, but some individual covariates may remain imbalanced. Optimizing on Mahalanobis distance is more likely to balance every observed confounding variable, though some may have a different balance than when using propensity scores. However, using Mahalanobis distance measures may produce poorer results if variables contributing to the distance are nonspherically distributed (Rosenbaum & Rubin, 1983). Nonspherical distribution among the variables can be seen if scatterplots of these variables do not follow an oval shape. Technically, this means the distribution of the errors do not uniformly get smaller near the upper and lower bounds of the scatterplot. The error variances are heteroscedastic. This is also possible if some of the variables are dichotomous with a lopsided distribution. Such data are typically not well behaved, and use of a nonparametric optimization procedure is recommended in this situation.

Figure 6.1 above is an example of two such variables. If we look at a bar chart of a similar variable, var004, we see that the distribution is definitely not normal (see Figure 6.5). It is clearly bimodal. Further evidence that the distribution

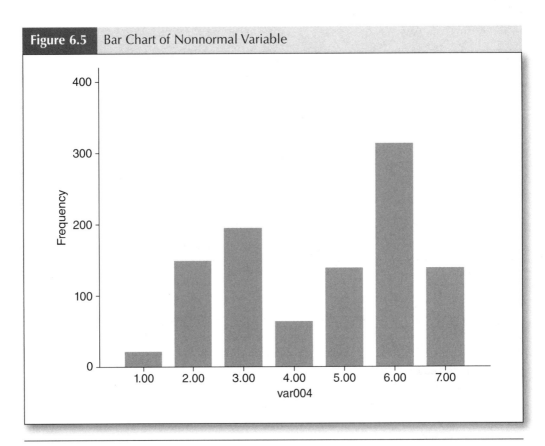

**Figure 6.5**  Bar Chart of Nonnormal Variable

*Note.* Mean = 4.6; Median = 5.0; Mode = 6.0; Skewness = −.303;[a] Kurtosis = −1.295.[a]

[a]Statistic is significant at $p < .01$; $N = 1,024$.

is not well behaved is provided by the fact that the mean, median, and mode are all different and the skewness and kurtosis statistics are statistically significant. In addition, the K–S test of normality indicates less than a 0.01% chance that the distribution is normal.

Optimization may also use calipers. This is equivalent in full matching to giving some estimates a weight of zero when the difference in propensity or difference exceeds some criteria. It is the opposite of requiring certain matches (i.e., constraining the matches) where the weight is set at a maximum value. When the caliper is set to zero, this is equivalent to requiring exact matching. When the caliper is set close to zero, it might be regarded as equivalent to coarsened matching. Larger values of a caliper may be used for extremely large differences (paired differences having extremely small weights) to exclude those matches that might undermine the credibility of the analysis. Such exclusion is not strictly required by the computational process, since the pairs have small weights. It might be necessary, however, to promote social acceptance of the findings. If the analysis is run with and without calipers and the results are very similar, it can be more easily argued that excluding such cases is statistically unnecessary.

## OPTIMIZING PROCEDURES

There is more than one procedure for obtaining an optimized solution, even though they may produce the same result. Full matching, derivative-based optimized matching, genetic matching, and matching with variable controls are the principal options. Full matching has been discussed already in this chapter. Derivative-based optimized matching utilizes the derivative of the propensity distribution to optimize the similarity of the groups (Sekhon & Mebane, 1998), a procedure that is here called standard optimization because it uses standard Newton–Ralphson matrix inversion procedures in its calculation. Standard optimization is mainly used with pairwise matching because it is the simplest optimizing procedure. In addition, the derivatives of the distributions with 1–many matching are more complex or may not exist. Full matching is available using the optmatch program available from Hansen (2004). It is available at http://gking.harvard.edu/matchit. Standard optimized matching is available from the R program matching developed by Mebane and Sekhon (2011). This program is available from http://cran.r-project.org/web/packages/Matching/Matching.pdf.

Other procedures use a genetic approach to optimizing the similarity (Sekhon & Mebane, 1998). A genetic approach is a sequential process of refining weights for the similarity of cases and for the covariance between the predictors of the propensities that minimize differences between the cases for the variables predicting the propensity scores. Genetic optimized solutions are also available from the matching program using the rgenoud software developed by Mebane and Sekhon (2011) available from the CRAN website (http:// cran.r-project.org/web/packages/rgenoud/index.html).

The alternative approaches to optimizing matches and minimizing group differences are because the distribution of the propensity scores in the two groups may not be symmetrical with one mode and because one must choose multiple search criteria for the program to use in calculating the total differences between the groups. The multiple criteria one may use are the number of choices evaluated for comparison, the caliper used for how close propensities need to be to be included among the choices compared, and whether one is using propensity scores or a multivariate distance measure (e.g., the Mahalanobis distance). One can choose between a supposition that the multivariate distance and the propensity score distributions are continuous and have a single mode or not (i.e., whether a derivative exists for the distribution) or deciding that the distribution appears discontinuous or has multiple modes. The genetic approach is also preferred when a probability distribution has multiple minima or local optima (or both). Full matching and standard optimization cannot necessarily achieve an optimal solution in these circumstances.

If the former supposition is supported by inspecting the frequency distribution for the initial distance or propensity function, then standard maximizing procedures, such as Newton–Ralphson or quasi-Newton, can be used to find a weighted combination of predictors that minimizes the total Mahalanobis distance or total propensity differences between the groups (Mebane & Sekhon, 2011). If inspecting the initial propensity or distance distribution suggests that the function is discontinuous or has multiple modes, then the genetic approach discussed below should be considered.

## OPTIMIZATION AND NETWORK FLOW

As noted by Rosenbaum (1989), optimizing procedures can be derived from network flow theory in which the costs of following a path to matching are minimized (see Figure 6.6). In figure 6.6, there are three intervention subjects (I) and three comparison subjects (C). In the optimal match, the path from the sample to the match links C1 to I1 and C2 to I3. This combination has a total distance of 9.65. In contrast, a greedy matching would link C2 with I2, with a total distance of 11.0.

**Figure 6.6** Optimal Network Paths

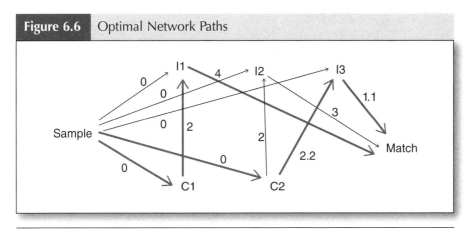

*Note.* Optimal paths are in bold and distances are in numbers next to the lines.

There are two commonly used methods for optimizing the similarity of matches using network flow theory. One is called minimum cost augmentation. The other is cost-reducing cycles (Rosenbaum, 1989). The minimum cost method starts with the best match and keeps adding additional matches sequentially, each time evaluating what is the best match among the remaining matches. The cost-reducing cycles method starts with a set of matches and searches for a better match for the worst match among the pairs already matched. If one is found, then a new match is made and a search begins for a better or equivalent match for the cases whose match was reassigned to the worst match. Both of these methods continue until no more acceptable matches are found, or the number of cycles for identifying better matches exceeds some defined maximum.

Both minimum cost and cost-reducing methods assume that derivatives exist for the distribution functions of variables whose distance is being minimized. If one is working with reasonably well-behaved data, either of these procedures can produce optimal results and they will converge toward the same value. If the data are not well behaved, however, these two approaches can converge on different values. If the two approaches do converge on identical values (or nearly identical), standard optimization is fully adequate.

When the minimum cost and the cost-reducing estimates do not agree, a genetic approach to matching is needed. It will find an optimal match in situations in which the minimum cost and cost-reducing approaches do not produce the same results. It can also reproduce results of randomized controlled trials (RCTs) when the research is replicated as an observational study in situations where standard optimized propensity matching fails to replicate the RCTs (Sekhon & Grieve, 2011).

## GENETIC OPTIMIZED MATCHING

Genetic procedures produce the best likelihood of optimized results. Genetic matching is more general in the sense that it does not assume that the multi-variate distance or the propensity score has a continuous distribution with a single mode (i.e., does not assume the distribution has a derivative). It can be used when a propensity score distribution is continuous and symmetrical, but it is not required to be so (Mebane & Sekhon, 2011). Genetic matching also combines the use of propensity scores with multivariate distance measures such as Mahalanobis distance or other distance measures. It thus uses more information than propensity scores alone. It is more likely to achieve balance in the confounding variables and replicate the results of RCTs.

For purposes of matching to reduce imbalance, it is used especially to mini-mize the distance between groups. Consequently, the results of genetic matching are indistinguishable from standard optimized matching when the propensity data are well behaved. It can produce different results if there is more than one optimized solution or the data are not well behaved—that is, if there is more than one combination of matches that produces the same average distance between the two groups.

The genetic method of optimizing uses a formula similar to the Mahalanobis distance, but it has an additional weighting factor. Cases having greater distance from either are given lower weights. Mebane and Sekhon (2011) provide the matrix form of the formula as follows:

$$D_{gw}(X_i, X_j) = \{(X_i - X_j)'(S^{-1/2})'WS^{-1/2}(X_i - X_j)\}^{1/2}, \qquad (6.2)$$

where $S^{-1/2}$ is the lower triangle matrix of $X$ and $W$ is a matrix of weighting factors. This can be reduced to weighting the Mahalanobis distance according to how different the cases are and how strong is the covariance between the predicting variables:

$$D_{gw}(X_i - X_j) = \{(X_i - X_j)((COV)W(W_i - W_j))\}^{1/2}. \qquad (6.3)$$

This matrix equation can be represented as a simple quadratic equation:

$$D_{\text{gw}(X_i - X_j)} = \{\Sigma(X_i - X_j)\text{COV}_{ij}(W_{ij}(W_i - W_j))\}^{1/2}, \qquad (6.4)$$

where $D_{\text{gw}(X_i - X_j)}$ is the weighted difference across the variables $X_i$ through $X_j$, $(X_i - X_j)$ is the difference between the paired $X_i$ and $X_j$ variables, $\text{COV}_{ij}$ is the covariance between $X_i$ and $X_j$, $W_{ij}$ is the weight for the $X_i$ and $X_j$ pair, and $(W_i - W_j)$ is the difference between the weight for $X_i$ and $X_j$.

The equation is estimated iteratively, each time selecting the variable having the greatest distance to have its weight adjusted. The process stops when an arbitrary maximum number of iterations is reached or a criterion for minimum distance is met. Because this process does not require the covariates estimating the propensity to be ellipsoidal, it can produce better solutions than other approaches. In general, if full matching or standard optimized matching do not sufficiently reduce imbalance, genetic matching may provide a better solution. This is a theoretical possibility. With real data, the author has yet to see a situation in which genetic matching does a substantially better job than full matching in finding matches that reduce imbalance and produce estimates that are more precise or significantly different.

Jasjeet S. Sekhon and Richard Grieve (2011) provide an example comparing nearest-neighbor versus optimized genetic matching (see Table 6.1, based on data from Sekhon & Grieve, 2011, table 1). Table 6.1 compares the imbalance of selected variables without matching, with nearest-neighbor matching, and with genetic matching for those who received pulmonary artery catheterization (PAC) with those who did not (non-PAC). With one exception, the genetic matching outperforms nearest-neighbor greedy matching in reducing imbalance. The exception is mean length of stay prior to use of the intensive care unit. This shows the aspect of genetic matching that it minimizes the total differences across all confounding variables, but there may be an individual variable where the mean distance is slightly higher. In this case, it is still not a significant difference, even though it appears to be larger than with nearest-neighbor matching.

The balance in the measures in Table 6.1 goes beyond differences in means or percentages. In the Sekhon and Grieve (2011) article, they also demonstrate that better balance is achieved using Q–Q plots and K–S statistics.

The comparisons of Sekhon and Grieve also show differences in the estimated mortality rates for those in the PAC and non-PAC groups (see Table 6.2). They also show that genetic matching produces results very close to those of an RCT that was done as part of the SWIFT study. The differences in the mortality rates between the PAC and non-PAC groups were statistically significant for the

| Table 6.1 | Selected Characteristics for PAC and Non-PAC Groups Before Matching and After Nearest-Neighbor and Genetic Matching | | |
|---|---|---|---|
| Characteristic | PAC | Non-PAC | p Value[a] |
| Mean age | | | |
| Unmatched | 60.1 | 61.9 | <.001 |
| Nearest-neighbor matching | 61.2 | 61.9 | .41 |
| Genetic matching | 62.0 | 61.9 | .61 |
| Mean LOS prior to ICU (days) | | | |
| Unmatched | 4.56 | 5.73 | <.001 |
| Nearest-neighbor matching | 5.58 | 5.73 | .91 |
| Genetic matching | 5.42 | 5.73 | .79 |
| Mean acute physiology score | | | |
| Unmatched | 17.9 | 27.7 | <.001 |
| Nearest-neighbor matching | 28.0 | 27.7 | .06 |
| Genetic matching | 27.6 | 27.7 | .77 |

Source. Based on Sekhon and Grieve (2011).

Note. PAC, pulmonary artery catheterization; LOS, length of stay; ICU, intensive care unit.

a. For the $t$ test of differences of means or percentages.

| Table 6.2 | Mortality Rates by Method of Estimation | | | |
|---|---|---|---|---|
| Method | N | Non-PAC (%) | PAC (%) | Difference (%) |
| Unmatched | 38,282 | 29 | 59 | 30[a] |
| After p score matching | 1,052 | 54 | 59 | 5[a] |
| After genetic matching | 1,052 | 57 | 59 | 2 |
| RCT | 1,013 | 66 | 68 | 2 |

Source. Based on Sekhon and Grieve (2011).

Note. PAC, pulmonary artery catheterization; RCT, randomized controlled trial.

a. Difference is significant at $p < .05$ with $t$ test of percentages.

unmatched groups and the nearest-neighbor propensity score matched groups, although the propensity score matched groups were substantially less different than the unmatched groups. Both the genetic matched and the RCT groups did not have significant differences between PAC and non-PAC. This clearly shows that genetic optimized matching can outperform nearest-neighbor matching some of the time.

## ADEQUACY AND SUFFICIENCY OF OPTIMIZED SOLUTIONS

The adequacy of standard pairwise, full, and genetic solutions depends on correct specification of the confounders and meeting the assumptions for use of the techniques. If all significant confounders have been measured and included in the propensity estimation, the results will be statistically adequate. As with other uses of propensity scores, including the appropriate confounding variables is also an issue here. The statistical adequacy of the optimization depends on using properly estimated propensities. The software can almost always find matches that meet the criteria specified using the available propensities. If the propensities were estimated omitting important variables, the estimated propensities will themselves not be statistically sufficient, and optimizing a match using them will not be statistically adequate or sufficient. The matches will not be adequate because the matches will be based on misspecified estimates. They will not be sufficient because adding the omitted variables to the propensity estimates will improve on the matches.

The assumption of ignorability is important to this result. If omitted confounders can be ignored, they will not add significant bias or improve on the matches. Under the assumption of ignorability, the results of optimizing software are adequate and sufficient. If there is evidence of significant omitted confounders and the assumption of ignorability does not hold, optimized matching should not be done. It will give the false impression that no better matches can be obtained. In such a situation, it is better to use a greedy solution where there is greater recognition of the potential risks involved and appropriate cautionary remarks are issued.

The assumption of a continuous, overlapping distribution with a single mode is also important to optimizing solutions that use derivates of the distribution for maximizing the results. This assumption is necessary for Newton-like algorithms to reach a stable, true maximum. The standard pairwise optimal matching makes stricter assumptions about the data. When the data are not well behaved, standard optimization does not produce statistically adequate results. When full matching and genetic matching are used, however, this assumption is not required. Either procedure will produce adequate results. If either procedure uses all the cases, they are both sufficient as well. If cases are dropped, it depends on whether using the dropped cases would change the results. If it does, the results are not sufficient.

This result is exemplified by the case of full matching. If the model for propensity estimation is properly specified and the data are well behaved, full matching has an excellent chance of obtaining the optimal match. If the model is not properly specified and the data are not well behaved, a stable optimization might still be found, but changing the criteria may produce a different result. One will have the appearance of having obtained an optimized result or, at least, a "best result," without reaching an optimal result—in the sense that no other information will change the result. To get true optimized results for propensity matches, one must have previously offered evidence that the propensity estimates were correctly specified, that the data are well behaved, that no cases have been dropped that will change the result, and that reasonable changes in criteria do not also change the result.

Similar conclusions apply to genetic matching, with an important exception. Since genetic estimation does not require the distribution to be continuous with a single mode, this assumption is not necessary. Violating it does not threaten the adequacy or sufficiency of the result. The adequacy and sufficiency of genetic matching does require that the estimation of the propensity scores did not leave out important variables. The ignorability assumption still has to be met. The only other thing that can jeopardize the sufficiency of genetic results is whether reasonable changes in the criteria for stopping the iteration produce a different result. If evidence is offered that this is not the case, genetic matching produces adequate and sufficient estimates.

# CHAPTER 7

## PROPENSITIES AND WEIGHTED LEAST SQUARES REGRESSION

This chapter presents the use of propensity scores in **weighted least squares** **(WLS)** regression. It presents different approaches to weighting and examines the trade-offs between them. Criteria for assessing the results of the regression, as well as judging the adequacy of the results of the weighting in reducing bias in the comparisons, are presented.

Weighted regression may be done using multiple regression (ordinary least squares regression (OLS), maximum likelihood solutions, or generalized least squares) or using logistic regression. The former is used when weighting is necessary and the outcomes are continuous variables. The latter is used when weighting is necessary and the outcomes are dichotomous or polychotomous variables.

## PROPENSITIES AS WEIGHTS

When one has a sample of cases and wants it to more closely resemble the population from which the sample was taken, the sample cases may be weighted. Those individuals who are underrepresented in the sample may be given more weight. Some of the cases may be counted more than once so that the percentage of a sample having a given characteristic will equal the percentage in the population. Individuals who are overrepresented may be given less weight. Some of those cases may be ignored. The result of sample weighting is that the distribution of characteristics in the sample closely resembles that of the population. For example, if men are overrepresented in a sample and women are underrepresented, some men could be deleted from the sample and some women could be counted twice to produce a balanced number of men and women.

In similar fashion, propensities may be used to derive weights for the cases in the treatment group and the comparison group so that the two groups have the same or closely similar characteristics. This is another way of removing pregroup differences. Take an example in which the intervention group is 60% male and the comparison group is 40% male. If the males in the first group are given a weight of 5/6 (83%) and the males in the second group are given a weight of 5/4 (1.25), this would result in both groups having 50% males. The weighted sample would use 83% of the males in the first group and count 25% of the males in the second group twice. This would change the sample to 50% male and 50% female.

Overrepresentation and underrepresentation are a result of random selection variation and of the influence of confounding variables on the selection process. Propensities, as a score summing the effect of multiple confounding variables, represent the multivariate effect of prior variables in causing some cases to be overrepresented or underrepresented in the treatment or control groups. If cases are given low weights for high propensities, this reduces the effect of the confounders in causing some cases to be overselected into one of the groups. If cases are given high weights for low propensities, this will counter the effect of the confounders in causing some cases to be underselected into one of the groups. The problem is how to select the weights that achieve the best balance for the prior variables.

Propensity scores may be used to weight samples or to weight data values. In the former case, a weighted sample is created to which multiple regression, logistic regression, or some other procedure may be applied. In the latter case, all the subjects are used and the values of each case are weighted in calculating the effect coefficients and standard errors. The former procedure is easier to use, but it has larger standard errors. The latter procedure is more difficult, but its standard errors are smaller. When weighting samples, one must be aware that the standard errors may be inflated by the weighting. Unless software explicitly says it produces unbiased standard errors with weighted data, the user should assume that the true standard errors are smaller than that provided by the computer program. Using a smaller significance probability may be appropriate.

Matching cases can be treated as a special case of sample weighting, where a weight of 1 is assigned to cases that are matched and a weight of 0 is assigned to cases that are not matched. The expected value for each group with this weighting scheme is the same as paired or 1–$k$ matching. The criteria for assigning 1 or 0 to cases depend on the matching procedure. Except for full or genetic matching, not all the cases will be used. With propensity weighting, where noninteger weights are permitted, all the cases are used. The only exception is in sample weighting where cases having weights close to 0 get excluded due to probability exclusion.

## WEIGHTING OPTIONS

There are several alternatives for weighting with propensity scores, inverse proportional weighting, rescaled inverse proportional weights, rescaled inverse proportional weighting, augmented inverse proportional weighting, trimmed inverse proportional weighting, and matched inverse proportional weighting. Each of these is described, and their strengths and weaknesses are discussed. Guidelines for choosing from them are then provided.

### *Inverse Proportional Weighting*

The simplest way to weight a sample to reduce imbalance is to make the weights inversely proportional to the propensities. It is referred to as the **inverse propensity weight (IPW)**. To estimate the average treatment effect (ATE), 1 is divided by the propensity score in the control group.

$$W_i = 1/P_i, \tag{7.1}$$

where $W_i$ is the weight for the $i$th case and $P_i$ is the propensity score for that case. This procedure will reduce overrepresentation and underrepresentation of the cases in the groups. It will produce more balance in the representation of the cases. However, it also inflates the sample size because the sum of the $1/P_i$ values is typically greater than 1.0 (Freedman & Berk, 2008).

Their solution for the ATE is that cases in the treatment group get weights of $1/(1 - P_i)$. See Equations 7.2 and 7.3,

$$W_{IPW} = (1/P_0 \mid X = 0) \text{ for the controls} \tag{7.2}$$

and

$$W_{IPW} = 1/((1 - P_1) \mid X = 1) \text{ for those in the treatment group,} \tag{7.3}$$

where $P_0$ is the propensity for cases in the treatment group, $P_1$ is the propensity for cases in the control group, and $X$ is a dichotomous variable taking 0 for comparison cases and 1 for intervention cases. If one wishes to estimate the average treatment effect for the treated (ATT), the weight for the treated group is set as 1.0, and the weight for the controls is set as $P/(1 - P)$ (Guo & Fraser, 2010, p. 161).

Calculating the weights with statistical software is straightforward. With SPSS, for example, two conditional IF statements are used as follows:

IF (treatmentgroup eq 0) IPWweight= 1/predps

and

IF (treatmentgroup eq 1) IPWweight= 1/(1 − predps),

where treatmentgroup is a variable coded 0 or 1 for control or treatment, respectively, IPWweight is the computed weight, and predps is the predicted propensity score.

Freedman and Berk (2008) examined the performance of weighted regressions using simulated data. The weighted data did not greatly reduce the imbalance. This appeared to be related to small propensities having large weights that inflated the variance of the estimates, to small sample estimates also having large variances (Glynn & Quinn, 2009), and to sensitivity of weighting to model misspecification. This approach does not always eliminate the sample inflation problem. If the weighted sample is larger than the unweighted sample, additional modification is necessary to eliminate the sample inflation.

## Rescaled Inverse Proportional Weighting

An alternative solution to the sample inflation problem was proposed by Imbens (2004). His solution is to rescale the inverse propensities so that the group weights sum up to 1.0, a process he refers to as **normalization**. This is accomplished by dividing the inverse of the propensities by the sum of the propensities for each group. The weights are then multiplied by the values of the outcome measures and summed up for each group. This result is called **rescaled inverse propensity (RIP)** weights. The difference in the sums for each group is the treatment effect. The formulas for the rescaled weights are as follows:

$$W_{RIP} = \left(1 / P_0 \mid X = 0\right) / \left(\sum W_0\right) \tag{7.4}$$

and

$$W_{RIP} = \left(1 / (1 - P_1) \mid X = 1\right) / \left(\sum W_1\right), \tag{7.5}$$

where $W_{RIP}$ is the rescaled inverse propensity weight, $P_0$ is the propensity for comparison cases, $P_1$ is the propensity for intervention cases, $P_i$ is the propensity of the $i$th case, $X$ is the indicator for treatment or control group membership, $W_0$ is the calculated IPW for the control group, and $W_1$ is the IPW for the treatment group.

For the above example in SPSS, the rescaled weight is calculated by dividing the previously calculated weight by the sum of the weights:

$$COMPUTE \ RIPweight = IPWweight/sumpred,$$

where IPWweight is the result of the previous calculations and sumpred is a variable containing the value of the sum of the propensity scores for the control or treatment groups, respectively, obtained from a frequency distribution or a descriptive summary for each group.

When one has calculated the rescaled weights, they may be used in the manner of Freedman and Berk (2008). To calculate the ATE, $1/P_i/(\sum P_i)$ is used as the weight for the comparison group and $1/(1-P_i)/(\sum P_i)$ is used as the weight for the treatment group. Each outcome value is multiplied by its respective weight. This approach tends to improve balance compared with the nonrescaled weights. The procedure does not necessarily eliminate all the imbalances. The standard errors, however, need to be adjusted to reflect the observed sample size, not the weighted sample size. In the simplest case, the adjustment is to multiply the error variances by $N_O/N_W$, where $N_W$ is the weighted sample size and $N_O$ is the observed sample size.

## *Rescaled Inverse Propensity Weighting*

A difficulty with the RIP procedure is that variance measures and significance tests are not automatically calculated while computing the weighted difference, although some recent R programs have added this feature. They are not available in the SAS, SPSS, or STATA programs. An alternative would be to rescale the weights so that the mean weight is 1.0. This rescaled weight is called **rescaled inverse propensity weighting** (**RIPW**). The formula for these weights is given in Equation 7.6:

$$W_{RIPW} = \left(1/P_0 \mid X = 0, 1/(1-P_1) \mid X = 1\right)/\left(\sum W_{IPW}/N\right), \qquad (7.6)$$

where $W_{RIPW}$ is the rescaled inverse propensity weight normalized to a mean of 1.0, $P_0$ is the propensity for comparison cases, $P_1$ is the propensity for intervention cases, $W_{IPW}$ is the IPW of the $i$th case, and $X$ is the dichotomy coded 1 for treatment or 0 for comparison group membership.

The calculation of RIPW is a modification of the IPW similar to the RIP weight. The only difference is that the IPW is divided by the mean IPW. For the SPSS example,

COMPUTE RIPWweight = IPWweight/ipwmean,

where IPWweight is the calculated IPW and ipwmean is the mean of IPW obtained from a frequencies or descriptive summary program.

These weights can be used in WLS regression. These weights are not multiplied by the $Y$ values. They are used to weight the sample, where the weighted number of cases will equal the observed sample size. Variances and significance tests will be automatically calculated by the regression program. The variances, however, may be slightly larger than with the Imbens procedure. This is because weighted regression that uses case weights employs a probabilistic procedure for selecting cases whose weights are not whole integers, whereas the Imbens procedure uses all the cases. With large samples, the two approaches to rescaling produce nearly identical results.

While RIPW is slightly less precise than the RIP procedure, it is much easier. If the estimates of treatment effects are statistically significant using this procedure, they will always be significant using RIP. If the results are borderline nonsignificant, the researcher can use RIP to see if the initial results from RIPW are an artifact of using the simpler procedure. With smaller samples, the results of the two approaches may differ; RIP is to be preferred in such a situation. Probability weighting of small samples produces larger variances in the estimates. An advantage of RIPW is that it can be used to weight a sample prior to using other statistical programs. It produces propensity weighting for any program that accepts weighted samples.

Using RIPW eliminates the problem of sample inflation. It retains weights that are inversely proportional to the propensities. The alternative approach normalizes on the mean of the weights. It adjusts the weighted sample size to be equal to the observed sample size. Rescaled weighting is becoming common when using propensities as weights, both for sample weighting and for weighted regression.

Lee, Lessler, and Stuart (2011) have noted that the performance of weights in reducing imbalance is improved by trimming cases having very large or very small propensities, a procedure that may be called trimmed weighting (TW). They compared this improvement with that resulting from revising the propensity estimation process. Reducing misspecification in the estimation of propensities improved balance as much as trimming outlier propensities, besides retaining more cases. While trimming outliers can improve balance if done judiciously, a similar benefit might be obtained by taking a closer look at the propensity estimation process to see if it can be improved. If, however, it does not appear that further revision of the selection model reduces imbalance, trimming might be considered.

Figure 7.1 compares imbalance for three variables from the General Social Survey that were used previously in estimating propensity scores. It visually displays the group differences for the unweighted, the IPW, and RIPW data. The unweighted data have strikingly larger differences than that resulting from either of the two weighting procedures. The imbalance indicated by the standardized differences is very small between IPW and RIPW, though Imbens (2004) indicates that on some occasions the differences are not always so small. RIP or RIPW should be used in preference to

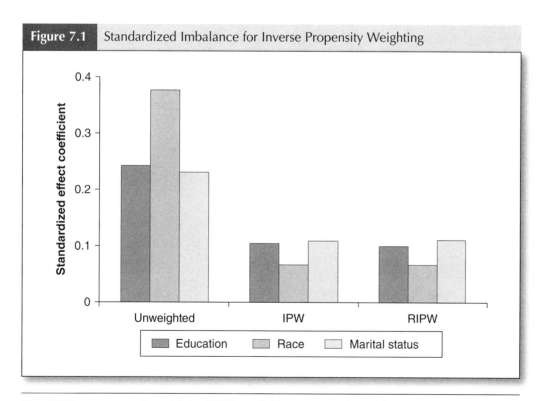

**Figure 7.1** Standardized Imbalance for Inverse Propensity Weighting

*Note.* IPW, inverse propensity weighting; RIPW, rescaled inverse propensity weighting.

unrescaled IPW because it removes the sample inflation problem and does better at reducing imbalance.

Table 7.1 provides the unweighted and weighted data results. For the unweighted data, all three differences between "treatment" and comparison groups are statistically significant at the .01 level using an analysis of variance (ANOVA) F test. For the IPW results, none are significant at the .01 level, but two variables remain significant at the .05 alpha level. The latter is mainly a result of inflated sample size, inasmuch as the estimated sample sizes for the unweighted data are 1,697 cases and 3,954 for the IPW cases.

Inspection of the standardized difference measures for the unweighted three variables shows that they all exceed a value of .20, a value commonly used to judge substantive significance of standardized differences. The standardized differences for the IPW data and the RIPW data are all below this value, implying that the weighted results are not a meaningful difference. The ANOVA F test on group differences for IPW and RIPW, however, produces conflicting results because the sample size for the two weighting procedures is not the same.

Unfortunately, the RIPW weighting scheme still doesn't always produce satisfactory balancing (Busso, DiNardo, & McCrary, 2009). It can produce estimated effects having large variances, especially with small samples. These error variances for the estimated effects are larger than those typically produced by a matching procedure. Even so, if the matching procedure chosen drops too many cases, its error variances will also increase. At present, it's an empirical question as to which procedure produces the smaller error variances. Since full

| Table 7.1 | Standardized Imbalance Results for Inverse Propensity Weighting | | | |
|---|---|---|---|---|
| | Education | Race | Marital Status | N |
| Unweighted | 0.245* | 0.376* | 0.230* | 1,697.00 |
| IPW | 0.102# | 0.067 | 0.074# | 3,594.00 |
| RIPW | 0.102 | 0.067 | 0.111 | 1,694.00 |

Note. IPW, inverse propensity weighting; RIPW, rescaled inverse propensity weighting.

*Differences between groups are significant at $p < .01$, using F test from ANOVA.

#Differences between groups are significant at $p < .05$, using F test from ANOVA.

matching and genetic matching can use all the cases and produce optimized estimates, an optimal weighting procedure would need to produce results equivalent to that of full matching or genetic matching, but at substantially less computational cost, to have a significant advantage over the optimizing matching procedures. The greater simplicity of optimized weighting over full or genetic matching would recommend itself if this occurs.

## *Augmented Inverse Propensity Weights*

Posner and Ash (2011) have proposed combining weighting with use of propensity strata. They have found that weighting within strata reduces error variances when the results between strata are combined (weighting strata proportionate to the number of cases in each stratum). The ATE and ATT estimates are weighted averages for the estimates produced by each stratum. Imbens (2004) has noted that this procedure doesn't use as much information as is present in the data. If the within-group variance is small, however, this approach may produce adequate results. The procedure has not been generally used, but it deserves further investigation.

Busso et al. (2009) have also noted that weighting procedures tend not to reduce imbalance as much as matching procedures, despite the fact that they theoretically can do so (Rubin, 1979). This has led Glynn and Quinn (2010) to argue that an augmented inverse propensity weight (AIPW) estimate should be used. This augmentation, proposed by Robins, Rotnitzky, and Zhao (1994), is an adjustment made to the RIPW estimated treatment effects based on the difference of weighted conditional regression equations. The conditional weighted regressions predict the treatment effect using the same confounding variables that estimated the propensity score. However, the weights in the adjusting regressions are the reverse of those for RIPW. $1/P$ is the weight for the treatment group, and $1/(1 - P)$ is the weight for the comparison group. The difference of two estimated effects is then averaged based on the number of cases in each group. The formula for the adjustment is given in Equation 7.7:

$$\tau_z = \left(\bar{Y}_{Z0} N_0 - \bar{Y}_{Z1} N_1\right) / \left(N_0 + N_1\right), \qquad (7.7)$$

where $\tau_z$ is the adjustment, $\bar{Y}_{Z0}$ is the mean predicted outcome for the comparison group cases, $\bar{Y}_{Z1}$ is the mean predicted outcome of the treatment cases, and $N_0$ and $N_1$ are the number of cases in the comparison and treatment groups, respectively.

This adjustment assumes that the coefficients predicting the outcome are similar for the two groups. If the regression coefficients differ between the two groups, that is prima facie evidence that there is an interactive effect between the confounding variable whose coefficient differs between groups and the intervention. Such interactive effects should have been incorporated in the original selection model. When interaction is found, the researcher must return to the selection model and revise it to incorporate those effects. Otherwise, the estimated propensity and the adjustment will both be biased. If the coefficients of the regressions are similar, the adjusted effects can be accepted.

This adjustment is subtracted from the treatment effect produced by IPW. The formula for AIPW is given in Equation 7.8:

$$\tau_{\text{AIPW}} = \tau_{\text{IPW}} - \tau_Z, \tag{7.8}$$

where $\tau_{\text{AIPW}}$ is the AIPW adjusted estimate of treatment effect, $\tau_{\text{IPW}}$ is the IPW estimate of treatment effect, and $\tau_Z$ is the adjustment. Glynn and Quinn (2010) provide the formula for calculating the AIPW estimate of treatment effects in matrix form when RIP weights are used in multiplying values, rather than weighting cases (see Equation 7.9).

$$\widehat{ATE}_{AIPW} = \frac{1}{n}\sum_{i=1}^{n}\left\{\left[\frac{X_iY_i}{\hat{\pi}Z_i} - \frac{(1-X_i)Y_i}{1-\hat{\pi}(Z_i)}\right] - \frac{(X_i - \hat{\pi}(Z_i))}{\hat{\pi}(Z_i)(1-\hat{\pi}(Z_i))}\right.$$
$$\left. \left[(1-\hat{\pi}(Z_i))\right]\hat{\mathbb{E}}(Y_i \mid X_i = 1, Z_i) + \hat{\pi}(Z_i)\hat{\mathbb{E}}(Y_i \mid X_i = 0, Z_i)\right\}, \tag{7.9}$$

where $\text{ATE}_{\text{AIPW}}$ is their notation for the AIPW estimated treatment effects, $\hat{\pi}(Z_i)$ are propensities estimated by the set of $Z_i$ variables, $Y_i$ are the outcome values, and $X_i$ is the treatment measure. In this case, $X$ takes on a value of 0 to indicate a comparison group and 1 to indicate receiving the treatment. Since AIPW is an adjustment to estimated treatment effects, those effects could also be estimated using RIP or RIPW procedures.

The AIPW results may not differ much from the RIP results, but they are doubly robust, compared with RIP. They provide consistent estimates if either the propensity score model or the regression estimate of the outcome are correct. If one procedure is not correct, but the other is, the ATE estimate is still consistent (Glynn & Quinn, 2009).

## *Matching Weights*

Similar to the AIPW approach, Li (2011) has proposed matching weights to create matching inverse propensity weights (MIPW). These are based on the formula for IPW where the numerator 1.0 is replaced with $\min(1 - P_i, P_i)$, that is, the lesser of the propensity or 1 minus the propensity. $P_i$ in this equation is given as $e_i$ in Li's notation. The formulas for the weights are $\min(1 - P_i, P_i)/P_i$ for the comparison group and $\min(1 - P_i, P_i)/(1 - P_i)$ for the treatment group. MIPW can be scaled to prevent sample inflation, since none of the weights can exceed 1.0. MIPW prevents very large weights. Li also offers theoretical justification for MIPW use. Proposition 1 in his paper suggests that this is an approach that produces optimal weights in the sense of minimizing imbalance while using all the cases. However, because no weight exceeds 1, the weighted sample size is smaller than the observed sample size. This deflates the sample size and calculated degrees of freedom. One could rescale MIPW so the weighted sample size becomes the observed sample size. Li does not discuss this option. He does note that MIPW optimizes both sample size and balance, so it may provide a solution to the need for optimized weighting. Because matched weighting is so recent and not used much yet, further examination of the performance of this weighting option is needed. If it performs as theory says it should, this will provide more consistent weighted regression results.

Figure 7.2 compares results for unweighted, RIPW, and MIPW. It shows that both RIPW and MIPW significantly reduce the imbalance. For the three variables in the example, the imbalance of the MIPW estimators is actually slightly larger than that for the RIPW and AIPW estimators. However, the variance of the estimators themselves are smaller, as noted below.

Table 7.2 shows the statistics for imbalance reduction resulting from MIPW usage. The data show substantial reduction of imbalance for the MIPW sample compared with the unweighted sample. However, the imbalance of the confounding variables for MIPW is little better than RIPW. If MIPW does not produce estimates of intervention effects with smaller error variances, it provides no significant advantage. Since it does provide estimates with smaller error variances, it may detect intervention effects that are more subtle than those identified by RIPW.

Li illustrates the imbalance reduction by comparing the histogram of the weighted propensity scores for the treatment group with that of the comparison group. This comparison is displayed in a mirror histogram (see Figure 7.3). In Figure 7.3, four histograms are displayed. Two above the horizontal line are the histograms for unweighted and matched weighted propensity scores for the comparison group. Two below the line are for unweighted and matched

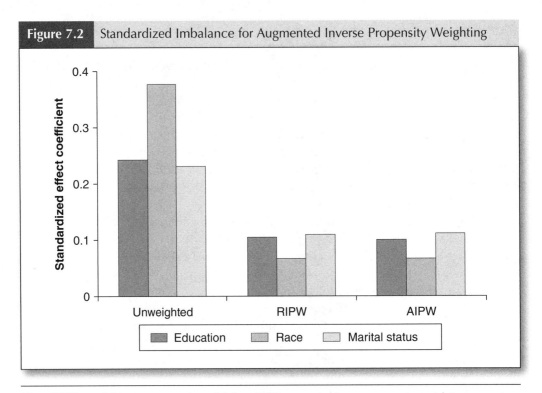

**Figure 7.2**    Standardized Imbalance for Augmented Inverse Propensity Weighting

*Note.* RIPW, rescaled inverse propensity weighting; AIPW, augmented inverse propensity weighting.

**Table 7.2**    Standardized Imbalance for Rescaled Matched Inverse Propensity Weighting

|  | Education | Race | Marital Status | N |
|---|---|---|---|---|
| Unweighted | 0.245* | 0.376* | 0.23* | 1,981.00 |
| RIPW | 0.102 | 0.067 | 0.111 | 1,965.00 |
| MIPW | 0.097 | 0.058 | 0.821 | 1,965.00 |

*Note.* RIPW, rescaled inverse propensity weighting; MIPW, matching inverse propensity weighting.

*Differences between groups are significant at $p < .01$, using $F$ test from ANOVA.

weighted propensity scores for the treatment group. The light colored histograms are for unweighted data. The darker histograms are for matched weighted data. The two histograms for the unweighted propensity scores are

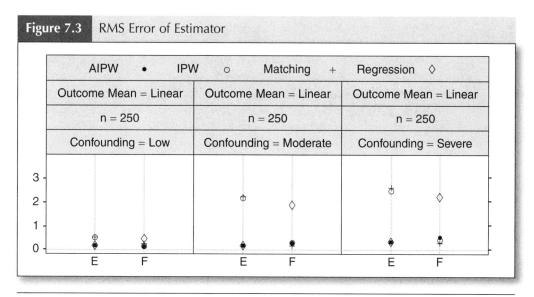

**Figure 7.3** RMS Error of Estimator

*Source.* Glynn and Quinn (2010, figure 5). Used with permission.

*Note.* RMS, root mean squares; AIPW, augmented inverse propensity weighting; IPW, inverse propensity weighting.

somewhat different. The two histograms for the matched weighted scores are mirror reflections of each other.

With relatively well-behaved data, the RIPW reduces imbalance as well as AIPW and MIPW. It may even produce better results in reducing imbalance in some cases. However, this does not necessarily mean that the variances of estimated treatment effects will be as good. It is claimed that the error variances will be smaller using AIPW and MIPW than using RIPW. Whether the gain in precision justifies the additional effort is a professional judgment by the researcher. Further usage will determine whether these weights produce estimates that match their theoretical performance. At present, it seems reasonable to continue using RIPW weights with well-behaved data. When the data are not so well behaved, statisticians might well explore the results of using AIPW or MIPW.

## Choosing Weights

For well-behaved data, using sums of conditional expected values for the group propensities produces results virtually identical to those of just using the average group propensities. In such a situation, the effect on imbalance may be the same as using RIPW. This procedure is more advantageous when working with poorly behaved data. In that case, error variances for the estimates may also be smaller for the AIPW estimates than for RIPW estimates. An example where the imbalance reduction is the same within rounding error is provided in Figure 7.4. In Figure 7.4, the results are virtually identical, except that the AIPW sample has fewer cases available (1,886 for AIPW vs. 1,995 for RIPW). The significance probabilities for the AIPW differences are higher than for RIPW because they are based on fewer cases.

Table 7.3 provides data comparing RIPW with AIPW in their ability to reduce imbalance. It shows that even though these data are not particularly well behaved, they are adequate, so the two methods produce nearly identical results. Both methods do equally well in reducing imbalance. For both, the standardized differences fall substantially below the .20 criterion. The fewer cases with the AIPW method in this case have to do with working with conditional groups rather than with pooled groups.

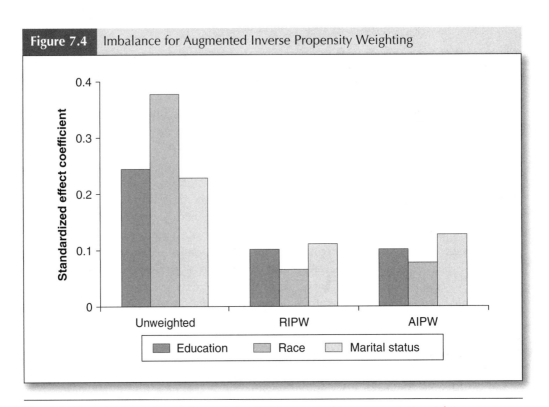

**Figure 7.4**    Imbalance for Augmented Inverse Propensity Weighting

*Note.* RIPW, rescaled inverse propensity weighting; AIPW, augmented inverse propensity weighting.

| Table 7.3 | Standardized Imbalance for Rescaled and Adjusted IPW | | | |
|---|---|---|---|---|
| | *Education* | *Race* | *Marital Status* | *N* |
| Unweighted | 0.245* | 0.376* | 0.23* | 1,981.00 |
| RIPW | 0.102 | 0.067 | 0.111 | 1,965.00 |
| AIPW | 0.102 | 0.067 | 0.067 | 1,886.00 |

*Note.* IPW, inverse propensity weighting; RIPW, rescaled inverse propensity weighting; AIPW, augmented inverse propensity weighting.

*Differences between groups are significant at $p < .01$, using $F$ test from ANOVA.

   Glynn and Quinn (2010) provide an example of how the AIPW estimator has smaller error variance than the IPW estimator. They conducted a Monte Carlo simulation in which treatment assignment was affected by confounding variables. In some cases, the assignment model was misspecified. In other cases, the outcome model was misspecified (see Figure 7.3). The figure plots the root mean squares for the outcome estimates under conditions of low, moderate, and severe confounding as estimated using AIPW, IPW, nearest-neighbor matching, and regression adjustment. Their simulation included estimates in which the confounding effects were nonlinear as well as linear. Figure 7.5 presents only the results for the linear confounding, since the results for nonlinear confounding were very similar. In all cases, the AIPW estimator produced the estimate with the smallest error variance. In some cases, matching, IPW, or regression did nearly as well. None of the alternatives did better than AIPW. The weights for the AIPW in the example somewhat stabilized the estimated ATEs. See Glynn and Quinn (2010) for more on this subject. Glynn and Quinn (2009) estimated their effects using an R statistical program, **CausalGam,** they wrote for that purpose.
   This approach has several desirable properties. The adjustment becomes zero when the true propensities and conditional treatment effects replace the estimated propensities and estimated conditional treatment effects. It produces consistent estimates when the propensity model is correctly specified or the conditional treatment effect models are correctly specified (Scharfstein, Rotnitzky, & Robins, 1999). The estimator is asymptotically normally distributed. AIPW seems to do better than IPW when the models are only slightly misspecified. This makes the estimators doubly robust. They are robust if either the selection model or the outcome model is correctly specified. While AIPW reduces the problems associated with propensities near 0 or 1, it does not

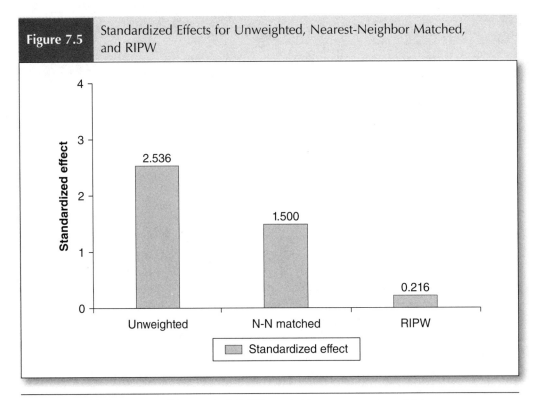

**Figure 7.5**   Standardized Effects for Unweighted, Nearest-Neighbor Matched, and RIPW

*Note.* N-N matched, nearest-neighbor matched; RIPW, rescaled inverse propensity weighting.

reduce the problem associated with small samples—though the smaller error variances makes AIPW more desirable than using RIPW with small samples.

The choice between weighting procedures may seem confusing, but several general principles can aid this process:

1. IPW is appropriate only if the sum of weights equals the sample size and the data are well behaved. If so, it can be used with any computer program that accepts weights. If not, other weights should be used.

2. RIP is only appropriate when using software that does proportional case weighting, rather than sample weighting, and the data are well behaved. WLS programs for SPSS, SAS, STATA, and R do proportional case weighting.

3. RIPW is appropriate when using software that does sample weighting and the data are well behaved. The general linear modeling programs of

SPSS, SAS, STATA, and R allow sample weighting. In addition, it can be used to weight samples prior to use with other programs.

4. AIPW is appropriate when confounding variables may have an interacting (moderating) effect on the outcome. By estimating separate conditional effects, the presence of interaction can be identified. With smaller samples, the smaller error variances are also desirable. It also does better than RIP and RIPW when the data are not well behaved.

5. MIPW is appropriate when the effects being estimated are expected to be subtle or weak. If the results of another weighting scheme are in the borderline, MIPW can be considered to provide further evidence regarding borderline results. In addition, it tends to produce more stable results when data are not well behaved.

6. Trimmed weighting is an add-on for other weighting procedures. If the calculated weights produce extreme values and the imbalance is not sufficiently reduced, trimming some extreme values may improve balance.

## WEIGHTED REGRESSION

Weighted regression is the same as OLS using a weighted sample when the assumptions for OLS are met. In this case, the sample is weighted using propensity scores. As noted above, whether one uses rescaled IPW, rescaled AIPW, or rescaled MIPW as the weights depends on how well behaved the data are, the extent to which imbalance is removed, and the extent to which the selection model might be misspecified.

The formula for weighted regression is given in Equation 7.10:

$$Y_i = \alpha + \beta X_i W_i, \tag{7.10}$$

where $Y_i$ is the predicted outcome; $\alpha$ is the regression intercept; $\beta$ is the treatment effect; $X_i$ is a dummy variable coded 0 for comparison group and 1 for treatment group, respectively; and $W_i$ is the weighting variable. The weight is used to select cases for the regression. Cases with a weight of 1.0 are selected as is. Cases with weights >1 are duplicated the number of times of the integer portion of the weight. Then, an additional duplication is made with a probability of occurrence equal to the decimal portion of the weight. If the weight is <1, then the case is selected with a probability equal to the weight. Once the cases are selected, the regression is run as a standard regression. If the sum of the weights is greater than the sample size, the program will base the calculations on a larger sample size than that observed, resulting in sample inflation and deflated standard errors. This approach to weighted regression is found in all major statistical packages.

Estimates of the baby effect using weighted regression are found in Figure 7.6. It provides standardized differences for unweighted, nearest-neighbor matched, and IPW regression.

The numerical results for this comparison are provided in Table 7.4. Both the matched and the weighted regression produce standardized effect estimates that are smaller than that with the unmatched and unweighted data (see Table 7.4).

This standard version of weighted regression is not appropriate for the Imbens normalization of the weights. When the weights are normalized to sum to 1.0, the standard weighted regression will usually select a single case, although the probability selection could result in zero or two cases selected. To use unitary weights, you must use either a regression program that selects all cases and does proportional weighting of each case's contribution to the result (a strategy used by most WLS programs) or an ANOVA or mean comparison

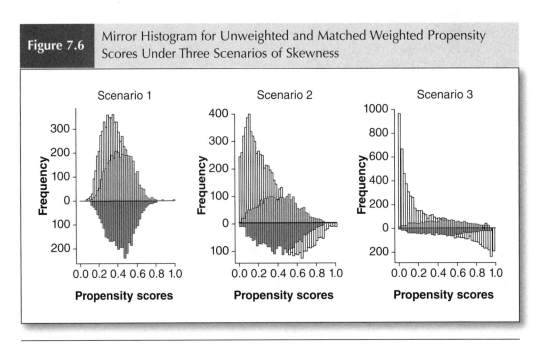

**Figure 7.6**   Mirror Histogram for Unweighted and Matched Weighted Propensity Scores Under Three Scenarios of Skewness

*Source.* From Li (2011). Used with permission.

*Note.* Histograms above the line indicate control group and the ones below indicate treatment group.

| Table 7.4 | Matched Versus Weighted Effect Estimates | | |
|---|---|---|---|
| | *Unmatched/Unweighted* | *Matched Only* | *Weighted* |
| Standardized difference | 2.536 | 1.500 | 0.216 |
| Unstandardized difference | 1.065 | 1.210 | 1.164 |
| Standard error | 0.274 | 0.317 | 0.272 |

program that calculates the sum of the outcome variable. The proportionally weighted regression is possible using the R statistical program. ANOVA or mean comparison programs that calculate the sum of Xs are found in most major statistical programs.

The sample weighting approach has advantages in that if the sample is weighted separately, any multivariate analysis program may be used appropriate to a particular research question. Another advantage of case weighting is that it allows direct inspection of imbalance reduction. With the weighted sample, one can use the same balance statistics and graphs used to detect the imbalance. It allows a clear examination of the imbalance reduction.

Fewer programs weight the values of the cases. If a program that weights values is appropriate, it will produce smaller error variances in its estimates. If one uses such a program, however, examining the balance of the antecedent variables may require creating a weighted sample separately so imbalance of the confounders can be examined.

A comparison of using case weighting versus proportional weighting is provided in Figure 7.7. This figure shows that either weighting procedure reduces prior differences in education, racial distribution, and marital status. The two approaches produce similar results, although the amount of reduction varies. Proportional weighting reduces racial differences more than sample weighting, whereas sample weighting reduces marital status differences more than proportional weighting. Unless one has a small sample, either procedure could be used. If one has a small sample, proportional weighted regression is preferred because it has smaller standard errors and uses all the cases.

## ASSESSING REGRESSION RESULTS

Standard logistic regression and multiple regression are traditionally evaluated by examining the significance of the coefficients, the explained variance, and an overall test of the regression equation. The distribution of residuals and their

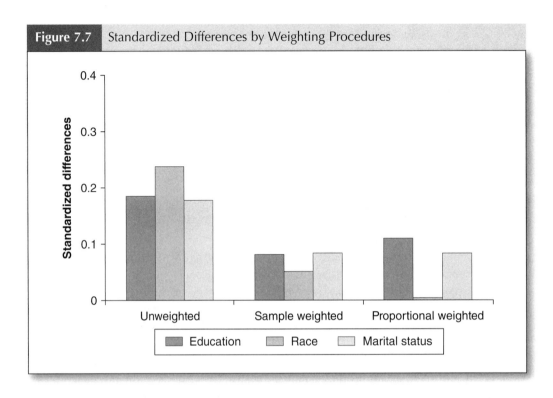

**Figure 7.7**    Standardized Differences by Weighting Procedures

correlation with antecedent variables may also be examined. With weighted regression, there is also a question of the extent to which the weighting reduces the imbalance of the confounding variables. This applies both for multiple regression and for logistic regression. The statistics vary between the two approaches, but the logic is similar.

It is important to first assess the extent of prior imbalance reduction. Running a propensity weighted regression is a poor strategy if the weighting doesn't reduce the prior imbalance. The results in Figure 7.7 show that either sample weighting or proportional weighting may be used to reduce imbalance, but you have to demonstrate that the imbalance is reduced. Assessing the imbalance reduction resulting from sample weighting is straightforward. Produce a weighted sample and run the same imbalance tests one runs with the unweighted sample. With proportional weighting, one must use either statistical procedures that allow proportional weighting or standard procedures with proportionally weighted values. This means multiplying each variable times its weight and using the result in the analysis. However, one must adjust for the weighting. For example, if a *t* test is used, the means produced do not follow the original scaling. One must multiply the computed means by the sample size to obtain a mean with the original scaling of the variable. Similarly, other statistics must be adjusted to produce a meaningful result. It is much more efficient to use a statistical procedure that allows proportional weighting if that is the approach one wishes to use. One should not use a weighted sample to test imbalance reduction if the analysis uses proportional weighting. The results can differ by the two weighting procedures, as illustrated in Figure 7.7.

If a continuous dependent variable is used, standard tests of regression are appropriate. An $F$ test of the overall R, $F$ or $t$ tests of the effect coefficient, checks on the distribution of errors, and their correlation with confounders or alternative causal influences are all necessary. One must also check to see if the association of confounders and alternative influences with the errors and the outcomes is heteroscedastic between the treatment and comparison groups. If heteroscedasticity is present, one must examine its source and modify the selection model or the intervention model accordingly.

If a dichotomous or categorical dependent variable is used, standard tests of logistic regression are appropriate. Overall, chi-square, likelihood, or $F$ tests or similar tests for the coefficients are used. The distribution of errors in classification can be examined. Although the procedure is uncommon, one can also treat errors in classification as variables and see if they are associated with confounding variables or alternative influences.

## ASSESSING ADEQUACY AND SUFFICIENCY OF WEIGHTING

The statistical adequacy of a propensity weighted analysis depends on several factors. First and foremost, the selection model used to estimate the propensities must itself be adequate. Providing evidence of the adequacy of this model was discussed in Chapter 2. Once a satisfactory selection model is used to estimate the propensities, one must address the adequacy of the weighting procedure. The discussion of the weighting options leads to the conclusion that the adequacy of a weighting procedure depends on characteristics of the data one has. For well-behaved data whose selection model is adequate, RIPW-based estimates are statistically adequate. The theoretical work of Rosenbaum and Rubin (1983) and Imbens (2004) clearly demonstrates that. It's only when the selection model or the estimation model is problematic that alternative weighting procedures are much superior.

How, then, can there be such mixed results from weighting? The simple answer is that selection models and outcome models are not always adequate. When the assumption of strong ignorability is violated, the selection model is not adequate and neither will be the weights based on the propensities estimated from that model. In this context, checking the ability of a weighting procedure to reduce imbalance is essential for judging the adequacy of the treatment effect estimated using that procedure. A weighted estimate effect is not adequate if the weights do not also reduce imbalance.

Similarly, the outcome model must also be adequate. The procedure used to estimate the treatment effect must meet the assumptions for that measure of effect. The difference between estimated and observed values should not form any identifiable pattern of association with any of the predictors of the propensity scores. The statistics corresponding to the treatment effect need not be statistically significant since there may be no such effect.

Assessing statistical sufficiency of the treatment effect depends on there not being additional information to improve the estimate. In principle, this means that one must use an optimized weighting procedure. However, the discussion of optimized weighting indicates how difficult it is to assess whether the weighting is optimal or not. If the weighting reduces the imbalance so that there is no significant imbalance, the weighting can be regarded as close to optimal.

# CHAPTER 8

# PROPENSITIES AND COVARIATE CONTROLS

This chapter examines the use of propensity scores with control variables and adjusting for bias. The trade-offs between matching and adjustment are discussed, as well as joint matching and adjustment. Criteria for judging the adequacy of the result of control variables are also presented and discussed.

Using statistical procedures to control prior group differences has a long history in the social and biological sciences. Data from quasi-experimental and experimental designs may have differences between intervention and comparison groups that confound estimation of treatment effects. Rosenbaum and Rubin (1983) showed that bias from prior differences can be removed by adjusting for differences in propensity scores. Such scores are a function of the prior confounding variables. Controlling differences in propensity scores also controls differences in the confounding variables.

There are several different ways in which confounding variables are used in controlling bias. Covariates of the selection process have been used as control variables in multiple regression, logistic regression (LR), analysis of variance (ANOVA), and analysis of covariance (ANCOVA), among other procedures. They have been used as adjusting variables prior to estimating intervention effects. They have also been used after estimating treatment effects to assess marginal effects of alternative influences.

Baseline measures of the outcomes have also been seen as confounding variables. They have been used either to adjust for initial differences between groups or to control differences simultaneous with estimating intervention effects. Baseline measures have not been used much after assessing treatment effects because they generally represent a situation prior to the intervention. In this case, the temporal ordering is not appropriate for using a baseline measure.

If the baseline measure occurs simultaneously with the intervention, it should be used as a simultaneous control—not as a postintervention control.

## CONTROLLING OPTIONS

When multiple variables are used simultaneously to estimate the effects of an intervention with the influence of confounding variables removed, those confounders are control variables. They are commonly used in multiple regression or LR. In ANOVA and ANCOVA, control variables are used when the factors are entered simultaneously with the independent variable. With ANCOVA, the use of covariates simultaneous with a factor for the intervention and treatment group is another use of the control variable approach.

Control variables are used because some variables affect the outcomes that are not confounding variables. These variables may have no causal influence on the selection process even though they do affect the outcomes being measured. They represent independent causal influences on the outcomes. They may be used to assess alternative influences that compete with the intervention effect. Such independent influences may precede, be simultaneous with, or follow the start of the intervention. When the control variables follow the start of the treatment and are also influenced by the treatment, these variables may be used to separate the direct effects of the treatment from the indirect effects that depend on mediating variables.

Propensity scores are not commonly used as control variables. This is mainly because a propensity score is conceived as a statistic (the conditional probability of selection into the treatment group) or as an indicator of multiple and diverse influences that doesn't correspond to a single construct in its own right. From the beginning of the use of propensity scores, however, Rosenbaum and Rubin (1983) have argued that a propensity score represents the process of selection into treatment. For example, if the confounders are variables such as race, gender, age, and ethnicity, it could be argued that the score is a measure of the extent to which prejudice and discrimination affect access to treatment or intervention programs. It is, after all, the conditional probability of receiving treatment. At the very least, it can be conceived as an access to treatment measure. Those with low propensity scores are less likely to be selected into treatment, but some of them receive treatment anyway (low propensity, but in the treatment group). Others may have high access but don't receive treatment (high propensity, but in the comparison group). Such conceptualizations of propensities may not apply in all cases. If they do apply, propensity scores may be used as a control variable like other variables.

Propensity scores are used as control variables less often, because the treatment effect estimate is the average treatment effect, unless a modification to the sample is made. Without a modification, using propensities as controls does not estimate the average treatment effect for the treated. If one wishes to estimate the average treatment effect for the treated, the modification needed is to select just treatment or intervention cases for the analysis.

Propensity scores summarize the result of the multivariate influences on receiving treatment. They summarize all the confounding influences on receiving treatment. Even if the conceptualization of what the propensity scores mean is unclear, they still can be seen as representing causal influences on selection. They can be used as a measure of these causal influences. If conceived in this manner, propensity scores may be used as a control variable.

Propensity score models are not always conceptualized as a causal model of the selection process. This is partly due to the difficulties in interpreting what construct(s) are represented by the propensity scores. This problem is similar to that of interpreting factors in factor analysis. One can use factor analysis to combine indicators sharing a common dimensionality, but then one must interpret what the construct means (Thompson, 2004). With confirmatory factor analysis, the indicators are selected as measures of a predefined construct. With propensity scores, this would imply selecting confounders according to a causal model of sample selectivity. In the earlier example where the confounders were variables associated with discrimination, the selection model could be seen as a model of discrimination with respect to receiving an intervention. With exploratory factor analysis, all the confounders would be included, and the interpretation of what the construct means would come after the statistical analysis. If no meaningful interpretation can be given for the propensity score, the analyst is left with using it as a statistical adjustment having no meaningful interpretation in its own right. This latter situation is less satisfactory, because the user has weak theoretical grounds for believing that the selection model represents the true model of selection.

Propensity scores can also be used as a control variable when the scores are conceived as statistics for removing prior group differences. Even if they are not seen as having a meaningful construct or representing a singular causal influence on selection, they still have statistical use to remove initial differences. This approach is relatively atheoretical. So the selection model cannot be conceived as a causal model of selection bias. It can be conceived as a form of statistical adjustment.

Take, as an example, parents who smoke. The Health and Retirement Study (HRS) data show that individuals whose parents smoked have an increased risk of acquiring measles before age 16. Since measles is an airborne disease and secondary smoke is known to affect the lungs of children, it may be that parents' smoking affects susceptibility to measles. The HRS data also show a correlation between having measles as a child and having breathing difficulty as an adult. Is this because secondary smoke from one's parents has damaged the lungs of these adults when they were children? Does parent smoking cause breathing difficulty indirectly by increasing the risk of measles, which then increases the risk of breathing difficulty of the children as adults? A hypothetical model of these interrelations is given in Figure 8.1.

To address these questions, one must control for confounding factors that affect parents' propensity to smoke and breathing difficulties as an adult. Experiencing stress, for example, may increase a desire to smoke as a way of relieving stress, a form of self-medication. Such stress may also impair one's immune system and make one more susceptible to diseases that can impair one's lungs. This and other factors confound the relationship between parents' smoking, having measles, and experiencing breathing difficulty as an adult. If one uses measures from the HRS to estimate a propensity score for parents' smoking, some of this confounding can be removed by matching, stratifying, or adjusting using the propensity scores.

However, having measles may intervene between parents' smoking and adult breathing difficulty. How much of the difficulty is a direct result of the parents' smoking and how much is indirectly from having measles? To answer these

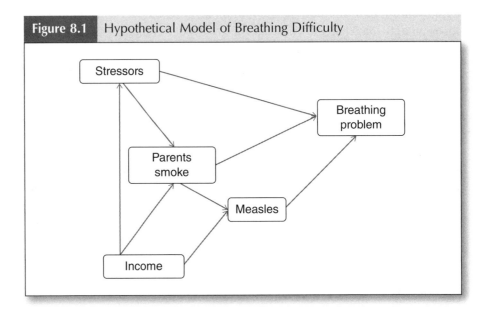

**Figure 8.1**    Hypothetical Model of Breathing Difficulty

questions, one would have to control for having measles. The child having measles is unlikely to cause parents' smoking. Measles in one's children usually comes after a parent has begun smoking. Thus, even though measles comes after parents' smoking, it needs to be used as a control variable.

Confounding the matter, stress, income, and other factors that affect smoking may also affect breathing difficulty independently of their effect on smoking. One can assess such factors individually or collectively. If one wants to look at the collective effect of such influences, propensities can be used as a control variable and also to estimate the collective effect of these variables in addition to the treatment effect.

The baseline or Time 1 value of an outcome may also need to be controlled. The earlier state of a condition may affect the later state of a condition independently of a treatment. Figure 8.2 provides a hypothetical example in which parents' smoking has a causal effect on adult smoking of their children. Other confounding factors are related both to parents' smoking and to smoking of their children as adults. In addition, parents' smoking affects the likelihood of the children smoking as children, which then affects smoking as an adult. To determine the direct effect of parents' smoking, childhood smoking needs to be controlled. This would also allow estimating how much less likely adult

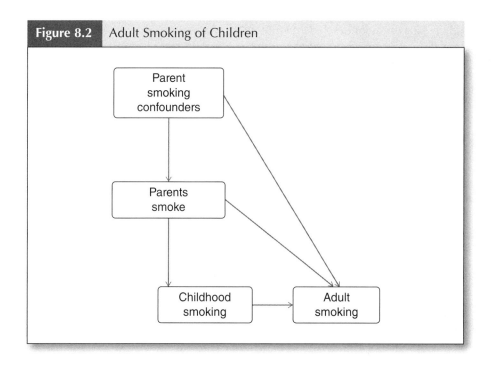

**Figure 8.2**     Adult Smoking of Children

smoking is if childhood smoking is prevented and assessing the independent effect of childhood smoking with other things controlled.

Data from the HRS allow examining this model. The propensity score variable is used in place of all the confounding variables to represent the effect if all the confounders were present. Table 8.1 contains correlations of indicators for the variables in Figure 8.2. All the variables have statistically significant correlations. Some variables were reverse coded so the signs of the correlation would be consistent. Correlations were used for initial screening of relationships because the categorical variables were dichotomies, and it is easier to summarize a set of correlations than odds ratios. The bivariate correlations are only used in this case for screening purposes. In any case, the coefficients controlling for the other variables would need to be examined before one could say that any of the hypotheses are supported or falsified.

Although correlations were used for a preliminary indication of whether associations might be present, the odds ratio is more appropriate as a measure of association when most of the variables are dichotomous. A LR was run with adult smoking as the dependent variable and the other variables as independent variables. The LR was also run using just the cases in the sample matched by propensity score for parents' smoking. Both LR results are found in Table 8.2.

Without propensity matching, the results find that the confounders that influenced smoking by one's parents had no influence on smoking by the child as an adult. This does not preclude the possibility that those confounders if measured at a later point in time might then have an influence, but the confounders that influenced the respondent's parents are not associated with this outcome. Childhood smoking has a borderline relationship with adult smoking. If the 10% alpha level had been selected, it would be judged to have a significant

**Table 8.1    Correlations for Figure 8.2 (N = 9,705)**

|  | Confounder Influence | Parents' Smoking | Childhood Smoking | Adult Smoking |
|---|---|---|---|---|
| Confounder influence | 1.00 | 0.155* | 0.862* | 0.073* |
| Parents' smoking | 0.155* | 1.00 | 0.137* | 0.071* |
| Childhood smoking | 0.862* | 0.137* | 1.00 | 0.070* |
| Adult smoking | 0.073* | 0.071* | 0.070* | 1.00 |

*Statistically significant at $p < .001$.

| Table 8.2 | Logistic Regression for Adult Smoking | | | |
|---|---|---|---|---|
| | B | Standard Error | Significance | Exp(B) |
| Without propensity matching (N = 12,217) | | | | |
| Confounder influence | 0.427 | 0.757 | .573 | 1.532 |
| Parents' smoking | 0.317 | 0.065 | .000 | 0.728 |
| Childhood smoking | 0.062 | 0.035 | .080 | 1.064 |
| Constant | 0.899 | 0.163 | .000 | 2.456 |
| With propensity matching (N = 1,144) | | | | |
| Confounder influence | −0.036 | 3.330 | .991 | 0.964 |
| Parents' smoking | 0.421 | 0.214 | .050 | 0.656 |
| Childhood smoking | 0.095 | 0.202 | .640 | 1.099 |
| Constant | 1.044 | 0.751 | .164 | 2.841 |

effect. This would increase the odds of smoking as an adult by about 6.4%. The intercept is also significant, suggesting that there is a tendency to smoke among these adults apart from the influence factors identified.

The unmatched result in Table 8.2, however, is open to criticism that it has inadequate controls over the factors that influence smoking. Using a matched sample of smokers and nonsmokers would provide a better test of the hypothesis of parents' smoking having an influence on the smoking of an adult child. These results are provided in Table 8.2 as the propensity matched sample results. The results are somewhat different. The effect of parents' smoking is itself borderline at the .05 alpha level. Childhood smoking is no longer borderline and is clearly nonsignificant. The constant is also nonsignificant, indicating that there is no tendency to smoke apart from the factors identified. It should also be noted that in this particular case, using a propensity score variable does not reduce imbalance beyond that provided by the matched sample, but that would not have been known had the propensity score variable been excluded from the LR.

The matched sample in Table 8.2 is a result of coarsened exact matching, with a criterion of .001. This small value was necessary to achieve balancing of the cofounders. 1–N greedy matching with a looser caliper produces a much larger sample, but the confounders are no longer balanced. A graph of the change in imbalance is illustrated in Figure 8.3.

| Figure 8.3 | Imbalance for Unmatched and Matched Samples[a] |

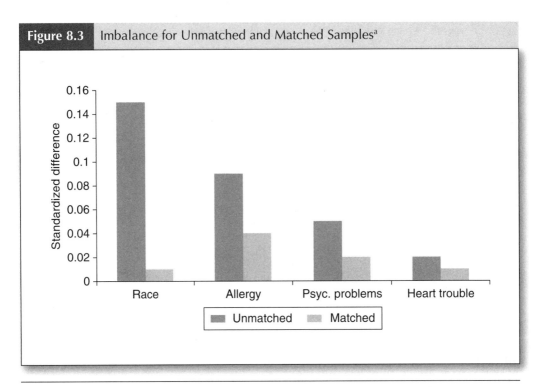

a. Imbalance is difference of means in parent smoking. All unmatched differences are significant at $p < .01$. No matched differences are significant. Unmatched $N = 12,000$. Matched $N = 1,440$. Psyc. problems, psychological problems.

## ADJUSTMENT OPTIONS

There are several options for using propensity scores for adjustment. They may be used to adjust the pregroup differences or to adjust the outcome estimates. Pregroup differences are adjusted using propensity scores primarily by adjusting the samples used to compare the intervention and comparison groups. Adjusting the outcome estimates is done primarily using statistical procedures within multiple regression, LR, ANOVA, and ANCOVA that allow such adjustment. The common thread of these procedures is that either the confounding variables are adjusted prior to the intervention factor (by adjusting the samples) or the influence of the confounders is subtracted while estimating the treatment effects (by adjusting during the estimation process).

Most of the approaches to adjustment attempt to adjust the prior differences between treatment and comparison groups. Matching can be seen as a form of adjusting for propensity scores. It selects matches so that differences in propensity scores are minimized. Rosenbaum and Rubin (1983) have referred to this as an adjustment process. This approach to adjustment was discussed in Chapters 5 and 6. With this approach, the selection of sample cases is adjusted to minimize prior differences. Different matching options represent alternative strategies for adjusting the prior differences. Optimized matching strategies represent the best possible adjustment for those cases selected in the matched samples, given the variables used to estimate the propensity scores.

Adjustment has been used to mean computing partial measures of association (in which case it is equivalent to controlling) or to mean computing part measures of association. A part measure of association occurs when two variables are correlated and a third variable correlated with the first two has its association with one of the two variables removed. This is done by using the regression coefficient between the first and third variables to subtract from the first variable the effect of the third variable, a process sometimes called residualizing. The association of the third variable with the second remains, but the association of the residualized first variable with the third no longer contains any association to do with the third variable. In the context of propensity score analysis, the first variable is the intervention. The second is the outcome, and the third is a confounder. If one is not interested in looking at the competing influence of confounders, adjustment procedures are appropriate. If one wishes to examine the alternative influence of a confounding variable, then propensity scores should be used as a control variable.

Stratifying may be used as an adjustment strategy. D'Agostino (1998) gives an example in which propensity scores are recoded into five categories. This categorical variable is used as a factor in a two-way analysis of variance in which use of an epidural during delivery is the treatment variable and propensity categories is used as an adjusting variable. He compared the $F$ statistics for imbalance in the means of the confounders before and after adjusting for propensity strata. All the confounding variables had nonsignificant imbalance after adjusting for propensity strata. The potential worth of this approach is indicated by the fact that he used a number of confounding variables to test the result, including some that were not included in the estimation of the propensity scores, and all of the prior imbalance became nonsignificant. D'Agostino also cites the work of Roseman (1994) that shows that the combined use of stratifying and adjustment is more statistically efficient than matching alone when response surfaces in the treatment and control groups are parallel.

This approach avoids having to compute a weighted average of the treatment effects. It can be obtained using any multivariate ANOVA program. All it requires is computing a recoded propensity score variable and entering it prior to entering the treatment factor. This procedure assumes that interactive effects of the confounding variables are included in the selection model. If there are interactive effects not included in the selection model, the calculation of treatment effects using this method may be inaccurate. It also assumes that the average treatment effects are the same between groups. If they are not, then the calculated value will have a larger error variance. When there are interactive effects, stratifying with generalized linear regression may be better done as a weighted average between groups than as an adjustment process. This process is discussed below.

Propensity weighted regression is also an adjustment strategy. The cases or the values are weighted so that the pregroup differences are minimized, given the propensity weights. With case weighting, the weighted sample is an adjustment to the original sample that minimizes imbalance. The adjustment occurs prior to estimating the treatment effects. With value weighting, all cases are used. The adjustment occurs simultaneously with estimating the treatment effects. The values of the outcome are weighted proportionate to the weights so that the proportions add up to one. The regression coefficient is the average difference of the weighted values in each group.

Adjusting the treatment effects estimated by rescaled inverse propensity weighting using an augmented inverse propensity weighting estimator (discussed in Chapter 7) is another form of using propensities as adjustment variables. In this case, the adjustment is based on the mean or expected value of the conditional weighted influence of the confounding variables on the outcome. With sufficient recoding, one can construct a control variable that takes on the appropriate conditional weights and use this as a control variable. This approach has not yet appeared in the literature.

The different adjustment strategies produce similar results only to the extent that the assumptions of an adjustment strategy correspond to characteristics of the data—that is, to the extent that it produces a statistically adequate estimate. When the data are well behaved, the alternative adjustment procedures produce very similar results. When the data are not well behaved, divergent results can be produced. These different strategies produce divergent results when their assumptions do not correspond to the data.

The trick for an adjustment strategy is to figure out what assumptions seem appropriate for a given set of data. This is why earlier chapters placed such emphasis on ex post facto checking of imbalance; symmetry, normality, and continuity of propensity distributions; and correlation of errors. Examining the sensitivity of the results to model specification and sample composition is also relevant to this issue. The previously reported differences in effect estimates are partly a result of differences in the appropriateness of the diverse procedures, given characteristics of the data. Even when the assumptions are not appropriate, however, some results may parallel those of an analysis whose assumptions are appropriate. To choose between similar results, one must focus in part on whose evidence is stronger and whose assumptions seem more credible.

All adjusting procedures subtract variance in the outcome variable attributed to the confounders and estimate the remaining variance attributed to the intervention. D'Agostino (1998) gives a formula for this process, which is equivalent to the formula for adjusting for a confounder given earlier:

$$\hat{\tau} = \left( \bar{Y}_t - \bar{Y}_c \right) - \beta \left( \bar{X}_t - \bar{X}_c \right) \tag{8.1}$$

In this case, $\beta$ is the effect of the propensity score, $\bar{X}_t$ and $\bar{X}_c$ are the mean scores for the treatment and comparison groups, and $\bar{Y}_t - \bar{Y}_c$ is the unadjusted treatment effect. This procedure works well when the covariance matrices of the confounders are equivalent in the treatment and control groups. A standard chi-square or likelihood ratio test of the equality of two covariance matrices can be used to examine this issue. This test is available in most statistical packages.

Using propensity scores as an adjusting variable in a multivariate model is an alternative approach to adjusting the estimated effect. Whether one is using ordinary least squares (OLS), maximum likelihood estimation, or LR, these procedures allow entering adjustment factors into the equation prior to entering the treatment factor. The propensity score is treated as a variable. It is forced into the equation in the initial step. The intervention measure is allowed (or forced) to enter afterward. The coefficient for the intervention measure will represent the treatment effect after the outcome measures have been adjusted for their association with the confounding variables (or, at least, those confounding variables that were used to estimate the propensity score). This stepwise approach to estimation has been very common when the confounding factors have separate measures. The only difference is that the propensity score measure is substituted for the multiple measures of the confounding variables. There is, however, a gain in degrees of freedom because only one adjustment measure is used instead of many adjustment measures.

This gain in degrees of freedom may not matter for very large data sets. However, even with large samples, increasing the number of covariates increases the risk of collinearity. Calculating the relative contribution of each confounding factor becomes less reliable. The selection model estimated may not reflect the selection process when collinearity is present. If the intent is to present a model of the selection process, this could alter one's conclusions about the nature of the selection process. If the intent is simply to predict propensity to receive an intervention, this is less of a problem. Even so, the predicted value of the propensity score may be accurate, but the estimate may not be efficient. The error variance for estimating the propensity score increases with the collinearity of the confounders. It is wise to be alert for collinearity among the confounders when estimating propensity scores. If collinearity is present, this implies that the dimensionality of the confounders is less than the number of indicators. Some simplification of the selection model may be possible.

In principle, using confounding variables as individual adjustors in an analysis of covariance prior to estimating treatment effects will result in the same estimate as using propensity scores as a variable—provided that all the assumptions for the ANCOVA or LR are met, especially those regarding multivariate normality of the covariates and linearity of their relationships with the outcome measure. When the assumptions are violated, using the confounders separately will produce different results.

Table 8.3 contains the results of the LR for adult smoking when one's own parents smoked—first, with propensity scores as a control, then with the individual items that created the propensity score using the total sample. These results are compared with those using matching and propensity scores as a covariate. This table has very similar results between the first two methods. When matching is added with propensity scores as a covariate, the results are somewhat different. It should be noted that there is a substantially smaller sample when matched cases are used and the standard errors for the coefficients are somewhat different.

| Table 8.3 | Parent Smoking Effect With Propensity, Individual Item, and Matching Controls | | | | |
|---|---|---|---|---|---|
| | B | Standard Error | N | Significance | Exp(B) |
| Propensity controls | −0.317 | 0.065 | 17,217 | .000 | 0.728 |
| Individual item controls | −0.326 | 0.066 | 17,217 | .000 | 0.722 |
| Matched and propensity controls | −0.421 | 0.214 | 1,144 | .050 | 0.656 |

To better assess the relative performance of these methods, the effect coefficients were converted into standardized scores by dividing the coefficient, *B*, by its standard error. The parameters for parents' smoking were divided by their respective standard deviations. The result is displayed in Figure 8.4.

This figure shows that differences remain when the effect estimates are standardized for comparison. Both of the control approaches produced larger effect estimates than the matching and propensity control approaches. In this case, they also had much larger samples. The work by Rosenbaum and Rubin (1983) supports accepting the matching plus propensity control estimates—even though it is a much smaller sample. The finding still is consistent with the hypothesis that parents' smoking influences their child's smoking as an adult. For purposes of generalizing from these results, however, it would be desirable to try a matching procedure that retained many more cases.

The data analyst can also consider combining adjustment procedures. The theoretical work of Rosenbaum and Rubin (1983), the simulations of Rubin (1979) and of Glynn and Quinn (2010), and the analysis reported by Shadish (2009) and Holmes and Olsen (2011) all argue that using propensity adjustors in addition to matching can outperform using either strategy alone. While

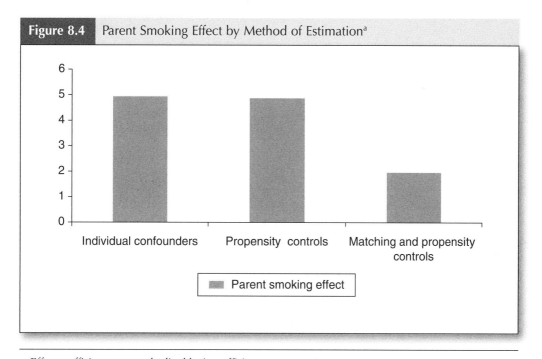

**Figure 8.4**    Parent Smoking Effect by Method of Estimation[a]

a. Effect coefficients are standardized logit coefficients.

matching alone or adjusting alone can sometimes produce results equivalent to combined matching and adjustment, the only way to know if this is the case is to try at least two of the strategies and compare the results. If matching alone and matching plus adjustment produce the same result, then one can use the matching alone result. If they produce different results, then the combined estimation process should be used. One can also compare adjustment versus matching plus adjustment. In similar fashion, if the results are the same, only one procedure need be used. If the results differ, the combined procedure should be used. If the results do not differ by much, then it's less clear which approach is most appropriate.

Figure 8.5 is a scatterplot of standardized residuals versus standardized predicted values for an OLS regression analysis using unmatched cases of the adult

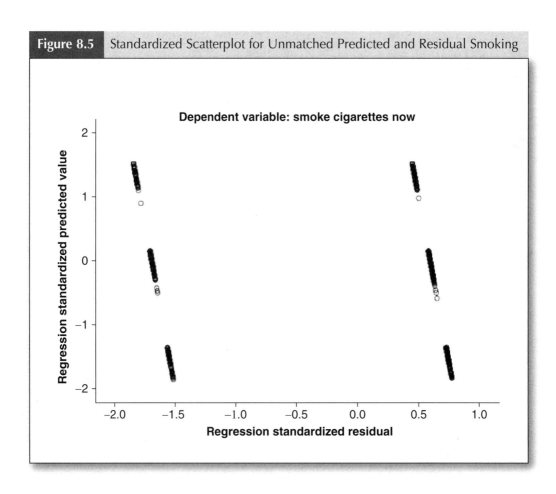

**Figure 8.5**    Standardized Scatterplot for Unmatched Predicted and Residual Smoking

smoking data previously analyzed with LR. This scatterplot shows two parallel lines of residuals that occur as a downward slope. This implies that there is a pattern in the scatterplot, even though the correlation between the two standardized variables is zero. The pattern is not linear. Something is wrong with this regression. The assumptions for OLS regression are poorly met because the dependent variable is dichotomous and so are two of the predictors. The only ratio level measure in the regression is the propensity score variable. This would argue against using these findings.

Despite violating assumptions for use of OLS regression, there is a similarity of its results with the LR result. Table 8.4 compares effect coefficients estimated by LR and by dummy variable OLS regression, with and without matching. The raw effect coefficients are completely different statistics: a regression coefficient of difference in probability of an outcome associated with the parent smoking and a ratio of the odds of adult smoking, given parent smoking. These statistics are standardized by dividing by their respective standard errors. The standardized results for the two different approaches are very similar.

## PROPENSITIES VERSUS TIME 1 CONTROLS

The baseline value of an outcome has been used as a control variable and as an adjustment factor for some time. In some cases, controlling for Time 1 value has had greater effects in reducing estimated treatment effects than using propensity scores (Shadish, 2010). There are two reasons why the baseline value may outperform propensities. First, the same confounding factors that influence the outcome are likely to influence those measures at an earlier point in time. Controlling the initial value of outcome measures partially controls those

| Table 8.4 | OLS and Logistic Regression of Adult Smoking | | | |
|---|---|---|---|---|
| | *Effect Statistic* | *Standard Error* | *Standardized Effect* | *N* |
| OLS unmatched | −.233 | 0.048 | 4.854 | 6,377 |
| LR unmatched | −.317 | 0.065 | 4.877 | 6,377 |
| OLS matched | −.288 | 0.146 | 1.973 | 1,034 |
| LR matched | −.421 | 0.214 | 1.967 | 1,034 |

*Note.* OLS, ordinary least squares; LR, logistic regression.

confounding factors, including the unobserved confounders that cannot be controlled by propensity scores. Even full matching and genetic matching, which are optimal procedures, do not employ information from confounders that were not measured. Second, many uses of propensity scores do not employ all the information present in the scores to reduce prior differences. The development of augmented inverse propensity weighting to use more information than rescaled inverse propensity weighting illustrates this issue.

Using baseline measures as controls does not always outperform using propensity scores. Sometimes, the two approaches produce similar results. Other times, the balance achieved by propensity use outperforms Time 1 values. Propensity scores are especially likely to outperform baseline values when the correlation of the confounder with selection into treatment is strong and the correlation with the outcome is moderate or weak. Such confounders improve the accuracy of the estimate of the propensity score without a similar effect on the estimate of their influence through Time 1 measures. When the correlation of the confounders with selection is weak and their correlation with the outcome is moderate or strong, then baseline measures may outperform propensity scores. If everything has a moderate or weak correlation, it's an empirical question as to whether one will outperform the other or produce the same result. In such a situation, one should try the alternative combinations to find out which works best.

Figure 8.6 provides an example where matching outperforms the baseline measure. It uses the respondent's smoking as a child as a Time 1 measure for adult smoking (Time 2). In this example, parents' smoking has a statistically significant effect on the odds of their child smoking as an adult. The respondent's behavior in smoking as a child does not have a statistically significant effect when the influences of parents' smoking and the confounders that influence parents' smoking are controlled. Parents' smoking also influences smoking by the respondent as a child. In causal terminology, this model supports an interpretation that the relationship between smoking as a child and smoking as an adult is a spurious effect. Because this model is illustrative and not tested against alternative models, this does not preclude alternative models in which such a causal effect is present.

## PROPENSITIES AND TIME 1 CONTROLS

The contribution of a baseline measure of the outcome to removing bias from sample selectivity depends on its correlation with both measured and unmeasured confounders. If all of the confounding factors are measured and used in

| Figure 8.6 | Adult Smoking Estimated Model (N = 1,044) |
|---|---|

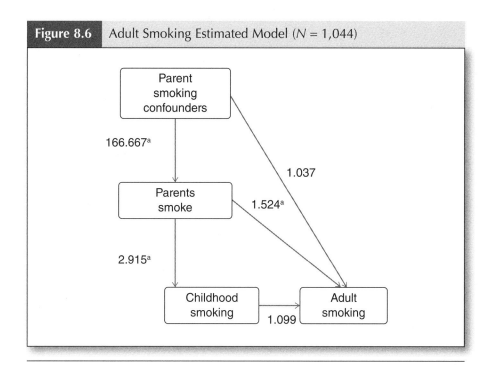

a. Coefficient is significant at $p < .05$. Coefficients are partial odds ratios. Some coefficients have been inverted to facilitate interpretation because they were coded in the opposite direction of interpretation. The smoking confounder odds is the ratio of all confounders present versus all the confounders absent.

the selectivity model that estimates the propensity scores (the assumption of strong ignorability), then the baseline measure may not add a great deal to getting an unbiased estimate of the treatment effect. If there are unmeasured confounders, however, using the baseline measure may well improve the estimate of treatment effects.

If some of the imbalance is a result of unmeasured confounders, they cannot be directly controlled. Some of this influence, however, can be removed by using Time 1 measures. Confounders that correlate with Time 2 measures are likely to also correlate with Time 1 measures. Time 1 measure can act as a surrogate measure of the unmeasured confounders. Controlling it removes some, but not usually all, of the bias of the unmeasured confounders. If a confounder has its effect through Time 1 measure (if Time 1 fully mediates the confounder), then controlling Time 1 will remove the bias from the confounder.

If all the imbalance is a result of measured confounders, adjusting or controlling for them will remove all the imbalance (Rosenbaum & Rubin, 1983). The baseline measure of the outcome, however, may still have an influence on the outcome apart from the confounders. Particularly, if the phenomenon dealt with is a developmental process or is subject to a feedback or reciprocal process, the variable at Time 1 may influence that variable at Time 2. In such a situation, there needs to be a baseline measure of the outcome to accurately estimate the treatment effect.

Take the adult smoking example. Adult smoking has bivariate correlations with smoking by one's parents and smoking as a child. Smoking as a child may lead to nicotine addiction, which can lead to adult smoking. The separate effects of the parent example and the nicotine addiction cannot be assessed without controlling for the baseline values of childhood smoking.

A baseline measure can be regarded either as another confounder or as an alternative causal influence. Given the correlation of the baseline measure with other confounders, it is hard to tell whether it should be treated separately or not. If one is interested in the relative effects of the treatment compared with that of the feedback or developmental process, one would have to treat the baseline measure as an alternative influence—not purely as a confounder. If one regards the baseline measure more as a surrogate for other confounders not measured, it should be treated as a confounder. Researchers may reasonably disagree on how it should be treated. Evidence may support either model as a reasonable estimator of the causal effect. This is particularly difficult if different evidence favors the alternative models. One must offer arguments why one set of evidence should be favored over another and hope the arguments are convincing to opposing viewpoints. When they are not, new studies may have to be designed to provide a more convincing test of the competing models. This means that the new studies must provide a direct test of both models with sufficient robustness that opposing results cannot be attributed to happenstance.

## ASSESSING COVARIATE RESULTS

Assessing the covariate results means examining the use of covariates as adjustors. When a propensity score variable has a statistically significant relationship with the treatment variable, adjusting or controlling will reduce the bias from pretest imbalance. When matching has been done first and the propensity variable is still associated with the intervention, then adjusting or controlling for the propensity variable will remove imbalance beyond that reduced by the matching process. When matching is the primary strategy and imbalance remains, one might also adjust or control for the propensity variable to see if the imbalance remains significant.

To examine imbalance after adjusting or controlling when matched samples have already been created, one residualizes the confounding variables (i.e., subtracts the value predicted by the propensity score from each confounder and uses the difference as a confounder). If the residualized confounders are no longer significantly different between the intervention and the control groups, then modification of the selection model is not required. One can, of course, continue to explore the selection model if one wishes; but it is not a statistical requirement.

When additional control variables have been added to the outcome or impact model, their coefficients represent their effect controlling not only for the intervention impact but also for all the confounders that were included in the selection model. This does not, however, control for effects that the confounders may have by interacting with the control variables. The interactive effects might be correlated with the additive effects of the confounders, but they still influence the outcome apart from their additive effects through the selection process. When control variables are used beyond the propensity variable, one must consider whether such interactive effects are possible. If they are, then one must compute multiplicative terms to use as control variables and must examine whether their coefficients are significant.

Control variables may also be used to treat certain characteristics as fixed effects within one's outcome model (D'Agostino, 1998). Using this approach to "fixing," a characteristic is simpler, less time-consuming, and cheaper than fixing a characteristic by research design—even though using the research design to produce fixed effects is generally preferable. Using design to fix effects is a well-known process and generally results in fixed effects. Using statistical controls to produce fixed effects, however, depends on meeting more statistical assumptions than fixing by design. If the assumptions are arguable, then using a design approach might be preferable. If the assumptions are reasonable, this statistical approach to fixed effects can be pursued. When using controls to produce fixed effect variables, the coefficients of these variables must be evaluated as fixed effects estimates, rather than as random effects estimates.

Control variables included in propensity analysis must also be assessed as they would be in OLS, ANCOVA, or LR models. The errors in predicting the outcome need to be examined to see if they correlate with the confounding variables or with any independent variables included in one's estimation equation. Even in the absence of correlation, visual inspection of the errors with the independents should be done to assess nonlinear relationships between the errors and the independents. An obvious pattern in those relationships indicates that the estimation equation did not fully capture all that is going on. The outcome model is misspecified. Control variables that have a patterned relationship with the outcome need to be examined further to try determining how the full relationship may be captured. This applies even if the correlation is zero, because the correlation only captures linear covariation—unless higher order terms, transforms, and multiplicative terms are also included.

When such terms are included and the patterned relationships with the errors in prediction appear to disappear, the next step is to consider whether these terms can be given theoretical or substantive interpretation. Adding additional terms to the prediction equation may improve the look of the relationship between the error terms and the control variables. However, if those terms cannot be given theoretical or substantive interpretation, this leaves open the possibility that some terms may have been added as a result of a false-positive decision—that is, that they don't represent any causal influence of any kind and are just unusual random variation. This implies that the model may be over-specified and that the true outcome model may have fewer terms in it than the model that was estimated. The decision to add or delete terms from a model cannot be a purely statistical one. That decision has to make sense, given one's theoretical understanding and substantive knowledge of the outcome being explained.

## ASSESSING ADEQUACY AND SUFFICIENCY OF COVARIATES

The statistical adequacy and sufficiency of using control variables depends on the selection and outcome models and on the procedures used to estimate those models. As was the case previously, both models must be correctly specified to meet the ignorability supposition. This also meets one of the adequacy criteria. A model cannot meet the ignorability supposition unless it is correctly specified. Correct specification of the selection model and the outcome model is also necessary for statistical adequacy.

Beyond correct specification, control and adjustment models must also use plausible assumptions for procedures that estimate the effects. This means that there must be correspondence between the level of measurement of the indicators (including control variables) and the level of measurement appropriate for a given statistical procedure. This is particularly a problem for control variables. It is common to convert categorical variables into dummy variables. This is perfectly reasonable if the split between the two categories is not too extreme. When the split between the two categories is extreme, the estimates of the means and variances for these variables are poor estimates of the expected value and variability of the measures. If dummy variables have extreme splits (say, outside an 80/20 distribution), it is better to use the categorical variables as categorical variables and not covert to dummy variables.

Not using categorical variables as dummy variables affects the degrees of freedom available for the analysis. If statistics must be computed as weighted averages among groups, this reduces the degrees of freedom and complicates the computation. With unequal distribution of cases among groups, some groups may have few or no cases. This can greatly expand the error variances of the estimated effects or make such estimation impossible.

If data are such that dummy variables are not recommended and using categorical variables is difficult or impossible, one must choose among undesirable alternatives. Either the assumptions for use are violated and the estimate is not adequate or the assumptions are met and the estimate is not very robust. One can, of course, estimate the effect both ways and hope that the results are in agreement. If they are, the results are adequate and probably reliable. If the results of the alternative methods do not agree, it is a difficult choice for which there are no agreed-on strategies. This author prefers the results that are statistically adequate. If that is not possible, cautionary remarks should be added to the not statistically adequate results.

The statistical sufficiency of analysis using control variables depends on there not being any additional information that would alter the result. For control variable analysis, this means that there must not be any omitted important control variables. The same is true for adjusting variables. The outcome model must include all important control and adjusting variables.

Beyond the issue of omitted variables, the procedure for estimating the treatment effect must be an unbiased estimator. No biased estimator is statistically sufficient. If the addition of information regarding the degree of bias can improve the estimate, then the estimator is not sufficient. In this situation, one cannot say that causal effects are clearly demonstrated. One might be able to say the results "are consistent with" a possible causal effect.

The use of estimation procedures whose assumptions correspond to the hypothesis and the data is a key element of having sufficient estimators. The example in which OLS regression was used to produce results similar to a more appropriate use of LR shows that nonsufficient statistics can sometimes produce results approximating a result estimated from a more sufficient analysis. In this example, even the LR is not sufficient because there are undoubtedly omitted variables. Yet, between the two approaches, the LR estimate is probably closer to the true sufficient estimate than the OLS estimate.

One's use of control variables or adjustors affects the sufficiency of the estimate. Strictly speaking, all confounding variables are control variables because you must remove their influence on selection and on the outcome. If you use such variables to adjust both, they function as control variables. Their influence is controlled. This is what matching does. On the other hand, if confounders are used to adjust only the intervention or the outcome, but not both, they are adjustors without being controllers. Such use is appropriate when the research question is asking about effects in special circumstances; that is, where one influence on a particular variable has been removed or where the effect without the presence of a particular characteristic is examined.

Different research questions or hypotheses require alternative uses of control variables and adjustors. To answer one research question may require using a variable as a control; while answering another may require using it as an adjustor. It is not inherent in the variables, whether their use as control variables or adjusting variables produces a sufficient statistic. It is the fit between the research question or hypothesis and how the variable is used that must be considered in deciding whether a control variable or an adjusting variable produces sufficient statistics.

# CHAPTER 9

# Use With Generalized Linear Models

This chapter examines the use of generalized linear models when propensity scores are used. It identifies issues for this procedure that arise with using propensity scores and discusses strategies for dealing with those issues. It presents and discusses criteria for judging the adequacy of the analysis when propensity scores are used.

Ordinary least squares (OLS) regression has been extended to the general linear model (GLM), which includes analysis of variance (ANOVA), analysis of covariance (ANCOVA), $t$ tests, and maximum likelihood estimation (MLE). GLM is a family of approaches used in analyzing data with propensity scores. GLM is applied mainly to outcomes that are normally or symmetrically distributed. GLM, in turn, has been generalized by Nelder and Wedderbom (1972) to apply to a larger class of data that are not normally distributed. This generalization of GLM is generalized linear models. It is also called generalized linear modeling (as opposed to general linear modeling) and generalized linear regression. The similarity of the names has caused confusion between them because they both have been abbreviated as GLM. Users of the general linear model commonly use GLM for that procedure. Users of the generalized linear model widely use GLM as an abbreviation for that procedure. Neither group is likely to give up using an abbreviation that has wide use among their group. For pedagogical reasons, the same abbreviation will not be used for both procedures. Some researchers have used the abbreviations GZM, GZL, or GZLM for generalized linear modeling to avoid this confusion. This book will use the abbreviation GZLM for generalized linear modeling because it is used a little more frequently than other abbreviations, except GLM, and it clearly differentiates it from general linear modeling. The book will use GLM only to refer to the general linear model, as there is a need to make comparisons and contrasts between GLM, GZLM, and logistic regression (LR)—particularly when binomial data are involved. GZLM includes both GLM and LR, as well as other techniques. The reader should keep in mind, however, that many authors still use GLM for both generalized and general linear modeling. All major statistical programs now have generalized linear modeling, as well as general linear modeling, programs. SPSS and SAS use GLM to stand for general linear modeling. The R program and Stata use GLM for generalized linear modeling. The Genlin program in SPSS and the Genmod procedure in SAS do generalized linear modeling. Linear model (LM) is used by the R program for general linear modeling. Stata uses GLM for both generalized linear modeling and general linear modeling. When reading articles that use general linear modeling or generalized linear modeling, the user is cautioned to pay close attention to which abbreviation is being used and what procedure is meant by it.

GZLM extends linear regression to nonnormal distributions. In particular, it extends linear modeling to the Poisson, binomial, exponential, inverse Gauss, and gamma distributions. This generalization expresses a variety of regression models as a linear equation. It does not require that the relationships of the variables in the equation themselves be linear. GZLM increases the range of outcome measures that can be used by the same procedure. MLE, Poisson regression (PR), binomial regression, probit regression, and LR are all included within GZLM.

GZLM does not include the analysis of repeated measures or correlated samples. That is provided by a further extension to GZLM, known as generalized estimation equations (GEE). The procedures for GEE will be discussed in Chapter 10.

## GENERALIZED LINEAR MODELS

GZLM can answer questions about treatment effects for which ANOVA, ANCOVA, OLS, and LR are not appropriate. When outcome measures are frequency counts, they may follow a Poisson distribution. If the average or expected value for a frequency count is close to zero, the distribution will be Poisson. As the expected value of frequency counts increases, it approaches a normal distribution. If the average frequency is greater than 3 standard deviations above zero, it generally doesn't matter whether one uses GLM or PR. If it is less than 3 standard deviations above zero, PR will give better results than GLM. There are distributions other than Poisson for which ANOVA, ANCOVA, or LR are not appropriate. GZLM can estimate treatment effects for most of them.

GZLM can be applied to a broader class of distributions, including normal, Poisson, and logit. However, one needs to know which distribution the data follow. One has to determine whether one should treat the outcome as having a Poisson, normal, exponential, inverse Gauss (also called a Wald distribution), or some other distribution to which GZLM applies.

This procedure does not assume that relationships are linear. It assumes that the relationships can be expressed in a linear equation. This equation is the generalization of the GLM. For GLM, the equation has the form of traditional linear regression:

$$Y = \alpha + \beta_1 X_1 + \cdots + \beta_n X_n, \tag{9.1}$$

where $\alpha$ is a constant and $\beta_i$ are the weights for the $X_i$ predictors.

The generalization adds an additional function to the basic equation that defines the relationship between the expected value in the GLM (usually, the mean) and the expected value of a specific type of distribution (often, not the mean). This function, referred to as a link function, is determined by the type of distribution in question. It transforms the linear relationships of the GLM into nonlinear relationships under GZLM. The formula under GZLM is as follows:

$$Y = \alpha + g(\beta_1 X_1 + \cdots + \beta_n X_n), \tag{9.2}$$

where $\alpha$, $\beta_i$, and $X_i$ are defined as in Equation 9.1; and $g$ is the link function (the transform) that converts the nonlinear relationships into linear relationships.

The Kolmogorov–Smirnov (K–S) one-sample test can be used comparing the observed distribution with one whose shape is specified. The K–S test was introduced to test whether a distribution was normal. It can also test whether the distribution corresponds to other distributions. In using a K–S test, one specifies what type of distribution is being compared with the observed distribution. The significance probability that they are the same is produced. One can also inspect a frequency distribution to get an idea as to the shape of the distribution and which type it is. In addition, the skewness and kurtosis of a distribution can be examined to get an idea as to the shape of the distribution. One can then test whether the distribution is more likely to be normal, Poisson, binomial, or some other shape and decide which estimation procedure and link function within GZLM is more appropriate. Many nonnormal distributions are skewed and have a tall peak (leptokurtosis) or extreme tail (skewness).

As noted in Table 9.1, using different link functions with GZLM results in estimating different models. LR and GLM models both can be estimated with a GZLM program by selecting the appropriate link function. A link function converts the mean of a specified nonnormal distribution into the mean of normal distribution, depending on the link function chosen. This also affects the shape of the distribution. Thus, different distributions use different link functions when GZLM estimates treatment effects.

Although the distribution of the outcome measures is an empirical question, it is related to the research question one is asking regarding treatment effects. As indicated in Table 9.1, if one asks about treatment effects that are scale values, the distribution produced can often be estimated using a GLM approach. If the treatment effects are frequency counts, the distribution may be Poisson, for which either PR (for small means) or GLM (for larger means) is appropriate.

If the treatment effects concern yes/no or dichotomous outcomes, then LR or probit regression will be appropriate. LR is used if one wishes to estimate treatment effects as number of outcomes out of possible outcomes (a Bernoulli

**Table 9.1    Distributions, Link Functions, and Estimation Procedures**

| Distribution | Typical Uses | Link Name | Link Function | Estimation Procedure |
|---|---|---|---|---|
| Normal | Scale response data | Identity | $X\beta = \mu$ | GLM |
| Exponential gamma | Exponential response data, scale data | Inverse or exponential | $X\beta = \mu^{-1}$ | GZLM |
| Inverse Gauss/ Wald | Brownian, random behavior | Inverse squared | $X\beta = \mu^{-2}$ | GZLM |
| Poisson | Counts of events | Log | $X\beta = \ln(\mu)$ | PR |
| Bernoulli | Outcome of dichotomous event or relative likelihood | Logit | $X\beta = \ln\left(\dfrac{\mu}{1-\mu}\right)$ | LR |
| Binomial | Count of number of "yes" events out of $N$ yes/no events | Logit | | LR |

*Note.* GLM, general linear model; GZLM, generalized linear model; PR, Poisson regression; LR, logistic regression.

distribution). It is also used if the question concerns the relative outcomes for intervention versus nonintervention (a binomial distribution).

There is an intimate relationship between GLM as an approach and the LR approach. As noted by Nelder and Wedderbom (1972), there is a linkage function that can represent these estimated outcomes in the same general, linear, functional form. The diverse procedures, however, produce results that have different interpretations. This is directly related to different questions being asked and different linkage functions being needed to answer those questions.

The ability of GZLM to perform GLM, PR, or LR depends on the linkage function used to create the corresponding linear model. Table 9.1 summarizes the data distribution, data type, and link function used to estimate various outcome effects. This table implies that a generalized strategy can be used for estimating many outcome effects. The version of the strategy depends on the distribution and type of the observed data. The type of data chosen, in turn, depends on the research question that is being asked. Consequently, the research question should be used to select both the measures of intervention effects and the analytical procedure used to estimate those effects. A summary of this relationship between research question, expected distribution of outcomes, and appropriate estimation procedure is stated in Table 9.2. It should be noted that if the observed distribution is at odds with the expected distribution, there is a need to reexamine why a particular distribution is expected and the choice of estimation procedure. It may mean revising the formulation of the research question.

When using GZLM software, one must specify the shape of the distribution and choice of the link function to achieve the appropriate estimation procedure. With OLS regression, the shape is normal and the link function is a simple identity. The mean equals the mean. It should be noted that GZLM will do MLE rather than least squares estimation in this case. If the normality assumption is correct, however, the regression coefficients will be the same. If the type of distribution and the link function are not specified, most GZLM programs use default values for the distribution and the link function—making inferences from the model specified.

It is better to specify a specific type of distribution and link function. This requires the user to recognize what type of distribution of data is expected as a result of the assumptions of the research question. If the data turn out not to have that distribution, this may require only changing the distribution and link function specification in the program to achieve a better result. Such change in the estimation procedure, however, implies a change in assumptions of the research question.

| Table 9.2 | Research Question, Outcome Distribution, and Estimation Procedure | | |
|---|---|---|---|

| Typical Research Question | Outcome Distribution | Appropriate Estimation Procedure |
|---|---|---|
| What is the level or scale of the effect with linear impacts? | Normal | GLM |
| What is the level of effect with exponential impacts? | Exponential/ gamma | GZLM |
| What is the level of effect with inverse exponential impacts (highly skewed tail on upper end)? | Inverse Gaussian | GZLM |
| What is the frequency or count of the outcome? | Poisson | PR |
| What is the likely outcome of a dichotomous event? | Bernoulli | LR |
| What is the expected outcome of dichotomous events? | Binomial | LR |

*Note.* GLM, general linear model; PR, Poisson regression; LR, logistic regression.

Changing the assumptions may have broader theoretical implications regarding the process that produces the effect under study. If one selects a different distribution and link function, one is implicitly saying that a different process produces the impact. If it is necessary to change the analytical procedure, it may require changing one's theory that produced the research question being studied. At the very least, the process said to have produced the result needs reexamining.

As indicated in Tables 9.1 and 9.2, when the outcome measures have a normal, gamma, exponential, or inverse exponential distribution, GLM or GZLM procedures are generally fine for estimating treatment effects. When the outcomes are frequency counts, PR procedures generally work best. When the outcomes are dichotomous, LR estimation is most appropriate. This does not mean that one cannot get useful or interesting results by using alternative procedures. It does mean that in these circumstances, there is a better match between the assumptions of a given technique, those of the research question, and the actual distribution of the data.

If there is no linkage between the questions, the data, and the estimation procedure, the assumptions for that procedure will not be met. While it is true that alternative estimation procedures can produce similar or identical results (as noted in the previous chapter), the only guarantee that this will be the case is if the techniques share the same assumptions. When different estimation procedures produce similar results, this argues that the correct estimate is somewhere in the vicinity of those estimates. This may allow establishing bounds within which the true estimate is likely to be found. This true estimate is more likely to be closer to that of the procedure whose assumptions are consistent with those implied by the research question.

All major statistical packages have programs for doing GLM, LR, and GZLM analysis. One may choose the package with which one is most familiar. It should be noted, as mentioned previously, the diverse packages may call different subroutines for performing the same tasks. Slightly different results can be produced. Small differences in the results produced by different packages can be regarded as random error in estimation. Larger differences require investigation. There may be differences in filtering or weighting cases or matrix inversion that produce different results with poorly behaved data. With well-behaved data, large differences should not occur. It may be a result of the well-known explanation for unusual computer results, "probable user error." A close examination of the commands used is warranted.

When doing GLM, one may choose a specialized program, such as an ANOVA program, a regression analysis program, or a PR program, or one may use the more general GLM program found in most packages. The choice is not arbitrary. Typically, there are options available in one program that are not necessarily available in another program that performs ostensibly the same analysis. The programs may even provide different additional statistics beyond what is regarded as the core information required for a particular kind of analysis. For example, one can do a two-sample comparison of means with a $t$ test, an ANOVA program, or GLM. However, the ANOVA program is likely to provide between-group sums of squares and within-group sums of squares that are not directly provided by the other programs. These can usually be calculated from the results presented, but they are not typically provided directly. Having the additional information can occasionally be useful, in this case for calculating Hedge's $g$ to estimate program effects. There may also be differences in how the results are plotted when producing charts from the programs.

The choice between different estimation procedures means specifying the alternative models that need to be estimated. The choice among models should also consider the convenience of estimating a model. If a model is difficult to estimate, it is more likely to result in errors. When the research questions imply that different estimation procedures are appropriate for different questions—for example, PR for a question dealing with frequency counts and LR for a question dealing with the likelihood of a dichotomous outcome—it is advisable to use whatever procedure encompasses all of the estimation approaches. This may require using a GZLM program to estimate ANOVA, ANCOVA, and LR models. Errors are less likely to be made when using a common program for multiple runs.

Table 9.3 provides an example where a model is estimated using OLS and GZLM. This model estimates household income using a propensity matched sample for presence or absence of babies in the household. The estimation also controls for the highest year of education of the respondent. The purpose of using the matched sample here is the same as before—to evaluate the effect of baby presence on household income. The model controls for education because education is related to income, and it was not included in the selection model that predicted baby's presence. The results between OLS and GZLM estimates of babies and education effects are identical within the precision reported on the output. However, the estimated value of the intercept, the standard errors for the parameters, and the significance probabilities differ between the two estimation procedures.

**Table 9.3    OLS and GZLM Estimation of Household Income**

| Program and Variable | Parameter | Standard Error | Significance Probability | No. of Cases |
|---|---|---|---|---|
| Ordinary least squares regression (OLS) | | | | 523 |
| Intercept | −48,414 | 14,081 | .001 | |
| Baby in household | −15,788 | 5,002 | .002 | |
| Education | 9,438 | 992 | .000 | |
| Generalized linear model (GZLM) | | | | 523 |
| Intercept | −64,202 | 14,290 | .000 | |
| Baby in household | −15,788 | 4,987 | .002 | |
| Education | 9,438 | 989 | .000 | |

The standard errors for the parameters estimated by GZLM are smaller than for OLS. This is largely due to OLS using least squares estimation for the parameters and GZLM using MLE. In this case, the end result is the same estimated parameters. For well-behaved data, the parameters will be the same, excluding rounding error. GZLM will have slightly greater precision because of MLE. It is difficult to say which procedure will outperform the other with poorly behaved data. If the problems with the data are multiple distinct modes, multiple inflection points, or gaps in a continuous relationship, the MLE may converge on the wrong values. If the problem is extreme skewness, OLS may give poor estimates by minimizing errors around a mean that is not the expected value for the distribution.

Figure 9.1 examines the similarity of the results further with a scatterplot of the residuals from the OLS estimate of income and the GZLM estimate. If the data are poorly behaved, curvilinear or discontinuous patterns will appear in this scattergram. In this instance, there is a perfect fit between the two residuals. The regression coefficient and the $R^2$ are 1.0. Only a single linear pattern is present. One may reasonably infer that the two methods produce the same result. If the relationship in the scatterplot were not linear, examination of the alternative regressions would be needed to determine the source of the problem.

It is better to use the same program when one has a number of models to estimate, even when unique aspects of a particular program's output might suggest that a different program be used for different models. If using a different program for a few runs is necessary, it should be replicated with the program used more often. This helps ensure consistency in the results produced. Using corresponding statistics for different relationships estimated by alternative programs can produce inconsistent results, unless one is careful.

## LOGISTIC REGRESSION

When outcomes are dichotomous events, a binomial or gamma distribution may result. LR applies when the outcomes are dichotomous and some of the predictors are dichotomous or categorical. It uses the odds ratio instead of correlations as a measure of association. The odds ratio is not normally distributed. Factors that lower the probability of an outcome have an odds ratio between 0 and 1.0. Factors that increase the probability of an outcome have an odds ratio between 1.0 and infinity.

To deal with the asymmetry of the odds ratio, it is transformed into a unimodal, symmetrical distribution by taking the natural log of the odds ratio

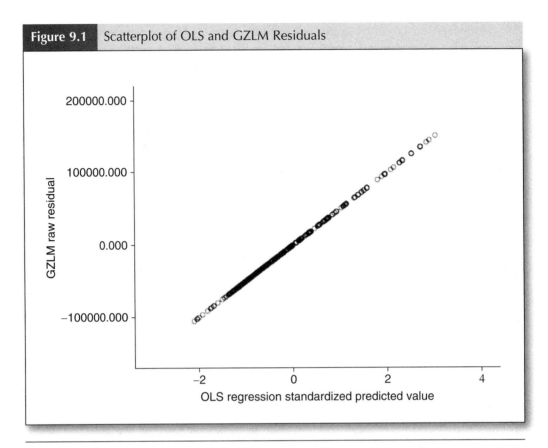

**Figure 9.1**    Scatterplot of OLS and GZLM Residuals

*Note.* OLS, ordinary least squares regression; GZLM, generalized linear model.

(log to the base *e*). This is the logit. A logit of 0 implies a factor has no effect on the likelihood an outcome will occur. A negative logit implies the factor decreases the likelihood of an event; a positive logit, that it will increase the likelihood.

A traditional format for the formula for LR estimation is given in Equation 9.3:

$$L_Y = \ln\left[\frac{\Pr\left(Y_i = 1 \mid X_i\right)}{\Pr\left(Y_i = 0 \mid X_i\right)}\right], \tag{9.3}$$

where $L_Y$ is the likelihood that an event will occur, Pr is the probability of event $Y$ conditional on the value of $X_1$, and ln is the natural logarithm transform to convert odds into logits. An alternative format for this equation is that of Equation 9.4.

$$L_Y = g(\alpha + \beta_1 X_1 + \cdots + \beta_F X_F), \qquad (9.4)$$

where $\alpha$ is a constant, $\beta_i$ are conditional probabilities of event $Y$ occurring given characteristic $X_i$, where $X$ is coded 0 or 1 for presence or absence of the characteristic, and $g$ is the logarithmic transform to convert odds ratios into symmetrical distributions. For LR, the transform is the natural logarithm. The form of Equation 9.4 reveals that an LR model with an appropriate transform can be expressed as a linear sum equation.

LR makes several assumptions to estimate effects. These are the following:

- The dependent variable is a dichotomy or polychotomy (a binomial variable or a multinomial variable).
- The probability of an event is a logistic function of the independent variables.
- All confounding variables are included.
- The errors in the measures of the independent variables are uncorrelated.
- The observations are independent.
- The independent variables are not linear combinations of each other.

Some of these assumptions are the same as those used to estimate propensity scores. They are justified by the theoretical grounding for the research question or hypothesis being studied. If the data do not seem to meet these assumptions, then LR estimation needs to be reconsidered. If the data seem to support these assumptions, LR may proceed. A key assumption is the one regarding the probability of an event being a logistic function of the independent variables. Logistic functions are often generated by a process of exponential growth or decay that is limited by some constraint (e.g., resources or population density) that is time dependent. In this situation, the likelihood of an event is a function of the values of the constraining variables (since they are also related to the number of events at a given point in time). An example of a logistic growth curve is given in Figure 9.2. A research question that might use LR to obtain an answer might be "What is the likelihood that a person given treatment will experience the specified outcome?" Alternatively, one might ask, "Does a person who has experienced the intervention have a higher likelihood of a specified outcome than a person who has not experienced the intervention?" For both these

**Figure 9.2** Cumulative Frequency for Logistic Curve[a]

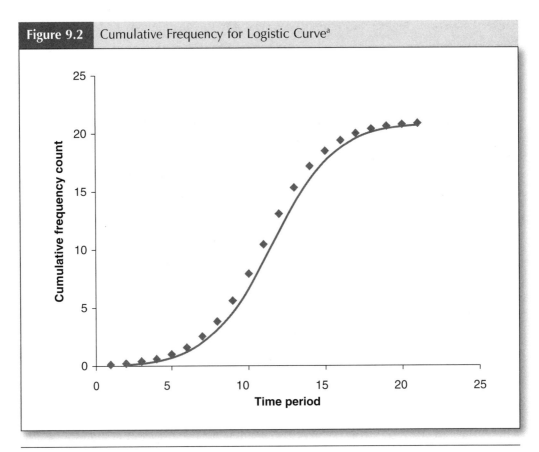

a. Cumulative frequency (cumulative density function, cdf) for $M = 12$, $SD = 2$, max = 21 (the constraint).

questions to be appropriate for LR, the treatment or intervention would theoretically have to affect those factors that constrain the specified outcome.

It is common that the binomial dependent variable is coded as 0 for condition or event absent and 1 for condition or event present. When the variable is coded as 0 and 1, interpreting the coefficients becomes easier as there is a direct conversion of the expected value of the outcome and the probability of the outcome. This is the same process as for estimating propensity scores. It is one of the reasons why LR is the procedure used most often for estimating propensity scores.

When doing LR, one may use either an LR program or a GZLM program. The estimated treatment effect should be the same for both programs. GZLM programs, however, provide more options for statistics produced as a result of having more estimation procedures. On the other hand, LR programs typically provide a classification table that compares observed classification with predicted classification, so that one can determine whether there are more errors in predicting the occurrence of the event or its absence. One must determine whether the LR program produces the statistics one needs. If it does and LR is the only procedure to be used for estimating outcomes, then using an LR program is fine. If one uses GZLM, a classification table can be constructed by computing the estimated probabilities of the outcomes and classifying on the basis of the probabilities and a chosen criterion for classification (often a probability >.50).

An example of using LR and GZLM is given in Table 9.4. This table summarizes an LR analysis using an LR program and a GZLM program when the same model is estimated. For this example, the SPSS programs LOGISTIC REGRESSION and GENLIN were used. The model uses the Health and Retirement Study (HRS) data to estimate the effect of parents' smoking on the likelihood of their child having respiratory problems before age 16. Parental smoking was recoded into a dichotomy of neither smokes and either smokes. Because these two groups differ in prior characteristics, the samples matched by propensity scores estimated in Chapter 5 were used to estimate the effects of parental smoking. The outcome was a dichotomy for the presence or absence of respiratory disorder before age 16 for the HRS respondent.

| Table 9.4 | LR and GZLM Estimation of Respiratory Disorder | | | |
|---|---|---|---|---|
| *Program and Variable* | *Parameter* | *Standard Error* | *Significance Probability* | *No. of Cases* |
| Logistic regression (LR) | | | | 1,034 |
| Intercept | 2.001 | 0.913 | .028 | |
| Parental smoking | 0.291 | 0.461 | .528 | |
| Propensity | 13.934 | 2.154 | .000 | |
| Generalized linear model (GZLM) | | | | 1,034 |
| Intercept | 1.711 | 0.776 | .027 | |
| Parental smoking | 0.291 | 0.461 | .528 | |
| Propensity | 13.934 | 2.154 | .000 | |

Since the matched sample was created for a situation that used a different outcome, the confounders might differ, leading to inadequate control of prior variables. The recommended strategy is to create new matched samples for each outcome when there are no other variables in the estimation equation. If there are other variables in the estimation equations and they are present for different outcomes, then using different matched samples can produce inconsistent estimates of the effects of the alternative variables. However, if the confounders identified for different outcomes are the same or mostly the same, then including confounders for all the outcomes in one estimated propensity score allows creating one matched sample that can be used for estimating the different effects. As noted previously, including additional prior variables in the confounder list does not bias the estimated effects. It reduces precision. If the estimated effects are significant, that is not a major problem. It is a problem if the confounder for one outcome is an intervening (mediating) variable for another outcome. In that case, separate propensity scores would need to be estimated for the different outcomes.

To increase the control over prior variables, the propensity score variable was also used as a covariate in the LR estimation. The results of this estimation are given in Table 9.4.

The results from the replicated analysis are virtually identical. The standard errors differ only at the fourth decimal point, except for the intercept of the equation. The significance probabilities differ by .001. Both analyses indicate that parental smoking does not affect respiratory disorder before age 16 for those in the HRS sample. Note, however, that those who had respiratory disorder prior to age 16 and whose parents smoked may have had increased mortality prior to the age for entering the HRS compared with those whose parents didn't smoke and had respiratory disorder. This would be a situation where there was an uncontrolled confounding variable, which might alter the findings. These findings are illustrative and do not provide causal evidence that parental smoking does not influence respiratory disorder among their children.

An example of respiratory disorder classification output is provided in Table 9.5. In this table, we see that all the errors in classification occur in a failure to predict those with respiratory disorder. None were predicted by the model. In contrast, 98% of those predicted as not having a disorder did not have a breathing disorder. This classification is notable in that none of the subjects were predicted as having a breathing disorder. This suggests that the model needs additional predictors, ones that are more strongly related to this outcome. This problem is especially likely to occur for infrequently occurring events.

The propensity variable is statistically significant for both estimation procedures. This indicates that adding the propensity as a covariate has reduced

| Table 9.5 | Classification Table for Breathing Disorder | | | |
|---|---|---|---|---|
| | | Predicted Breathing Disorder | | Percent Correct |
| | | Yes | No | |
| Observed breathing disorder | Yes | 0 | 26 | 0.0 |
| | No | 0 | 1,035 | 100.0 |

influence of the confounding variables beyond that produced by the matching procedure. Had the propensity not been included, the estimated effect on child's respiratory disorder would have been different.

In the circumstance where one is using a .001 alpha level and the effect was barely significant, the two procedures might lead to a different conclusion. In this circumstance where alpha of .05 is used, that is not the case. Estimates from either program lead to the same conclusion and the same parameter estimates. When one has findings that are barely significant or barely fail significance criteria, however, a little caution is warranted.

The choice between GLM and LR is sometimes a clear-cut decision. If all the propensity confounders, control variables, and outcomes are continuous, symmetrical measures (interval or ratio), GLM is preferred. If most of the variables (especially the outcome) are categorical, LR is preferred. When the measurement level of confounders and control variables is mixed, however, the choice is less clear. Categorical variables can be converted to dummy variables and used in GLM. Continuous variables can be used in LR or, even, recoded as categorical variables. The choice between the two approaches depends on the question one is trying to answer, statistical properties of the indicators, and personal preferences of the data analyst.

A research question may ask whether an outcome occurs more often as a result of an intervention (a frequency or percentage question), or it may ask whether an outcome is more likely to happen (an odds ratio or logit question). These two questions are very similar. Given one question, one can always reword it to become the other. However, they are not the same question. They require different information to answer. The former is concerned with the distribution of events. It is concerned with how many events will occur. The latter question is concerned with the likelihood of an event— whether it is more or less likely than some other event. It asks whether an outcome is more likely for those given a treatment than those not given a treatment. Both of these questions are important, but they are not the same. If one asks the first question, GLM will often provide the answer. If one asks the second question, LR will often provide the answer. GZLM can answer either question.

More specifically, the nature of the research question affects whether one uses PR or LR. A question that asks about the probability of an outcome is more appropriately answered using PR procedures—supposing assumptions for PR are met. A question that asks about whether one outcome is more likely than an alternative outcome is more appropriately answered using LR procedures. The distinction between these two questions is not trivial. One is more likely to ask the former question when one wants to know the average treatment effect on the treated. The latter question is more concerned with the relative effects between the untreated and the treatment groups—that is, the average treatment effects.

Both procedures can allow one to calculate average treatment effect on the treated and average treatment effects from the results. Slightly different inferences, however, may be made from using percentages versus using logits or odds ratios. They have a curvilinear relationship. The cutting points for judging strong, moderate, or weak effects are not strictly comparable. In some circumstances, an impact less than 30% may be regarded as weak. The corresponding odds ratio or logit would not necessarily be given that interpretation.

The relationship between odds ratio and percentage (or proportion) difference is illustrated in Figure 9.3. The figure shows that there is a curvilinear relationship between the percentage difference and the corresponding odds ratio, under the assumption that the percentages are occurring around a midpoint of 50. To achieve similar conclusions between percentages and odds ratios, the criteria for one would have to bear a curvilinear relationship to the other. For example, if 30% difference is judged to be the cutting point for weak relationships, then an odds ratio of 3.44 would have to be used, whereas if a 50% difference is judged moderate, an odds ratio of 9.0 would have to be used. The increase in the percentage difference is two thirds. The increase in the odds ratio is by a factor >5.5 because the relationship between the two statistics is curvilinear.

The situation is not greatly improved by switching to logits. The relationship between percentages and logits is illustrated in Figure 9.4. The relationship is also curvilinear, though not as curvilinear as that between percentage differences and odds ratios. If one is going to be discussing percentages and odds or logits, one needs to set consistent criteria prior to analyzing the data. As above, if one chooses a percentage difference of 30 for a moderate relationship, one should choose logits of 1.22 or odds of 3.44 to use a corresponding value. If one chooses a percentage difference of 60 for a strong relationship, values of 2.77 and 16 should be used for the logit and odds ratio.

| Figure 9.3 | Percentage Difference and Odds Ratio |
|---|---|

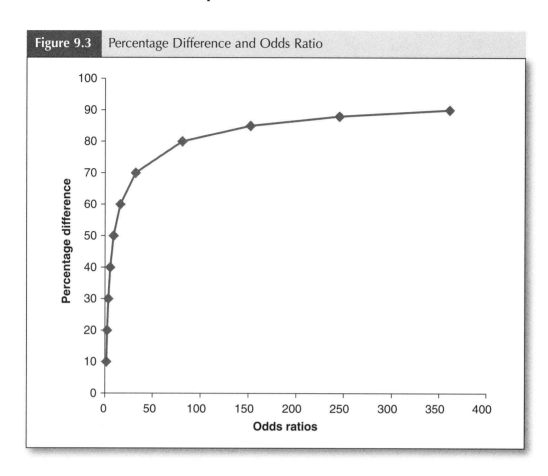

A summary of the relationships between percentage difference, odds ratios, and logits is given in Table 9.6. The reader can use the criteria offered for weak, moderate, or strong relationships or alternative ones. These are based on percentage differences. They may be applied to the other measures by selecting the corresponding value for an alternative statistic. Despite the curvilinearity, interpolating between adjacent numbers will give reasonable approximations of intermediate values.

## MATCHED DATA WITH GZLM

The examples in Tables 9.4 and 9.5 were based on cases that matched subjects on parental smoking propensity scores. This introduces greater control over the confounding factors that influence the outcomes. As argued in the chapter on

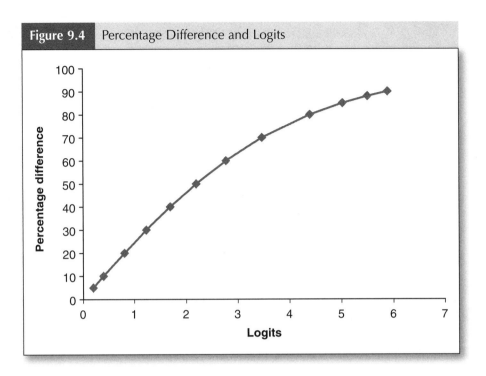

**Figure 9.4**    Percentage Difference and Logits

**Table 9.6**    Percentage Difference, Odds Ratios, and Logits

| Strength Characterization | Percentage Difference | Odds Ratio | Logit |
|---|---|---|---|
| Weak | 10 | 1.49 | 0.40 |
| | 20 | 2.25 | 0.81 |
| Moderate | 30 | 3.45 | 1.24 |
| | 40 | 5.44 | 1.69 |
| | 50 | 9.00 | 2.20 |
| Strong | 60 | 16.00 | 2.77 |
| | 70 | 32.11 | 3.47 |
| | 80 | 81.00 | 4.39 |
| | 85 | 152.11 | 5.02 |
| | 88 | 245.44 | 5.50 |
| | 90 | 361.00 | 5.89 |

control variables, even though using the confounders as covariates provides statistical control, more control is provided when confounders are also used to create matched cases for the variable whose causal influence is in question. It is not a question of either or. Including both uses of confounders can produce better controls than using either procedure alone.

When only one hypothesis is being tested, the procedure is straight-forward.

1. Create matched samples for the intervention and comparison groups. Use the matching procedure that seems to produce an acceptable match—remembering that with well-behaved data a greedy matching can produce good results, but optimized matching may produce better.

2. Use the matched cases as the analytical sample.

3. Check the distribution of the outcome measure and the hypothesis to determine which GZLM procedure is most appropriate for estimating those effects.

4. Estimate the effects using the chosen GZLM procedure.

5. Examine goodness-of-fit statistics, residuals, and graphic displays from estimation or prediction to assess the adequacy of the model.

6. Revise and repeat if necessary.

When more than one hypothesis is being tested or more than one research question is being addressed, the procedure is more complicated.

1. If the same variables confound multiple outcomes, use a single matched sample.

2. If different variables confound alternative outcomes, create alternative matched samples.

3. If some confounding variables do not correlate with alternative outcomes, create alternative matched samples.
   a. If the alternative samples greatly overlap (better than 90%), use the common cases for estimating effects for the alternative outcomes.
   b. If the alternative samples do not greatly overlap, use them separately.

4. Check the distribution of the outcome measure and the hypothesis to determine which GZLM procedure is most appropriate for estimating those effects.

5. Estimate the effects using the chosen GZLM procedure using either the common sample or the alternative samples, as appropriate, for the different outcomes.

6. Examine goodness-of-fit statistics, residuals, and graphic displays from estimation or prediction to assess the adequacy of the model.

7. Revise and repeat if necessary.

Caution should be used when alternative matched samples are used to estimate causal effects. When estimates of the intervention effects are based on different cases, those estimates might not be statistically consistent. This is especially true if the outcomes are themselves correlated with each other. When the outcomes have moderate to strong correlations among themselves, every reasonable effort should be made to estimate the effects using a common sample. Sometimes, every reasonable effort is not enough. Using different samples may be the only alternative available. This is not desirable when the outcomes intercorrelate, but it may be the only choice available. The results in this case should not be characterized as strong or highly reliable results. They may, however, be characterized as being consistent or inconsistent with a given hypothesis. It may be the best available evidence, even though it is not strong evidence.

The potential magnitude of the problem of matched samples for the same intervention not being equivalent is illustrated by comparing the matched samples created to illustrate the outcomes of parental smoking. One matched sample looked at the effects of parental smoking on the likelihood of their child's smoking (see Chapter 5). This matched sample had 1,144 cases out of 17,217. An alternative matched sample was created to examine the effect of parent's smoking on respiratory disorder in adult children. This matched sample had 372 cases. The second sample used exact matching. A cross-tabulation of the two matched samples reveals that there were only 26 cases common to the two samples (see Table 9.7). This was 7% of the smaller sample and 2% of the larger sample. The principal reason for the great disparity of the two samples was that different confounders were identified for the two different outcomes. As a result, the estimated propensities were somewhat different. When combined with the use of different matching criteria, the result is divergent samples.

This is not just a statistical problem. Different confounders imply different models of selectivity. Yet both are models of the process of selection into parent's smoking. Can the model of selectivity change with a switch in outcome? Since the outcome is supposed to be an effect, it cannot be a cause of the intervention or selection thereto. In such a case, a serious reexamination

| Table 9.7 | Cross-Tabulation of Alternative Matched Samples | | | |
|---|---|---|---|---|
| | | Matched Sample 1 | | |
| | | Not Matched | Matched | N |
| Matched Sample 2 | Not matched | 15,727 | 1,118 | 16,845 |
| | Matched | 346 | 26 | 372 |
| | N | 16,073 | 1,144 | 17,217 |

of the selectivity model is needed. Even so, a resolution of this conundrum is not always identifiable. When it occurs, the consequence is uncertain and tentative results.

Choosing the appropriate GZLM procedure with matched samples requires examining the distribution of the outcome measures and the corresponding hypotheses. Different outcomes may have different distributions, have different hypotheses concerning the effect, and be a result of different processes. This means different GZLM procedures may be necessary for alternative outcomes. In the case of LR, the outcomes are dichotomies or polychotomies. There is no question about the distribution. The only choice within GZLM is LR. Log linear analysis is a special case of LR. While probit regression can also handle dichotomous outcomes, it needs multiple, continuously distributed, independent variables. This is normally not the case when using matched samples for the intervention variable. If there were numerous ratio or interval-level alternative influences, PR should have been selected from the beginning. Consequently, choosing alternative estimation procedures is an issue mainly for GZLM procedures other than LR.

## WEIGHTED DATA WITH GZLM

Weighted regression is often done with GZLM. Whether using OLS, ANCOVA, PR, or LR procedures, they all allow weighting. Any GZLM procedure may use weighted samples. All statistical packages allow creating weighted samples. Some GZLM procedures allow using the weighted data computation method. As noted in the chapter on propensity weighting, both methods produce nearly identical results for symmetrical distributions. They also work well for dichotomous distributions. However, there are some situations with GZLM in which weighting poses special issues.

Weighting data can alter the distribution of a variable. It is possible to change a distribution from a symmetrical distribution to a skewed one or the reverse, depending on the weights used. This means a GZLM procedure that is appropriate for an unweighted sample might become inappropriate for a weighted sample. Usually, this is not the case; but it is possible. The distribution of the weighted sample needs to be checked to ensure the proper choice of the GZLM procedure. If the distribution is not greatly altered, one may proceed with the GZLM procedure selected. If the distribution is greatly altered, another estimation procedure or another weighting procedure needs to be selected. An alternative estimation procedure might be selected if there are alternative causal influences on the outcome that have nonnormal distributions, that is, if the change in distribution can be attributed to the effect of a variable other than the principal one whose effect is being studied. In this case, the change in the distribution reflects the distribution of the outcome when the confounders are controlled.

If the change in the distribution in the outcome cannot be attributed to the confounders, this raises questions about the distribution of the outcome appropriate for estimating the effect of the intervention or treatment. It also raises questions about the process that produces the outcome. The distribution might be inappropriate if the wrong weighting scheme was used. As noted in Chapter 7, there is more than one propensity weighting procedure. If augmented inverse propensity weighting (AIPW) is not used and the distribution changes, AIPW should be tried. If the change does not occur with AIPW, then the change can be attributed to an artifact of weighting. In that case, the AIPW weighted sample should be used. If AIPW is used and the change in distribution still occurs, it is likely a result of nonnormal distributions among the confounders. The predicted value of a regression, in this case a propensity score, cannot be nonnormal unless one or more of the predictors are nonnormal. This may require adding powers or transforms of the nonnormal confounder to obtain a better distribution of the propensity score. Alternatively, if the nonnormal distribution can be identified, an appropriate linkage function may be used in GZLM to obtain a better estimate of the intervention effect.

## COVARIATE DATA WITH GZLM

Except for simple two-sample comparisons, all the different GZLM procedures admit the use of covariates when estimating intervention effects. These covariates may be used either as control variables or as adjustors.

They may be used in the estimation of the selection model or in the outcome model or both.

When a covariate is seen solely as a confounder, the variable is used only in the selection model estimation. In this case, it is seen as a source of error in estimating the intervention effect. If the relationship between it and the outcome is linear, all of its influence is encompassed by the propensity score. It is not used as an alternative causal influence on the outcome.

When a covariate is seen as an alternative causal influence on the outcome unrelated to the intervention, the variable is used only in the outcome model. It is not included in estimation of the propensity score because it is not believed to be an influence on the selection process.

When a covariate is seen as both an influence on the selection process and an additional influence on the outcome, the variable may be used to estimate both models—depending on several factors. Either the propensity score or the variable may be used as control variables to encompass this alternative influence, if any.

## STRATA AND GZLM

Stratifying propensity score groups can be done in either of two ways with GZLM. The GZLM model may be estimated in each of the stratified propensity groups, and a weighted average may be calculated. Alternatively, a categorical variable may be introduced that identifies in which stratum each case belongs. The categorical variable is used as a control in the GZLM estimation. In the former case, the weights may represent either the number of cases in each group or the variances in each group. Weighting by variances gives results closer to that of using a categorical strata variable. For some procedures, it may be necessary to break the categorical variable into dummy variables if the procedure does not allow entering categorical variables (e.g., OLS). In the later procedure, only one GZLM model is estimated. Each approach has its advantages and disadvantages.

The former procedure is preferred when the results are expected to be somewhat different between groups. The categorical variable allows seeing the results for all the groups, including both propensity groups at the extreme ends. This often is where divergent effects lie, if there are any. On the other hand, using dummy variables is a simple, well-known procedure; but it depends on having enough cases in each group, and one of the groups is omitted from the dummies as a "reference group." So the effects in all groups are only available by computing what the reference value is in a separate procedure. It is better to use the strata as a categorical variable, since that most closely reflects the measurement level of the strata. Ex post facto contrasts allow identifying differences between the strata, as does comparing the coefficients of the dummy variables.

## ADEQUACY AND SUFFICIENCY OF GZLM

Statistical adequacy of GZLM estimates depends on the completeness of the selection model for estimating propensity scores used in the GZLM and in the completeness of the outcome model estimated. In addition to estimating a selection model for the propensity scores and an outcome model for the treatment effects, the GZLM estimator must also be selected using knowledge of the research question to be answered and information about the distribution of the outcome variable.

This typically comes down to two issues: (1) which procedure most closely reflects the assumptions of the research question and (2) whether there is evidence that the suppositions of that procedure have been violated. Matching the assumptions has been previously discussed. Evidence of supposition violation has been only partly discussed. When using GZLM, there is a common strategy that can be used to offer evidence supporting claims that the suppositions have been met; but the statistics used to provide that evidence depend on the procedure selected within GZLM.

Evidence used to support claims of its appropriateness was covered in the discussion of GLM and LR. The evidence needed to support use of a specific GZLM procedure concerns two issues: (1) Is there evidence of systematic error when estimating the outcome using the procedure? and (2) Is there evidence that the outcome distribution is consistent with suppositions of the model? The procedures for examining patterns of errors in estimation (whether continuous or discrete) address the first issue. The procedures mentioned previously for examining the distribution of the outcome address the second issue.

Sometimes a researcher will have to transform the measure into a format appropriate to testing the outcome. For example, with LR, the outcome is typically measured as a binomial variable. The cumulative distribution across time, however, should be examined to determine whether the distribution is logistic or not. If it is not, then LR (or any other procedure whose distribution is not supported by evidence) cannot be regarded as a statistically sufficient procedure.

This can be a problem if the data collection does not permit such examination. If all the subjects have the same duration of exposure to the intervention and the same length of time to measuring outcome, evidence of the distribution supporting the procedure chosen may not be available. One can, of course, provide references to other studies in which such evidence might be available and provide theoretical arguments for why it is credible to believe that the outcome has the distribution supposed. Even if the findings cannot be regarded as strong evidence of a causal impact, the analysis may produce results that have some utility. Such results should not necessarily be discarded. They may be used with words of caution and not be regarded as offering strong causal evidence. They may still offer suggestive evidence and descriptive findings.

# CHAPTER 10

## PROPENSITY WITH CORRELATED SAMPLES

**T**his chapter examines issues unique to correlated samples that arise with propensity score use. The correlation of samples may be cross-sectional or across time. Propensity scores may be used in either situation, but adjustments need to be made in the procedures used. The correlation of the samples can alter the variances and covariances between the outcomes, the confounders, and the intervention. It can bias the estimate of the treatment effect. Propensity scores can control some of the bias resulting from correlated data. Additional procedures, however, may be necessary to obtain consistent and unbiased estimates of intervention effects.

The issues associated with using propensity scores with various correlated samples are examined for different types of correlated samples. The chapter covers paired samples tests, repeated measures, panel studies, geographic correlation, longitudinal analysis, Cox regression, and variants thereof. Strategies for dealing with the issues are discussed. Recommendations for resolving these issues are provided.

## PAIRED SAMPLES

Paired samples arise when comparing the same units across time or in different circumstances. They also arise when comparing closely related subjects whose characteristics are known to be similar (e.g., siblings or businesses that are part of some conglomerate). Correlated samples, also called dependent samples, pose an analytical problem because their error variances may be smaller than unrelated or independent samples, the degrees of freedom when analyzing such samples are smaller compared with independent samples, and the correlations among variables may be inflated or deflated.

Randomized controlled trials (RCTs) are rarely cross-sectional paired samples. A situation when this is not the case with RCTs is if one starts with related pairs and then randomly assigns one of each to the intervention and control groups, respectively. Such groups may be balanced on measured characteristics. The presence of related subjects in each group, however, means that the samples are correlated. The estimate of the mean difference may be correct, but the estimate of the variance may not be correct. When propensity-based analysis involves comparisons of the same subjects across time or in different situations, it is uncontested that a correlated sample test should be used (Stuart, 2008).

There is disagreement about the need for correlated sample tests for some propensity matched samples. It has been argued by Austin (2008) that all matched samples should be treated as correlated samples. It is not agreed that propensity matched samples should be treated as correlated samples solely because they are propensity matched samples. It has been noted that pairs of cases matched by propensity scores do not necessarily have the same individual characteristics (Rubin, 2006; Stuart, 2008). Propensity matching balances the aggregate distribution of characteristics, not those of individual pairs—unless constraints are placed on the pairs to have individually matched characteristics such as gender, symptomatology, or occupational achievement. In this latter case, a reasonable argument can be made that correlated sample procedures should be used because unmeasured confounders may correlate with the fixed, correlated characteristics. If it were demonstrated that propensity matched samples must be dependent, perhaps as a function of the degree of closeness of the match, then there would be agreement that correlated sample procedures should be used.

Whether one favors using correlated sample tests for some or all matched samples, there is a need for such tests. There are situations when the samples will be correlated for reasons other than the fact that the members of the groups are matched. With quasi-experimental designs where the same subjects or related subjects may appear in multiple groups, correlated tests should be used. Panel data and longitudinal studies unquestionably require dependent sample procedures.

Using a correlated sample test may require reformatting the data. For many programs that analyzed quasi-experimental data, correlated sample tests require specifying the outcome variable for the treatment group and the outcome for the control group. This means that the matched cases are stacked side by side—that is, on the same record. To accomplish this, each matched pair must have a common ID. Consequently, treatment and outcome information is available for each subject. For independent sample tests, the outcome is specified as a variable and an intervention/treatment variable is specified. The matched cases are stacked as separate records. Treatment and comparison information is not available for each case. Only one set of information is available for each case. A treatment flag variable indicates for which group information is available. See Tables 10.1 and 10.2 for examples of the two formats.

It takes a sample twice as large if one wishes to have the same number of cases in groups subject to independent sample tests as there are in correlated sample tests, but half as many cases to have the same degrees of freedom. There are only half as many degrees of freedom available to the correlated sample tests because the same or similar cases appear in the intervention and comparison groups. In Table 10.1, there are four cases in each group, but there are

| Table 10.1 | Data Format for Correlated Sample Test[a] | | |
|------------|------------------|------------------|------------------|
| ID | Propensity Score | Treatment Outcome | Comparison Outcome |
| 101 | .65 | 25 ← | → 30 |
| 102 | .63 | 37 | 41 |
| 103 | .59 | 29 | 35 |
| 104 | .67 | 30 | 35 |

a. Arrow indicates direction of comparison.

| Table 10.2 | Data Format for Independent Sample Test[a] | | |
|------------|------------------|------------------|------------------|
| ID | Propensity Score | Outcome | Treatment Variable |
| 101 | .65 | 25 ↑ | 1 |
| 105 | .65 | 30 ↓ | 0 |
| 102 | .63 | 37 | 1 |
| 106 | .63 | 41 | 0 |
| 103 | .59 | 29 | 1 |
| 107 | .59 | 35 | 0 |
| 104 | .67 | 30 | 1 |
| 108 | .67 | 35 | 0 |

a. Arrow indicates direction of comparison.

not eight cases for computing degrees of freedom. There are only four. In Table 10.2, there are also four cases in each group, but there are eight cases in total for computing degrees of freedom.

## *Paired Sample t Test*

The paired sample $t$ test is the simplest correlated sample test. Although the $t$ test by itself does not provide much information, many software programs allow producing a one-way analysis of variance (ANOVA) table also when doing a $t$ test. This provides additional information such as between- and within-group sums of squares and the eta coefficient. This additional information is useful if one wishes to compute standardized effect measures, such as Hedges' $g$ or Cohen's $d$, as part of an RCT or an intervention evaluation. These are not currently provided in existing paired sample $t$ test programs.

The paired sample $t$ test can be used with propensity scores if all prior imbalances are removed by the score used, and the data are organized as matched pairs. Propensity matching is one of the few ways one can control other variables while doing a $t$ test. If the two groups do not differ on any significant factor—if strong ignorability is met—a $t$ test can be justified. However, it does not allow adding additional, nonconfounding, causal variables. If the additional causal influence can be conceptualized as a confounding variable, it can be included in the selection model for estimating the propensity score. Its inclusion in propensity score matching will control the influence of that causal variable. If the alternative causal influence is uncorrelated with the intervention, including it in the propensity score calculation will do little to control the alternative influence.

Another way of controlling other factors while doing a $t$ test would be to stratify the data into categories of a third or more variable(s) and computing Hotelling's $T^2$ across the groups. While it is more usual to use $T^2$ to test across multiple outcome variables, rather than across multiple causal groups, there is no reason one cannot do so. It allows testing multiple variables for balance without running an inflated risk of a false positive. This statistic is distributed as a chi-square statistic with $p - 1$ degrees of freedom, where $p$ is the number of groups. $T^2$ can be transformed to an $F$ distribution by the following equation, with $p$ and $(N - 1) - p$ degrees of freedom:

$$F = ((n_1 + n_2) - (p - 1)/(n_1 + n_2 - 2)P)T^2, \tag{10.1}$$

where $n_1$ is the number of cases across all treatment groups, $n_2$ is the number of cases across all comparison groups, and $N$ equals $n_1 + n_2$.

An illustration of this situation is provided in Table 10.3. This table describes the pre–post household income change of the Health and Retirement Study respondents between 2006 and 2008 for propensity, greedy matched samples, and conditional on whether babies are present in the home. This says that income change from 2006 to 2008 does not significantly vary by whether babies are present in the home.

Table 10.3 does not address whether there were alternative causal factors that might have affected income independently of the presence of the babies. Only the alternative influence of the confounding variables is controlled by the propensity score matching. If the selection model has included all likely alternative causes, then propensity matching would have controlled those influences.

To examine differences in the paired samples for the intervention group and the comparison group with a *t* test, we need to convert the 2006 and 2008 income values into a change score and compare the changes between the groups. Table 10.3 does not show statistically significant changes in income between the two groups, despite the fact that income levels were previously shown to be related to group differences. This could imply that presence of babies might affect the level of household income and that it does not subsequently affect the rate at which the income increases or decreases.

Hypothetically, it will be supposed that the effect of the respondent's education has not been controlled. How can we empirically test whether it has an alternative influence after the propensity matching? Either we abandon the use of *t* tests and specify a multivariate model to allow simultaneous control of babies' presence and education or we do a bivariate regression of income change on education for each of the two groups and compare the results.

The results of the regressions appear in Figure 10.1. This scatterplot displays the regression line for each of the two groups. They are not identical, but they may be similar. To more definitively determine whether these two regression slopes are the same, a paired sample *t* test of the difference of the two slopes was performed.

The *t* test on the difference in the regression slope was not significant. This additional evidence supports the view that the presence of babies in the

| Table 10.3 | Income and Babies' Presence, 2006–2008 | | | |
|---|---|---|---|---|
| | Mean Income Change | Standard Deviation | N | Significance |
| Babies not present | 22,008 | 35,229 | 1,510 | .624 |
| Babies present | 20,973 | 28,934 | 318 | |

**Figure 10.1**    Regression Slope Comparison

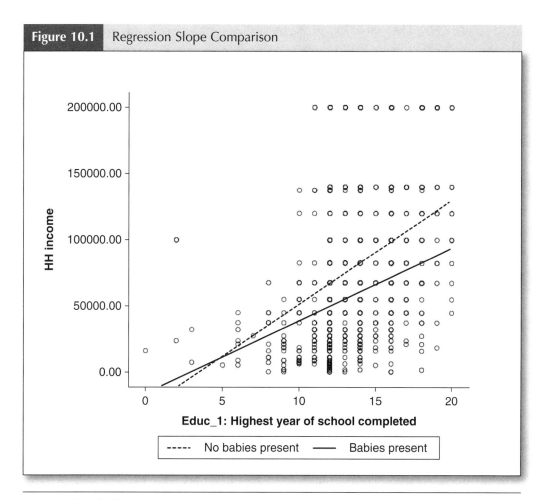

*Note.* HH, household.

household does not affect changes in income. Without the additional evidence, the *t* test would have been open to the claim that education level had an alternative effect that confounded the comparison for babies and income change.

## *Paired Sample ANOVA and ANCOVA*

The paired sample test for ANOVA and analysis of covariance (ANCOVA) provides more information than the *t* test. They provide sums of squares by default. They allow comparing more than just two groups. They have a built-in option for doing paired sample tests, either by using change scores for pre–post comparisons or by specifying two repeating groups.

ANOVA and ANCOVA both allow entering additional factors to control confounders and alternative causal influences. They allow adjusting data for these influences by entering them prior to entering the treatment variable. They provide good results with simple designs and normally distributed data. However, ANOVA and ANCOVA do not work well with nonnormally distributed data. The generalized linear model (GZLM) was created specifically to work with nonnormal data, but some GZLM programs do not have a repeated measures estimation option. R and Stata use alternative programs for estimating generalized estimation equations (GEE) than for estimating GZLM. SPSS and SAS provide GEE within their GZLM programs. Conditional logistic regression (CLR) procedures are also available in these packages, discussed below.

One can use dummy variable outcomes with ANOVA and ANCOVA instead of GEE or CLR if the distribution of cases between groups is not too extreme, but the results are not always satisfactory. Cell combinations may be empty. Variances and covariances may be biased. However, this approach may provide useful descriptive information for suggestive results. It does not provide a basis for estimating causal effects that are statistically adequate or sufficient.

## REPEATED MEASURES

Repeated comparisons may have two or more groups being compared across time. If there are only two groups for an intervention, pre and post, and two for a comparison group, this is the pre–post design with comparison. If there is a treatment group and a control group with several measures across time, this is the panel study. If the comparisons are done with multiple measures across time, this is the longitudinal comparison design. The distinction between panel studies and longitudinal comparison designs, however, is obscured by the fact that both use measures across time. Panel studies may or may not compare the same units across time. Longitudinal studies usually do.

Propensity score contributions to four types of repeated measure analysis are discussed below: (1) pre–post comparisons, (2) panel studies, (3) longitudinal panels, and (4) mixed repeated designs. For each type of analysis, alternative procedures are described and the role of propensity scores in enhancing the results is explained. The trade-offs between alternatives are also discussed.

## Pre–Post Comparisons

One may use a *t* test, an ANOVA, an ANCOVA, McNemar's test, CLR, GZLM, or GEE to do a pre–post comparison. The paired sample *t* test can examine bivariate change with continuous outcomes. When difference scores are used for the outcome, it examines effects between paired samples. When the intervention and comparison groups have been matched by propensity scores, it introduces controls for all of the measured confounders. Repeated measures tests are included in ANOVA and ANCOVA programs. Controls can be introduced either by including confounders in the selection model or by adding them as factors or covariates, as appropriate.

The McNemar test can be used to analyze pre–post data with discrete outcomes. It is associated with some cross-tabulation programs or with two-sample nonparametric tests. All four packages have McNemar's test. Examples appear in the appendixes.

Another approach for analyzing discrete outcomes is to use CLR. The CLR approach is equivalent to testing the ratio of proportions of groups having a specified outcome using logistic regression (LR). Like most other repeated measures tests, however, the multiple observations may need to be stacked vertically, rather than horizontally, to perform an LR repeated measures test. However, only one of the LR programs considered (SAS) allows a repeated measures factor to be included in LR. The other programs included it as a separate conditional logit procedure (clogit in R and Stata, nomreg in SPSS). To get CLR results, one may use difference measures as the outcome. It will produce the same result (Kasule, 2003).

The McNemar test is a bivariate test. Controls, however, can be introduced by using propensity scores to select cases matched on confounders for the pretest groups. Like the *t* test, however, this is not an elegant solution to doing pre–post comparisons with controls. A generalization to the multivariate case to allow examining multivariate outcomes and additional causal effects has been developed by Klingenberg and Agresti (2006), but the computation is somewhat complex. It has not been incorporated into many statistical programs. It does, however, reduce the likelihood of a false positive by not testing multiple outcomes separately.

Both the multivariate McNemar test and the CLR results can be converted into statistics produced by a repeated measures GZLM program or by GEE. Repeated measures GZLM and GEE produce equivalent results. GEE is available as a component of most statistical packages. R and Stata have separate GEE programs. SPSS and SAS include GEE in their GZLM programs. GEE can also estimate treatment effects produced by any GLM approach for the analysis of correlated data (e.g., *t* test and repeated measures ANOVA and ANCOVA).

In other words, the GEE approach for estimating intervention effects with correlated samples within GZLM provides a general solution that applies both to discrete outcomes and to continuous outcomes. Instead of applying a variety of procedures to estimate treatment effects between groups for different types of data, one can use an integrated approach that estimates differences between dependent groups. This applies to discrete and continuous outcomes. GEE, however, does not estimate effects on individuals as well as multilevel regression models (MRM). MRM is a form of mixed repeated designs discussed below.

## *Generalized Estimation Equations*

GEE was proposed by Liang and Zeger (1986; Zeger, Liang, & Albert, 1988). The procedure was developed because of the limited development of tools for analyzing longitudinal data when the outcomes were not normally distributed (non-Gaussian) and because standard GZLM procedures did not fully model situations in which cases were correlated across time.

GEE is designed to provide a general approach for dealing with the biasing effects of correlated samples. The biasing effects of these samples on estimates of the variances and covariances of the variables can be considerable. It depends on how strong the correlation is and whether it is positive or negative. At the bivariate level, positive correlations between samples tend to reduce the true variance and increase the observed variance. Negative correlations tend to have the opposite effect. At the multivariate level, however, it is difficult to tell whether the net effect will be inflation or deflation or a mixture of both.

GEE uses an iterative procedure to obtain increasingly better estimates of the true variances and covariances (or their analogs for non-GLM situations). It estimates the outcome effects based on the improved estimates of the variances and correlations. It calculates the effects based on aggregate differences between groups. The formula developed by Liang and Zeger (1986) is based on a quasi–maximum likelihood estimate that assumes independence or low correlation between groups. Because of the complexity of the computation, it is presented in matrix form:

$$U_I(\beta) = \sum_{i=1}^{K} X_i^T \Delta_i S_i = 0, \tag{10.2}$$

where $\Delta_I = \text{diag}(d\theta_{it}/d\eta_{it})$ is an $n \times n$ matrix and $S_i = Y_i - \alpha'_i(\theta)$ is of order $n \times 1$ for the $i$th subject. $\beta_I$ is the estimated effect assuming independence, and $\text{diag}(d\theta_{it}/d\eta_{it})$ is the diagonal of the $n \times n$ matrix.

When the samples are not independent, the formula takes into consideration the improved estimates of the variances and covariances. The formula begins with computing the effect coefficient based on the assumption of independence. Then, Liang and Zeger revise the estimate based on the variances, covariances, and effects estimated on the preceding step:

$$\hat{\beta}_{j+1} = \hat{\beta}_j - \left\{ \sum_{i=1}^{K} D_i^T \left( \hat{\beta}_j \right) \tilde{V}_i^{-1} \hat{\beta}_j D_i \left( \hat{\beta}_j \right) \right\}^{-1} \left\{ \sum_{i=1}^{K} D_i^T \left( \hat{\beta}_j \right) \tilde{V}_i^{-1} \hat{\beta}_j S_i \left( \hat{\beta}_j \right) \right\}, \qquad (10.3)$$

where $V$ is the previously estimated variances and $D_i = d\{\alpha'_i(\theta)\}/d\beta = A_i \Delta_i X_i$. Given the revised estimate of the effects, new estimates of the variances and covariances are computed as follows:

$$\tilde{V}_i(\beta) = V_i \left[ \beta, \hat{\alpha} \left\{ \beta, \hat{\phi}(\beta) \right\} \right], \qquad (10.4)$$

where $\beta$ is the effect estimated on the preceeding step and $V$ is the prior estimated variance–covariance matrix.

This process is repeated until the estimated effects do not differ between steps according to the criteria chosen or a specified maximum number of steps is reached. Liang and Zeger (1986) provide a proof that these estimates converge on the true effect. Zeger et al. (1988) also demonstrate that this procedure generalizes to discrete outcomes as well as continuous outcomes using GEE. Proofs of these above equations are provided in Liang and Zeger (1986) and Zeger et al. (1988).

Estimation of GEE follows a procedure parallel to that of GZLM. One specifies the variables, distribution, and link function. The program then starts with initial estimates based on the observed values for the variances and covariances of the items to provide initial estimates of the effects. The estimates of the effects are used to compute new estimates of the variances and covariances. When the outcomes are normally distributed and there is no correlation between the groups, this procedure is the same as standard maximum likelihood estimation. An example of GEE applied to repeated income measures by presence or absence of babies in the household is provided in Table 10.4.

The repeated measures analysis was performed using a repeated ANOVA specification within a GLM program. It was replicated for GEE with a propensity matched sample for the babies present variable and for GEE with matching and the propensity score as a covariate. The ANOVA gives a smaller estimate of the difference in income between 2006 and 2008 compared with the matched sample ($9,726 vs. $10,455 for GEE with matching), but a larger value compared with the GEE matching and propensity covariate ($8,826).

| Table 10.4 | Repeated Measures Income by Presence of Babies | | | | | |
|---|---|---|---|---|---|---|
| Procedure | B | SE | Sig. Coefficient[a] | df | Sig. | N |
| Repeated ANOVA | | | | | | |
| Babies present | 9,726 | 2,746 | 14.104 | 2,745 | <.001 | 2,746 |
| GEE, matching | | | | | | |
| Babies present | 10,455 | 3,840 | 7.411 | 1 | .006 | 1,844 |
| GEE, matching and propensity covariate | | | | | | |
| Babies present | 8,826 | 3,884 | 5.163 | 1 | .023 | 1,844 |
| Propensity covariate | 47,419 | 18,224 | 6.770 | 1 | .009 | 1,844 |

Note. SE, standard error; df, degrees of freedom; Sig., significance; ANOVA, analysis of variance; GEE, generalized estimation equations.

a. Significance coefficient is F value for ANOVA and Wald $\chi^2$ for GEE.

Since the ANOVA estimate was not done with a matched sample, the GEE estimates would be preferred. The similarity of the repeated measures ANOVA to the two GEE estimates is not coincidence. If the repeated measures ANOVA had been done using the same matched sample as the GEE, results closer to those of GEE would be obtained. However, adding propensity as a covariate, in addition to using it for matching, reduces the GEE estimated difference by $1,600. The large coefficient for the propensity covariate is mainly a result of a reduction in the magnitude of the intercept for the prediction equation (not included in the table), but part of it is at the expense of the estimated baby effect. The significance of the propensity coefficient indicates that matching alone did not remove all the prior imbalance between households that had and did not have babies present. The estimate with the propensity covariate is a better estimate. If the repeated ANOVA had been repeated ANCOVA with propensity covariate, those results would have been very similar to that for the GEE with propensity covariates—but only if the data are normally distributed. Income is not, which is why GEE results are a better estimate of the impact on income of having babies in the household.

The contribution of propensity scores is to reduce the degree of confounding. It also speeds up the estimation process with more accurate convergence on the true values. This happens because the reduction in confounding is also likely to reduce the degree of correlation among the samples. The common association of the confounders with the measures across time or between groups is a factor in producing some of the correlation between the samples. Zeger et al. (1988) demonstrate that the degree of original bias is a function of this correlation. With the correlation of the samples reduced, the degree of bias is smaller and fewer iterations are needed for the estimates of the effects to converge on a stable value.

## *Panel Studies*

Panel studies obtain a particular benefit from using matched samples or adjustment by confounders. The matching or adjustment process reduces the degree of dependence of the samples (Nielsen & Sheffield, 2009). As noted above, this reduces bias in estimation of treatment effects. It also reduces the number of variables that need to be included in the analytical equations. Confounders included in the propensity score estimation may be uncorrelated with outcome variables within the matched sample. This simplifies the analytical process.

Propensity matching, however, has special problems with panel data. In a previous example, matching on the baseline data for a pre–post comparison was used to select cases for the matched samples. This works well because there are no intermediate variables that need to be considered—no mediating variables. With panel studies, there can be multiple baselines if different time lags of influence are included. If one uses all the cases across time, however, this means that intermediate cases may be dropped if a measure is missing from any point in time. This forces the statistician to drop all observations for that case, analyze with missing data, or substitute some imputed or estimated value. All of these approaches have their problems, though they are not necessarily insurmountable.

One approach with panel data is to do propensity matching for the earliest baseline of the panel and not intermediate measures. This avoids having to develop separate selection models for multiple measures of the intervention and results in fewer dropped cases. This can be justified if differences remaining on intermediate measures can be attributed to intervening measured variables in the model. If intermediate imbalance remaining after balancing the baseline is a result of external influences, however, separate selection models may be needed for each occurrence of a measured intervention. This requires balancing using the propensity scores from all points of measurement. Instead of matching two propensity scores, one must match two to the *n*th propensity scores, where $n$ is the number of selection models. Because of the difficulty of this process and the likelihood of dropping many cases, this approach has not been used a great deal. In principle, generalized matching algorithms could be developed to simplify the process.

Nielsen and Sheffield (2009) have developed two balance scores for use when there are multiple observation points prior to the intervention. They calculate the Mahalanobis distance of all the prior observations within a specified time frame and use the average of that, the mean Mahalanobis distance of a panel of observations. Similarly, they estimate propensity scores for a panel using all observations prior to the intervention within the specified time frame. The reason for using a specified time frame is to prevent loss of too many cases in the estimation and to maintain consistency of the estimate. With only one prior observation, this produces a result identical to using the standard Mahalanobis distance and propensity scores. With multiple prior observations, this uses more information than the standard procedure. By including more observations of the confounding variables, more confoundedness is likely to be removed.

The procedure of Nielsen and Sheffeld (2009) allows that subjects may enter and leave treatment status, provided there are sufficient prior observations. If four observations are needed prior to the intervention, then four observations are needed during intervention prior to a subject's transition to nonintervention.

Nielsen and Sheffeld also require a fixed number of observations or a fixed time period after transition to intervention or nonintervention. The purpose is to maintain a comparable time period after intervention. This might not be required if duration between transition and outcome observation were included in the analysis. Further work on these procedures is needed.

Using propensity weighting avoids dropping these cases; but as noted above, the results of weighting are not always satisfactory. The work by Nielsen and Sheffeld indicates that the appropriate method for estimating propensity scores with panel data is still being discussed. If only one set of data prior to intervention is available and there is no transition in status during the study, standard procedures may be used. If multiple prior observations are available or transition between treatment and nontreatment occurs, the procedures of Nielsen and Sheffeld would seem to be a better approach. If weighting by standard propensity scores or if panel level propensity scores produce satisfactory balancing, this would seem to be a much more viable strategy. It doesn't result in dropping cases.

## Longitudinal Panels

Adding more measurement points across time complicates the analysis and use of propensity scores further. If there is a single baseline measure of the intervention, however, matching or weighting may be done in the usual fashion. The multiple measures are all consequent to the treatment. They may all be treated as outcomes from the intervention. In this case, the principal issue is whether there are repeated measures of these outcomes. In some cases, the measures represent proximal, intermediate, and distal outcomes. There might not be multiple measures, in which case a multivariate GZLM model may be used to estimate the outcomes. If there are repeated measures, GEE is a reasonable procedure to use.

The Wald chi-square is the most commonly used significance test of the effect coefficients for GEE, rather than an $F$ test or a likelihood ratio. This is because GEE estimates the coefficients using "quasi-likelihood" procedures. It is not strictly equivalent to maximum likelihood estimation, except in the special case where the variables are multivariate normally distributed, having linear relationships. The Wald chi-square is appropriate for whatever distribution the GEE is estimating.

Data for GEE need to be organized for a correlated sample analysis. Each measure of a subject needs to be treated as a separate case or row in the data file. In contrast to repeated ANOVA, subjects may have a variable number of observations. Every row should have the subject ID and an indicator of the time point or circumstance to which the case applies. See Table 10.2 for an example format.

As with panel studies, longitudinal data may have multiple prior observations. If that is the case, the approach of Nielsen and Sheffield (2009) may be used. Mean Mahalanobis distances and panel propensity scores may be calculated and used for matching or weighting.

## Mixed Repeated Designs

A mixed repeated design contains sampling at different levels of aggregation and across time. Samples of individuals may be nested within organizations or geographical units. When data are collected across time for multiple sites (including characteristics of each site) that are combined with individual subject data, the analysis usually includes hierarchical linear modeling (HLM), also called multilevel response (MLR) analysis.

Estimation of an MLR model begins with the GZLM equation in linear form:

$$\eta_{ij} = x'_{ij}\beta + \mu_j^{(2)}, \tag{10.5}$$

where $\eta_{ij}$ is the effect coefficient, $x$ stands for explanatory variables (including interventions), $\beta$ is the link function, and $\mu_j^{(2)}$ is the error term (either normal or exponential, depending on the distribution specified). Additional terms are added to this equation for estimating multilevel responses:

$$\eta = x'\beta + \sum_{l=2}^{L} z^{(l)}\mu^{(l)}, \tag{10.6}$$

where the original terms are as before, but the additional term $\sum_{l=2}^{L} z^{(l)}$ is added. This additional term represents the covariates that influence outcomes at higher levels of aggregation. If there are only two categories in a higher level, the term reduces to a constant that is added when one level applies to a given case, rather than the other.

There are a variety of procedures for estimating the effects of higher levels—such as marginal quasi-likelihood (MQL), penalized quasi-likelihood (PQL), Markov Chain Monte Carlo (MCMC), Gaussian quadrature (GQ), and adaptive Gaussian quadrature (AGQ; Rabe-Hesketh, Skrondal, & Pickles, 2002). GQ, MQL, and PQL tend to work better with normally distributed data or those for which GLM is applicable, but they can also be estimated using GZLM. MCMC works relatively well for binomial data for which Bayesian assumptions are appropriate, but it sometimes does not achieve a stable solution. GQ tends to work well with binomial data for situations in which MCMC does not. It does not do well when the cluster sizes are small and the intraclass correlation of the groups is high (Rabe-Hesketh et al., 2002). MQL and PQL provide some evidence as to whether the estimation model is properly identified. MCMC does not. None of these approaches produces uniformly optimal estimates. Although the estimates provided by these procedures may be reasonable approximations of the causal effects, none of these procedures are statistically sufficient if there are correlations between characteristics at different levels (Rabe-Hesketh et al., 2002). The adaptive Gaussian quadrature procedure tends to work well in situations in which the other approaches do well and in situations in which the other approaches do not. However, it has not been incorporated in all of the software packages. At present, it can be done using stand-alone programs MLwiN (Goldstein, 2003) and HLM (Bryk, Raudenbush, & Congdon, 1996).

SPSS and SAS use the procedure "Mixed." R uses the packages "multilevel" and "nlme." Stata uses "xtmixed."

## GEOGRAPHICALLY CORRELATED SAMPLES

Geographic units may either be the units of analysis or be contextual variables for the units of analysis. In either case, there may be dependence among the cases due to factors correlated with the geographic units. Statistically, it is very similar to mixed repeated designs. The difference is that a mixed repeated design usually has dependence in the samples of individuals, whereas geographically correlated samples have dependence in the samples of geographic units. This type of data can be analyzed using the same software as for MLR or HLM. The geographic units are specified as an additional level in the analysis.

### Adjacent Geographic Units

Correlation among geographic units may occur because the areas are adjacent to each other. Theories of ecological growth, diffusion, segregation, adaptation to physical environment, and functional specialization offer many reasons why adjacent areas may have similar characteristics. Such units are especially likely in ecological research and in studies that compare policies in adjacent political units.

Adjacent geographic areas that have common social, cultural, economic, political, or health characteristics are likely to have such correlation. If propensity matched adjacent areas are used, a correlated sample approach should be considered.

### Geographic Units Sharing Commonalities

Geographic areas may share characteristics for reasons other than adjacency. Functional specialization may be dispersed over several areas that are not adjacent, but within which similar activities are performed. The growth of regional shopping, entertainment, and financial centers illustrates this principle. Areas that concentrate on crime, health issues, poverty, or wealth may also have geographic correlation. In these cases, the ecological context may be used either to control for contextual variables or to provide a basis for contrasting different contexts. GEE with propensity matched pairs can help control for the geographic dependence.

## REPEATED VARIABLE ANOVA

While repeated variables ANOVA and ANCOVA still exist as programs within statistical packages, GEE is growing in use as a replacement for stand-alone ANOVA and ANCOVA programs. As illustrated above, anything that can be done with an ANOVA or ANCOVA program can be done with GZLM or GEE, plus more. The repeated measures component of GZLM programs produces results equivalent to GEE estimates. In fact, SPSS and SAS use the same subroutines whether one selects GZLM with repeated measures or selects GEE as an estimation procedure. R and Stata, having separate procedures for GEE, do not use the same subroutines, but they are based on the same algorithm.

### *Traditional Repeated ANOVA*

The traditional repeated ANOVA assumes normally distributed data and the absence of confounders. Using GEE to estimate such effects produces results identical to ANOVA and ANCOVA repeated measures estimates. The advantage of using GEE, however, lies in the same rationale for selecting GZLM over ANCOVA estimates. It provides estimates for a broader class of distributions than ANOVA or ANCOVA. Even if the data are normally distributed, nothing is lost by using the GEE procedure.

Propensity scores enhance a repeated ANOVA or ANCOVA by reducing the effect of confounding variables that occur at the baseline of the experiment or quasi-experiment. Even with a traditional ANOVA program, if matched samples are used for the intervention and comparison groups, this reduces the likelihood that the resulting estimated treatment effect is confounded.

Traditional ANOVA and ANCOVA programs, however, are predicated on normally distributed outcomes. They assume that the errors in estimation are also normally distributed and that the relationships between covariates and an outcome are linear. Deviations from this are dealt with on an ad hoc basis by transforming the covariates so that the relationships become linear or the errors are normal. In contrast, GEE doesn't require the errors to be normally distributed or the relationships to be linear.

One of the biggest risks with repeated measures ANOVA is the possibility that error terms will be correlated across time. This problem was introduced in the discussion of two-stage least squares estimation in Chapter 2. With repeated measures, error in the baseline measure of a variable is likely to be correlated with error in subsequent measures. Confounders contribute to this correlation. It is reduced by controlling or adjusting for the confounders. GEE estimation allows dealing with such correlation, either as specified fixed effects in the covariance matrix or as random effects estimated by the program.

## Propensity-Adjusted Repeated ANOVA

Propensity-adjusted repeated ANOVA uses propensity scores to control or adjust for confounding influences on the estimate of treatment effects. Matched samples can be created for which repeated ANOVA estimates are generated. Propensity scores can be used to adjust ANCOVA estimates. Both matching and adjustment can be done. Weighting to remove imbalance is also available.

What differentiates propensity-adjusted repeated ANOVA from traditional ANOVA is that propensity-adjusted repeated ANOVA uses the propensity score measure to control confounders. Traditional ANOVA and ANCOVA use the confounders separately. In addition to all these reasons, why propensity scores might be preferred over individual control variables that were discussed previously is that propensity scores also reduce the risks of errors in the outcomes being correlated with errors in the confounders. Since the treatment and control groups are balanced on the confounders, they are balanced on the errors in the confounders. Such errors cannot differentially affect the outcomes.

Problems with repeated data are also reduced because balanced confounders at the baseline tend to reduce the imbalance of the confounders at subsequent measurement points. The baseline measures of the confounders are often correlated with subsequent measures of the confounders. This is necessarily the case for fixed effect. Few people change their racial identification or gender across time. Those effects fixed by design are also unlikely to change. This also tends to be the case for random effects. Thus, confounders in subsequent measures tend to become more balanced when the baseline confounders are balanced.

## COX REGRESSION

The contribution of propensity scores to the analysis of correlated samples has so far examined situations in which the correlation is linear, either with or without transformation. The assumption is that the amount of effect between time periods is constant. A different assumption applies when the effect between time periods is a proportion, rather than a frequency or a scalable amount. This is the situation to which **proportional hazards analysis (PHA)** applies (Cox & Oakes, 1983). When the proportion of a population experiencing an event is a constant between points in time and applied to the number of cases in a population that have not yet experienced the event, this produces what is called the proportional hazards function—a curvilinear pattern over time that is increasing or decreasing at a decreasing rate (see Figure 10.2). The rate overall is decreasing because the probability of the event is applied only to those who have not yet experienced the event. When the event is positive, the function is called a survival function. A finite population and proportional hazards imply that there is a limit to which the cumulative density function (cdf) for the event approaches. The pattern of the cdf is displayed in Figure 10.2.

This figure implies increasing hazard and decreasing survival. If the risk is negative (if the hazard is decreasing or survivorship/cure rate is increasing), the

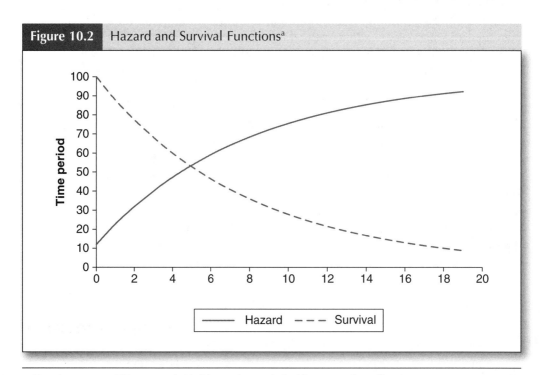

**Figure 10.2    Hazard and Survival Functions[a]**

a. Functions assume 100 cases and .12 risk per time period with no covariate effects.

hazard and survivor functions swap positions. These functions are represented by Equations 10.7 and 10.8.

The equation for hazard is

$$h_i(t) = e^{X_i \beta} h_0(t), \qquad (10.7)$$

where $h_i(t)$ is the total hazard at time t, $h_0(t)$ is the baseline hazard, $X_i$ is the value of a covariate, and $\beta$ is the effect of the covariate. For experiments and quasi-experiments, $\beta$ is the treatment effect. When there is no intervention, the value of $\beta$ equals 1 and drops out of the equation.

The equation for survival is

$$S_i(t) = e^{-X_i \beta} h_0(t), \qquad (10.8)$$

where the terms are defined as in Equation 10.7. These equations show that the sum of hazards and survival always equals the population size.

A data analyst may be concerned with how many have experienced the event, what proportion have experienced the event, or the average length of time to the event. Knowing how many of a population or sample have experienced the event at each point in time allows calculating the average length of time to when the event occurs, the proportion that have cumulatively experienced the event or experienced the event between two points in time, and the number or proportion remaining who have not yet experienced the event.

The contribution of propensity scores to PHA also applies to hazards analysis and survival analysis. The principal difference is in the conceptualization of the outcome. Hazards analysis applies to negative outcomes. Survival analysis applies to positive outcomes. Both cases assume that there is a finite population for which a fixed percentage of cases will exhibit the hazard or survival from among those that have not yet experienced the result. Both imply that there is a limit to which the cumulative density function approaches—assuming nothing alters the probability of the event occurring.

## PROPORTIONAL HAZARDS AND QUASI-EXPERIMENTS

Experiments and quasi-experiments use PHA to determine whether a treatment or intervention alters the probability of the event occurring. The functions in Figure 10.3 show a hazard function with and without an intervention.

**Figure 10.3**    Survival Function With and Without Intervention[a]

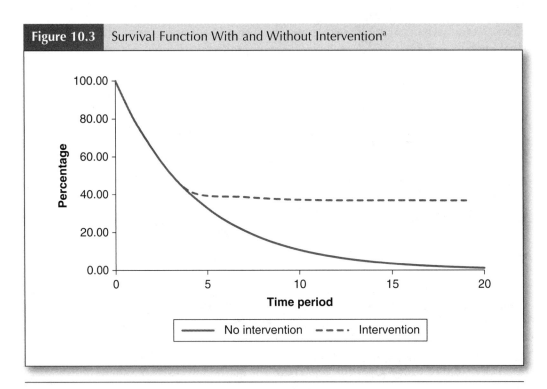

a. Risk is .20. Intervention occurs at Time 5. Risk reduces from .20 to .02. At Time 10, the risk reduces further to .001. The assumed population size is 100 with 20 time periods.

The intervention occurs at Time 5, where the risk reduces for those receiving treatment from .20 to .02. The risk further reduces to .001 at Time 10 (a delayed impact). The divergence of the two lines at Time 5 indicates a treatment effect. Computer programs estimate the functions for the treatment group and the comparison group separately and compare any differences.

When there is no effect, the effect coefficient equals 1.0. In this example, it is not equal to 1. It equals .10, which is why the risk reduces from .20 to .02. The value of $X_i$ is $1/\beta$ or $1/.02$ before the intervention occurs and 1.0 after the intervention occurs. The value of $1/\beta$ is used so that when multiplied by $\beta$, the product becomes 1.0 and drops out of the exponent. The equation with a treatment effect is

$$h_i(t) = e^{X_i \cdot 10} h_0(t). \tag{10.9}$$

In this equation, $X_i$ has the value of $1/.10$ prior to the intervention at Time 5. It has a value of 1 at Time 5 through 9 and a value of $1/200$ for Times 10 through 20.

When PHA is used with data from an experiment that successfully controls all confounding factors by randomization, the cdf for the data may well resemble those in Figures 10.2 and 10.3. With broken experiments and quasi-experiments, however, the confounders are not fully controlled. The data points across time will have some scattering above and below the line. They may even diverge away from the line. This is why PHA includes using control variables. The effects of confounders can be removed and make it easier to see and to estimate the parameters for hazard and survival functions. Using propensity scores enhances the estimation of the functions beyond that produced by using the confounders as control variables. It also enhances the ability to see the pattern across time.

*Censored Data and Propensity Scores.* Censoring of data in PHA occurs because information is available for some subjects for shorter periods of time than other subjects. This may occur from subjects dropping out of the study. The study may have been terminated before the subject had been in it for the full amount of time as other subjects. Confounding variables may cause the data to be not available. Propensity score use helps deal with censored data.

With propensity scores use, the matched subsamples of cases are likely to have complete or nearly complete data. Using the matched samples allows selecting a subset of cases that have complete data without creating bias from some confounding variable. It removes bias from differential missing data. Even when censoring of data is present, the balancing of the samples tends to reduce the proportion of the sample that has missing data and to make it less likely to confound the results.

An example is illustrated in Table 10.5. This table summarizes a survival analysis of time to initiation of smoking by Health and Retirement Study respondents when their parents smoked or did not smoke. To do this analysis, it is necessary to have variables for the length of time to initiation from birth (age at initiation) and age of the respondent (to allow computing age for those who did not initiate smoking). An age variable is computed that takes on the value of age at initiation (for smokers) or current age (for nonsmokers). It is also necessary to have dummy variables indicating whether the respondent smoked and whether his or her parents smoked. The computed age variable is the dependent variable. The dummy for whether the respondent smoked is called a status variable. The dummy for parents smoking is a covariate in the model. Table 10.5 shows that there are far more censored cases and cases with

| Table 10.5 | Survival Analysis With and Without Matching | | |
|---|---|---|---|
| *Samples* | | *N* | *Percentage* |
| All cases available | | | |
| Event[a] | | 231 | 1.3 |
| Censored | | 11,993 | 69.7 |
| Cases with missing values | | 4,993 | 29.0 |
| Total | | 17,217 | 100.0 |
| Matched sample cases | | | |
| Event[a] | | 167 | 44.9 |
| Censored | | 205 | 55.1 |
| Cases with missing values | | 0 | .0 |
| Total | | 372 | 100.0 |

a. Dependent variable: initiated smoking.

missing data when the analysis is performed using all the cases available than when matched samples are used.

Since confounding variables used in estimating the propensity score for parents smoking are controlled by the balancing, the survival curve without matching is somewhat different from that when matching is done (see Figures 10.4 and 10.5). When confounders are controlled, the survival rate drops off more steeply. The sharp drop-off at the end reflects the proportion who initiated smoking in their nineties.

The estimated parameter (Beta) for the two analyses is different (see Table 10.6). The matching results are more statistically significant than the nonmatching. This is partly due to matching making the groups more homogeneous, having less systematic error coming from the confounding variables. As a result, the proportion of systematic variance explained by the model increases.

*Frailty Models of Proportional Hazards.* Propensity scores assume that no important variables are omitted from the selection model. Standard PHA also assumes that important factors that affect the hazard or survivorship have also not been omitted from the outcome model. To know whether this is the case, diagnostic tests on the difference between the predicted and observed outcomes

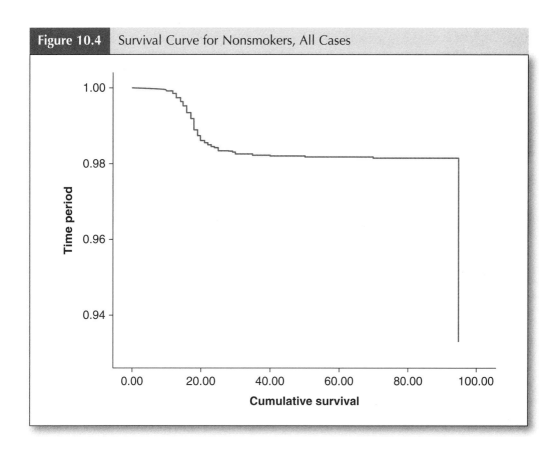

**Figure 10.4**   Survival Curve for Nonsmokers, All Cases

need to be done. If the significance tests on the errors are not significant, one can say that there is no evidence of unmeasured or latent factors confounding the results of the PHA.

There are several different error measures available for testing. If the one chosen is not significant, the model is said to not to be subject to frailty. If the measure does produce a significant test, frailty is said to be present. This implies that at least one unmeasured or latent variable is also affecting the pattern of risk or survival across time. This means that the hazard function and covariates do not adequately describe the outcomes. The equation for the hazard function needs to be modified to take into consideration this frailty (Weinke, 2003). This modified equation is as follows:

$$\mu(t,Z,X) = Z\mu 0(t)e^{(\beta TX)}, \tag{10.10}$$

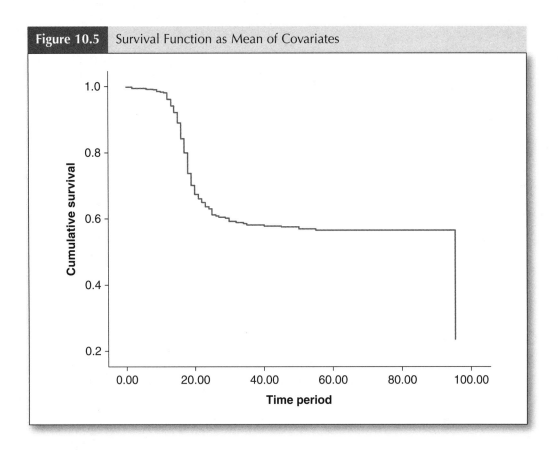

**Figure 10.5    Survival Function as Mean of Covariates**

**Table 10.6    Survival Parameter With and Without Matching**

| Method | β | SE | Wald Chi-Square | df | Sig. | $e^B$ | n |
|---|---|---|---|---|---|---|---|
| No matching | 0.384 | 0.146 | 6.955 | 1 | .008 | 1.469 | 17,217 |
| Matching | 0.834 | 0.162 | 29.020 | 1 | .001 | 2.397 | 372 |

*Note. SE,* standard error; *df,* degrees of freedom; Sig., significance.

where the terms common to Equation 10.9 mean the same as above. The new term, Z, is a multiplier that modifies the hazard function. Z is not measured. It can, however, with certain assumptions, be estimated.

Estimating the effect of the unobserved variable $Z$ requires assuming that $Z$ has a particular distribution. It is common to assume that the latent variable has a gamma, Poisson, linear, or log-normal distribution. The choice of distribution depends on what kind of process one thinks is present. The discussion of GZLM in the previous chapter noted how different processes produce different distributions. One may use theory, substantive experience with the phenomenon under study, or inspection of the distribution of the errors to make this choice. Once a distribution is chosen, a computed variable is added having that functional form and its parameters estimated from the errors. This produces an estimated latent variable that can then be used in a revised survival analysis.

The results of the survival analysis in Table 10.6 were examined by performing Kolmogorov–Smirnov one-sample tests on whether the residuals were distributed normally, log-normally, or Poisson. None of these distributions corresponded to that of the residuals. In Figure 10.6, we see a bar chart of these residuals grouped in 15 equally spaced categories.

The bar chart shows an unusual distribution. There are two points at which a large number of errors occur. This could be an artifact of the dichotomous covariate in the survival equation or it could mean that there are unobserved variables not included in the model that correspond to discrete events—perhaps being in high school or graduating from high school. One would need to examine what age ranges or events correlate with these errors. If identified, appropriate covariates could be added to the model. If not identified, frailty analysis (discussed below) may be necessary.

Propensity scores can simplify the process of dealing with unobserved or latent variables. If matched samples are used when treatment is a covariate, it promotes homogeneity of the groups in the covariate. Since homogeneity of the groups is an assumption of PHA, the analysis is more likely to meet the assumptions required for use of this technique. Propensity matched samples also increase the precision of the estimated effects. This occurs because the error variance of the parameters is smaller (unless one loses so many cases that this offsets the reduction from matching).

Propensity scores reduce the role of unmeasured variables in two ways. The propensity scores may be used as a measured covariate in the PHA, similar to what can be done with GZLM, either with or without the use of matching. To the extent that the confounding variables are also correlated with the unmeasured or latent variable, it will reduce the impact of the unmeasured variable. In addition, the ability of propensity score use to reduce error variance implies that the errors from prediction will be smaller. The unobserved variable will have less variance that it can influence. This variance will also tend to be more

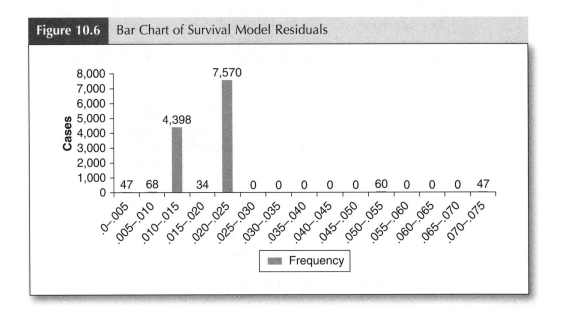

**Figure 10.6**    Bar Chart of Survival Model Residuals

homogeneous across groups because the propensity score use reduces between-group heterogeneity. Greater homogeneity will make it easier to estimate the hypothetical effect of the latent variable and determine whether it has any effect on the variance not accounted for by the baseline process, the measured covariates, and the confounding variables.

*Nonproportional Hazards.* PHA requires that the baseline hazard or survival rate be constant across time. The same percentage of those not experiencing a hazard succumb to the hazard at each point in time. Sometimes this assumption is not credible. The risk may be high initially and taper off over time. The risks of criminal recidivism and disease recurrence both have instances in which the risk is high within the first few years but then gets much lower later on. Box-Steffensmeier, Reiter, and Zorn (2003) provide examples in political science, psychology, biology, and economics. These are known as time-dependent factors. They alter the risk continuously across time, rather than at a point of intervention or occurrence of an event.

When the hazards change continuously across time, they are known as nonproportional hazards (NPH). If a time-dependent variable is identified, it can be treated as a multiplicative effect, where the effect decreases or increases across time. It can then be added in the survival or hazards analysis to better estimate effects across time.

Time-dependent variables can be identified by tracking their effects across time. This can be done by correlating variables with time (for effects that change linearly) or using transforms of the variables (for effects that have curvilinear changes, such as sigmoid curves or decreasing exponential curves). Variables having a log transform or some other curvilinear transform may be used when the change is curvilinear. Scatterplots with time may be useful. Plotting survival functions for treatment and comparison groups separately may also suggest NPH if the two curves are not parallel. NPH can also be identified by plotting the percent change for each time period. Proportional hazards have a constant percent change for every time period. If the percent change varies considerably, it either is perturbed by covariate factors or is not a proportional hazards process.

Propensity scores can facilitate NPH analysis by creating homogeneous time-dependent samples. The trends associated with confounding variables will be controlled by creating samples matched by propensity scores. The same trends associated with the confounders should be found in each. The only time-dependent variables remaining are nonconfounding, alternative covariates and unmeasured variables. If the assumption of ignorability needed to estimate the propensity scores is met, frailty is reduced and the unmeasured variables are less likely to have time-dependent effects.

## ADEQUACY AND SUFFICIENCY WITH CORRELATED SAMPLES

All of the techniques noted above for analyzing correlated data require making additional suppositions about the nature or pattern of the correlation. Given the variety of possible suppositions, it is especially important that evidence be offered that these suppositions have been met. If such evidence is not available, then strong theoretically based arguments are needed to provide confidence that the suppositions are reasonable. If neither evidence nor strong theoretical arguments are advanced to support the suppositions for the analysis of correlated data, the results cannot be said to be statistically adequate. Adequacy requires that assumptions of the data match assumptions of the techniques. If neither evidence nor strong arguments are provided justifying that linkage, there are not sufficient grounds for saying they are present.

Even if evidence or arguments are offered, statistical sufficiency requires that the technique chosen can produce estimates that are unlikely to be superseded by applying an alternative technique to the same data. Sometimes, this may require replicating the analysis using alternative techniques and showing that they produce the same result or that the alternative results have evidence of being more problematic estimates. The bottom line is that one needs to use the technique that provides the best possible estimate. Less than that can still produce useful results, but they won't be statistically sufficient and may be superseded by those of an alternative procedure.

# CHAPTER 11

## Handling Missing Data

This chapter examines problems of missing data when using propensity scores. Procedures for identifying missing data and their risk to the analysis are described. Strategies for handling, estimating, and imputing missing data are presented and discussed. Criteria are presented for judging the results when missing data are present.

It is common to regard missing data as being either random or nonrandom. If it is random, researchers might ignore it or use any of a variety of techniques for estimating or replacing it—often, without clear theoretical or substantive reasons for choosing a technique, other than the fact that "it seems to work." Using propensity scores, however, requires a more carefully considered response to missing data. Rubin (1976a) distinguishes between three types of missing data: (1) missing completely at random (MCAR), (2) missing at random (MAR), and (3) missing not at random (MNAR). Missing data that are MCAR are uncorrelated with any of the observed variables. They are unlikely to introduce bias into the analysis. Missing data that are MAR have randomly deleted values, but the variables for which they are missing are correlated with other observed variables in the data set being analyzed. Such missing data might introduce bias into the analysis, but not necessarily. Missing values that are MNAR are correlated with other observed variables. Of the three types of missing data, these are most likely to introduce bias into the analysis and pose the most problems for using propensity scores.

Different types of missing data require different actions by the researcher. Each of these types of missing data requires different procedures for diagnosing the impact of the missing data on the analysis and conclusions. Each may require a different strategy to prevent bias. Each may require a different response when using propensity scores.

The estimation of propensity scores is particularly affected by missing data because the default procedure for handling missing data by the programs that most commonly estimate propensity scores (Poisson regression, logistic regression, and discriminant function analysis) all use listwise deletion of cases as the default. These programs, per se, do not offer procedures for handling missing data that are commonly used in estimating intervention effects—that is, prediction or imputation of the missing values. While prediction is generally treated as a type of imputation (Barnard, Du, Hill, & Rubin, 1998), the strategy discussed below is distinct from the usual imputation process. It rests on developing a plausible causal model of the missing data. Theoretical grounds are required for believing that the predicted values correspond to the true values. Prediction based on other than a causal model is referred to below as estimation. The basis for accepting the estimated values is purely statistical and does not rest on a theoretical causal model.

These procedures have to be used prior to selection model estimation. Such procedures provide more complete estimation of propensity scores for use in one's analysis. As discussed below, the propensity scores estimated initially, though having missing data, can also be used to improve the prediction or the imputation process. This leads to even better estimation of the propensity scores.

Typically, analysis of missing data has to be done prior to and separate from the estimation of one's outcome model. It may need to be done in conjunction with estimation of propensity scores. Those scores may exhibit patterns of missing data, which could imply that the scores are not MCAR and may need further examination.

The statistical packages considered in this text all have modules for performing missing data analysis. They not only determine patterns of missing data but also provide tests as to whether missing data are MCAR or not. They have procedures for estimating missing data using a procedure called expectation-maximization (EM) estimation, which is discussed below. This allows choosing different responses, depending on the type of missing data and the effect the missing information has on estimates of central tendency, variation, and covariation. These packages also allow imputing missing values.

The different responses to missing data include predicting, estimating, or imputing the missing values and weighting the data. Predicting missing values means developing a causal model of the missingness and using it to predict what the values should be. Estimating missing values means using observed variables to develop a model based on statistical criteria to predict what the missing values would be. Imputing missing values means selecting a value from among the possible values (or selecting a set of values and computing an average of the results from multiple models that use the different values) based on probability criteria. Weighting nonmissing data means the cases with missing data are deleted, and the remaining sample is weighted to resemble the original sample before deleting missing cases.

The first procedure requires developing a model for predicting individual items based on causal theory. The second procedure requires developing a model based on statistical fit criteria. The third procedure requires simulating or estimating possible values and selecting from among them, producing results using the alternative simulated values, and averaging the multiple results. The last procedure requires identifying key characteristics in the original sample that the weighted sample characteristics should resemble. The trade-offs between these four approaches are discussed below.

Researchers need to plan for issues of missing data prior to data collection. The literature review should include noting which variables seem most subject to missing data and whether prior research has noted correlates of the missing data. If prior research has tried estimating or imputing missing data, the results for the imputation of missing value estimation should be noted as well.

Reviewing prior research identifies which measures are most likely to have missing data and what problems this might create. When designing the data collection process, protocols may be added to reduce the likelihood or amount of missing data. Like the issue of control variables, it is better to control by design than to use ex post facto efforts to compensate for missing data.

These protocols may include follow-up or probe questions for problematic measures, additional training for interviewers on difficult items, clarification information on self-administered questionnaires, and the inclusion of items known to correlate with missing data. The latter will help identify the reasons for missing data and provide variables for predicting or estimating the missing data.

Table 11.1 has an example of missing value codes. Note that the table differentiates between information that is missing due to nonresponse and that due to structural inappropriateness. The former means that no response was given on the questionnaire, was given during the interview, or was recorded by the observer. The latter means that no response is possible because that information does not apply to the research subject. If more than one reason can be identified as to why the information is not available, then separate codes should be provided for each reason.

Multiple codes are used for the different reasons why someone may not indicate they are employed. Codes 0 and 6 through 10 allow differentiating those not in the labor force because they are not looking for work, disabled people, retired people, and those for whom being in the labor force is structurally inappropriate, as well as those for whom no information is available.

| Table 11.1 | Possible Missing Value Codes | |
|---|---|---|
| Variable | Code | Meaning |
| Employment status | 0 | Unemployed, not looking |
| | 1 | Unemployed, looking |
| | 2 | Employed 20 or fewer hours per week |
| | 3 | Employed 21 to 39 hours per week |
| | 4 | Employed 40 or more hours per week |
| | 6 | Disabled |
| | 7 | Retired |
| | 8 | Not in labor force, student |
| | 9 | Not in labor force, inappropriate |
| | 10 | No response indicated |

## IDENTIFYING MISSING DATA

On the surface, identifying missing data is a simple task. Most variables have codes that are assigned to missing values. If this is not the case, the researcher should go through the data set and identify what codes should be assigned to or treated as missing data. An example of this occurs when blank fields appear in a record. This may mean that a check box was not checked, that no responses were checked, that the person refused to provide the information, that a 0 should be substituted for the blank field, or that no response is appropriate and the field should be left blank. Various statistical programs handle this issue differently. Some treat blanks as zeros. Some treat them as missing. There should be consistency between the program default and the intent of the researcher on how these are treated.

Missing data pose a special problem for use of propensity scores. If information is missing from a confounding variable, it must be estimated or imputed, or the case must be deleted from the analysis. The estimation and imputation of missing data are discussed below. If cases are deleted, this may allow preserving internal validity of the analysis at the expense of generalizability of the findings. If the missing data are MCAR, the missing cases can be deleted and the propensity score use will still be valid—so long as the sample size is not greatly reduced. If the data are MAR, this may or may not bias the results of using propensity scores. Prediction, in the sense discussed above, is not usually done for missing confounding variables because they are often exogenous to the system being analyzed. A causal framework for predicting these may not be available.

If the missing data in the confounding variables are correlated with the propensity scores, the missing data will create bias. For example, suppose those having less income in the comparison group are more likely to withhold information on their income than those in the intervention group. This will create correlation between missing income information and selection into treatment. This can occur in quasi-experimental designs where either the comparison group individuals were not eligible for the alternative intervention or there are reactive effects between the alternative intervention (not the treatment) and the subjects. The new intervention may have been developed because the existing intervention had such reactive effects.

Generating a frequency distribution for the variables is an easy, but cumbersome, way to identify missing data. The number and percentage of missing cases is tabulated for each variable separately. If summary statistics are produced for the variables, it will also summarize missing data. However, if the number of variables is large, this can be tedious. Inspecting a large number of tables increases the likelihood of making errors in judging the presence and seriousness of missing data.

Missing data analysis programs are only slightly more complex to use than those for frequency distributions. They provide a lot more information about the amount and patterns of missing data. They also provide significance tests as to whether the missing data seem to be MCAR or not. Table 11.2 provides an example of the output of a missing value analysis program present in the SPSS package. It summarizes the amount of and patterns in missing data for selected General Social Survey (GSS) variables.

Table 11.2 shows variation in how much data are missing from the variables. Education and financial view both have less than 1.0% of data missing. On the other hand, information is available for only about half the cases on knowledge of genetics. In analyses involving the first two variables, missing data are not much of an issue. For the genetics knowledge and age at first child's birth variables, the missing data cannot simply be ignored. Prediction, estimation, or imputation will need to be done. Age data for childless respondents will need to remain missing.

Table 11.2 also shows variation in the distribution of extreme cases. Knowing if there are extreme cases is useful in handling missing data because it affects

| Table 11.2 | Missing Value Analysis of General Social Survey Variables |
| --- | --- |

| Univariate Statistics | | | | | | | |
| --- | --- | --- | --- | --- | --- | --- | --- |
| | | | Standard | Missing | | Number of Extremes[a] | |
| | N | Mean | Deviation | Count | Percentage | Low | High |
| Education | 1,997 | 13.48 | 3.103 | 3 | 0.2 | 61 | 0 |
| Knowledge of genetics | 1,039 | 1.25 | 0.435 | 961 | 48.1 | 0 | 0 |
| Age at first kid's birth | 1,431 | 23.79 | 5.604 | 569 | 28.5 | 0 | 36 |
| View of finances | 1,984 | 2.86 | 0.854 | 16 | 0.8 | 0 | 36 |

*Note.* IQR, interquartile range.

a. Number of cases outside the range (Q1 − 1.5 × IQR, Q3 + 1.5 × IQR).

| Tabulated Patterns | | | | | |
| --- | --- | --- | --- | --- | --- |
| | Missing Patterns[a] | | | | |
| Number of Cases | Education | Financial View | Age When First Kid Born | Knowledge of Genetics | Cases Complete If[b] |
| 722 | | | | | 722 |
| 694 | | | | X | 1,416 |
| 258 | | | X | X | 1,981 |
| 307 | | | X | | 1,029 |

*Note.* Patterns with less than 1% cases (20 or fewer) are not displayed.

a. Variables are sorted on missing patterns.

b. Number of complete cases if variables missing in that pattern (marked with X) are not used.

the choice of procedure for estimating missing values. The table provides the percentage of cases that are defined as extreme. They fall outside a range from the first quartile minus 1.5 times the interquartile range up to the fourth quartile plus 1.5 times the interquartile range. For normal distributions, this is about plus or minus 1.7 standard deviations, a range encompassing about 92% of the cases. With normal distributions, about 4% of the cases would be at each end of the distribution. By this definition, less than 3% of these variables' cases are extreme. The interquartile range is used to determine extreme cases because the distribution of the variables is not always normal.

Table 11.2 also provides information on the pattern of missing data. It identifies how many cases are missing data for one or more variables and tabulates how many cases are missing which pattern of missing data. This table shows that there are 481 cases missing data for all four of the variables in the table. There are 447 cases missing data only on knowledge of genetics and 154 cases missing data only on age at first child's birth. In addition, there are 125 cases missing information on two variables: age at first child's birth and knowledge of genetics. The table shows how many cases would be available for analysis if each pattern of cases were excluded from the analysis. This can help decide whether some combinations of missing data should be replaced with estimated or imputed values and whether other cases should simply be excluded.

Only recently have missing data analysis programs begun incorporating visual displays of missing data. The Virtual IO Module of the R statistical program is a notable exception. It allows graphic displays of missing data in a variety of formats. Figure 11.1 provides an example of the graphic display of the frequency of missing data between variables.

In this figure, it is much easier to see the relative proportions of missing data among the variables. It was created from the variables that indicate presence or absence of missing data discussed above. A stacked histogram constrained to sum to 100% produced the image.

The pattern of missing data can also be graphed. Figure 11.2 shows the patterns for four variables: (1) education, (2) financial view, (3) age at first child's birth, and (4) knowledge of genetics. The white area in the graph indicates how many cases are missing data in comparison. It can be produced by missing data programs within all the statistical packages discussed in the text.

*Predicting Missing Data.* The propensity score in the GSS data in Table 11.2 was missing some predicted values because confounding variables were missing data. Several options are available for predicting these values. The mean or median of the distribution can be substituted for the missing value for a continuous variable. If the distribution is symmetrical, the mean would be substituted. If the distribution is skewed or ordinal, the median might be used. Substituting the mean preserves the mean of the distribution, but it reduces the variance. Substituting the median may slightly alter the mean of the distribution.

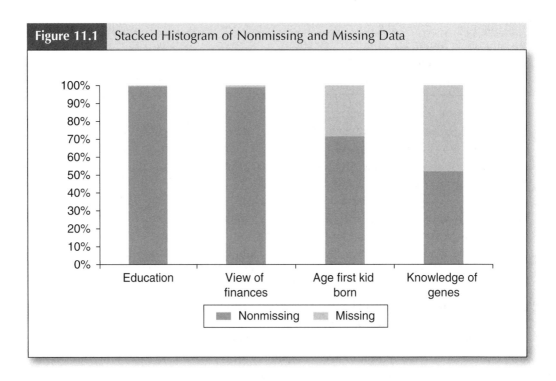

**Figure 11.1**    Stacked Histogram of Nonmissing and Missing Data

If a distribution is extremely skewed, a strategy other than substitution should be used. Substituting a fixed value for the missing data is called deterministic substitution.

Substituting the mean or median is often called an imputation procedure. It is discussed in this section because it shares a commonality with predictive models. With symmetrical distributions, the mean and median are the expected values for the distribution. They are also the maximum likelihood value for the distribution. The mean is the predicted value in the special case where no other variables provide information for prediction. To the extent that all substitution procedures are regarded as imputation, substituting the mean or median can also be regarded as imputation.

Substituting the mean preserves the mean value, but it reduces the standard deviation of the distribution. This can inflate correlations with this variable, since the correlations are a function of the ratio of the covariances to the variances; and the variances are being reduced. This can increase the risk of a Type I error, a false-positive inference. If the correlations before mean substitution are close to those after mean substitution, the risk of a Type I error is not inflated, and this procedure may be an acceptable strategy. Mean substitution

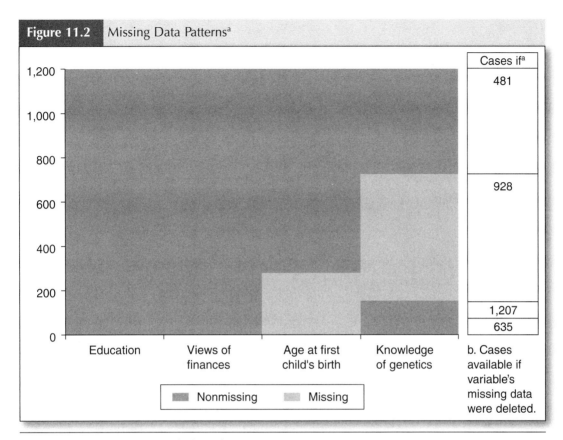

**Figure 11.2**    Missing Data Patterns[a]

a. Parent smoking, propensity matched sample. N = 1,207.

is the grossest and least accurate strategy possible. If no other strategy works, however, it can be considered—provided that checks are made to be sure the correlations are not altered.

The missing values can be predicted using information from the observed data matrix. When certain conditions are met, an equation can be developed to predict the missing value, and the predicted value is substituted for the missing value. The conditions are as follows: (a) some other variables must have nonmissing information for the cases that are missing information on the variable to be predicted, (b) the variables with nonmissing information must correlate or be associated with the variable having missing data, and (c) a plausible reason must be offered for why these variables are associated with the target variable.

As an example, let us consider the respondent's highest level of education reported in the GSS. This indicator has 3,068 cases with this information and 2 cases missing this information. With such a small amount of missing data, those 2 cases would usually be dropped from the analysis and their missing data ignored. However, their missing data illustrates the options for predicting these values.

To find other variables having information for the cases with missing education data, a dummy variable needs to be constructed indicating absence or presence of missing education information. This was done with 0 indicating education data not missing and 1 indicating education data missing. This variable was correlated with noncategorical variables for which there was a plausible argument that they might be correlated with education. These variables are the following: having knowledge of genetics, mother's occupational prestige score, believing that one's standard of living will increase, confidence in the educational system, respondents' age when their first child was born, total family income, respondents' perception of the adequacy of their income, and how fundamentalist respondents regard their religious beliefs. These correlations appear in Table 11.3. The purpose of this table is to determine whether there might be an association between these variables and the missing educational information. One could do the same thing by cross-tabulating the dummy variable with possible categorical predictors.

Some of these variables do not have correlations computed because they have no data for the cases missing the educational information. Other variables have extremely low correlations with missing data. These variables can be deleted from the equation predicting the missing values. Further screening can be done by doing an analysis of variance (ANOVA) of the possible predictors by the dummy variable. This will tabulate how many of the predictor variables have information for both cases where education is missing (see Table 11.4).

Some of the plausible predictors have information for one of the two cases. The rest have information for all four cases. Those having information on both cases are the variables that can be used for predicting the missing data. The nine variables having data for the missing cases were entered in a general linear model estimating education for all cases. The estimated years of education were saved as a new variable, truncating decimal points. The missing education information was then replaced with the predicted education, providing complete education for the entire sample.

This predictive process works well when one has sufficient plausible predictors with data for the cases missing information to be predicted. This does not always work because sometimes there are insufficient predictors with information for the right cases. One or two predictors are not enough. With so few predictors, the

| Table 11.3 | Correlates of Missing Educational Data |
|---|---|
| *Possible Correlates* | *Missing Educational Data* |
| Age when first child was born | .325* |
| Knowledge of big bang | −.196* |
| Knows father's genes determine sex of child | −.097* |
| Confidence in education | .088* |
| R's highest degree | .848* |
| R's highest degree earned | .752* |
| Opinion of family income | .308* |
| Believes standard of living will improve | −.030 |
| Happiness of marriage | −.078* |
| Total family income | .243* |
| Mother's highest year of school completed | .426* |
| Mother's occupational prestige score | .341* |
| How fundamentalist is R | .176* |

*Correlation significant at .05 level.

predicted value becomes dominated by a single variable. The predicted value with one or two predictors is not meaningful as a separate variable.

The procedures for estimating propensity scores can also be used to estimate missing values. The most reliable and valid estimates of propensity scores are made when the predictors are causal influences on the selection process. The same holds for predicting missing data. Including causal variables provides theoretical grounds for expecting the predicted values to resemble the true values. While estimation models might also include consequent variables, the inclusion of such variables has predictive credibility if they also have a plausible causal relationship with the variable being predicted.

If the predictors of the missing data account for all the known causal influences on a particular variable, the estimation equation based on these predictors can produce statistically sufficient estimates of the missing data. This requirement is rarely met because the causal influences on a given variable are

| Table 11.4 | ANOVA of Predictors of Education by Missingness of Education Data | | | |
|---|---|---|---|---|
| | *Missing Education Information* | | *Not Missing Education Information* | |
| *Predictors* | *Mean* | *N* | *Mean* | *N* |
| Age when first child born | 20.0 | 2 | 23.8 | 1,109 |
| Knowledge of big bang | 1.0 | 1 | 1.5 | 644 |
| Knows father's genes determine sex of child | 1.0 | 1 | 1.3 | 809 |
| Confidence in education | 2.0 | 2 | 1.9 | 1,018 |
| R's highest degree | 0.0 | 2 | 1.6 | 1,534 |
| View of family income | 2.0 | 2 | 2.9 | 1,522 |
| Believes standard of living will improve | 2.5 | 2 | 2.3 | 1,018 |
| Happiness of marriage | 2.0 | 2 | 1.4 | 764 |
| Total family income | 11.0 | 2 | 11.0 | 1,021 |
| Mother's highest year of school completed | 18.0 | 1 | 11.0 | 1,346 |
| Mother's occupational prestige score | 44.0 | 2 | 42.0 | 938 |
| How fundamentalist is respondent | 2.0 | 2 | 2.0 | 1,469 |

*Note.* ANOVA, analysis of variance.

usually in dispute. If one can select most of the major influences on a variable, however, very good estimates are produced.

If a prediction equation for all the missing cases cannot be developed, several strategies are possible. It may be possible to develop an equation for some of the missing cases. This is less satisfactory than predicting all the values, but it may provide enough cases to improve the statistical power of the analysis. The substitution procedures discussed above are an option if a prediction equation cannot be developed; but substitution is best used when exploring one's findings, rather than when trying to produce estimates of treatment effects. If one is estimating intervention effects and predictive substitution is not feasible, the only reliable alternative is imputing the missing data.

*Weighting Nonmissing Data.* This procedure weights a sample from which missing cases have been deleted listwise. The weights are chosen so that the weighted sample resembles the original sample. Meng (1994) has identified situations in which weighting can outperform prediction and imputation. Two conditions have to be met for this to be the case. The amount of subjects lost by listwise deletion of cases with missing data must not be a large percentage of the original sample. In addition, key variables must be identified to adequately describe the sample.

Since the percentage of missing cases is a continuum, there can be no clearly defined cutting point at which there is too much missing data. Instead, sensitivity analysis will need to be done to assess the effect of this procedure compared with alternative procedures. If the sensitivity analysis suggests that the results of weighting are less sensitive than the results of prediction or imputation, those results should be preferred.

The best choice of weights is also not clearly defined. When the sample has been selected using probability criteria, as with many surveys, there are known parameters. Weights can be selected to approximate those parameters. The sample weights are divided by the percentage of nonmissing cases after listwise deletion to obtain weights that approximate the population parameters. The formula is simply

$$W_{sn} = W_s/P_n, \tag{11.1}$$

where $P_n$ is the proportion of nonmissing cases and $W_s$ is the sampling case weight. The weighted sample with complete data will approximate the total sample size with parameters similar to the population from which it was drawn (Bloom & Idson, 1991).

Not weighting may bias estimates of standard errors and measures of association. The frequency with which this occurs varies from sample to sample and depends, in part, on the extent to which there is variation in the sample weights themselves. If all cases were weighted the same, the results would be no different than if the data were unweighted. Without sample weighting, the covariance matrix of the confounding variables can produce biased estimates of the propensity scores (Imbens & Wooldridge, 2009).

This weighting procedure is fine for population estimation. It doesn't work for estimating intervention effects because it doesn't use weights to control the influences of confounding variables. Matching samples, propensity weighting, adjusting covariates, and/or stratifying will still have to be done to balance the confounding effects.

If propensity weighting is the strategy chosen, the weighting procedures to compensate for missing data can be combined with using propensity weights. In this case, propensity scores will need to be estimated using the completed data file. These propensity weights can be applied to the nonmissing data weights to obtain a balanced sample that approximates a balanced, complete sample with no missing data. The combined weight is

$$W_{snp} = W_{sn} \, W_p, \tag{11.2}$$

where $W_{snp}$ is the combined weight, $W_{sn}$ is the sample nonmissing weight, and $W_p$ is the propensity weight. As previously discussed, there are a variety of choices for propensity weights, and the data analyst will have to choose the one that is most appropriate for the situation.

It is not known how combined propensity weighting performs compared with prediction or imputation propensity use. No simulation studies or mathematical derivations have been published making this comparison. No empirical studies have used all three procedures and compared the results. If combined propensity weights are used, the results should be compared with either prediction or imputation use to handle missing data. If the results are similar, this can add confidence that the results are not an artifact of missing data handling procedures. If the results are dissimilar, this can be a warning flag to more closely examine the missing data and procedures for handling it.

## IMPUTING MISSING DATA

Five forms of imputation are examined here: (1) hot deck, (2) cold deck, (3) single, (4) multiple, and (5) propensity. Hot deck imputation (HD) requires substituting one of the observed values of a variable for the missing data using the same data set. Cold deck imputation (CD) substitutes an observed value from a data set not being currently analyzed. It may be a holdout, validation subsample, or a similar data set. Single imputation (SI) requires simulating or identifying one plausible value of a variable. Multiple imputation (MI) requires simulating multiple values for a variable and averaging the multiple results. Propensity imputation (PI) uses homogeneous propensity strata to improve the accuracy of the imputed values. When a credible causal model of missing data is not available to predict the missing values (and this is often the case), imputation is generally the best alternative strategy.

Both hot deck and cold deck imputation have mostly been replaced by SI and MI procedures. The former procedures have been found to underestimate the population variances slightly in comparison with SI and MI procedures. The SI procedure tends to produce slightly less precise estimates than the MI procedure. Consequently, MI is now the principal imputation procedure used.

If MI is used, values are substituted for each replication. In this case, the analysis is replicated using the alternative values to produce multiple results. The results from the replications are combined to produce a fairly reliable estimate. When a credible causal model of missing data is not available to predict the missing values, MI generally performs better than other methods at providing substitute values for missing data (Rubin, 1996)—except in the special case mentioned above for propensity imputation.

Ideally, imputing missing data produces results that are consistent with findings from data with complete cases. When the two agree, the results with imputation provide greater confidence since they are based on larger sample sizes. When the two do not agree, this discrepancy is known as inferential uncongeniality (Meng, 1994). The imputation may be done by others prior to the analyst receiving the data, as in the case with public use data sets. There may be a discrepancy between the imputation done by the producers of the data and those of the analyzer of the data. This also leads to uncongeniality. When there is such a discrepancy, the imputations of the producers of the data are generally to be preferred—unless the simulations that led to the imputations explicitly left out a variable the analyst considers important. In this latter case, the researcher should replicate the analysis with the alternative imputations, acknowledge the discrepant findings produced, and provide his or her argument as to why one set should be accepted over another.

MI begins by simulating the process that accounts for variation in a variable. This is similar to the process of developing a prediction equation, except that unobserved random data are used to predict possible values rather than observed nonrandom data. The simulation uses two primary alternative strategies: (1) the monotone method and (2) the fully conditional specification (FCS) method.

As noted above, the number of variables in the matrix to impute the plausible alternative values should include any variable likely to be included in the analysis, even if it has limited association with the variable being predicted. Interactive terms among these variables may also be included if they retain any association with the target variable after controlling the additive effects of the variables. There is nothing to be gained by adding variables or predictive terms that have no relationship with the target variable at all. It can even add random error variance to the predicted values, which affects the estimate of the variance of the simulated distribution.

This approach is contrary to that for developing a causal predictive model. With the latter, one wants to include only predictors having a plausible causal relationship with the target variable. With the former, one wants to include as many of the known correlates and variables that might be used in the analysis as one can. This is because their omission may weaken the ability to fully examine the effects of variables that were omitted from imputation.

## Monotone Selection

This method sorts the cases by missing data. If the cases cannot be ordered to meet the monotone criteria mentioned above, computer programs for which a monotone procedure was selected will abort the estimation process and print out an error message. When data do meet the monotone criteria, the variables are ordered with those that have no missing data being listed first, followed by the variable having the least amount of missing data. The variables having complete data are used to predict values for the first variable with missing data. Multiple values are imputed by creating a random distribution having the mean and standard deviation of the distribution of values predicted by the complete data variables. Values are then randomly selected from this simulated distribution. The values selected are proportionate to their frequency in the distribution. The number of selections is specified by the analyst, unless default values of a specific program are used. Three to five imputations are often selected.

The monotone method can only be used if the variables can be ordered and sorted so that if a given variable has data for a case, all variables preceding that variable also have data. Conversely, if a variable is missing data for a given case, then all variables following it on the list are also missing data for that case. An example of a hypothetical monotone data file is given in Table 11.5. This table assumes that the cases have been sorted so that the missing values come last and the variables have been ordered with those variables having the fewest missing values coming first.

In Table 11.5, VAR3 and VAR5 would predict values for VAR2. The mean and variance of the predicted values for VAR2 are used to create a distribution of random data having the mean and standard deviation of the predicted distribution. Imputed values would be randomly selected from this distribution for the cases having missing data. The imputed values would replace the missing values. Once imputed values for the first variable having missing data are selected, these are inserted in multiple files completed by the imputed data. This allows going to the second variable having missing data. It is predicted by the preceding variables, including the previous variable that used to have missing

| Table 11.5 | Monotone Data File | | | | |
|---|---|---|---|---|---|
| ID | VAR3 | VAR5 | VAR2 | VAR1 | VAR4 |
| 103 | 38 | 6 | 12 | 33 | 1 |
| 107 | 26 | 4 | 14 | 13 | 0 |
| 102 | 42 | 8 | 15 | 21 | 0 |
| 105 | 21 | 2 | 16 | 19 | 1 |
| 101 | 51 | 1 | 14 | 25 | Missing |
| 104 | 19 | 5 | 11 | Missing | Missing |
| 106 | 23 | 7 | Missing | Missing | Missing |

data. VAR3, VAR5, and VAR2 would be used to predict values for VAR1, continuing until all the variables have either complete data or imputed values.

This creates multiple imputed files. The number of files equals the number of values imputed for each variable. If single imputation was being done, only one imputed file would be produced. The analysis is replicated for each set of data, and the results are pooled. The means are averaged, and the variances are weighted proportional to the size of the variances.

## FCS Method

The FCS method uses either a Markov Chain Monte Carlo (MCMC) procedure or an EM procedure to estimate the selected values. The former is a semi-Bayesian procedure that revises the imputed values by successive iteration. It is not completely Bayesian because the observations are not completely independent. The latter procedure is also iterative and revises the imputations until the mean and variance of the imputed distributions are the same as the observed distribution.

Initial information is used to produce revised estimates of what the selected values should be. The starting point for both procedures is to create a simulated data set with a mean and variance equal to the observed values. MCMC then uses probability selection in choosing imputed values, whereas EM uses regression (ordinary least squares or logistic) to estimate the imputed values. The estimates are revised in subsequent iterations by using all the variables, inasmuch as they have all nonmissing cases (observed or imputed). The process stops when the distributions of the imputed data files do not change between iterations.

MCMC has been preferred when the distribution of the variables is unknown or is nonnormal. EM has been preferred when the distribution is known or is normal. This distinction, however, is breaking down, because generalized estimating equation procedures allow identifying and estimating nonnormal distributions, which may be applied to EM. MCMC procedures, however, have proven more efficient than generalized estimating equation procedures. The only situation in which MCMC has a clear strength over EM is when the distribution is completely unknown, when tests have verified that it does not have any distribution that can be estimated with generalized linear models. Either of the procedures can estimate missing values for any identifiable distribution. Sensitivity analysis of the results may be necessary to know which procedure produces the best estimates.

The imputation process is illustrated with the education variable whose missing values were estimated using a predictive model above. The same variables in the prediction equation were included in a data matrix used for imputation. Table 11.6 displays predicted and imputed values for the two cases. MI was used for five imputations. The FCS method was used because the data were not monotone. MCMC simulation was used to obtain the values. An EM estimate of the missing values is also provided.

The maximum likelihood (ML) prediction and the EM estimation are in complete agreement. Only one of the imputed values was the same as the ML and EM values. The average of the five imputed values also differed from ML and EM. Although imputation can be applied to small samples, the number of values imputed in this case is insufficient for the averages to converge on the sample value. When there are very few cases with missing values, it may be better to predict them, estimate them, or delete them. Even so, the findings will not be greatly altered with just a few imputations.

**Table 11.6  Predicted and Imputed Missing Values**

| CASE | ML Pred. | EM Est. | Imputed 1 | Imputed 2 | Imputed 3 | Imputed 4 | Imputed 5 | Mean Imputed |
|---|---|---|---|---|---|---|---|---|
| 1 | 16 | 16 | 16 | 11 | 11 | 9 | 13 | 12 |
| 2 | 12 | 12 | 15 | 10 | 11 | 15 | 18 | 14 |

Note. ML Pred., maximum likelihood prediction; EM Est., expectation-maximization estimation.

## *Propensity Imputation*

Propensity scores can be used to improve the performance of adjustment cells. If propensity scores are initially estimated using simple substitution without using adjustment cells, strata can be constructed based on similarity of propensity scores. This will create cells that have multivariate homogeneity, rather than being homogeneous on just a small number of variables. Substitution can be made within each cell for the initially substituted missing data. The propensity scores can be reestimated and the procedure repeated until the estimated propensity scores for the cases having substitution converge according to whatever criterion is selected.

## IMBALANCED MISSING DATA

Assessing imbalance of missing data can be done in a fashion similar to that for nonmissing data. Dummy variables can be created indicating whether a given case is missing information on a variable or not. A matrix of such dummy variables for all the confounders is commonly named an R matrix.

Additional procedures may be needed to assess the effect of the missing data on the imbalance. Using dummy variables indicating missing data is one strategy. The missing value dummy variables can be correlated, cross-tabulated, or run in an ANOVA to explore associations among missing data and confounding variables. When such associations exist, the missing data are not random. The missing values need to be predicted, estimated, or imputed.

An example where the missing data are correlated with another variable is given in Figure 11.3. This is a scatterplot of GSS household income with the respondent's education for observed data and for data estimated using the EM procedure.

The observed data are plotted in black circles. The estimated data are plotted in white triangles. Regression lines that are drawn show the relationship between the education indicator and the household income. The estimated data that replaced the missing data occur more in the middle of the distribution and have a different relationship with household income than do the observed data. Including these estimated values will produce an estimated relationship between education and household income that is different from using just the nonmissing data alone. When there is a significant amount of missing data, including estimated values may alter the findings—unless checks are made to verify that the estimated data do not have different covariances than the observed data.

| Figure 11.3 | Scatterplot of Observed and EM Estimated Education by Household Income |

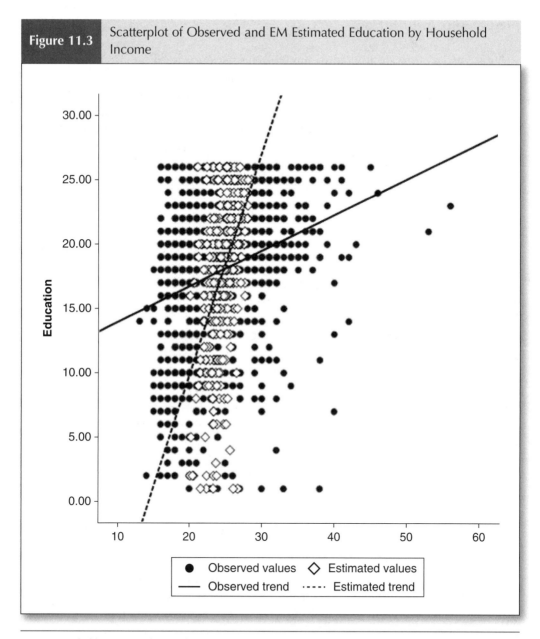

*Note.* Household income in thousands. EM, expectation-maximization.

Examining the association of dummy missing variables with the outcomes is another strategy. Any association of this nature implies differential mortality or differential nonresponse. Some researchers have tried using the dummy variables as control variables to remove the influence of differential missing data on estimates of treatment effects. However, in some circumstances, it produces biased estimates of regression coefficients and mean differences between groups. Prediction, estimation, and imputation appear to be better strategies (McKnight, McKnight, Sidani, & Figueredo, 2007).

## Imputation of Missing Data

Imputation is the process by which missing value codes are replaced with values that are simulated. Rubin (1976a) has shown that randomly replacing missing data by selecting from a small number of simulated values can produce good results in increasing the sample size while preserving the interrelations of the observed variables.

Two elements are especially important for getting good results with imputation. The model that produces the simulated results must be a plausible model, and the variables used to simulate the results must have a plausible relationship with the variable being simulated. Factors that research has shown to have a causal relationship with the target variable are essential to include. Variables that correlate with the target variable and that have theoretical justifications for believing that they are related to the target variable should be included. Variables that prior research has shown to have a consistent correlation with the target variable should also be added if a plausible rationale can be offered as to why they are correlated with the target.

In addition to the above variables, those that appear in one's outcome model should also be included if they are correlated with the target. Such variables may have weak or no theoretical justification for inclusion in a simulation of the target variable. One can initially exclude such unjustified variables and examine the correlations of the simulated data with the observed variables and determine whether they are the same. If so, they may be left out. If the correlations of the simulated data with the observed data are different from the correlations of the observed data alone, these additional variables may need to be added into the simulation. If they are added to the simulation, the correlations of the simulated data with the observed data should be reexamined to see if those without the simulated values are still the same.

It is possible that none of these strategies produce results for the simulated data that replicate the correlations among the observed data. This may happen when there is an important unobserved variable. Such omission violates the ignorability assumption. The imputation approach should not be done when ignorability is violated. Another factor that may prevent replication is the inclusion of variables that correlate with the target variable, but for which no theoretical justification exists to think they have a causal relationship with the target. These "implausible" variables may add to the predictive power of the simulation, but the simulated values may then not have the same correlations with either observed data or simulated data for other variables. One must empirically examine these correlations to have assurance that they don't produce inconsistent results.

Although imputation originated by simulating individual values, it is common now to have the simulation process produce several values, insert them in alternative models, and combine the results of estimating the alternative models. This process is called MI. All major statistical packages have the capacity for MI.

Maximum likelihood estimation (MLE) provides a common alternative to the MI approach. Rather than simulating multiple values, estimating multiple models, and combing the results, MLE develops an equation that directly estimates the missing values. A Bayesian version of this process was developed by Dempster, Laird, and Rubin (1977) that has been shown to work well with missing data. This approach has been called EM. It is so called because this algorithm alternates between using expectations and MLE to iteratively converge on a single estimated value. All major statistical packages have the capacity for EM estimation. EM estimation can be incorporated as part of the MI estimation process. This dual strategy tends to produce imputed distributions whose parameters are closer to those of the observed distribution.

## PROPENSITY ESTIMATION WITH MISSING DATA

It is not clear how the propensity score should be estimated when some covariate values are missing. The missingness itself may be predictive about which treatment is received. Any technique for estimating propensity scores in the presence of covariate missing data either will have to make a stronger assumption regarding ignorability of the assignment mechanism or will have to make an assumption about the missing data mechanism.

There is no agreed-on procedure for estimating propensity scores when confounding variables have missing data. The pattern of data missing from the confounders may be correlated with the selection process. Either the researcher must assume that the missing data is uncorrelated with the selection process, that it is ignorable, or the researcher will need to develop a model for the process creating the missing data. In the latter case, this means developing an estimation or simulation model that corresponds to the supposed process creating the missing data.

## GENERALIZED PROPENSITY SCORES

Propensity scores were originally developed for variables with two categories: treatment and control. Interventions, however, may have more than one value. There may be alternative doses used to determine the one having maximum efficacy with minimum side effects. There may be different interventions used, based on alternative theories, funding levels, or legal requirements. There is also a question of how to handle missing data when multiple categories are present. This is particularly a problem when the missing data are correlated with background characteristics of the respondents or with confounding variables. Generalized propensity scores (GPS) were developed to handle these problems.

Hirano and Imbens (2004) provide an example in which the missing data for lottery winners is correlated with the amount of their winnings. As a random lottery, the amount of winnings should be uncorrelated with background characteristics. Those winning large, intermediate, or small amounts should be balanced on their background characteristics. However, those who won more were less likely to respond to the survey or to provide complete information when they did respond. The background characteristics were imbalanced.

Hirano and Imbens (2004) address this imbalance by creating a GPS, the formula for which is in Equation 11.3:

$$R = r(T; X_i),$$
(11.3)

where $r(T; X)$ is the conditional probability of treatment given the characteristics of the covariates $X_i$, and the subscript $i$ indicates that there are multiple strata of the treatment variable. The value can vary between strata but is homogeneous conditional on characteristics within strata. Hirano and Imbens indicate that GPS has a balancing property similar to the standard propensity score. When there are only two groups, GPS is the same as the standard propensity score.

The GPS is used to estimate a dose–response function for the different levels of intervention. It can also be used to estimate dose–responses for discrete interventions. The GPS can be estimated by a three-step process. First, the GPS is estimated:

$$R_i = \left(\frac{1}{\sqrt{2\pi\sigma^2}}\right) \exp\left(-\left(\frac{1}{2\pi\sigma^2}\right)(T_i - B_0 - B_1'X_i)^2\right),$$
(11.4)

where $R_i$ is the GPS, $T_i$ is the standard propensity score estimated from the covariates, and $B_0$, $B_i'$, and $\sigma^2$ are maximum likelihood estimates of the effect of the covariates on each group. They can be estimated by a maximum likelihood regression in which $T_i$ is the dependent variable. A value for $\pi$ and the estimated value of $\sigma^2$ for each stratum are substituted in the equation. They are constants for each time the equation is estimated. In effect, propensity scores are estimated within each stratum and adjusted using $\pi$ and the variance for each stratum.

Second, the conditional treatment effect for each group is estimated using ordinary least squares regression:

$$(Y \mid T_i, R_i) = \alpha_0 + \alpha_1 T_i + \alpha_2 T_i^2 + \alpha_3 R_i + \alpha_4 R_i^2 + \alpha_5 T_i R_i, \qquad (11.5)$$

where $T_i$, $T^2$, $R_i$, and $R^2$ are the predictor variables. This provides estimated treatment effects for each level or category of the intervention, balanced by the GPS.

If one wishes to create a dose–response curve, the expected outcomes for each treatment level can be estimated by regression procedures:

$$Y_t = \alpha_0 + \alpha_1 t_i + \alpha_2 t_i^2 + \alpha_3 r_i + \alpha_4 r_i^2 + \alpha_5 t_i r_i, \qquad (11.6)$$

where $\alpha_0$ is the intercept, $\alpha_1$ through $\alpha_5$ are regression coefficients, and $t_i$ are dummy treatment variables and $r_i$ are GPS propensities for the $i$th treatment, which is conditional on the covariates $X_i$.

Given that the missing data are correlated with the predictor variables, adjusting using the GPS also adjusts for the effect of missing data. This holds under the assumption of weak ignorability. To be fully effective, all of the dummy missing data variables that have a significant amount of missing data need to correlate with the confounding variables. If they do not (if weak ignorability is violated), this procedure does not remove the biasing effects of missing data.

Hirano and Imbens (2004) applied GPS to the lottery data for intervals of winnings. They estimated the marginal income of winners of the Massachusetts lottery with and without GPS adjustment. The results of this are given in Figure 11.4, which displays dose–response curves of the marginal income by winnings.

The curve after adjusting with GPS and removing the missing data effects produces a more curvilinear trend than without adjusting for such effects. Hirano and Imbens (2004) interpret this to mean that those with lower incomes are more sensitive to winnings effects than those with larger incomes.

## MATCHING WITH MISSING DATA

Creating matched samples with propensity scores is complicated by missing data. If the missing data are correlated with the covariates, they are not completely at random (not MCAR). D'Agostino and Rubin (2000) have shown that propensity adjustment with MNAR data can produce biased results. This means samples matched using propensity scores when the data are MNAR will not remove the entire imbalance. If one uses only complete data and standard matching procedures, the resulting samples will produce biased estimates of treatment effects. If one uses GPS for matching, however, the imbalance can be removed, and the results may not be biased. As with any matching procedure, there is still a need to check for imbalance after matching.

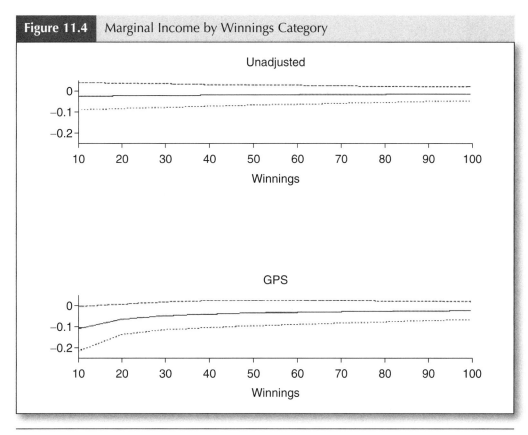

**Figure 11.4**    Marginal Income by Winnings Category

*Source.* Hirano and Imbens (2004).

*Note.* GPS, generalized propensity score.

## STRATIFYING WITH MISSING DATA

Since strata are based on propensity scores whose data are not missing, differential nonresponse can produce strata that are not balanced. Approaches for dealing with this problem are to use prediction, estimation, or imputation to fill in the missing data. Prediction and estimation work well when the variables used in the prediction and estimation are those with which the missing data are correlated. Imputation works well when the data are MAR.

Weighting is an alternative approach for handling missing data within strata. Propensity weights can be used to remove any remaining imbalance within strata. Combining propensity weights with the proportion of data not missing also allows creating strata with complete data.

## COVARIANCE CONTROL WITH MISSING DATA

Adding covariates with missing data decreases the sample size when the covariates have missing data. The defaults on most programs that allow use of covariates are listwise deletion of cases having missing values. The trade-offs in handling missing data with covariates have been discussed above.

A combined strategy of imputing or estimating values for missing confounding variables and estimating propensity scores with complete records is an alternative strategy for dealing with covariates that add to the missing data. The covariates with missing data can have those values filled in by imputation or estimation. Prediction is not likely to be a viable strategy because covariates in this case may well be exogenous variables in one's models. There may be no plausible causal variables for predicting the values.

When one has estimated or imputed values of covariates, the stability of the parameters of the model need exploration. A model estimated using complete data should be compared with a model having missing data filled in. If the parameters are similar, it is common to assume that the estimation or imputation results should be accepted. Strictly speaking, such results only fail to prove that the data are MNAR. They can be accepted as the best available information. They can offer evidence consistent with a causal hypothesis. Because of the questions that may be left unanswered, however, definitive results in the face of MNAR data are problematic. It takes strong evidence to say that problems from MNAR have been eliminated or made ignorable.

# WEIGHTS WITH MISSING DATA

Propensity weighting can reduce the problem of cases missing data on control variables. If the missing data are correlated with the confounding variables, then weights based on GPS will adjust for the missing data. If missing data are not correlated with confounding variables or with outcomes, they may be assumed to be MCAR. In this case, weighting with standard propensity scores may be used. In these two situations, propensity weighting can reduce or eliminate biasing effects of missing data.

When the missing data are correlated with unmeasured confounders, then neither of the weighting schemes mentioned above produce unbiased results. Some progress has been made in treating the missing data as due to a latent variable. Sensitivity analysis can be used to explore the effects of supposing the existence of a particular latent variable and examining what the consequences would be for the parameters of the model and the estimated treatment effects.

If assuming the existence of a particular missing data factor seems to result in more stable estimates of treatment effects, the tendency is to accept that as having accounted for bias from missing data. While one can make a strong argument in favor of a particular model as having accounted for the missing data, it is impossible to completely rule out MNAR missingness so long as some missing data are present. The most that can be obtained is to offer evidence that is consistent with a model in which MNAR data are ignorable.

# CHAPTER 12

## REPAIRING BROKEN EXPERIMENTS

This chapter discusses problems with experimental and quasi-experimental data when random assignment is either impossible or not achieved. It considers departures from research protocol. Nonrandomization, noncompliance, and nonresponse are the principal consequences when research protocol is broken. This results in problems for analysis and inference. The chapter presents procedures for diagnosing the magnitude of these problems and for reducing their impact.

*Broken experiment* is a term coined by Barnard, Du, Hill, and Rubin (1998). It means that deviations from the ideal standard of random assignment and complete data raise questions about the internal validity of a study. These deviations may or may not introduce bias into the analysis. The data must be examined to determine whether the deviations bias the results.

Problems of implementation, between-group imbalance, differential missing data, and noncompliance are the four principal issues that need examination to determine if an experiment is broken. Procedures for examining imbalance were discussed in Chapter 4. Techniques for assessing missing data were considered in Chapter 11. Strategies for dealing with noncompliance when it results in missing data were also examined in Chapter 11. However, noncompliance can result in bias by means other than differential missing data. This chapter focuses on assessing when implementation and noncompliance jeopardize the research protocol. It discusses strategies for dealing with the problems created, particularly using propensity scores. The strategies do not always eliminate the problems of broken experiments. They generally improve the quality of the analysis so that false conclusions are less likely to result. When strategies are used that are both statistically adequate and sufficient, no better results can be obtained from the data at hand.

The reader is reminded that it is not always possible to design a perfect experiment—even if one has unlimited resources. Legal and ethical constraints, side effects of interventions, and variability of human willingness make this impossible with human experiments—except in very restricted situations. While the goal is to use design to maximize control over confounding and other relevant factors, analytical techniques need to be used when the design cannot cover everything. They are needed when ethical or legal constraints prohibit some options, the implementation has difficulties, and subjects assert their human choice.

## WHEN THINGS GO WRONG

Barnard, Frangakis, Hill, and Rubin (2003) provide an example of a broken experiment from their study of a school choice voucher program in New York City. The program randomly provided vouchers to applicant families where the probability of selection was a function of design variables: period of application, current school, family size and income, and propensity scores estimated from background variables for the families. Families that had low income or whose children were in public schools had a higher probability of selection. Families that had high income or whose children were in private schools had a lower probability of selection.

There were 20,000 families who applied for vouchers. These families were asked to attend a meeting to collect background information to be used in the selection process. One thousand families were randomly selected from strata defined by family size (one child or multiple) and performance criteria for schools. A control group was selected by matching families with propensity scores similar to those selected. The propensity scores were estimated for the 20,000 applicants based on when they applied, their current school, family size, and other background characteristics.

The selection of control families was impaired principally by five issues.

1. Some families offered a scholarship did not subsequently accept the scholarship and sent their children to a private school.

2. Some families not offered a scholarship sent their children to a private school anyway.

3. Some families invited to attend data collection and testing sessions 1 year after the baseline survey did not show up.

4. Some parents and students did not complete all items in their questionnaire.

5. Some students did not complete enough items in the standardized reading and math assessments to be given a score.

These issues create problems for some of the approaches to estimating intervention effects. In particular, they create problems with intent to treat studies, per protocol analysis, and as treatment analysis. The intent to treat studies compare those assigned to treatment who received treatment with those assigned to control who received the controls. They exclude those assigned to treatment or control who did not receive the treatment or placebo to which they were assigned.

Per protocol analysis compares those assigned to treatment with those assigned to control. It includes those assigned to a group who did not receive the treatment or placebo assigned. It assumes that the proportion of subjects not receiving their assigned treatment will be the same in the experimental group as in the real-world implementation. It also assumes that compliers and never takers in the comparison group are the same before intervention. In particular, it assumes that the reasons compliers and never takers drop out of a study or refuse to answer some questions are the same reasons. Given the above five issues, it seems unreasonable to make this assumption. Without this supposition, however, the estimated treatment effects are likely to be biased.

Analysis of the as treated group compares those who received intervention or not, without regard to whether they were assigned to receive or not receive the intervention. It includes those who were assigned to treatment or control and received something other than that assigned. It assumes that the effect of receiving the intervention is not related to whether they were supposed to receive the intervention. With noncompliance or differential missing data, those for whom the intervention is not appropriate might have received the intervention and be expected to have the same effect as those for whom the intervention is appropriate. It is not reasonable to make this supposition.

The New York School Voucher program had both missing data and noncompliance. Groups were imbalanced in background characteristics. To deal with this, missing data were estimated using the expectation-maximization algorithm discussed in Chapter 11. Propensity scores were obtained using complete data estimation. Control cases that had the closest scores to those of an intervention family were selected (nearest-neighbor matching). When multiple control cases had the same propensity score, the Mahalanobis distance from the treatment case was calculated for each candidate. The family having the smallest Mahalanobis distance was then selected as the study control case. This balanced those variables used in calculating the propensity scores.

When the control or comparison group is larger than the intervention group, this approach to fixing the imbalance that occurred is a feasible strategy. The existence of ties in the control group is not a problem if the Mahalanobis distance of those cases from the treatment case is not the same. The one having the smallest Mahalanobis distance can be selected. If the Mahalanobis distances are also tied, the action depends on whether one wants equal-sized treatment and control groups or not. If the goal is to have equal-sized groups, one can select a key variable and see if they are also tied. If not, the comparison case can be selected that matches the key characteristics. If even key characteristics are tied, then the selection can be done by random probability. If equal-sized groups are not part of one's design, all of the cases tied on propensity scores and Mahalanobis distance can be used (1–many matching).

Measuring factors that might go wrong is key to this approach. Even if it is likely that something won't go wrong (e.g., in assigning random numbers), information should be collected to verify that the procedure was implemented correctly and produced the result expected. For example, one might check that the distribution of random numbers assigned for sampling follows what is required by the selection criteria. In a quasi-experiment, the randomness of the distribution of cases can still be examined. The shape of the distribution and its parameters can be examined to see if they conform to that expected by a particular probability selection procedure. This is sometimes done as part of the normal process of examining imbalance in the characteristics of the intervention and comparison groups.

## Incomplete Randomization

Sometimes randomization is not possible for all of the subjects in the pool of cases from which treatment and control groups are drawn. In the 1981–1982 study of domestic violence cases in Minneapolis, Sherman and Berk (1984) originally intended to randomly assign cases of domestic disturbance to mandatory arrest or separation of the parties. It was quickly realized, however, that some cases posed extreme risk of assault, injury, or death of the victim if the alleged perpetrator was not arrested. All of those cases were assigned to arrest, even when the random number associated with the case said it was a control case. It would have been illegal not to do this. The police have a legal obligation to protect victims from immediate risk of death if this can be done by arresting the offender. It was also unethical for the researchers to allow subjects to be faced with extreme risk of death under their human subject protection obligations.

When the reason for incomplete randomization is known, it can be addressed by analytical procedures. If the reasons are discrete and confounding variables are balanced between groups for those who were nonrandomly assigned, it can be assumed that the reasons for nonrandom assignment are uncorrelated with the confounders and that the nonrandom assignment has not biased the results. If there is imbalance between treatment and comparison groups in the nonrandom assignees, propensity score matching, weighting, or adjusting can be used to control for this area of imbalance.

If standard propensity score use does not achieve balancing, additional measured variables or latent variables need to be considered. Additional measured variables can be identified using the procedures discussed in Chapter 2 for identifying control variables. If any are identified, they can be used to revise the selection and outcome models. For the selection model, this entails revising the propensity score estimation.

Multiple uses should be considered, such as matching and weighting, matching and covariate adjustment, and so on. These procedures will handle most instances of incomplete randomization when the nonrandomness is not correlated with confounding variables. When the nonrandomness is correlated with confounding variables, as is often the case with differential compliance, one of the procedures from Chapter 11 may help. Sometimes, none of these procedures help. If that happens, the principal stratification method discussed in the next section can be attempted.

## Differential Compliance

Differential noncompliance is always a possibility. The research design should include variables that directly measure or are correlated with compliance. The level of involvement or participation in the intervention might be used as a measure of differential compliance. Skillful debriefing after an intervention can also provide indications of noncompliance. These measures can be used to improve the selection and outcome models. Such variables may be associated with selectivity or with the outcomes. Holmes and Olsen (2010), for example, used involvement in a dose–response model that looked at different levels of participation as it affected outcome of a family service program. Compliance measures can remove bias associated with differential noncompliance. They can be used following the procedures of Chapter 2.

If none of these procedures remove the imbalance, principal stratification can be explored as a method for reducing differential bias from nonrandom assignment. Principal stratification divides the samples into four groups: (1) compliers, (2) never takers, (3) always takers, and (4) defiers (Barnard et al., 2003). The compliers are those who accept the assignment given when it differs from their baseline status (already taking or not yet taking). If they are assigned to the intervention and not yet taking it, they receive the intervention. If they are assigned the control and are taking the intervention, they receive the control. The never takers are those not receiving treatment at any point. They're not participating in the intervention at the baseline. If they are assigned to the comparison group, they continue to not receive the intervention. The always takers are those always using the intervention. They are participating in the intervention at the baseline. If they are assigned to the intervention group, they continue participating in the intervention. Defiers do the opposite of whatever is assigned. If they receive treatment and are assigned to treatment, they stop treatment. If they do not receive the treatment and are assigned to control, they reject control and seek treatment. These four groups are displayed in Figure 12.1.

These four strata are referred to as principal strata. They derive from post-treatment information. They have two important properties. They are not affected by the treatment process. They are determined after treatment is received or not received. They also allow examining estimated effects whose properties are well-known. These effects estimated within principal strata are known as principal effects (Barnard et al., 2003). Estimating principal effects better represents the effect of an intervention in the presence of noncompliers than can be done using standard procedures.

**Figure 12.1    Principal Stratification Groups**

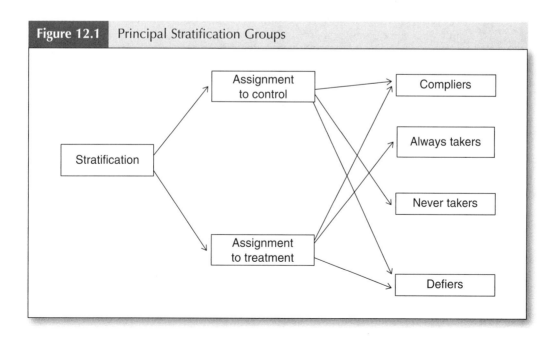

Principal effects estimation rests on several suppositions. The always takers will be continuing the intervention. They should not have any change in their outcome measures compared with their baseline measures. The never takers will continue to not participate in the treatment. They, too, should not have a change in their outcome measures. Defiers and compliers are the only groups that will have a change in their outcome if the intervention has an effect. The compliers who were assigned to a group other than that in which they were already will have a change in their outcome. The defiers who were assigned the same group as that in which they were already will switch groups. They also have a change in their outcomes.

Effects are estimated within each group. For notation, the four groups can be numbered from 1 to 4; with 1 = *compliers*, 2 = *always takers*, 3 = *never takers*, 4 = *defiers*. With this notation, two estimates of treatment effects are available (see Equations 12.1 and 12.2):

$$\tau_c = E(Y_{1t}) - E(Y_{1c}),\tag{12.1}$$

$$\tau_d = E(Y_{4t}) - E(Y_{4c}),\tag{12.2}$$

where $\tau_c$ is the treatment effect estimated for the compliers, $\tau_d$ is the treatment effect for the defiers, $E(Y_{1t})$ and $E(Y_{1c})$ are the expected values for the treatment and control groups within the compliers, and $E(Y_{4t})$ and $E(Y_{4c})$ are the expected values for the treatment and control groups within the defiers. With normally distributed data, these are the differences of the means conditional for the compliers and the defiers, respectively.

Within compliers and defiers, the intervention and comparison groups are compared to estimate treatment effects. If these two estimates are the same, this is the estimated treatment effect. If these two estimates are significantly different, subject characteristics are likely to be interacting with the treatment. Different effects are produced for different subjects.

The always takers can also be compared with the never takers. No effects are expected from this comparison. If there are effects estimated, this means the two groups probably did not start off the same in the outcome measure or that some other variable was uncontrolled—an observed or latent confounder. Further investigation will be needed if this occurs.

For principal stratification to work, it is crucial to know whether individuals received the treatment prior to the start of the study. If it is known, subjects can be classified into one of the four groups, given intervention assignment and monitoring of implementation. It is also crucial to know if they received the treatment whether or not they were assigned to treatment.

In the New York School Voucher evaluation, private schools were already available. The never takers and always takers could be identified by finding out what schools the children in the family attended. In the Vitamin C study discussed in Chapter 1, some in the sample may have been taking vitamin C supplements already. If principal stratification methodology had been available at the time of the study, it may have allowed a better approach to repairing the experiment than was used (analyzing just those who did not break compliance by tasting the capsule contents—in effect, using just the uncontaminated complete cases). In the evaluation of job training programs, some in the population may have already tried a job training program.

Principal stratification only works for treatments that are already in use. New interventions that have not been previously tried by the subject population cannot use this approach because there are no "always takers" when the treatment is new nor can there be always defiers. Those not receiving the treatment at the start may or may not wish to not receive it. Half the "defiers" are missing as well (those who were taking the treatment, were assigned to treatment, and stopped taking the treatment).

A modification to the four-group approach can be tried for new interventions. Three groups can be used. The always takers are excluded because no one has yet had the new intervention. Half the defiers are also excluded. This complicates the analysis, and some questions cannot be addressed. It may provide usable results, depending on whether the research questions are those that can be answered with the reduced groups.

Adequate groups are available for compliers and never takers. The compliers are composed of those who were not taking the intervention, were assigned to treatment or control, and complied with the assignment. The defiers group is composed only of those who were not participating in the intervention at the beginning, were assigned to treatment or control, and chose the option other than that to which they were assigned. In this situation, there are no always takers and no never takers. Analysis is done within the groups of compliers and defiers. This produces valid estimates of intervention effects for those groups—provided that the groups being compared are relatively homogeneous at the start. Since the never takers and the always takers are presumed to have no treatment effect, the compliers and defiers are the only source of estimated effects. In contrast to full principal stratification, one cannot test whether any effects emerge by comparing between always takers and never takers. It is presumed that there are no effects. There is no possibility of determining whether something more is going on by observing this difference (if any) because no information is available for these groups.

Another modification to the principal stratification approach occurs if some members of a sample receive a treatment prior to the experiment or quasi-experiment for reasons other than those for which the new treatment is being tried. This occurs in drug treatments where a drug may be prescribed for a use other than that for which it was licensed (off-label or investigational). It also occurs where folk practices or innovative actions in a community are targeted for experimental or quasi-experimental study. Demonstration projects fall in this category, since they are often designed to provide rigorous evaluation of innovative project efforts.

For example, Barber and Odean (2000) did a quasi-experimental study in which they compared the performance of investment clubs with that of market index investing. Investment clubs that followed their own strategy were compared with those who invested in index funds that followed the market average performance. The researchers were not able to randomly assign investment strategies, but the clubs were investing prior to the start of their study. Clubs could have been divided into those who followed an indexing strategy and those who did not. This would have allowed creating groups similar to those needed for principal stratification.

The Sherman and Berk (1984) study could also have been modified for principal stratification. Mandatory arrest was in use by some police departments prior to their study. It was the local practice of some communities. Tracking individuals with domestic disturbance calls prior to the study and identifying offenders who had previously been arrested in a domestic disturbance in communities that did and did not have such a policy may have allowed principal stratification of the subjects in the study. For this to occur when policies are already in place, however, some communities with the policy would have to select some potential arrestees and assign them to an alternative intervention. Even then, there would be cases in which they could not be assigned to nonarrest because of the legal and ethical constraints on the study.

## Differential Mortality

Sample attrition refers to those who leave a study and do not return to it. This is also called sample mortality. The subjects may become ineligible for the study. They may have reactive effects from the treatment. They may move away or die. So long as this happens equally in both groups and is unrelated to the outcomes, the attrition is missing completely at random (MCAR). If the mortality is more frequent in one group or characteristics of those leaving the study are associated with the outcomes, this may bias the findings. This is differential mortality. The mortality is imbalanced between the groups. This leads to imbalance in outcome characteristics and is a breakdown in research protocol.

A common method of dealing with sample mortality is to create a dummy missing variable and see if it is associated with baseline characteristics of the subjects. If it is, a characteristic that might have been balanced at the beginning of the study has become imbalanced during the study. If the missing data are not too large, prediction, estimation, or imputation may be used to replace the missing values—provided that the cautions mentioned above regarding their use are kept in mind.

## Differential Events

If something can go wrong, it will go wrong. This applies to the events research subjects experience. When intervention and comparison groups experience different events or experience the same event in different ways, this creates differential events. They become confounding factors. This is accepted as a normal aspect of the analysis of quasi-experimental data. When research protocols do not anticipate or do not adequately respond to external or internal events, the effects of such events are compounded.

Table 12.1, based on the Health and Retirement Study data, shows evidence that high blood pressure is associated with missing treatment information and missing educational information. Those with high blood pressure have more missing data than those without high blood pressure. Research would be needed to determine why this is the case.

Propensity matching for the treatment and control groups reduces the missing data differential for intervention information. The differential declines from 6.8% with unmatched data to 4.0% with matched data (see Figure 12.2). The

| Table 12.1 | High Blood Pressure and Percentage Missing Data | | | | |
|---|---|---|---|---|---|
| | *Intervention Information Not Missing* | *Intervention Information Missing* | *Education Information Not Missing* | *Education Missing* | *Total* |
| No high blood pressure | 73.7%, 7,668 | 26.3%, 2,735 | 0.6%, 60 | 99.4%, 10,743 | 100.0%, 10,403 |
| High blood pressure | 66.9%, 4,541 | 33.1%, 2,247 | 1.2%, 83 | 98.8%, 6,705 | 100.0%, 6,788 |
| Totals | 71.0%, 12,209 | 29.0%, 4,982 | 0.8%, 143 | 99.2%, 17,048 | 100.0%, 17,191 |

small differential for missing education information remains at 0.6%, but it is already so small that there is a boundary issue in detecting further declines.

Propensity weighting of the sample is an alternative to propensity matching for reducing the missing data differential. Figure 12.2 displays the reduction in differential missing data due to propensity weighting. The result is similar to that for matching.

## Differential Missing Data

Missing data were discussed in Chapter 11, mainly from the viewpoint of random missing data. As noted above, missing data are not always random. Some procedures from Chapter 11 are applicable to missing at random data if

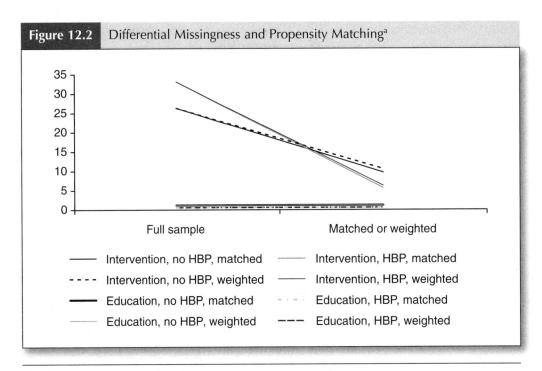

| Figure 12.2 | Differential Missingness and Propensity Matching[a] |

*Note.* HPB, high blood pressure.

a. Vertical axis is percentage missing data. Full sample has 17,191 cases, matched sample has 1,141 cases, and weighted sample has 1,142 cases.

measures of those factors are available. If measures of nonresponse are available, it allows much better management of missing data bias than assuming the data are missing at random or MCAR. It allows empirical examination of this issue and specific procedures for dealing with it when detected.

Differential missing data can be introduced due to the structure of the design of the study. Certain questions may not be asked of some groups. Other questions may be inapplicable to a group. Some data may not be collected because it is thought to be impractical for a group. The New York School Voucher study did not collect baseline information on kindergartners because it was thought that the children would have to know how to take tests before data could be collected from them. However, standardized observational measures of school readiness and reading readiness were widely available at the time of the study. Such information was likely to be in the children's school records. Yet it was not collected. Given the objectives of the study, it was probably not an important omission. The New York study also asked some questions of multichild families, but not single-child families, because those questions pertained to siblings. These examples illustrate how missing data can be created by the design of the study.

Research designs should include variables predictive of nonresponse. While specific socioeconomic predictors may vary from study to study, education, professional association, linguistic ability, alcohol dependence, childhood conduct disorder, expenditures on health care, saliency of the topic, and potential for embarrassment are among those commonly mentioned (Barclay, Todd, Finlay, Grande, & Wyatt, 2001; Hawkes & Plewis, 2006; Heath et al., 2001; de Winter et al., 2005). Collecting information about these variables, even when they are thought not relevant to the outcome, can aid building nonresponse models, and adding nonresponse adjustors that can remove some of the differential nonresponse.

In addition, design characteristics are known to affect response rates. Such factors as offering appropriate inducements, holding interviews in convenient and pleasant locations, having news stories about a study, sending friendly and informative cover letters, and using postage stamps on mailings have long been known to affect response rates and differential nonresponse (Hawkes & Plewis, 2006). If only some subjects get follow-up letters or phone calls or vary by other design characteristics, missing data analysis should be done to empirically determine whether this variation is associated with selectivity or outcomes. When they are associated, they should be incorporated into the missing data models.

One strategy for detecting whether differential missing data have occurred is to correlate the missing data dummy variables with themselves, the treatment indicator, and the outcome measures. There should be no significant correlations with the treatment indicator and the outcomes. If the missing data are MCAR, the correlations among the missing data indicators should also be low, with only a few significant within the bounds of what would be expected from multiple tests. An example of this approach is provided in Table 12.2, correlations of the treatment indicator, household income, and missing data indicators for the General Social Survey data. Correlations among these dichotomous variables are not Pearson correlations, even though they were computed using a standard correlation program. They are more like point biserial correlations or phi coefficients. With even splits between the categories, they approximate Pearson coefficients. In this case, they are used for diagnostic purposes—not as point estimates of the relationship between two variables. A similar table can be generated for Kendall's tau or phi coefficients.

The correlations in Table 12.2 show three things. First, there are no significant correlations among the missing data indicators for the variables predictive of income. There is no differential missing data among those variables. Second, the intervention indicator (babies present) is correlated both with missing financial information and with missing information on the age of respondents when the first child was born. This is a warning that there is differential missing data among these three variables. Further examination of these relationships will be needed to determine the nature and strength of the pattern and what corrective actions, if any, are needed. These are discussed in the sections below on assessing strength and nature of differential effects.

| Table 12.2 | Missing Data Correlations With and Without Matching[a] | | | | | |
|---|---|---|---|---|---|---|
| | Babies Present | HH Income Missing | Education Missing | Age First Kid Born Missing | Financial View Missing | Gene Knowledge Missing |
| Babies present | | | | | | |
| Without matching | 1.000 | −0.045* | −0.016 | −0.212[a] | −0.001 | 0.015 |
| With matching | | −0.033 | [b] | −0.276[a] | −0.030 | 0.030 |
| HH income missing | | | | | | |
| Without matching | −0.045[a] | 1.000 | 0.003 | 0.024 | 0.003 | 0.039 |
| With matching | −0.033 | | [b] | −0.032 | 0.011 | 0.004 |

| | Babies Present | HH Income Missing | Education Missing | Age First Kid Born Missing | Financial View Missing | Gene Knowledge Missing |
|---|---|---|---|---|---|---|
| Education missing | | | | | | |
| Without matching | −0.016 | 0.003 | 1.000 | 0.004 | −0.003 | −0.037 |
| With matching | b | b | b | b | b | b |
| Age first kid born missing | | | | | | |
| Without matching | −0.212[a] | 0.024 | 0.004 | | −0.019 | −0.037 |
| With matching | −0.276[a] | 0.071 | b | | −0.037 | −0.039 |
| Financial view missing | | | | | | |
| Without matching | −0.001 | 0.003 | −0.003 | −0.019 | 1.000 | 0.015 |
| With matching | −0.030 | 0.018 | b | −0.037 | | 0.020 |
| Gene knowledge missing | | | | | | |
| Without matching | 0.015 | 0.039 | −.037 | −0.030 | 0.015 | 1.000 |
| With matching | 0.030 | 0.000 | b | −0.039 | 0.020 | |

*Note.* HH, household.

a. Correlations significant at $p < .05$, two-tailed test. N of significant correlations without matching is 1,990; with exact matching is 718.

b. No missing cases with exact matching.

The third thing the correlations show is that the differential missing data are reduced by creating propensity score matched samples (in this case, 1–many exactly matched on propensity scores). The reduction in differential missing data is, in part, a result of antecedent variables that are confounders becoming more homogeneous and less likely to have their missing data be differential across groups. Balancing reduces differential missing data when the missingness is correlated with variables that contribute to estimating the propensity score.

The third result does not necessarily eliminate differential nonresponse bias. Propensity score matching may need to be used in conjunction with additional procedures—such as multiple imputation to replace missing values—to more fully deal with missing data from protocol breakdown.

## Reactive Effects

Treatments and interventions often have side effects. Some of these can be anticipated. When they are anticipated, the research design can introduce procedures for dealing with them. One of the principal issues that human subjects review committees deal with is whether an intervention has effects other than those intended and what needs to be done about them.

In Chapter 1, an example was given of a vitamin C experiment. The health professionals in the study were inquisitive about what they were receiving. They opened the capsules and identified whether they had ascorbic acid (vitamin C) or powdered sugar (the placebo). Knowing which group they were in affected their subsequent responses to the questionnaires. Their actions became part of the experimental conditions. They were reacting to knowledge that they were in the treatment or control group.

Side effects of the intervention itself can create subject–experiment interaction. Those in a job training program may decide to practice their skills outside of the program. Those not in the program may decide to get training elsewhere. This could intensify or suppress the estimated effect of the program. It may also lead some individuals to drop out of the program, rather than other individuals.

## Subject Communication

In strict experiments, there may be little opportunity for subjects to communicate with each other. It is especially difficult for those in the treatment group to communicate with those in the control group because treatment and controls are either done separately or done blind so the subjects can't tell in which group they are. Any opportunity for those in the two groups to interact with each other, however, can lead to a breakdown in the research protocol.

In quasi-experiments, there is much more of an opportunity for participants to speak with each other. In many research studies, it is common to draw the comparison group from the same school, organization, census block, or neighborhood. They may know the person in the intervention group. The researcher would not tell the subjects whom they are paired with, but the control person may discover that by attending a school activity, an organizational event, a block party, or a neighborhood gathering. The researcher can swear the subjects to silence regarding their involvement in the research; but friends and family who observe subjects' behavior may well discover this even without the subject divulging involvement in research. Once it becomes known, there is little control over those to whom the information is communicated.

Debriefing can provide information on the plausibility of this happening. Ask about who else knew their involvement, what they did, and what the effects seemed to be. Did they discover or meet any other participant in the project? Did these others have the same role, activity, or effects as themselves? Collecting this information can help determine whether subject communication has occurred and whether it may have altered behavior of the subjects.

Analyzing the association of these measures with selection, outcome, and missing data can help assess the impact of subject communication and suggest possible remedies. If the measures of communication and interaction are associated with selectivity and outcomes, then subject communication has impaired the experiment or the quasi-experiment.

## Strong Placebo Effects

Placebos can alter behavior by themselves. The belief that a pill will make one feel better can make a person feel better—even if the actual reason for the intervention has not improved. If a policy creates an expectation that the economy will improve, people may spend more money, improving the economy. If politicians say a policy will be bad for the economy, people may reduce spending and impair the economy.

The best way to prevent placebo effects from causing a breakdown in research protocols is to manage the expectations of the subjects. Provide them neutral expectations. Provide the same expectations to those in both groups. Questions can also be asked at the baseline as to what kinds of expectations the subjects have for the program, what they hope will happen, what they fear will happen, and what they think will actually happen. The association of these measures of baseline expectations with selection and outcomes can be examined to determine whether placebo effects are likely. If any of these measures are associated with group membership, outcomes, or presence of missing data, something may have gone wrong in managing the expectations of the subjects.

When the comparison group or intervention group is constructed after the fact, it is not possible to manage their expectations. This is especially true when analyzing data collected by others. The most that can be achieved is to hope positive and negative expectations of the groups cancel each other out. This is purely an assumption on the part of the researcher. If there are any measures of expectations at the baseline, however, they can be examined to see their association with selection, outcomes, or missing data.

## *Propensities and Breakdowns*

It might be thought that if propensity use can fix things that go wrong, the researcher may be more sloppy when using propensities. If there is a mistake, propensity analysis can fix it. This author contends that breakdowns in research protocol are less likely to occur if the design includes the use of propensity scores. This text has emphasized that propensity score use doesn't always fix everything. It is not a hammer with which you can bang on anything. It is a tool to be used in appropriate situations. Even then, the problems may be so great that propensity score use cannot resolve them.

The model of propensity score use requires measures of things that affect selectivity and compliance. Designs that incorporated propensity score use are encouraged to include measures of these factors. In addition to allowing propensity score estimation, such measures allow determining whether there are problems in the implementation of the research protocol—at least with respect to selection, assignment, and compliance of cases.

When propensity score use is involved in other aspects of data analysis, it encourages addition of measures of noncompliance, techniques for analyzing missing data, and imputation of missing values. Researchers have to monitor nonrandomness, noncompliance, and missingness to use propensity scores to their full extent. This results in more attention to designing research protocols that are less likely to fail and observing factors that may contribute to failure. The result is research that is less likely to break down. It still happens. There is still a need for these techniques for dealing with broken experiments and quasi-experiments; but the researcher will be better able to deal with these problems when they occur.

## ASSESSING THE DAMAGE

Some deviations from research protocols have no effect on the study. They represent extraneous events that have no consequences. Others may have an impact. It is necessary to assess the presence, nature, strength, and implications of these deviations on the ability of the research to answer the questions with which it began.

## *Presence of Impact*

Determining whether nonrandomness, noncompliance, and nonresponse are present in the data is basic to assessing the presence of design breakdown.

Univariate and bivariate approaches are commonly used to determine this. The univariate approaches look at the distribution of the missing data. The bivariate approaches look at the relationships among missing data indicators with the intervention and outcome indicators.

Examining the percentage missing is the principal univariate statistic used for assessing the potential impact of missing data. Small percentages are thought to have little impact. It is common to think that variables with less than 10% missing cases pose less risk of having missing data distort their relationship with other variables. This is, however, an empirical question that can be addressed directly with bivariate statistics. When more than 10% of the cases are missing data (except for structurally inappropriate missing data), bivariate relationships should be examined. A smaller percentage can be chosen when a data analyst believes it appropriate.

Cross-tabulation, analysis of variance (ANOVA), and correlations can all provide useful information for assessing whether missing data have a differential pattern between groups or with continuous variables. Table 12.3 summarizes cross-tabulations between the missing data indicator for household income and the intervention measure, comparing unmatched and matched samples.

Table 12.3 shows that with the unmatched data there is a statistically significant, though weak, relationship between the treatment variable and missing

| Table 12.3 | Cross-Tabulation Between Income Missing and Intervention | | |
|---|---|---|---|
| | *Babies Not Present (%)* | *Babies Present (%)* | *N* |
| Unmatched samples | | | |
| Income info not present | 30.6 | 24.6 | 276 |
| Income info present | 69.4 | 75.4 | 1,714 |
| Column total | 100.0 | 100.0 | 1,990 |
| Matched samples | | | |
| Income info not present | 27.2 | 23.9 | 189 |
| Income info present | 72.8 | 76.1 | 527 |
| Column total | 100.0 | 100.0 | 716 |

*Note.* Unmatched samples, $\chi^2 = 4.01$, $df = 1$, $p = .045$, $\Phi = -.045$; matched samples, $\chi^2 = 0.77$, $df = 1$, $p = .380$, $\Phi = -.033$.

income data. The missing data are differentially distributed across the intervention and comparison groups. The difference in missing data between the two groups is 6%. When samples are created by exact matching, however, this relationship becomes even weaker and nonsignificant. The difference in missing data is 3% in the matched data. The propensity matched sample is more homogeneous than the unmatched sample. Some, but not all, of the differential missing data will be removed from the matched sample.

Correlation use was demonstrated in Table 12.2. The significant probabilities are only approximations, due to the use of dummy variables. Nevertheless, those whose significance probabilities are less than .05 with these correlations are also likely to be significant with a cross-tabulation—unless one is dealing with a small number of cases. The correlation of babies present with missing data for the age when the respondent's first child was born was significant. That relationship needs to be examined more closely. Procedures for such an examination are discussed below.

ANOVA can be used to look at the association of missing data with continuous variables. The dummy variable missing indicator is treated as a factor and the continuous variable is the dependent variable. Table 12.4 presents one-way ANOVAs for the education variable with the age when the respondent's first child was born. The missing data from education previously mentioned has, in this example, been imputed using the expectation-maximization algorithm. As in Table 12.3, it also compares with and without matching.

The significant $F$ statistics indicate that missing age data were associated with the education of the respondent. Those with missing information on age at first child's birth had a higher mean education than those who were not missing age information. It might be that those with more education felt

| Table 12.4 | ANOVA of Age at First Child's Birth Missing With Education | | | | |
|---|---|---|---|---|---|
| | *Means* | *N* | *F* | *p* | η |
| Unmatched | | 2,000 | 61.375 | .000 | .173 |
| Age not missing | 13.14 | 1,431 | | | |
| Age missing | 14.33 | 569 | | | |
| Matched | | 718 | 13.078 | .000 | .134 |
| Age not missing | 13.25 | 534 | | | |
| Age missing | 14.01 | 184 | | | |

embarrassed by having children at a young age and did not report the age information. Those with missing age at first child's birth had an average 1.2 years of education more than those who had the age information. There was differential noncompliance in reporting this information (although a small amount).

Under the supposition that this differential noncompliance was a concern to the analysis of the impact of babies being present in the household, the same ANOVA was rerun using samples matched on propensity scores for households with and without babies present. The degree of differential non-response was reduced when the matched samples were used. The eta value changed from .173 to .134. The difference in mean education for those reporting and those not reporting age changed from 1.2 years to 0.7 years. The standardized difference changed from .407 to .308. These changes were modest, but they show a consistent pattern.

The differential nonresponse was reduced when using propensity matched samples. This change in differential missing data is displayed in Figure 12.3.

Mean substitution, propensity matching, and multiple imputation were used to replace the missing age information. The difference in education for missing data in Figure 12.3 is before the procedures were used. The difference for no missing data is after the procedures were used. Creating matched samples and multiple imputation both eliminated the differential data problem for this variable. Mean substitution does not eliminate the differential missing data. Without this differential missing data analysis, however, the presence of differential missing data would not have been known, nor would the extent to which imputation or matching might have fixed the missing data problem resulting from noncompliance.

## Nature of Impact

When design breakdown is present, it is necessary to determine the nature of the breakdown. A breakdown in protocol can increase Type I and Type II errors (false positives and false negatives), or it may have no impact on answering the question being asked. One aspect of the nature of the impact concerns whether the probability of a Type I or Type II error is increased. Another aspect concerns whether the relationship is positive or negative.

The potential impact on Type I or Type II error is a result of the sample size being inflated or deflated or the measure of association being inflated or deflated. Either affects the statistical power of any tests run and, thus, the likelihood of a Type I or a Type II error.

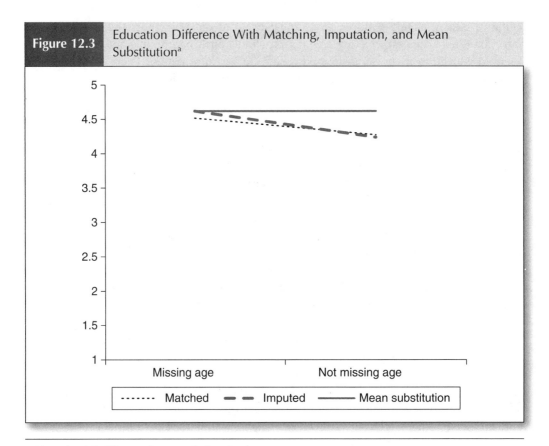

**Figure 12.3** Education Difference With Matching, Imputation, and Mean Substitution[a]

a. Vertical axis is difference in years of education between groups.

Design breakdowns are much more likely to result in having fewer cases, but they can have the opposite effect. Respondent data may be entered twice. Blank records may be created. File merging may duplicate records. These issues are normally dealt with by having research protocols to check for duplicate or blank records. When that protocol is not fully followed, additional cases are added to the file. This does not usually create differential missing data. However, if cases are duplicated by merging in records that already have differential missing data, this will strengthen the effect of the missing data. It will increase the bias. Repeating checks for duplicate and blank records for the file from which analysis will be done will reduce or eliminate this problem.

The presence of babies and missing data on age at first child's birth are negatively associated in Table 12.2. This indicates that the households with babies present had less missing information on age when the first child was born than did households where babies were not present. The presence of babies might jog the memory of their caretakers regarding the age at which they had their first child. Strategies for imputing missing data were discussed in Chapter 11.

The relationship between babies present and missing age information are shown in the cross-tabulation of these two variables in Table 12.5.

## Strength of Impact

Even when an impact inflates or deflates a relationship, it may be sufficiently weak that estimated effects are not greatly distorted. The exact point estimate of the intervention effect may be off, but not by much. The strength of the impact can be judged either by looking at standardized effect coefficients or by looking at raw effect coefficients. In Table 12.4, the two groups in the unmatched samples differed in their education by 1.2 years. That may or may not be regarded as having substantive significance. The eta coefficient for this difference was .17, a value that is commonly regarded as weak.

When the groups are compared as propensity matched samples, the strength of association declines (see Figure 12.4). The raw difference is about three quarters of a year. The eta is .13, a weaker association than with the unmatched data. These changes are not large, but boundary effects prevent them from becoming so. They illustrate how propensity use can reduce the inflation of effects resulting from broken research protocols.

| Table 12.5 | Babies Present and Missing Age Information | | |
|---|---|---|---|
| | *Babies Not Present (%)* | *Babies Present (%)* | *N* |
| Unmatched samples | | | |
| Age info not present | 30.1 | 16.3 | 561 |
| Age info present | 69.9 | 83.7 | 1,418 |
| Column total | 100.0 | 100.0 | 1,979 |
| Matched samples | | | |
| Age info not present | 27.9 | 16.3 | 182 |
| Age info present | 72.1 | 83.7 | 531 |
| Column total | 100.0 | 100.0 | 713 |

## *Implications of Impact*

Does the breakdown in protocol affect the conclusions? Noncompliance, nonresponse, and nonimplemented procedures affect the conclusions by inflating or deflating an estimated effect and by leading to Type I or Type II error.

Bias from a broken experiment may increase or decrease the differences between the intervention and the comparison group. This may lead to false conclusions about how strong or weak the effect is. Inflation of effect may lead to a Type I error, a false conclusion that an intervention has an effect. Deflation of effect may lead to a Type II error, a false conclusion that the intervention has no effect.

As demonstrated above, propensity score use leads to fewer false conclusions by reducing the bias in estimated effects. Inferences about how strong or weak are the effects will be more accurate. Conclusions about whether the treatment has an effect are more likely to be correct. It is not a panacea.

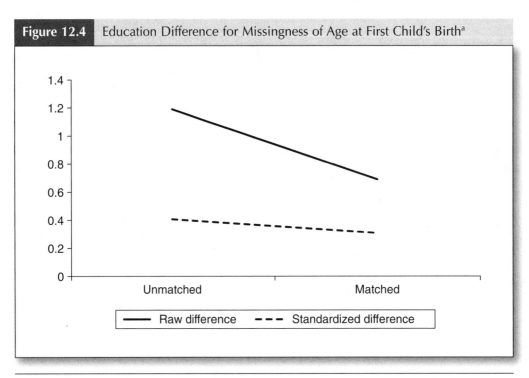

**Figure 12.4** Education Difference for Missingness of Age at First Child's Birth[a]

a. Vertical axis is difference in years of education by missingness of age at first child's birth. The raw difference in years of education and the standardized difference are reported.

Propensity score use does not always eliminate imbalance. It does not always eliminate bias.

## DEVELOPING A STRATEGY

This section discusses six strategies for repairing broken experiments: (1) ex post facto matching, (2) propensity score weighting, (3) principal stratification, (4) instrumental variable use, (5) multiple imputation, and (6) getting missing data. After describing a strategy and its trade-offs, conditions under which it might be tried are discussed. Sensitivity analysis can examine this possibility.

### Ex Post Facto Matching

Propensity scores allow for removing this imbalance ex post facto. Those background factors correlating with attrition can be used to create propensity scores for the sample at a later point in time. A matched sample can then be created from among the cases remaining in the study, provided that sample attrition has not been so large that the remaining sample becomes underpowered.

Ex post facto matching is a useful strategy when matching was previously done with baseline information (ex ante matching). If matching removed imbalance at the beginning, rematching may remove imbalance later on. Variables associated with selection have already been identified. They may be associated with subsequent imbalance. There is still a need to check whether other variables are associated with the new imbalance. The procedures for doing this and for the matching, however, will already have been worked out if ex ante matching was done.

### Propensity Score Weighting

The complete case approach for repairing broken research is still widely utilized. However, it doesn't resolve issues of nonrandom sampling, noncompliance, or nonresponse. Like propensity score matching, a weighting procedure using propensity scores reduces the severity of the problems. It helps for the same reason. It makes the samples more homogeneous for the intervention and comparison groups.

The weights to be used are the same as those used for standard propensity score weighting to improve balance. They have the same issues. Rescaled inverse propensity score weights work for most purposes. In some cases, augmented inverse propensity weighting may produce superior results. An example is given below in the discussion of differential missing data that compares propensity score matching with propensity score weighting in their ability to reduce that problem.

Propensity score weighting is more complicated to use than either principal stratification or multiple imputation. Unless one is already using propensity scores in the analysis, it would not be a primary strategy to use in repairing a broken experiment. However, when the missing cases are differentially missing, weighting by propensity scores can remove or reduce resulting bias.

### Principal Stratification

Using principal stratification to repair problems in a study requires being able to create the four groups (compliers, always takers, never takers, and defiers). If the study is looking at a treatment or intervention that is already used in some circumstances, the four groups can usually be identified. If the intervention is new and no subjects are already involved in it, this produces the problems with the three groups discussed above.

A principal stratification procedure is a useful strategy for repairing broken experiments or quasi-experiments, when all four groups can be identified. This means that the treatments or interventions must already be available. There must be some subjects in the sample who are already participating in the treatment. With a new intervention that no one has yet experienced, principal stratification use can be questioned. Ex post facto matching, multiple imputation, or instrumental variable use may be a better choice. However, some questions can still be answered given three groups. If the research questions can be answered using principal stratification, it is a viable option.

### Instrumental Variables

Using instrumental variables was introduced in the section on two-stage least squares regression. The instruments are variables that influence the selection process and are not associated with the outcome measures. It is helpful, in this case, if they are associated with the causes of the breakdown as well (differential compliance, nonresponse, or nonrandomization).

Instruments may also be used in some cases to reduce bias from a breakdown in the experiment or problems with quasi-experiments. Tan (2006) summarizes instrumental variable use. The effect of the intervention is given as the ratio of the differences between groups, conditional on the instrumental factor. When the instrument is binary, the formula is as follows:

$$(E(Y|Z = 1) - E(Y|Z = 0))/(E(D|Z = 1) - E(D|Z = 0)) \qquad (12.3)$$

It is the differences in the outcomes for the two instrumental groups versus the differences in treatment status for the two instrumental groups. Tan (2006) characterizes this as "the average difference in $Y$ relative to that in $D$ between the two instrument groups" (p. 1607). Tan provides a generalization of this to continuous instruments.

The procedures for using instrumental variables to repair this breakdown involve identifying correlates of the problem that do not correlate with the outcome. The selection of the correlates for this purpose is similar to that for two-stage least squares. It is best if these variables are plausible causes of selectivity, but unrelated to the outcome. They should also be variables correlated with the missing data dummy variable. These variables might be thought of as extraneous to the outcomes, but they may appear to have a bivariate correlation with the outcome. This is because they may have indirect causal effects on the outcome through the treatment or intervention. They must not be thought of as having any direct effects on the outcome.

Debriefing respondents and project staff may provide useful information on the causes of breakdown. Coding their responses may provide measures of those causes. Debriefing may provide instrumental variables that were not originally included in the project design. In particular, if measures of factors associated with noncompliance and nonresponse were not collected as part of normal data collection, they should be included in the debriefing process.

The ideal situation for instrumental variable use is if the causes of noncompliance, nonresponse, or nonrandomization have been measured. Those measures that are not also associated with the outcomes can be used as instrumental variables. If the causes of breakdown are correlated with the outcomes, the instrumental variable approach should not be used.

## *Multiple Imputation*

The analysis that produced Figure 12.4 showed that propensity matching and multiple imputation can both reduce bias from research breakdown. Multiple imputation has an additional advantage in that it increases the available sample size by increasing the number of cases having complete data. It also requires less work than propensity matching. A separate selection model doesn't need to be constructed, evaluated, revised, and used. Its use to repair broken experiments has been established (Rubin, 1987).

The advantages of multiple imputation recommend the strategy. If multiple imputation does not reduce bias from noncompliance and differential missing data, however, prediction, estimation, propensity matching, or propensity weighting strategies can be tried. They may be used individually or in combination.

## *Getting Missing Data*

A research design can plan for augmentation of the data after the first round of data collection. Researchers sometimes plan to have a round of phone calls, interviews, Internet chats, or e-mail exchanges with subjects after initial data collection to clarify ambiguities and obtain missing data. The design of the study can create the opportunity for obtaining data that were initially missing. It needs coordination between reviewing the instrument (the interview schedule, questionnaire, Internet response record, etc.) and contacting the respondents. Callbacks need to contact some respondents who have no missing data to verify that data were really collected, rather than fabricated. However, some callbacks can be reserved for those missing data on key variables.

A callback represents an immediate repair for a problem before the research has gone on so long that the subject is no longer available. Callbacks may be especially useful because they have hope of obtaining true information, rather than plausible imputations. They should not be neglected in the design of experiments and quasi-experiments. The process of repairing broken research should begin in the design stage of that research.

# APPENDIXES

# APPENDIX A
## STATA COMMANDS FOR PROPENSITY USE

Shenyang Guo and Mark W. Fraser (2010) have written an excellent book on propensity score analysis that provides many Stata commands. While their treatment is more technical than this book, the Stata commands are quite useful. The *Stata Journal* article by Becker and Ichino (2002) provides a good overview of propensity score use and extensive commands with Stata. It can be accessed at http://www.stata-journal.com/sjpdf.html?articlenum=st0026.

## NORMALITY TESTS

The CAPABILITY procedures provide normal plotting, ppplotting, and qqplotting, as well as the Kolmogorov–Smirnov test. Some of these are also available in the UNIVARIATE procedure.

PROC CAPABILITY DATA = masil.normality NORMAL;

VAR random;

QQPLOT random/NORMAL(MU = EST SIGMA = EST COLOR = RED L = 1);

PPPLOT random/NORMAL(MU = EST SIGMA = EST COLOR = RED L = 1);

HISTOGRAM/NORMAL(COLOR = MAROON W = 4) CFILL = BLUE CFRAME = LIGR;

INSET MEAN STD/CFILL = BLANK FORMAT = 5.2;

## IMBALANCE ASSESSMENT

Imbalance may be assessed with the ANOVA command or *t* test.

.anova confounder1 treatm

.ttest confounder1 treatm

# PROPENSITY ESTIMATION

Propensities may be estimated with logistic regression or with discriminant function analysis commands.

.logistic confounder1 confounder2 confounder3 i.treatm

.candisc confounder1 confounder2 confounder3, group(treatm)

# MATCHING

The psmatch2 program provides a means for propensity score matching within Stata. Alternative matching programs may be accessed with the R interface for Stata.

## Exact and Coarsened Exact

See psmatch2 within Stata

## Nearest Neighbor and Caliper

See psmatch2 within Stata

## One-to-Many

See psmatch2 within Stata

## Optimized, Full, or Genetic

To do optimized, full, or genetic matching within Stata, the R interface must be used to access the corresponding R programs.

## STRATIFYING

Creating propensity strata can be done with the recode command, using the range of estimated scores.

recode propen 0/.19999 = 1 .2/.39999 = 2 .4/.59999 = 3 .6/.79999 = 4 .8/.99999 = 5, gen(propenstrata)

## REGRESSION AND THE GENERAL LINEAR MODEL

Regression and General Linear Model estimation may be done with the regress and glm commands.

.regress outcome1 i.treatm

.glm outcome1 i.treatm, family(gaussian) link(identity)

## TWO-STAGE LEAST SQUARES

2SLS regression can be done with the ivregress command.

.ivregress 2sls outcome1(treatm = instrument1), vce(robust)

## SAMPLE WEIGHTING

Sample weighting is done within the analytical commands using pweight. For example, with a logit analysis, the command would be as follows:

logit treatm confounder1 confounder2 [pweight = ipw]

## WEIGHTED LEAST SQUARES

Weighted least squares may be done within an analytical program (see sample weighting above) or with the wls0 command.

.wls0 outcome treatm, wvar(ipw) type(abse) noconst graph

## GENERALIZED LINEAR MODEL

.glm income educ jobexp i.black, family(gaussian) link(identity)

## MISSING DATA ANALYSIS

Analysis of missing data can combine mdesc with mvpatterns or with the misstable command.

mdesc confounder1 confounder2 confounder3

mvpatterns confounder1 confounder2 confounder3

.misstable summarize

## IMPUTATION OF MISSING DATA

Multiple imputation can be done with the mi impute command. Variables to be imputed must first be registered. The example below imputes five values with a random seed of 123. Estimation of imputed data in Stata may be done with the mi estimate command.

.mi register imputed confounder1 confounder2

.mi impute regress confounder1 confounder2 confounder3, add(5) rseed(123)

.mi estimate: logit treatm confounder1 confounder2 confounder3

# APPENDIX B
# R COMMANDS FOR PROPENSITY USE

**R** is the most extensive, internationally used statistical analysis program (R Development Core Team, 2007). There are many ways to use R to perform propensity analysis. These are some of them. Alternative ways are possible. The commands in R are usually printed in lowercase.

## NORMALITY TESTS

Normality of a distribution can be tested with the rnorm function or with the ks test, where the number is the sample size.

```
rnorm <- rnorm(500, mean(confounder1), sd(confounder1))

cc <- cbind(rnorm, confounder1)

g <- goodfit(cc, method = "MinChisq")

summary(g)

z<-rnorm(500)

ks.test(z,pnorm, .5, .2)
```

## IMBALANCE ASSESSMENT

Imbalance assessment can be done with oneway or with the MatchBalance function.

```
oneway.test (confounder1 ~ treatment)

mb <- MatchBalance(treatm ~ confounder1 + confounder2 + confounder3)

summary mb
```

## PROPENSITY ESTIMATION

Propensity estimation may be done with the multnom function or with the lda function. Those familiar with boosted regression may use the ps package. Propensity estimation for logistic and discriminant analysis are as follows:

result <- MULTINOM(treatm ~ confounder1 + confounder2, ABSTOL = 1.0e-20, data=mydata, na.action="na.omit")

fit <- lda(treatm ~ confounder1 + confounder2, data = mydata,

na.action = "na.omit")

## MATCHING

The match and matchit functions perform a variety of different matching procedures.

### Exact and Coarsened Exact

Exact and coarsened matching is included in the match function. An example with 1–1 matching is given below. It can also be done with the Matchit function.

rr <- Match(Y = Y, Tr = Tr, X = X, M = 1);

summary(rr)

m.out <- matchit(treat ~ propen, data = mydata, method = "exact")

summary (m.out)

m.out <- matchit(treat ~ propen, data = mydata, method = "cem")

summary (m.out)

### Nearest Neighbor and Caliper

There are a variety of nearest-neighbor matching packages in R. These include the matchit function.

```
m.out <- matchit(treat ~ propen, data = mydata, method = "nearest")
```

```
summary (m.out)
```

### One-to-Many

The Matching package does a variety of 1–many matches, as well as 1–1 matching and genetic matching. It uses the match function (see above). Set the parameter "m" to the number of matches desired.

```
m.out <- matchit(treat ~ propen, data = mydata, m = 2, method = "nearest")
```

```
summary (m.out)
```

### Optimized, Full, and Genetic Matching

The matchit and optmatch perform optimized, full, and genetic matching. The genmatch function performs genetic matching.

```
m.out <- matchit(treat ~ propen, data = mydata, method = "optimal,"
ratio = 2)
```

```
summary (m.out)
```

```
m.out <- matchit(treat ~ propen, data = mydata, method = "full")
```

```
summary (m.out)
```

## STRATIFYING

A stratifying variable can be computed with a series of conditional assignment statements.

```
mydata$propenstrata[propen > .80] <- ".80+"
```

```
mydata$propenstrata[propen > .60 & propen <= .80] <- ".60-.80"
```

```
mydata$propenstrata[propen > .40 & propen <= .60] <- ".40-.60"
```

```
mydata$propenstrata[propen > .20 & propen <= .40] <- ".20-.40"
```

```
mydata$propenstrata[propen <= .20] <- "0-.20" detach(mydata)
```

## REGRESSION AND THE GENERAL LINEAR MODEL

Within R, regression and GLM can be done using the lm function.

```
lm.r = lm(treatm ~ confounder1 + confounder2 + confounder3)
```

## TWO-STAGE LEAST SQUARES

The systemfit package can be used for two-stage least squares (2SLS) in R.

```
Fit2sls <- systemfit(treatm, method = "2SLS,", inst = ~instrument1 + instrument2 + instrument3)
```

## SAMPLE WEIGHTING

Sample weighting is done within the survey analysis package.

```
mydataweighted <-svydesign(id = ~1, weights = ~ipw, data = mydata)
```

## WEIGHTED LEAST SQUARES

Many analysis programs allow a weights parameter. The linear modeling, lm, function gives an example:

```
Outcomepred <- lm(outcome ~ treatm, weights = ipw)
summary outcomepred
```

## GENERALIZED LINEAR MODEL

Generalized linear model estimation in R is done with the glm function.

```
Outcomepred <- glm(formula = outcome ~ treatm, family = gaussian)
```

## MISSING DATA ANALYSIS

Analysis of missing data requires using the summary program and the missingness map function within the Amelia package. See creation of a.out under imputation.p summary(confounder1, confounder2, confounder3)

missmap(a.out)

## IMPUTATION OF MISSING DATA

Imputation of data can be done with the Amelia package.

a.out <- amelia(confounder1, m = 5)

# APPENDIX C
# SPSS COMMANDS FOR PROPENSITY USE

**M**any uses of propensity scores are possible with SPSS commands. The following presents some of these commands. There may be other ways of accomplishing the same result. Some uses of propensity scores are not possible by directly using SPSS commands. However, with an add-on R extender for SPSS, any procedure that is not possible within SPSS directly can be executed through R.

## NORMALITY TESTS

Testing whether the distribution is normal or some other shape can be done with the Kolmogorov–Smirnoff onesample test within NPAR (Thoemmes, 2011). The EXAMINE command also provides normality statistics and plots.

NPTESTS/ONESAMPLE TEST (confounder1, confounder2)

KOLMOGOROV_SMIRNOV(NORMAL = SAMPLE EXPONENTIAL = SAMPLE

POISSON = SAMPLE)

/MISSING SCOPE = ANALYSIS USERMISSING = EXCLUDE.

EXAMINE VARIABLES = confounder1 BY TREATMNT/PLOT = NPPLOT.

## IMBALANCE ASSESSMENT PROCEDURES

Imbalance tests with SPSS can be done with the MEANS program (for ANOVA statistics) or T-TEST.

MEANS TABLES = confounder1, confounder2, confounder3, confounder4

BY treatment/CELLS MEAN STDDEV VARIANCE COUNT

SUM/STAT ANOVA.

T-TEST GROUPS = treatment(0 1)/MISSING = ANALYSIS

/VARIABLES = confounder1, confounder2, confounder3, confounder4

/CRITERIA = CI(.95).

## PROPENSITY ESTIMATION

Propensity scores can be estimated using a REGRESSION program, LOGISTIC REGRESSION, GLM, or DISCRIMINANT.

REGRESSION/MISSING LISTWISE/STATISTICS COEFF OUTS R ANOVA

/CRITERIA = PIN(.05) POUT(.10)/NOORIGIN/DEPENDENT treatment

/METHOD = ENTER confounder1, confounder2, confounder3, confounder4

/SAVE PRED (propen).

LOGISTIC REGRESSION VARIABLES treatment/METHOD = ENTER confounder1, confounder2, confounder3, confounder4/SAVE = PRED (propen)

/CRITERIA = PIN(.05) POUT(.10) ITERATE(20) CUT(.5).

GLM

DISCRIMINANT/GROUPS = treatment0 (1)/VARIABLES = confounder1, confounder2, confounder3, confounder4/ANALYSIS ALL

/save PROBS (propen)/PRIORS EQUAL/STATISTICS = MEAN STDDEV

UNIVF COEFF/CLASSIFY = NONMISSING POOLED.

## MATCHING

Most matching with SPSS has to be done using the R extender add-on to execute R programs that do matching. A version of exact or coarsened matching and of greedy matching are two exceptions.

### Exact and Coarsened Exact

Break the file into treatment and comparison group files containing propensity scores. Aggregate each file. Merge the aggregated control file into a disaggregated treatment using propensity scores as IDs, trimmed to as many significant digits as desired. Add cases of the comparison disaggregated file to the treatment file. Create a flag for cases having merge matches. Select the cases meeting the flag. This produces a 1–many match. For a 1–1 match, purge comparison cases having duplicate propensities.

## Nearest Neighbor and Caliper

Painter (2010) has created an SPSS macro to do nearest-neighbor matching. It has been extended by Clark (2012). The Painter macro is available from http://www.unc.edu/~painter/SPSSsyntax/propen.txt. It requires an input file containing a propensity score named propen and an intervention variable named treatm. You must also specify the number of cases. Instructions are contained in the file propen.txt. The Clark version and instructions are posted at http://faculty.umb.edu/william_holmes/clarkmacro.htm.

## One-to-Many

This is currently available through R programs via the R extender add-on.

## Optimized, Full, and Genetic

Optimized, full, and genetic matching within SPSS commands is not currently possible. Optimized programs can be executed within SPSS using the R extension add-on.

## STRATIFYING

Stratifying using propensity scores is achieved in SPSS by recoding the propensity score into five groups whose range of values are equal. The new, variable groups are the strata.

RECODE propen (.20 THRU .29 = 1)(.30 THRU .39 = 2)(.40 THRU .49 = 3)

(.50 THRU .59 = 4)(.60 THRU .69 = 5) INTO propenstrata.

## REGRESSION AND THE GENERAL LINEAR MODEL

These procedures can be accomplished in SPSS with the GLM program or the REGRESSION program.

> REGRESSION/MISSING LISTWISE/STATISTICS COEFF OUTS R ANOVA
>
> /CRITERIA = PIN(.05) POUT(.10)/NOORIGIN/DEPENDENT treatment
>
> /METHOD = ENTER confounder1, confounder2, confounder3, confounder4
>
> /SAVE PRED (propen).
>
> GLM INCOME BY TREATMENT/EMMEANS TABLES(TREATMENT)
>
> /PRINTDESCRIPTIVES PARAMETER.

## TWO-STAGE LEAST SQUARES

Two-stage least squares (2SLS) may be done with either 2SLS or weighted least squares (WLS) procedures.

> 2SLS INCOME WITH TREATMENT/INSTRUMENTS AGE/CONSTANT
>
> /SAVE PRED RESID.
>
> WLS INCOME WITH TREATMENT/INSTRUMENTS AGE/CONSTANT
>
> /SAVE PRED RESID.

## SAMPLE WEIGHTING

> COMPUTE IPW = 1/PROPEN.
>
> IF (TREATMENT EQ 1)IPW = 1/(1-PROPEN).
>
> WEIGHT BY IPW.

## WEIGHTED LEAST SQUARES

This may be done with either the WLS procedure or the GLM procedure.

> GLM INCOME BY TREATMENT/EMMEANS TABLES(TREATMENT)
>
> /REGWGT IPW/PRINT DESCRIPTIVES PARAMETER.

## GENERALIZED LINEAR MODEL

GZLM is done with the GENLIN PROGRAM. The following produces logit predicted propensity scores.

GENLIN TREATMENT (REFERENCE = LAST) BY CONFOUNDER1

CONFOUNDER2 (ORDER = ASCENDING)/MODEL CONFOUNDER1

CONFOUNDER2 INTERCEPT = YES DISTRIBUTION = BINOMIAL

LINK = LOGIT/CRITERIA METHOD = FISHER(1) SCALE = 1 COVB = MODEL

MAXITERATIONS = 100 MAXSTEPHALVING = 5 PCONVERGE = .001

(ABSOLUTE) SINGULAR = 1E-012 ANALYSISTYPE = 3(WALD) CILEVEL = 95

CITYPE = WALD LIKELIHOOD = FULL/MISSING CLASSMISSING = EXCLUDE

/PRINT CPS DESCRIPTIVES MODELINFO FIT SUMMARY SOLUTION

/SAVE MEANPRED (PROPEN).

## MISSING DATA ANALYSIS

Missing value analysis is done in SPSS with the MVA command. It also allows expectation-maximization (EM) estimation of missing values that can be saved as an output file. It can also be done with the multiple imputation command.

MVA VARIABLES = educ_1 boyorgrl_1 agekdbrn_1 finrela_1/TPATTERN

PERCENT = 1 DESCRIBE = agekdbrn_1/EM(TOLERANCE = 0.001

CONVERGENCE = 0.0001 ITERATIONS = 25)/EM

(OUTFILE = "c:\spssdata\gss\emdata.sav").

MULTIPLE  IMPUTATION  CONFOUNDER1  CONFOUNDER2 CONFOUNDER3 CONFOUNDER4/IMPUTE METHOD = NONE

/MISSINGSUMMARIES VARIABLES (MINPCTMISSING = .001).

## IMPUTATION OF MISSING DATA

Multiple imputation in SPSS is done with the multiple imputation command. A new data file is saved containing imputed values. Running subfiles for a command on this file calculates the results with average imputed results.

MULTIPLE IMPUTATION confounder1, confounder2, confounder3, confounder4

/IMPUTE METHOD = FCS/CONSTRAINTS confounder1

(RND = 1 MIN = 1)/CONSTRAINTS confounder1 (MAX = 20)

/OUTFILE IMPUTATIONS = IMPUTEDDATA.

# APPENDIX D
# SAS COMMANDS FOR
# PROPENSITY USE

An overview of SAS commands for propensity score use is given in http://support.sas.com/resources/papers/proceedings12/314-2012.pdf. There are multiple ways for using SAS commands for this purpose. These are only some of them. SAS also has an interface for running R commands, so they may be employed as well.

## IMBALANCE ASSESSMENT

Imbalance assessment can be done with the ANOVA procedure or with the GLM procedure.

```
proc anova data = mydata;

class treatm;

model treatm = confounder1, confounder2, confounder3;

run;
```

## PROPENSITY ESTIMATION

Estimation with logistic regression can be done with the proc logistic procedure or discriminant function analysis (proc candis).

```
proc logistic;

model treatm = confounder1, confounder2, confounder3/lackfit outroc = ps_r;

output out = ps_p XBETA = ps_xb STDXBETA = ps_sdxb PREDICTED = propen;
```

```
run;

proc candisc data = mydata out = outcan distance anova;

class treatm;

var confounder1 confounder2 confounder3;

output out = ps_p PREDICTED = propen;

run;
```

## MATCHING

Some matching can be done with SAS macros and commands. Other matching options are available through the R interface.

### Exact and Coarsened Exact

The web page http://support.sas.com/resources/papers/proceedings12/314 -2012.pdf contains SAS commands for 1–1 exact matching.

### Nearest Neighbor and Caliper

The web page mentioned under exact and coarsened matching also contains SAS commands for 1–1 caliper matching.

### One-to-Many

One-to-many matching is only available through R matching programs. These can be used with the R interface for SAS.

### Optimized, Full, or Genetic

These forms of matching are available through the R matching programs. They can be used with the R interface for SAS.

## STRATIFYING

Strata are created by creating a recoded propensity score variable.

Propenstrata = ;

IF (propen < .2) THEN propenstrata = 1;

IF (propen >= .2) and (propen < .4) THEN propenstrata = 2;

IF (propen >= .4) and (propen < .6) THEN propenstrata = 3;

IF (propen >= .6) and (propen < .8) THEN propenstrata = 4;

IF (propen >= .8) THEN propenstrata = 5.

## REGRESSION AND THE GENERAL LINEAR MODEL

Regression and general linear model (GLM) estimation may be done with the GLM program.

proc glm data = mydata;

class treatm;

model outcome = treatm covariate1

means treatm;

run;

## TWO-STAGE LEAST SQUARES

Two-stage least squares regression may be done with the syslin proc.

proc syslin data = mydata 2sls;

endogenous treatm;

instruments instrument1 instrument2 instrument3;

effects: model outcome1 = treatm instrument1 instrument2 instrument3;

run;

## SAMPLE WEIGHTING

```
wt = 0;

if treatm = 0 then ipw = 1/propen;

if treatm = 1 then wt = 1/(1-propen);

proc freq data = mydata.new;

tables counfounder1, confounder2, confounder3;

weight ipa;

run;
```

## WEIGHTED LEAST SQUARES

The simplest form of weighted least squares regression in SAS can be done with the regression procedure. More complicated models can be estimated with the GLM procedure. The "p" option in the MODEL line below calculates the estimated dependent variable.

```
PROC REG DATA = mydata;

MODEL outcome1 = treatm covariate1/p;

VAR outcome1 treatm covariate1 ipw;

WEIGHT ipw;

OUTPUT OUT = mydataout PREDICTED = outcome1pred.;

BY variables;
```

## GENERALIZED LINEAR MODEL

Generalized Linear Model estimation (GZLM within the text) can be done with the genmod procedure. The example estimates a logistic regression.

```
PROC GENMOD;

MODEL outcome1 = treatm/link = logit dist = binomial;

RUN;
```

## MISSING DATA ANALYSIS

Missing data analysis can be performed with the missingpattern macro or the mianalyze procedure. The mianalyze procedure produces mda as part of a multiple imputation procedure.

```
%macro missingPattern(datain = mydata, varlist = confounder1 confounder2
confounder3,

Exclude = "FALSE," missPattern1 = "TRUE," dataout1 = mydatam1, miss-
Pattern2 = "TRUE,"

dataout2 = "mydatam2," missPattern3 = "TRUE," dataout3 = mydatam3,

missPattern4 = "TRUE," dataout4 = mydatam4);

proc mianalyze;

modeleffects confounder1 confounder2 confounder3;

stderr sconfounder1 sconfounder2 sconfounder3;

run;
```

## IMPUTATION OF MISSING DATA

Imputation can be done with both the multiple imputation (MI) and the mianalyze procedures.

```
proc mi data = mydata seed = 12345 out = mydatami simple;

var confounder1 confounder2 confounder3;

run;

proc mianalyze;

modeleffects confounder1 confounder2 confounder3;

stderr sconfounder1 sconfounder2 sconfounder3;

out = mydatami;

run;
```

# REFERENCES

Abadie, A., & Imbens, G. W. (2006). Large sample properties of matching estimators for average treatment effects. *Econometrica, 74,* 235–267. doi:10.1111/j.1468-0262.2006.00655.x

Allison, P. D. (2008, March). Convergence failures in logistic regression. *Proceedings from SAS Software Global Forum 2008* (Paper No. 360), San Antonio, TX. Retrieved from http://citeseerx.ist.psu.edu/viewdoc/download?doi=10.1.1.176.2077&rep=rep1&type=pdf

Angrist, J., Imbens, G., & Rubin, B. (1996). Identification of causal effects using instrumental variables. *Journal of the American Statistical Association, 91,* 444–455. doi:10.1080/01621459.1996.10476902

Austin, P. C. (2008). A critical appraisal of propensity-score matching in the medical literature between 1996 and 2003. *Statistics in Medicine, 28,* 2037–2049. doi:10.1002/sim.3150

Austin, P. C. (2010). Comparing paired vs non-paired statistical methods of analyses when making inferences about absolute risk reductions in propensity-score matched samples. *Statistics in Medicine, 30,* 1292–1301. doi:10.1002/sim.4200

Austin, P. C., Grootendorst, P., & Anderson, G. M. (2007). A comparison of the ability of different propensity score models to balance measured variables between treated and untreated subjects: A Monte Carlo study. *Statistics in Medicine, 26,* 734–753. doi:10.1002/sim.2580

Balke, A., & Pearl, J. (1997). Bounds on treatment effects from studies with imperfect compliance. *Journal of the American Statistical Association, 92,* 1171–1176. doi:10.1080/01621459.1997.10474074

Barber, B. M., & Odean, T. (2000). Too many cooks spoil the profits: Investment club performance. *Financial Analysts Journal, 56,* 17–25. Retrieved from http://www.jstor.org/stable/4480219

Barclay, S., Todd, C., Finlay, I., Grande, G., & Wyatt, P. (2001). Not another questionnaire! Maximizing the response rate, predicting non-response and assessing non-response bias in postal questionnaire studies of GPs. *Family Practice, 19,* 105–111.

Barnard, J., Du, J., Hill, J., & Rubin, D. B. (1998). A broader template for analyzing broken randomized experiments. *Sociological Methods & Research, 27,* 285–318.

Barnard, J., Frangakis, C. E., Hill, J. L., & Rubin, D. B. (2003). Principal stratification approach to broken randomized experiments: A case study of school choice vouchers in New York City. *Journal of the American Statistical Association, 98,* 299–311. Retrieved from http://www.jstor.org/stable/30045238

Baser, O. (2006). Too much ado about propensity score models? Comparing methods of propensity score matching. *Value in Health, 9,* 377–385. doi:10.1111/j.1524-4733.2006.00130.x

Becker, S. O., & Ichino, A. (2002). Estimation of average treatment effects based on propensity scores. *Stata Journal, 2*(4), 358–377.

Blalock, H. M. (1971). Causal models involving unmeasured variables in stimulus-response situations. In H. M. Blalock Jr. (Ed.), *Causal models in the social sciences* (pp. 334–347). Chicago, IL: Aldine Press.

Bloom, D. E., & Idson, T. L. (1991). The practical importance of sample weights. *Journal of the American Statistical Association, 86,* 620–624.

Bollen, K. A. (1996). An alternative two stage least squares (2SLS) estimator for latent variable equations. *Psychometrika, 61,* 109–121. doi:10.1007/BF02296961

Box-Steffensmeier, J. M., Reiter, D., & Zorn, C. (2003). Non-proportional hazards and event history analysis in international relations. *Journal of Conflict Resolution, 47,* 33–53. Retrieved from http://www.jstor.org/stable/3176181

Bryk, A. S., Raudenbush, S. W., & Congdon, R. T. (1996). *HLM: Hierarchical linear and nonlinear modeling with the HLM/2L and HLM/3L programs.* Chicago, IL: Scientific Software International.

Busso, M., DiNardo, J., & McCrary, J. (2009). *New evidence on the finite sample properties of propensity score matching and reweighting estimators* (IZA Discussion Paper 3998). Bonn, Germany: Institute for the Study of Labor. Retrieved from http://ftp.iza.org/dp3998.pdf

Clark, M. H. (2012). *SPSS matching macro* [Computer macro]. Unpublished computer code.

Cochran, W. G. (1968). The effectiveness of adjustment by subclassification in removing bias in observational studies. *Biometrics, 20,* 205–213. Retrieved from http://www.jstor.org/stable/2528036

Cochran, W. G., & Cox, G. M. (1957). *Experimental designs* (6th ed.). New York, NY: Wiley.

Conniffe, D., Gash, V., & O'Connell, P. J. (2000). Evaluating state programs: Natural experiments and propensity scores. *Economic and Social Review, 31,* 283–308.

Cook, T. D., & Campbell, D. T. (1979). *Quasi-experimentation: Design and analysis for field settings.* Chicago, IL: Rand McNally.

Cox, D. R., & Oakes, D. (1983). *Analysis of survival data* (Monographs on statistics and applied probability). London, England: Chapman & Hall/CRC Press.

Cramer, J. S. (1987). Mean and variance of $R^2$ in small and moderate samples. *Journal of Econometrics, 35,* 253–266. doi: 10.1016/0304-4076(87)90027-3

D'Agostino, R. B., Jr. (1998). Tutorial in biostatistics propensity score methods for bias reduction in the comparison of a treatment to a non-randomized control group. *Statistics in Medicine, 17,* 2265–2281.

D'Agostino, R. B., Jr., & Rubin, D. B. (2000). Estimating and using propensity scores with partially missing data. *Journal of the American Statistical Association, 95*(451), 749–759. doi:10.1080/01621459.2000.10474263

Davis, J. A., Smith, T. W., & Marsden, P. V. (2010). *General social surveys, 1972–2008* [Cumulative and Panel File; Computer file]. Storrs: University of Connecticut, Roper Center for Public Opinion Research. doi:10.3886/ICPSR25962

Dehejia, R. H. (2005). Practical propensity score matching: A reply to Smith and Todd. *Journal of Econometrics, 125*(1/2), 355–364. doi:10.1016/j.jeconom.2004.04.012

Dehejia, R. H., & Wahba, S. (2002). Propensity score-matching methods for nonexperimental causal studies. *Review of Economics and Statistics, 84*(1), 151–161. doi:10.1162/003465302317331982

Dempster, A. P., Laird, N. M., & Rubin, D. B. (1977). Maximum likelihood from incomplete data via the $EM$ algorithm. *Journal of the Royal Statistical Society: Series B (Methodological), 39,* 1–38. Retrieved from http://links.jstor.org/sici?sici=0035-9246%281977%2939%3A1%3C1%3AMLFIDV%3E2.0.CO%3B2-Z

de Winter, A. F., Oldehinkel, A. J., Veenstra, R., Brunnekreef, J. A., Verhulst, F. C., & Ormel, J. (2005). Evaluation of non-response bias in mental health determinants and outcomes in a large sample of pre-adolescents. *European Journal of Epidemiology, 20,* 173–181.

Diamond, A., & Sekhon, J. S. (2006). *Genetic matching for estimating causal effects: A general multivariate matching method for achieving balance in observational studies* (escholarship). Berkley: University of California, Institute of Governmental Studies. Retrieved from http://escholarship.org/uc/item/8gx4v5qt

Dollfus, C., Patetta, M., Siegel, E., & Cross, A. (1990). Infant mortality: A practical approach to the analysis of the leading causes of death and risk factors. *Pediatrics, 86,* 176–183.

Durbin, J. (1954). Errors in variables. *Review of the International Statistical Institute, 22,* 23–32. Retrieved from http://www.jstor.org/stable/1401917

Freedman, D. A., & Berk, R. A. (2008). Weighting regressions by propensity scores. *Evaluation Review, 32,* 392–409. doi:10.1177/0193841X08317586

Glynn, A. N., & Quinn, K. M. (2009). *Estimation of causal effects with generalized additive models.* Vienna, Austria: R Foundation for Statistical Computing.

Glynn, A. N., & Quinn, K. M. (2010). An introduction to the augmented inverse propensity weighted estimator. *Political Analysis, 18,* 36–56. doi:10.1093/pan/mpp036

Goldberger, A., & Duncan, D. (Eds.). (1973). *Structural equation models in the social sciences.* New York, NY: Academic Press.

Goldstein, H. (2003). *Multilevel statistical models* (3rd ed.). London, England: Arnold.

Gu, X. S., & Rosenbaum, P. R. (1993). Comparison of multivariate matching methods: Structures, distances, and algorithms. *Journal of Computational and Graphical Statistics, 2,* 405–420. doi:10.1080/10618600.1993.10474623

Guo, S., & Fraser, M. W. (2010). *Propensity score analysis.* Thousand Oaks, CA: Sage.

Hansen, B. B. (2004). Full matching in an observational study of coaching for the SAT. *Journal of the American Statistical Association, 99,* 609–618. doi:10.1198/0162 14504000000647

Hansen, B. B. (2008). The essential role of balance tests in propensity-matched observational studies: Comments on "A critical appraisal of propensity-score matching in the medical literature between 1996 and 2003" by Peter Austin. *Statistics in Medicine, 27,* 2050–2054. doi:10.1002/sim.3208

Hansen, B. B., & Klopfer, S. O. (2005). Optimal full matching and related designs via network flows. *Journal of Computational and Graphical Statistics, 15,* 1–19. doi:10.1198/106186006X137047

Hawkes, D., & Plewis, I. (2006). Modelling non-response in the National Child Development Study. *Journal of the Royal Statistical Society: Series A, 169,* 479–491. Retrieved from http://ccsr.ac.uk/methods/events/attrition/documents/ANR16.pdf

Health and Retirement Study. (2011). *HRS tracker 2008 file codebook* (Produced and distributed by the University of Michigan with funding from the National Institute on Aging; Grant No. NIA U01AG009740). Ann Arbor: University of Michigan.

Heath, A. C., Howells, W., Kirk, K. M., Madden, P. A. F., Bucholz, K. K., Nelson, E. C., ... Martin, N. G. (2001). Predictors of non-response to a questionnaire survey of a volunteer twin panel: Findings from the Australian 1989 Twin Cohort. *Twin Research, 4,* 73–80.

Heckman, J. J. (1989). Causal inference and nonrandom samples. *Journal of Educational Statistics, 14,* 159–168. Retrieved from http://www.jstor.org/stable/1164605

Heckman, J. J. (2005). The scientific model of causality. *Sociological Methodology, 35,* 1–97. doi:10.1111/j.0081-1750.2006.00164.x

Heckman, J. J., & Navarro-Lozano, S. (2004). Using matching, instrumental variables, and control functions to estimate economic choice. *Review of Economics and Statistics, 86,* 30–57. doi:10.1162/003465304323023660

Heckman, N. E. (1986). Spline smoothing in a partly linear model. *Journal of the Royal Statistical Society: Series B, 48,* 144–248. Retrieved from http://www.jstor.org/stable/2345719

Hedges, L. V. (1981). Distribution theory for Glass's estimator of effect size and related estimators. *Journal of Educational Statistics, 6,* 107–128. doi: 10.3102/10769986006002107

Heinrich, C. J. (1998). Returns to education and training for the highly disadvantaged. *Evaluation Review, 22,* 637–667.

Hirano, K., & Imbens, G. W. (2004). The propensity score with continuous treatments. In A. Gelman & X. Ming (Eds.), *Applied Bayesian modeling and causal inference from incomplete data perspectives* (pp. 73–84). New York, NY: Wiley. Retrieved from http://www.ipc-undp.org/evaluation/aula10-dosagem/Hirano%20%26%20Imbens%20-%20GPS.pdf

Holland, P. W. (1986). Statistics and causal inference. *Journal of the American Statistical Association, 81,* 945–960. doi:10.1080/01621459.1986.10478354

Holmes, W., & Olsen, L. (2010). *Using propensity scores with small samples.* Presented at annual meetings of the American Evaluation Association, San Antonio, TX. Retrieved from http://www.faculty.umb.edu/william_holmes/usingpropensityscoreswithsmallsamples.pdf

Holmes, W., & Olsen, L. (2011, November). *Minimizing pregroup differences with matching and adjustment.* Presented at the annual meetings of the American Evaluation Association, Anaheim, CA. Retrieved from http://www.faculty.umb.edu/william_holmes/minimizingpregroupdifferences.pdf

Imbens, G. W. (2004). Nonparametric estimation of average treatment effects under exogeneity: A review. *Review of Economics and Statistic, 86,* 4–29. doi: 10.1162/003465304323023651

Imbens, G. W., & Wooldridge, J. M. (2009). Recent developments in the econometrics of program evaluation. *Journal of Economic Literature, 47,* 5–86. Retrieved from http://www.jstor.org/stable/27647134

Kasule, O. H. (2003, September). *Conditional logistic regression for paired data.* Paper presented at the annual SAS Users' Malaysia Conference, Kuala Lumpur, Malaysia.

Klingenberg, B., & Agresti, A. (2006). Multivariate extensions of McNemar's test. *Biometrics, 62,* 1–7. doi:10.1111/j.1541-0420.2006.00525.x

Lee, B. K., Lessler, J., & Stuart, E. A. (2011). Weight trimming and propensity score weighting. *PLoS ONE, 6*(3), e18174. doi:10.1371/journal.pone.0018174

Li, L. (2011). *Propensity score analysis with matching weights* (COBRA Preprint Series, Working Paper No. 79). Retrieved from http://biostats.bepress.com/cobra/ps/art79

Liang, K., & Zeger, S. L. (1986). Longitudinal data analysis using generalized linear models. *Biometrika, 73,* 13–22.

Long, J. S., & Ervin, L. H. (1998). *Correcting for heteroscedasticity with heteroscedasticity consistent standard errors in the linear regression model: Small sample considerations.* Retrieved from http://www.indiana.edu/~jslsoc/files_research/testing_tests/hccm/98TAS.pdf

MacKinnon, J. G., & White, H. (1985). Some heteroskedasticity consistent covariance matrix estimators with improved finite sample properties. *Journal of Econometrics, 29,* 305–325. doi: 10.1016/03044076(85)901587

Mahalanobis, P. (1936). *Proceedings from the National Institute of Sciences of India '36: The generalized distance in statistics.* Kolkata, India. Retrieved from http://www.new.dli.ernet.in/rawdataupload/upload/insa/INSA_1/20006193_49.pdf

McKnight, P. E., McKnight, K. M., Sidani, S., & Figueredo, A. J. (2007). *Missing data: A gentle introduction.* New York, NY: Guilford Press.

Mebane, W. R., & Sekhon, J. S. (2011). Genetic optimization using derivatives: The rgenoud package for R. *Journal of Statistical Software, 42*(11), 1–26. Retrieved from http://www.polmeth.wustl.edu/conferences/methods2009/resources/papers /Mebane-genoudtalk.pdf

Meng, X. (1994). Multiple imputation inferences with uncongenial sources of input. *Statistical Sciences, 9,* 538–573. Retrieved from http://www.jstor.org/stable/2246252

Miller, J. Z., Nance, W. E., Norton, J. A., Wolen, R. L., Griffith, R. S., & Rose, R. I. (1977). Therapeutic effects of vitamin C: A co-twin control study. *Journal of the American Medical Association, 237,* 248–251. Retrieved from http://www.mv .helsinki.fi/home/hemila/CC/Miller_1977_ch.pdf

Mill, J. S. (1848). *Principles of political economy with some of their applications to social philosophy.* London, England: Routledge.

Moser, C. A. (1952). Quota sampling. *Journal of the Royal Statistical Society: Series A, 115,* 411–423. Retrieved from http://www.jstor.org/stable/2343021

National Institute on Aging. (2008). *Health and Retirement Study* (Data file HRS_Text_ WEB.zip). Retrieved from http://hrsonline.isr.umich.edu

Nelder, J. A., & Wedderbom, J. A. (1972). Generalized linear models. *Journal of the Royal Statistical Society: Series A, 135,* 370–384. Retrieved from http://www.jstor .org/stable/2344614

Nelson, D., & Noorbaloochi, S. (2010). *Sufficient dimension reduction summaries.* Unpublished manuscript. Retrieved from http://citeseerx.ist.psu.edu/viewdoc/down load?doi=10.1.1.147.3774&rep=rep1&type=pdf

Neyman, J. (1935). Statistical problems in agricultural experimentation. *Journal of the Royal Statistical Society: Series B, 2,* 107–154. Retrieved from http://www.jstor.org /stable/2983637

Nielsen, R., & Sheffield, J. (2009, July). *Matching with time-series cross-sectional data.* Paper presented at Polmeth XXVI, Yale University, New Haven, CT. Retrieved from http://www.polmeth.wustl.edu/conferences/methods2009/resources/papers/Nielsen-PanelMatching2009-poster.pdf

Painter, J. (2010). *SPSS propensity matching program description.* Retrieved from http:// www.unc.edu/~painter/SPSSsyntax/propen.txt

Pearl, J. (1995). Causal diagrams for empirical research. *Biometrika, 82,* 669–710. Retrieved from http://bayes.cs.ucla.edu/R218-B.pdf

Posner, M. A., & Ash, A. S. (2011). *Comparing weighting methods in propensity score analysis.* Retrieved from http://www.stat.columbia.edu/~gelman/stuff_for_blog/ posner.pdf

Rabe-Hesketh, S., Skrondal, A., & Pickles, A. (2002). Reliable estimation of generalized linear mixed models using adaptive quadrature. *Stata Journal, 2,* 1–21.

Rassen, J. A., Glynn, R. J., Brookhart, M. A., & Schneeweiss, S. (2011). Covariate selection in high-dimensional propensity score analyses of treatment effects in small samples. *American Journal of Epidemiology, 173,* 1401–1413. doi:10.1093/aje/kwr001

Rassen, J. A., & Schneeweiss, S. (2012). Using high-dimensional propensity scores to automate confounding control in a distributed medical product safety surveillance system. *Pharmacoepidemiology and Drug Safety, 21,* 41–49. doi:10.1002/pds.2328

R Development Core Team. (2007). *R: A language and environment for statistical computing.* Vienna, Austria: R Foundation for Statistical Computing.

Robins, J. M., Rotnitzky, A., & Zhao, L. P. (1994). Estimation of regression coefficients when some regressors are not always observed. *Journal of the American Statistical Association, 89,* 846–866.

Roseman, L. (1994). *Using regression and subclassification on the propensity score to control bias in observational studies* (Unpublished report). Harvard University, Boston, MA.

Rosenbaum, P. R. (1989). Optimal matching for observational studies. *Journal of the American Statistical Association, 84,* 1024–1032. Retrieved from http://www.jstor .org/stable/2290079

Rosenbaum, P. R., & Rubin, D. B. (1983). The central role of the propensity score in observational studies for causal effects. *Biometrika, 70,* 41–55. Retrieved from http://links .jstor.org/sici?=0006-3444&28198304%2970%3A1%3C41%3ATCROTP%3E2.0 .CO%3B2-Qhttp://sisla06.samsi.info/ndhs/dc/Papers/RosenbaumPropensityScore.pdf

Rosenbaum, P. R., & Rubin, D. B. (1984). Reducing bias in observational studies using subclassification on the propensity score. *Journal of the American Statistical Association, 79,* 516–524. doi:10.1080/01621459.1984.10478078

Rosenbaum, P. R., & Rubin, D. B. (1985). Constructing a control group using multivariate matched sampling methods that incorporate the propensity score. *The American Statistician, 39,* 33–38. doi:10.1080/00031305.1985.10479383

Rubin, D. B. (1974). Estimating causal effects of treatments in randomized and nonrandomized studies. *Journal of Educational Psychology, 66,* 688–701.

Rubin, D. B. (1976a). Inference and missing data. *Biometrika, 63,* 581–592. doi:10.1093/ biomet/63.3.581

Rubin, D. B. (1976b). Matching methods that are equal percent bias reducing: Maximums on bias reduction fixed sample sizes. *Biometrics, 32,* 121–132. Retrieved from http://www.jstor.org/stable/2529343

Rubin, D. B. (1976c). Matching methods that are equal percent bias reducing: Some examples. *Biometrics, 32,* 109–120. Retrieved from http://www.jstor.org/stable/2529342

Rubin, D. B. (1977). Assignment to treatment group on the basis of a covariate. *Journal of Educational Statistics, 2,* 1–26. doi:10.3102/10769986002001001

Rubin, D. B. (1979). Using multivariate matched sampling and regression adjustment to control bias in observational studies. *Journal of the American Statistical Association, 74,* 318–328. doi:10.1080/01621459.1979.10482513

Rubin, D. B. (1987). *Multiple imputation for nonresponse in surveys.* New York, NY: Wiley.

Rubin, D. B. (1996). Multiple imputation after 18+ years (with discussion). *Journal of the American Statistical Association, 91,* 473–489. doi:10.1080/01621459.1996.10476908

Rubin, D. B. (2006). *Matched sampling for causal effects.* New York, NY: Cambridge University Press.

Rubin, D. B. (2010). Reflections stimulated by the comments of Shadish (2010) and West and Thoemmes (2010). *Psychological Methods, 15,* 38–46.

Scharfstein, D. O., Rotnitzky, A., & Robins, J. M. (1999). Rejoinder to adjusting for nonignorable drop-out using semiparametric nonresponse models. *Journal of the American Statistical Association, 94,* 1135–1146.

Schumacker, R. E. (2009). Practical issues to consider before using propensity scores. *Multiple Linear Regression Viewpoints, 35,* 1–3.

Sekhon, J. S. (2007). *Alternative balance metrics for bias reduction in matching methods for causal inference* (Working paper). Berkley: University of California, Political Science Department. Retrieved from http://polmeth.wustl.edu/media/Paper /SekhonBalanceMetrics.pdf

Sekhon, J. S. (2011). Multivariate and propensity score matching software with automated balance optimization: The matching package for R. *Journal of Statistical Software, 42,* 1–52.

Sekhon, J. S., & Grieve, R. (2011). A nonparametric matching method for covariate adjustment with application to economic evaluation. *Health Economics, 21,* 695–714.

Sekhon, J. S., & Mebane, W. R., Jr. (1998). Genetic optimization using derivatives: Theory and application to nonlinear models. *Political Analysis, 7,* 189–203. doi:10.1093/pan/7.1.187

Shadish, W. R. (2009, November). *Issues in selecting covariates for propensity score adjustments.* Paper presented at the meetings of the American Evaluation Association, Orlando, FL.

Shadish, W. R. (2010). Randomized controlled studies and alternative designs in outcome studies: Challenges and opportunities. *Research on Social Work Practice, 21,* 631–643. doi:10.1177/1049731511403324

Shadish, W. R., Cook, T. D., & Campbell, D. T. (2002). *Experimental and quasi-experimental designs for generalized causal inference.* Boston, MA: Houghton-Mifflin.

Sherman, L. W., & Berk, R. A. (1984). The Minneapolis domestic violence experiment. *Police Foundation Reports, April, 1984,* 1–13. Washington, DC: Police Foundation. doi: 10.1.1.115.9494

Stuart, E. A. (2008). Developing practical recommendations for the use of propensity scores: Discussion of "A critical appraisal of propensity score matching in the medical literature between 1996 and 2003" by Peter Austin. *Statistics in Medicine, 27,* 2062–2065. doi:10.1002/sim.3207

Stuart, E. A. (2010). Matching methods for causal inference: A review and a look forward. *Statistical Science, 25,* 1–21.

Stuart, E. A., & Green, K. M. (2008). Using full matching to estimate causal effects in non-experimental studies: Examining the relationship between adolescent marijuana use and adult outcomes. *Developmental Psychology, 44,* 395–406.

Tan, Z. (2006). Regression and weighting methods for causal inference using instrumental variables. *Journal of the American Statistical Association, 101,* 1607–1618. Retrieved from http://www.stat.rutgers.edu/home/ztan/Publication/ivDec06.pdf

Thoemmes, F. (2011). *Propensity score matching in SPSS.* Ithaca, NY: Cornell University Press. Retrieved from http://arxiv.org/ftp/arxiv/papers/1201/1201.6385.pdf

Thompson, B. (2004). *Exploratory and confirmatory factor analysis.* Washington, DC: American Psychological Association.

Wald, A. (1940). The fitting of straight lines if both variables are subject to error. *The Annals of Mathematical Statistics, 11,* 284–300. Retrieved from http://www.jstor.org/stable/2235677

Walter, S. D. (1988). The feasibility of matching and quota sampling in epidemiologic studies. *American Journal of Epidemiology, 130,* 379–389.

Weinke, A. (2003). *Frailty models* (MPIDR working paper 2003-032). Rostock, Germany: Max Planck Institute for Demographic Research.

Wright, S. (1921). Correlation and causation. *Journal of Agricultural Research, 20,* 557–585. Retrieved from http://www.ssc.wisc.edu/soc/class/soc952/Wright/Wright_Correlation%20and%20Causation.pdf

Zeger, S. L., Liang, K., & Albert, P. S. (1988). Models for longitudinal data: A generalized estimating equation approach. *Biometrics, 44,* 1049–1060.

# Author Index

# SUBJECT INDEX

Adaptive Gaussian quadrature (AGQ), 230
Adequacy and sufficiency
  of causal inference, 20–23
  with correlated samples, 243–244
  of covariates, 188–190
  of generalized linear models, 214–215
  of matching, 74–76, 125–126
  of optimized solutions, 145–146
  of propensity estimates, 100–102
  of weighting, 167–168
Ad hoc controls, 32
Adjacent geographic units, 231
Adjusting, 25–27, 29
  covariates as, 186–190
  options, 176–183
AGQ. *See* Adaptive Gaussian quadrature
  (AGQ)
AIPW. *See* Augmented inverse
  probability weight (AIPW)
Always takers, 278–279
Analysis of covariance (ANCOVA),
  27, 30, 98–99, 100, 180
  control variables, 170
  estimating propensity scores using, 79
  generalized estimation equation and,
    225–226
  paired sample, 221–222
  pre-post comparisons, 223–224
  propensity-adjusted repeated, 233
  repeated variable, 232–233
Analysis of variance (ANOVA), 4, 5
  adequacy and sufficiency of propensity
    estimates and, 101
  assessing damage from broken
    experiments using, 289–291
  assessing matching results using, 69
  classic experiment, 7–10
  dropout rate and, 54
  generalized estimation equations and,
    225–226

generalized linear models and,
  192–199
Hedges' g and, 92
inverse proportional weighting and, 154
paired sample, 221–222
paired sample t test, 219–221
predicting missing data using,
  254, 256 (table)
pre-post comparisons, 223–224
propensity-adjusted repeated, 233
repeated variable, 232–233
stratifying and, 97–98
weighted regression and, 164–165
ANCOVA. *See* Analysis of covariance
  (ANCOVA)
ANOVA (analysis of variance). *See*
  Analysis of variance (ANOVA)
Antecedent variables, 15–16, 30, 48–49,
  165–166, 285
Assessment
  of adequacy and sufficiency of
    weighting, 167–168
  covariate results, 186–188
  of damage from broken experiments,
    288–295
  of matching results, 68–73
  regression results, 165–167
As treatment analysis (ATA), 274
ATE (average treatment effect). *See*
  Average treatment effect (ATE)
Attrition, 280–281
Augmented inverse probability weight
  (AIPW), 99, 212
  choosing weights for, 159–163
Augmented inverse propensity weights
  (AIPW), 155–156
Average treatment effect (ATE), 2, 99,
  149, 155
Average treatment effect for the treated
  (ATT), 150, 155

330

# ⑤SAGE research**methods**

The essential online tool for researchers from the world's leading methods publisher

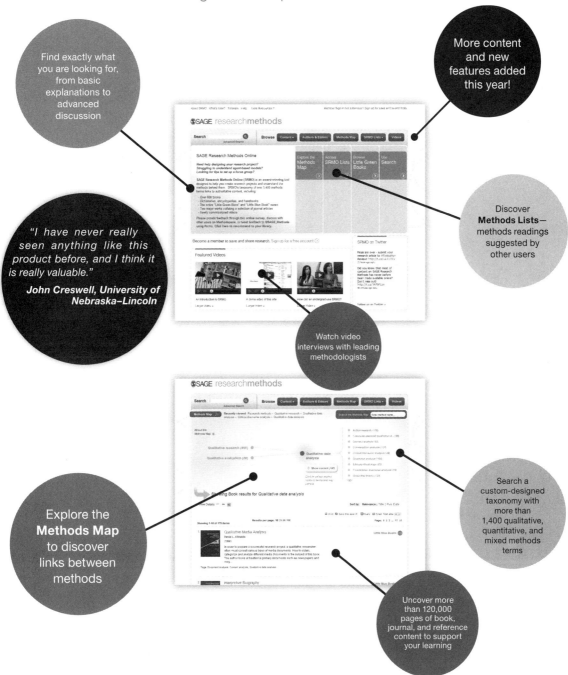

Find exactly what you are looking for, from basic explanations to advanced discussion

More content and new features added this year!

"I have never really seen anything like this product before, and I think it is really valuable."

**John Creswell, University of Nebraska–Lincoln**

Discover **Methods Lists—** methods readings suggested by other users

Watch video interviews with leading methodologists

Explore the **Methods Map** to discover links between methods

Search a custom-designed taxonomy with more than 1,400 qualitative, quantitative, and mixed methods terms

Uncover more than 120,000 pages of book, journal, and reference content to support your learning

# Find out more at
# www.sageresearchmethods.com